# QATAR
TRAVEL GUIDE

Arabesque

QATAR: Travel Guide

Copyright - Published by Arabesque Travel

Note on Transliteration

Arabic names and terms in this text follow local Gulf conventions, using the capitalised 'Al' and spacing distinct from the hyphenated lowercase standard often found in academic texts.

All rights reserved No part of this publication may be reproduced, stored in a retrieval system, or transmitted in any form or by any means, without the prior written permission of the copyright owner.

Disclaimer: every effort has been made to ensure the accuracy of the information in this book at the time of going to press. However, details such as opening hours, prices, visa regulations, and local conditions are subject to change, often with little or no notice. You should factor your own fitness, experience, and circumstances into any decisions made based on this guide. The author and publisher accept no liability for loss, inconvenience, or injury arising from reliance on this guide.

A Request to the Reader

Reliable intelligence is the currency of independent travel. As an independent publisher, we do not have the marketing algorithms of the corporate giants to remain visible. If this guide proved authoritative and genuinely useful during your journey - providing the context that separates a tourist from a traveller - please consider leaving a brief review on the retailer's website. A few honest lines about what worked for you will help others decide with confidence and ensure we can continue documenting Qatar with the depth it demands.

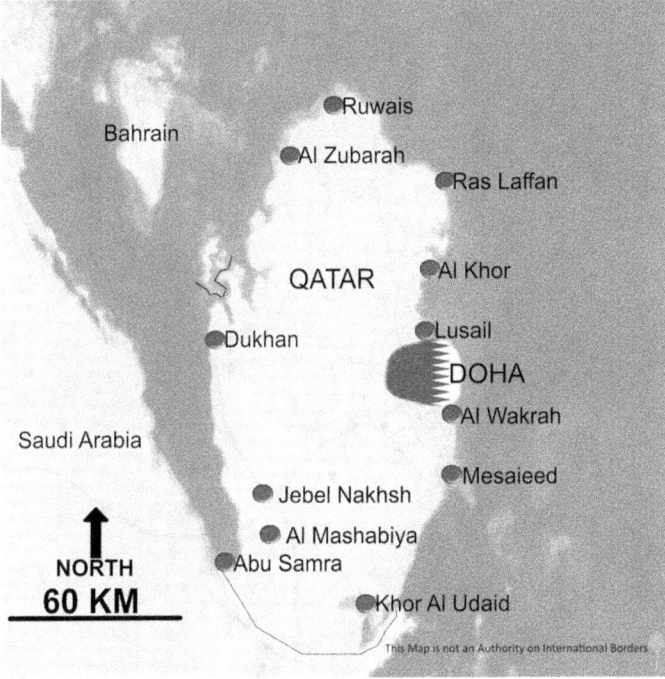

# INTRODUCTION

While most visitors will encounter no issues when visiting Qatar, understanding that Qatar has distinct laws and culture is essential. Unlike the UK, or many other wester countries, where public commentary regarding the government or head of state is a common feature of civil life, in Qatar such discourse is strictly regulated; indeed, these protections extend to the privacy and reputation of any private individual. Authorities efficiently enforce these regulations. Show the same politeness, courtesy, and common sense you would if visiting a person's home, and you will find Qatar a welcoming and safe environment.

Please use this guide as a starting point and double-check details for your trip. This book does not provide medical, financial, legal or other professional advice. For such matters, consult the appropriate authorities in your country. The publisher is not responsible for any loss resulting from the use of this guide. British English spelling is used throughout. Dates follow the BC/AD Gregorian system rather than BCE/CE to avoid confusion with the the the assumption that it is "before the current" Hijri era. The term 'Arabian Gulf' is used here, as it is the standard in Arab countries. This approach is similar to the use of 'English Channel' in English-speaking countries. France uses 'La Manche' (The Sleeve), Bretons in France use 'Mor Breizh' (The Sea of Brittany), and Germany uses 'Der Ärmelkanal' (The Sleeve Channel).

Some information is repeated where appropriate – so that its not necessary to flick though pages to get it.

**Review Request**
**THANK YOU for buying this Qatar guide I do hope you found it useful.**
**A review will help let others know if it's right for them compared to other guides to Qatar.**
**It will also let us know what we need to improve.**

I first arrived in Qatar at the turn of the millennium, when the National Museum was the Old Amiri Palace, which itself is now an exhibit within the current National Museum and the Sheraton Hotel was the most prominent building. Changes have been constant since then; both physical and regulatory. These will continue.

This guide is designed for practical use. It favours clarity over descriptive prose, and information over atmosphere. It is intended for independent travellers, and for those checking arrangements made by others - with an emphasis on realistic expectations rather than a curated, glossy Instagram-like portrayal of the country.

For some visitors, Souq Waqif and a desert drive will be great for a visit. However Doha has some great cultural attractions to visit, if time is available. Locations in this book are presented in the order you might reach them on a visit - using the Metro means its possible to jump from the National Museum to Katara without see other options.

The maps in this book are for general orientation, not Ordnance Survey-level precision. Accommodation and dining listings are intentionally selective. The hospitality market changes fast: properties open, rebrand, and close with little warning. The places included are sensible options for their price band in that specific location.

This book offers information which can also be checked against your own government's foreign ministry for current travel advice. For wider political and cultural context, outlets such as the BBC, Guardian, and Der Spiegel provide ongoing coverage, CNN may also be considered.

Spellings here, are hopefully, British English - and styling is my own.

# CONTENTS

1. ARRIVAL IN QATAR — 1
   *AND INFORMATION TO HELP*
   ENTRY REQUIREMENTS & VISAS — 2
   AIR ARRIVALS AND DEPARTURES — 6
   SEA ARRIVAL- The Cruise Terminal — 8
   LAND ARRIVAL The Saudi Arabian Border — 10
   MOBILE CONNECTIVITY & SIM CARDS. — 12
   GENERAL TRANSPORT INFORMATION — 14
   HEALTH and SAFETY CONSIDERATIONS — 32
   DIGITAL CONDUCT AND PRIVACY — 39
   PUBLIC HOLIDAYS IN QATAR — 47

2. WHERE TO GO — 50
   *AND WHAT TO SEE*
   CORNICHE AREA — 60
   SOUQ WAQIF — 73
   MSHEIREB — 83
   THE DOHA GRAND PARK: AL BIDDA, AL RUMAILA, AND WADI AL SAIL — 88
   IMAM MOHAMMED BIN ABDULWAHHAB MOSQUE — 90
   WEST BAY — 93
   DOHA SOUTH AND EAST: SPORTS AND LOW-COST SHOPPING — 96
   AL WAKRAH and SOUTHEAST QATAR — 98
   SOUTHEAST QATAR KHOR AL UDAID — 104
   EDUCATION CITY AND RAYYAN — 109
   ASPIRE — 121
   KATARA — 129
   THE PEARL — 136
   LUSAIL AND NORTHEAST DOHA — 139
   AL KHOR — 146
   NORTHERN QATAR — 152
   GHOST VILLAGES OF WESTERN QATAR — 159
   AL ZUBARAH — 167

| | |
|---|---|
| CENTRAL QATAR | 179 |
| SERVICE PROVIDERS - Tours, Events | 187 |
| **3. HOTELS AND RESTAURANTS** *OPTIONS TO CONSIDER* | 194 |
| RESTAURANTS | 198 |
| HOTELS | 224 |
| **4. BACKGROUND** *AND WHAT TO SEE* | 240 |
| NATURE | 244 |
| POPULATION & MAJOR PROJECTS | 265 |
| GOVERNMENT, POLITICS AND INTERNATIONAL RELATIONS | 270 |
| GDP, ECONOMY & MONEY: BANKS, ATM AND MONEY IN GENERAL | 271 |
| Food Production | 281 |
| CULTURE | 282 |
| DO'S AND DON'T'S | 290 |
| OTHER NATIONALITIES IN QATAR | 294 |
| ISLAMIC RELIGION IN QATAR | 295 |
| UNESCO LISTING | 298 |
| **5. HISTORY** | 310 |
| **6. THE AL THANI FAMILY** | 324 |
| **7. EXPLORERS OF QATAR** | 330 |
| **8. ARABIC LANGUAGE** | 334 |
| **9. INDEX** | 344 |

## CHAPTER 1
# ARRIVAL IN QATAR
## AND INFORMATION TO HELP

Introduction to Qatar

*Qatar Airways*

Qatar is a wonderful place to visit. The infrastructure is remarkable, and the government wants to make it easy for people to visit. I hope this book will inspire you explore the country. The book is organised into a short section on the practicalities of getting into the country [PAGE 2]. Then places to visit [PAGE 50], a selection of restaurants [PAGE 198], and some hotel options [PAGE 224]. If you want to learn more about the country you will visit, there is a section on the geography [PAGE 242] & history of the country [PAGE 310]. You will then have a better idea of what has contributed to Qatar's development. It's best to check the Qatari government websites listed below for the latest situation.

Qatar's arrival regulations have evolved quickly through 2026 and continue to change. Reference these key sources: Ministry of Public Health - https://www.moph.gov.qa/english/Pages/default.aspx; Visit Qatar - https://www.visitqatar.qa; Qatar Airways - https://www.qatarairways.com/en-gb/visa-and-passport-requirements.html ; Immigration: Hamad International Airport - https://dohahamadairport.com/airport-guide/at-the-airport/visas-immigration

**Diplomatic Missions** – If you need consular advice or long-stay permits, contact the relevant embassy directly: London: https://london.embassy.qa/en ; Washington: https://washington.embassy.qa/en ; Canberra: https://canberra.embassy.qa/en ; Berlin: https://berlin.embassy.qa/de (many pages are available in English)

ENTRY REQUIREMENTS & VISAS

Qatar's entry system is now highly digitalised. The core remains consistent, though updates occur regularly.

**Passport Validity** - Passports must be valid for at least 6 months from the date of entry. While some official sources occasionally cite three months for specific electronic visas, having a six-month validity. I suggest to add to a couple of weeks buffer which helps safeguard against flight delays or unforeseen changes to your itinerary.

**Visa on Arrival** - Nationals from over 100 countries can currently obtain a visa on arrival. The duration of stay is determined by reciprocal agreements: **Schengen Members (including Germany & France):** Typically permitted to spend up to **90 days** in Qatar within a 180-day period. **UK & USA:** Generally permitted a **30-day** stay, which can often be extended for an additional 30 days. Holders of passports from Israel should check the situation if they wish to visit.

**Extensions & Fees**; Should you require an extension, the fee is QAR100, payable by credit or debit card only. This is processed through the Ministry of Interior (MOI). While you can visit the dedicated Ministry of Interior Office located near the check-in area (between Rows 2 and 3), many travellers now manage extensions and inquiries via the official portal: https://portal.moi.gov.qa or the Hayya portal (if that was original used for visa entry) mobile app. Or **MOI Service Centres:** Ministry main building 25.305, 51.504.

The **Hayya** Platform; The 'Hayya' scheme (https://hayya.qa) has transitioned from a World Cup fan ID portal into a comprehensive digital portal for all visitors. It streamlines the entry process and provides access to e-Gates at the airport, letting you bypass manual immigration queues. UK, USA, or EU passport holders can register and then use the eGates at Hamad International Airport. Check with staff before you join the queue. By using the Hayya A1 (Tourist not qualifying for visa-free entry) or A3 (Electronic Travel Authorisation for those holding a UK, USA, or Schengen Area visa or residency) categories in advance, your details are already vetted in the system. This gives faster processing. At the border, the officer scans your passport, and your pre-approved status appears instantly.

**Visa on Arrival** (VoA): Visitors from the UK, USA, and the EU are currently exempt from the mandatory insurance requirement for the first 30 days of their stay. While entry is permitted without it, the **Ministry of Public Health** (MOPH) moph.gov.qa/english/Mandatory-Health-Insurance advises purchasing the standard QAR50 policy to avoid large out-of-pocket expenses at private clinics or Hamad Medical Corporation facilities. If you intend to extend your stay beyond the initial 30 days, purchasing this policy is a mandatory prerequisite for the extension.

**Hayya Platform** & Pre-approved Visas: For those arriving via the Hayya platform or a pre-approved **Ministry of Interior** (MOI) visa (such as for citizens of India or the Philippines), insurance is a requirement. The MOI portal will typically redirect you to the MoPH insurance gateway. You cannot finalise the visa without a valid policy number.

The GCC **Grand Tours Visa** (GTV) – a unified, Schengen-style permit designed to revolutionise travel across the six member states – is currently slated for a pilot launch by Q4 2026. This initiative will allow tourists to move freely between Saudi Arabia, Bahrain, Kuwait, Oman, Qatar and UAE, on a single authorisation, possibly valid for 30 to 90 days. While originally targeted for late 2025, the rollout is postponed ensuring the integration between the sovereign interior ministries. Crucially, the One-Point Air Travelers project is now under current testing; its "a Eurostar type domestic departure-style" passport control between Abu Dhabi and Bahrain. Once operational, the GTV visa is expected to cost USD100-130. Bahrain: evisa.gov.bh; Kuwait: evisa.moi.gov.kw, Qatar: hayya.qa; Oman: evisa.rop.gov.om; Saudi Arabia: ksavisa.sa; UAE: gdrfad.gov.ae; icp.gov.ae;

**Mandatory Health Insurance** is a broad requirement for all non-residents entering the State of Qatar. While the enforcement mechanism varies by visa category, the underlying principle remains: the state intends that every visitor is covered for medical emergencies.

Authorised Digital Providers The following "digital-first" providers are recognised for their efficiency: Qatar Insurance Company (QIC): The most streamlined digital portal (qic.online/en/visitors), allowing for a policy to be issued in under two minutes. QLM Life & Medical Insurance: A specialist with an extensive network of private hospitals. Their interface (qlm.com.qa) is highly functional for those seeking rapid confirmation. Beema (Damaan Islamic Insurance): Offers a minimalist, mobile-optimised experience (beema.com.qa) tailored for quick turnarounds.

Key Insurance Policy Facts - Cost: Fixed at QAR50 per 30-day period. Coverage: Limited to Emergency and Accident services. The limit is QAR150,000 for the policy period, with a QAR50,000 sub-limit for COVID-19 related treatments. Validity: The policy is active immediately upon issuance. It covers the visitor only within the borders of Qatar.

## INSURANCE FROM YOU OWN COUNTRY

It is advisable to also purchase travel insurance from a reputable "A-rated" company within your own home country. This might cover you (after mentioning existing medical conditions) from general travel disruption, accidents you receive, or cause to others (blood-money Diyya), lost property – repatriation flights and so on. Importantly they should cover for any activity you might engage in. Compensation claims might vary in how you deal with them if you have booked all your journey independently or as a package holiday. If you have booked through an aggregator (Booking.com etc) or direct to a hotel - contacting the entity you have booked through may resolve issues with travel disruption. Airlines often offer insurance for each flight, as might your own credit card.

Your government's travel advice is also critical. Many policies contain an Exclusion Clause that renders them invalid if you travel to a region against the 'Do Not Travel' warnings (or similar notifications) of your Foreign Ministry – or perhaps the government where the insurance company is based. Ensure you review the policy for notifications concerning *Vis Major* or *Force Majeure* – or indeed an 'Act of God' (wars or natural disasters) – any of which may render a policy void if in a region covered by them.

Qatar has a legal system distinct from many Western nations; consequently, medical and accident insurance structures obtained within Qatar differ significantly – including regarding compensation following any accidental injury.

**Other Countries Visa** For citizens including from the Indian subcontinent and the Philippines, research into specific visa categories and pre-approvals should be conducted via official channels such as https://www.qatarvisacenter.com (a government site) or the Hayya portal.

**Customs & Prohibited Items**

Qatar enforces strict customs checks to uphold its cultural and security standards. Navigating through Hamad International Airport (HIA) is straightforward if you comply with the country's import regulations.

**Prohibited & Restricted Items** The following items are strictly forbidden and will be confiscated, often resulting in fines or legal proceedings: **Alcohol:** The personal import of any alcohol - including 'Duty Free' purchased in transit - is entirely forbidden. **Pornography:** this is as viewed by Qatari authorities, not those of your own country. **Pork Products:** All forms of pork, including food items containing pork fat or gelatin, are prohibited. **Vaping & E-cigarettes:** As of 2026, the import of electronic cigarettes, vapes, and their associated liquids remains prohibited for personal entry. **Narcotics:** Qatar has a zero-tolerance policy. This includes seeds, such as poppy seeds, and any substance containing trace amounts of opiates. Such substances include **Codeine** and popular over-the-counter brands in the UK, such as **Solpadeine** or **Nurofen Plus**.

**Prescription Medication** If you have been prescribed medication that is controlled by Qatar (https://www.moph.gov.qa/arabic/Pages/default.aspx - look for PDF download Guideline-of-Controlled-Drugs-for-Travellers.pdf), you must be able to present: Original Documentation: The original prescription (in English or Arabic). **Medical Letter:** An official letter from your GP or consultant, signed and stamped, detailing the diagnosis and treatment plan for any controlled or 'psychotropic' medication. **Packaging & Volume:** The medication must be in its original packaging. Ensure you carry no more than a **30-day supply**. Note: Qatari pharmacies will not issue prescription medication against non-Qatari prescriptions. If you require more, you must consult a locally licensed physician.

**Duty-Free Allowances** For adult travellers (18+), the following exemptions apply for personal use: **Tobacco:** 400 cigarettes - OR - 20 cigars - OR - 300g of pipe tobacco. **Gifts & Personal Items:** A maximum value of **QAR3,000**. **Currency:** Any cash or precious metals exceeding **QAR50,000** in value must be declared upon arrival.

**Practical Customs Links;** For the most current list of restricted commodities, consult the official portals: **HIA Security & Customs:**https://dohahamadairport.com/airport-guide/at-the-airport/security-customs **General Authority of Customs:** https://www.customs.gov.qa

## AIR ARRIVALS AND DEPARTURES

Hamad International Airport (HIA) is a global aviation hub. While Qatar Airways dominates, the airport hosts multiple major international airlines.

As of 2026, the following airlines (and others) provide frequent direct services to Doha: **Major Carriers:** British Airways (London-Heathrow), Emirates (Dubai), Pegasus Airlines (Istanbul), and Turkish Airlines (Istanbul). **Qatar Airways Hub:** Operating from over 180 destinations, including: **UK:** London-Heathrow, London-Gatwick, Manchester, Birmingham, and Edinburgh. **Germany:** Frankfurt, Munich, Berlin (Brandenburg), Düsseldorf, and Hamburg. **France:** Paris (Charles de Gaulle) and Nice. **USA:** New York (JFK), Washington (Dulles), Chicago (O'Hare), Dallas/Fort Worth, Houston, Los Angeles, Miami, Atlanta, San Francisco, Boston, and Seattle.

**Navigating the Terminal.** The airport is large, with many high-end shops and modern art displays.

**Immigration (Arrivals):** Lines can be longer during early mornings and late evenings. If you have registered under the Hayya scheme or visit often, use the e-Gates for faster entry. These kiosks scan your passport and biometrics, letting you skip the manual desks. If you are unsure which line to join, ask an official near the immigration area for help. **Emigration (Departures):** Allow plenty of time to reach your gate when leaving Qatar. The central 'Orchard' and the 'Lamp Bear' are good landmarks, but some gates in the D and E concourses are a long walk or require a short ride on the shuttle train. Signs are modern but can be easy to miss, so always check the overhead digital displays for the latest gate information.

*The Orchard - HIA*

Hamad International Airport offers **Internet Access:** Complimentary, high-speed Wi-Fi is available throughout the terminal.

*Bear Lamp - HIA*

**Digital Assistance & Connectivity**. Airline apps are helpful for tracking your baggage. Many will tell you which baggage carousel to use soon after you land. If your bag is delayed, you may get a notification before you reach the hall, so you can go straight to the service desk instead of waiting at the belt.

**Currency & Banking:** Inside the baggage (luggage) reclaim area, you will find ATMs and a Travelex currency exchange (https://www.travelex.qa). Note that exchange rates at the airport are typically not as good as at money changers in Doha – though of course immeasurably more convenient – they are probably better than in your home country. Use the **ATM**s inside the baggage area; they are significantly less crowded than those in the public arrivals meeting hall. **Arrivals Hall:** Once through customs, the main hall provides toilets, further ATMs, currency exchange, and coffee shops for those awaiting transport.

Contact Points. **HIA Main Switchboard:** +974 4010 6666; **Lost Property Offices:** +974 3307 2482 or +974 4462 6531; **Email (General):** contact-us@hamadairport.com.qa or hialostproperty@hamadairport.com.qa; **Non-Qatar Airways Airlines:** llqas@qataraviation.com; **Qatar Airways Baggage:** https://haqiba.qatarairways.com.qa/ReportInquiry; **Flight Status:** https://dohahamadairport.com/airlines/flight-status

**Art & The "Orchard".** HIA is famed for its "Art Programme," featuring museum-quality installations that serve as useful landmarks. **The Orchard:** A standout 10,000-square-metre indoor tropical garden located in the northern expansion (Concourse C). It features over 300 trees and a vast water feature, providing a tranquil "oasis" ambiance under a glass roof. **The Lamp Bear:** The iconic yellow teddy bear by Urs Fischer is situated in the central Departure/Transit area (Concourse B) and acts as the airport's primary mascot. **Small Lie:** Created by American artist Brian Donnelly (KAWS), this 32-foot wooden marionette is located in the North Node near Concourse E, adjacent to the **sleep 'n fly** lounge. **Other Works:** Look for sculptures by Tom Claassen (the "Oryx" family) and the playful "Playground" installations by Tom Otterness.

**Internal Transit.** Due to the airport's vast footprint, an automatic internal shuttle train connects the South Node (near the Lamp Bear) to the North Node (near the Orchard and Concourse D/E). The train runs 24 hours a day, significantly reducing the time to reach a gate.

## SEA ARRIVAL- THE CRUISE TERMINAL

Doha has rapidly established itself as a premier destination for winter sun cruising in the Arabian Gulf. It's a round trip program based out of Dubai. Ships typically call into Dubai, Abu Dhabi, Muscat, and Bahrain. Major operators such as AIDA, Costa, MSC, and TUI (Mein Schiff) are frequent visitors between November and May.

*Aida in Port*

Regional maritime schedules can be subject to alteration due to geopolitical shifts in the Arabian Gulf or the Red Sea-Suez Canal route. **Doha Port** (Old Port) & The Cruise Terminal. Cruise ships dock at the Grand Cruise Terminal at Old Doha Port [PAGE 64].

This facility is a notable architectural feature, with over 1,000 arches and a terminal building that houses a large aquarium and the City Art Gallery. **Facilities:** The port area, known as the **Mina District**, is a pastel-coloured 'village' containing over 50 restaurants, 100 retail outlets, a fish market, and the **Mina Hotel & Residences**. **Logistics:** You will find foreign exchange services, taxi ranks, and a duty-free shop at the terminal complex.**Transit to the City**.

The port is situated at the southern tip of the Doha Corniche, making it an easy springboard for cultural exploration. **Shuttle Services:** Most cruise lines offer complimentary shuttle buses to the **Museum of Islamic Art (MIA)** [PAGE 65]. From the MIA, it is a pleasant **1.5km walk** along the promenade to **Souq Waqif** [PAGE 73]. The **National Museum of Qatar** [PAGE 60] is less than a 15-minute drive from the terminal. If you prefer to walk between the two museums, the distance is roughly **2km**. **Taxis & Apps: Taxis** are readily available at the terminal. Using the Sila/Karwa or Uber apps is the most efficient way to get around for short hops to West Bay or Msheireb.

**Entry Formalities when arriving by sea**

For most cruise passengers in 2026, the entry process is streamlined: **Visa Requirements:** A 96-hour transit visa or a visa-on-arrival is generally available to many nationalities (including UK, USA, and EU citizens). **Liaison:** Your cruise line typically handles the manifest and immigration formalities using the passport details you provided at embarkation. **Health Insurance:** While short-term transit passengers are often covered under the ship's protocols, those embarking or disembarking in Doha (turnaround passengers) are required to purchase the mandatory **QAR50** national health insurance. Shore Excursions: Popular choices include a half-day "Doha Express" city tour or a desert safari to the inland sea of Khor Al Adaid.

LAND ARRIVAL THE SAUDI ARABIAN BORDER

The only land gateway into the Qatari peninsula is the **Abu Samra** border crossing, located in the southwest of the country. On the Saudi Arabian side, the frontier is known as the **Salwa** border. For those driving from Riyadh or transit passengers from the wider GCC, transits from the vast Saudi interior to the Qatari coast.

**Documentation & Pre-Registration.** In 2026, the border has become significantly more digitalised. To ensure a swift crossing, the following are ideal. Pre-Registration: This can save time and reduce uncertainty. Qatari residents can use the Metrash app, while international visitors should use the Hayya Portal (https://hayya.qa). Pre-clearing your vehicle and passenger details allows you to use dedicated fast lanes at the border.

**Vehicle Insurance (MSAR).** As of February 2026, the process for vehicle insurance to visit Qatar has effectively transitioned to the MSAR digital platform (https://msar.com.qa). For short-term visits (between one and four weeks), physical insurance counters at the Abu Samra border have been suspended. You must now purchase your insurance electronically. While some regional insurance policies offer "GCC extensions", ensure yours specifically fulfils the Qatari Third-Party Liability requirement. The MSAR system is the most reliable way to guarantee compliance and avoid being turned back at the gates. For stays of one month or longer, on-site counters remain available, though using the digital system is still advised to access the dedicated fast lanes at the border.

**Passports & Visas:** Passports must be valid for at least six months. Non-GCC nationals must ensure they are eligible for a Qatari visa (or Hayya permit) and, crucially, a **Saudi Transit or Tourist Visa** when driving through the Kingdom. If you are a foreign resident in Saudi Arabia, ensure your exit/re-entry permit is active, and your residency card (Iqama) has at least three months of validity. **Vehicle Registration** documents must be in the vehicle. If the car is not in your name (e.g., a company car or a borrowed car), you must have a notarised No Objection Certificate (NOC) for its international use. **Driving Licences** and International Driving Permit (IDP). The originals are essential for non-GCC license holders to ensure insurance validity and smooth police inspections.

**The Crossing Experience.** The border complex is large and modern. While there are separate lanes for GCC nationals and other passport holders, officials may occasionally direct traffic to balance the load. Allow around an hour – for visa, customs and vehicle inspection. **Exit Requirements:** If you are a foreign resident in Saudi Arabia, ensure your **Exit/Re-entry Visa** is valid and that your Iqama (residency permit) has at least three months of remaining validity. **Fuel & Provisions:** There are petrol stations on both sides of the border. Because the drive between Abu Samra and the next major towns crosses long stretches of desert, it is wise to fill your tank near the border.

**International Bus Services (SAPTCO).** The Saudi Arabian Public Transport Company, SAPTCO (https://www.saptco.com.sa), has historically operated a Riyadh-Doha service. While the availability of this route has fluctuated, 2026 has seen a resurgence in regional bus connectivity. **Status:** Services have been reintroduced on a seasonal basis. I recommend checking the SAPTCO app or their website for the most up-to-date timetable, as these services are often added or adjusted in response to demand for major regional events.

## MOBILE CONNECTIVITY & SIM CARDS.

If you are staying in Qatar for more than a short layover, getting a local SIM card is a good idea. International roaming can be expensive, but local data rates in 2026 are affordable. Having a Qatari number also makes it easier to book restaurants and use local transport apps. Internet speeds may be faster than those in many western countries.

**Providers & Purchase Points.** The market is a duopoly between two established operators, both offering extensive 5G coverage across the peninsula. **Ooredoo** (https://www.ooredoo.qa)**:** The national carrier. Their 'Hala' visitor SIMs are specifically tailored for tourists. You can find their kiosks immediately after immigration in the baggage reclaim area and at Exits 2, 3, and 4 in the Arrivals Hall. **Vodafone Qatar** (https://www.vodafone.qa) are a reliable alternative with similar pricing and coverage. They maintain a prominent presence at Hamad International Airport (HIA) and in major shopping malls, including Villaggio and Doha Festival City. **Registration & Setup**; By law, all SIM cards must be registered against a valid passport (ID). Staff at airport kiosks are well-versed in this process and can usually activate the card and configure your handset within minutes. **eSIM Option:** If your device is compatible, both Ooredoo and Vodafone offer eSIMs. These can often be purchased and activated via their respective apps or websites before you even land, allowing for immediate connectivity upon touchdown.

**Communication Apps & Privacy.** Digital communication in Qatar is tightly regulated by the government: **WhatsApp:**

Messaging, including text, photos, and voice notes, functions perfectly. However, **Voice over IP (VoIP)** - specifically WhatsApp voice and video calling - is frequently restricted on local networks. **VPN Usage:** While travellers often use Virtual Private Networks (VPNs) to bypass these calling restrictions, be aware that connectivity can be unstable. **Monitoring:** You should assume that authorities monitor social media and messaging platforms. Do not share anything that could be seen as politically sensitive or culturally offensive under Qatari law. This may include social media posts of incident the government might consider detrimental to Qatar's image.

Hamad International Airport provides complimentary high-speed Wi-Fi. Numerous "Internet Desks" and help kiosks are scattered throughout the terminal if you require assistance with local connectivity or downloading the Sila app.

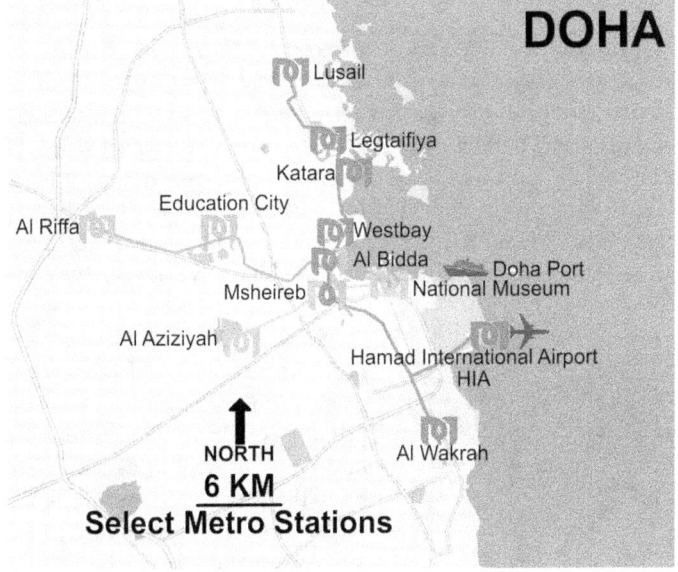

**Emergency Services**

For any life-threatening situation, criminal activity, or fire, the following numbers are operative 24 hours a day:

Unified Emergency Service (Police, Fire, Ambulance): 999

Emergency Service for the Deaf and Hearing-Impaired: 992 (Accessible via 3G video call, SMS, or email at 992@moi.gov.qa)

Coast Guard: 999 (The operator will transfer you to the relevant coastal patrol unit)

Assistance for Women and Children (Domestic Abuse): 919

Environmental Violations Reporting: 998

**Transport and Travel**

For issues on the road or enquiries regarding public transport:

Traffic and Patrol Police Department (Non-emergency): 4489 0666

Mowasalat (Karwa Taxi and Bus Services): 4458 8888

Qatar Rail (Doha Metro and Lusail Tram): 105

Hamad International Airport Enquiries: 4010 6666

Qatar Assist (Roadside Assistance): 5545 5252

## GENERAL TRANSPORT INFORMATION

A key payment and information system for Qatar's transport sector is Sila (www.sila.qa). App or a Card. **The Sila Card:** A unified "smart travel card" that you can tap on readers across different modes of transport. **The Sila App:** A journey planner and digital wallet. It allows you to plan routes, check real-time schedules, and pay using a **QR-Code** on your phone if you do not wish to carry the physical card. It also supports direct payment via contactless credit/debit cards (Visa/Mastercard) and mobile wallets like Apple Pay and Google Pay.

*Metro Card*

**Services Covered by Sila.** Sila has successfully unified several services under one payment and planning umbrella: Under the Sila integration, if a passenger transfers from the Metro to a bus within a specific time window, the total fare is often capped or discounted to reflect a single journey. Ask specifically about this time window when buying a card. The Karwa card and app currently function – choose Sila for a new purchase.

The Public Transport Network in Doha, public transport provides reliable access to most sites of interest. A historical frustration for travellers was the need for separate fare cards; however, the integrated Sila platform aims to unify the Metro, Lusail Tram, and Karwa buses under a single payment framework. Despite this, it is prudent to check if specific legacy Karwa cards are still required for certain regional routes.

**Doha Metro**. Sila Card, App QR-Code, or Contactless Bank Card

**Karwa Public Buses**. Sila Card, App QR-Code, or Contactless Bank Card

**Lusail Tram**. Sila Card, App QR-Code, or Contactless Bank Card

**Karwa Taxis**. Sila App (linked payment) or Sila Card (in some vehicles)

**Metrolink** (Feeder Bus). Free, but requires a tap with a Sila/Metro card for statistics.

**Msheireb & Education City Trams**. Integrated for planning, though they are free to use

However – perhaps the most practical method to pay is by debit card (tap in and tap out using the same card) if you have a Starling type card (transaction charge free). This is especially convenient from the airport as it saves dealing with a ticket machine. The same fare structure applies as with the Sila system. However, a debit card currently cannot be used on the Karwa buses.

Many bank cards will have a disproportionately high transaction fee for small costs like a metro journey. Check your card's conditions of use. Always ask Metro staff to verify what options are available to you.

*Karwa Ticket Machine*

**Where to Purchase and Recharge travel cards**. Sila cards are available at all **Doha Metro and Lusail Tram stations** (via Ticket Vending Machines - TVMs), **Hamad International Airport**. Ask staff for support if needed. **Recharging: In-person:** Use the TVMs at any Metro or Tram station. **Digital:** Top up instantly via the **Sila**

**App** or the official website using a credit or debit card. **Third-party:** Many "Authorised Merchants" (local grocery stores with the Sila logo) and **Ooredoo Self-Service Machines** also offer top-up services.

*Doha Metro Carriage*

## THE DOHA METRO

The backbone of Doha's transit is the Metro system www.metrotram.qa/, managed under the Sila integrated network. For most visitors, the combination of the Metro, MetroLink feeder buses, and the Education City, Lusail and Msheireb Trams provides a comprehensive way to navigate the capital.

The metro system currently operates three primary lines - Red, Gold, and Green - covering 37 stations. While the network is largely subterranean in the dense heart of Doha, it emerges onto elevated tracks as it strikes out towards the periphery. Plans for a Blue Line, connecting Hamad International Airport directly to West Bay, are projected for completion within the next decade.

**Carriage Classes and Access**. Each passenger aged 5 or older requires a valid TravelCard. The trains are divided into three distinct sections: **Standard:** Open to all travellers. **Gold Club:** Requires a specific premium Gold TravelCard; these carriages offer better seating. **Family/Female:** Reserved for women and families; men are not permitted unless accompanied by a female relative. Pets are not allowed. The trains are driverless – with the front and rear carriages having panoramic widows at each end.

## Fares and Timing

The Metro's efficiency is reflected in its pricing. A single standard journey is QAR2.00, with daily expenditure capped at QAR6.00. For those preferring the Gold Club, a single journey is QAR10 with a QAR30 daily cap. Standard cards cost QAR10 and Gold cards QAR100, both requiring additional credit for travel. Journeys are strictly timed; the maximum trip duration is 90 minutes. The Metro operates on the following schedule: **Saturday to Thursday:** 05:00 - 01:00 (the following day); **Friday:** 09:00 - 01:00 (Saturday morning) timings are often extended during major events.

*Metro Entrance Souq Waqif*

Trains from the **Airport Metro Station** run from around 05:10-00:20 from Sun-Thurs, and 09:00 to 00:10 on Friday and Saturday 05:10-00:20 (other stations will have slightly different timings within the general Metro timings).

The HIA Metro station is found after exiting airport arrivals - turn right and diagonally opposite you take the lifts and follow the signs via travellator & lift/escalator. The route though essentially straight changes floor level several times.

The Metro stations in Doha are extremely spacious, most especially Msheireb station and other hubs. They are also clean, and litter free.

**The Metro Lines**

The Red Line (Coast Line). This north - south artery connects Hamad International Airport to Lusail QNB station. It offers vital interchanges at Al Bidda and Msheireb. From these hubs, the alleys of Souq Waqif are less than a 1.5 km stroll. The metro then passes under the skyscraper forest of West Bay. The Gold Line (Historic Line) runs east-west and links Ras Bu Aboud to Al Aziziya. It is the essential route for culture seekers, serving the National Museum of Qatar and the Museum of Islamic Art (via the Souq Waqif station). The Green Line (Education Line) stretches from Al Mansoura in the south and cuts west to Al Riffa. It provides access to Education City and the Qatar National Library.

The Metro is bolstered by the **Metrolink feeder bus service** as a last-Kilometre Service within a 2-5 kilometre radius of most stations and are free, though passengers must "tap in and out" with a travel card to provide the authorities with usage statistics. **MetroExpress** works within specific central zones, and offers an on-demand passenger van service. This complimentary feature can be requested via the Karwa Taxi App and serves six major stations, acting as a flexible bridge between the station doors and your final destination – again ask staff as this service will be reassessed.

A proposed high-speed rail project, intended to traverse the sands at 300kmph between Doha and Riyadh, signals a significant pivot in regional connectivity stitching the Qatar peninsula closer to the Saudi heartland.

**PUBLIC BUS SERVICES**

The public bus network, operated by Mowasalat under the turquoise coloured Karwa brand, remains a vital artery of the Sila integrated transport system. While the Metro serves the city's primary hubs, the bus network reaches into the city's more granular corners and stretches across the peninsula to industrial and residential outposts https://www.mowasalat.com/mowasalat/public-transportation/routes/ In line with Qatar's sustainability mandates, in 2026, the fleet is almost entirely electric - moving silently through the city. More information - www.mowasalat.com

*Karwa Bus*

**Key Airport Bus Routes.** While many routes primarily serve industrial or residential nodes, the following are of particular interest to visitors: **Route 757:** Operates 24 hours a day, connecting the airport to the **Al Mansoura** district. This is a useful alternative if the Metro has closed for the night. **Route T612:** Provides a 24-hour service to the **Industrial Area**. **Route T613:** Connects the airport to **Al Wakrah** and the industrial city of **Mesaieed** (operating 24/7).

**Bus Fares and the TravelCard System**

Cash is not accepted on board a bus (currently debit cards do not work either); all fares must be paid using a Sila (or Karwa) Smart Card or a digital E-Ticket via the Sila App. These are available at airport vending machines and throughout the city. **Classic Card:** Costs **QAR 30** (which includes **QAR 20** pre-loaded credit). This is the most pragmatic option for those staying several days or taking varied trips. **Limited Card:** Costs **QAR 10** and is valid for two single journeys within a 24-hour period. **Unlimited Card:** Costs **QAR 20** and provides unlimited bus travel across the entire network for 24 hours. For a more modern experience, you may skip the physical card entirely by using the **Sila App to generate a QR-Code for each journey**. This also allows you to link your card for automatic top-ups. Karwa cards are available at Ticket Vending Machines (TVMs) at Hamad International Airport, all major bus stations, and via Ooredoo outlets. For convenience, larger supermarket chains such as Lulu and Carrefour also stock them. See above for payment – always check with staff regarding the possibility of using the Sila Card, or a debit card (noting that many cards may levy a transaction chard for each use).

*Metro Matar Al Qadeem and MetroLink Bus*

Buses utilise a "tap on, tap off" system (meaning you must scan your smartcard when boarding and when leaving). Fares are distance-dependent, typically ranging from QAR2.50 for short inner-city hops to QAR9 for longer excursions beyond the Doha city limits. The Sila Card works for Metro, Tram, Karwa bus and maroon Metrolink feeder buses.

Most newer buses are equipped with the hardware for contactless bank cards – however currently they do not accept them. The **Metrolink feeder bus service** is free, but you must use your Metro Travel Card or the Karwa app to "verify" your journey.

**Bus Operations and Infrastructure**

Bus stops are easily identified by large red boxes painted onto the asphalt and modest vertical signage. Operating hours generally run from 05:00 to 23:00, Saturday through Thursday. On Fridays, services are significantly curtailed - with some routes suspended entirely. However, routes serving the airport often operate 24 hours a day.

The **HIA Mowasalat Bus Station** GPS 25.259, 51.612 is signed; turn right after exiting immigration – ticket machines are just before the actual bus parking area. Karwa is increasingly used for the Mowasalat brand name of their transport bus/taxi service.

For real-time navigation, the Sila App and the Karwa Journey Planner are good digital tools for tracking these turquoise fleets, though local commuters often need to exercise patience when waiting for suburban connections.

## DRIVING IN QATAR

Qatar uses left-hand drive (drive sits on the left of the vehicle as in Europe and much of the world). The road network in the city is a sophisticated, often dizzying for Europeans, mix of traffic-light junctions, multi-lane roundabouts, and expansive flyovers. Signage is bilingual in Arabic and English, with distances and speeds marked in kilometres using the standard Indo-Arabic numerals common in the West. Rental vehicles are almost universally automatic and equipped with powerful air-conditioning.

Regulations generally mirror Western standards, enforcement is rigorous. Penalties for jumping a red light are severe (QAR6,000), and leaving the scene of even a minor accident is a serious offence. Front-seat occupants must wear seat belts, it is now standard practice and increasingly enforced for rear seat passengers. Children under 10 - or those shorter than 145 cm - are prohibited from the front seat.

The national speed limit is 120 km/h, this drops significantly in urban zones to 60 or 80 km/h.

**Fuel and Services**

Qatar's petrol stations are more than just refuelling points; they are community hubs operating under the state owned brand "Woqod". In the majority stations there are convenience stores " Sidra". These will have small takeaway food & coffee offerings. Larger stations will have other services such as restaurants and extensive car wash and oil change facilities, Fuel prices are regulated by Qatar Energy (formerly Qatar Petroleum) and adjusted monthly. An attendant will fill up your vehicle with petrol. It is customary to offer a small tip or "round up" the change (e.g., to the nearest QAR5), particularly if they have cleaned your windscreen - a nice service given the persistent desert dust. Current Petrol Rates (February 2026): **Premium (91):** QAR1.80 per litre. **Super (95):** QAR1.85 per litre. **Diesel:** QAR1.90 per litre

**Road Surveillance and Restrictions**

The state employs a network of fixed and mobile **radar units**. These sophisticated systems use facial and license plate recognition to detect not only speeding but also mobile phone use and seat belt violations. Do not expect warning signs for speed traps; they are designed to be felt through the wallet rather than seen on the road. Similarly, "speed tables" and aggressive speed bumps often lack visibility; hitting one at speed can easily damage a vehicle's chassis.

Heavy vehicles are strictly regulated to manage the city's traffic flow. Trucks are prohibited from Doha's roads during peak hours: 06:00 - 08:30 / 12:00 - 15:00 / 17:00 - 22:00. Crucially, trucks and large buses (over 25 passengers) are permanently banned from February 22 Street, a primary north-south artery that is notoriously congested even without heavy traffic.

**Strategic Routes** - For the visitor, navigating Doha is easier once the logic of its ring roads is understood. The core is encircled by the A Ring Road (now Al Diwan St), with subsequent rings - B, C, D, E, F, and G - expanding outwards. The D and E rings eventually merge into the Doha Expressway. Two routes are key to visitors: **The Corniche:** A 7 km coastal curve that is as scenic as it is functional. It provides the most direct access to the **National Museum of Qatar**, the **Museum of Islamic Art**, and **West Bay**. **The Inner Loop:** This bypass skirts the heavy traffic of the traditional centre. Formed by the **Ras Abu Abboud Expressway**, **B Ring Road**, and the

**Lusail Expressway**, it allows for swift transit from the port area towards **Katara** and **The Pearl** [PAGE 136].

Renting a vehicle in Qatar is an efficient way to explore the peninsula. Most visitors find the process familiar, though it is governed by specific timelines that dictate the validity of foreign documentation.

**Licensing and Eligibility**

The minimum age for hiring a car is generally 21, though many agencies restrict premium or 4x4 fleets to drivers aged 25 and above who have held a full licence for at least one year. The legal validity of your documents is strictly time-bound: **Your National Licence:** Can be used for a hire for **7 to 15 days** from your date of entry (this varies by car hire company; always verify their specific grace period). **International Driving Permit (IDP):** If you carry a **1968 Convention IDP** alongside your national licence, you may drive for up to **6 months**. **Temporary Qatari Licence:** For stays exceeding these limits, you must apply for a temporary licence at the **Traffic Department Headquarters** in **Madinat Khalifa**. You will need your passport (plus photocopies), three colour passport-style photos, and a fee of **QAR160**. Note that an eye test at an accredited centre is usually required. **GCC Licences:** Licences issued by other Gulf Cooperation Council states are valid for short-term use without an IDP.

**Hire Companies** - there are approximately 20 car rental providers in the airport, concentrated in the terminal's ground transport area. After exiting the Arrivals hall, the car rental counters are located across the road, accessible via the pedestrian crossings. Qatar offers a balance of global franchises and long-standing local specialists. International Brands: Well-established global firms with multiple branches, including **Hamad International Airport**: **Europcar:** www.europcarqatar.com; **Avis:** www.avisqatar.com; **Hertz:** ; www.hertz.com ; Local Specialists: Qatari firms often provide competitive rates and a deep understanding of local logistics: **Al Mana Leasing:** Part of a major national conglomerate, offering a modern fleet. almanaleasing.com; **Mustafawi:** A reliable choice that has operated in the country since 1976. www.mustafawi.qa ; **Strong Rent A Car:** Known for a diverse fleet ranging from compacts to high-end SUVs. www.strongrentacar.com

Estimated Rates (2026): **Compact/Economy:** QAR120 -

QAR180 per day. **Intermediate/SUV:** QAR250 - QAR450 per day. **Full-size 4x4:** QAR500+ per day.

Before accepting a vehicle, check it carefully, you will have left the country before any security deposit etc might be refunded, or not. Use your phone to photograph any existing dents, scratches, or interior marks. Ensure the vehicle is equipped with a functioning spare tyre, jack, and tools – having a charger or working cigarette lighter (power adaptor needed) to power mobile phones is ideal. Critically, ask the agent to verify that the vehicle has no outstanding traffic fines via the Metrash app. If fines are pending, request a different vehicle; Qatari police may hold the current driver responsible for unpaid violations incurred by previous occupants.

The Metrash app (previously Metrash2 app) was developed by Qatar's Ministry of Interior (MOI) to provide citizens and residents with direct access to government e-services. Part of its service is to allow users to view and settle traffic fines and submit photographs to report minor traffic accidents.

Driving without a valid licence is a crime that voids all insurance coverage. Other non-negotiable rules include: **Child Safety:** Children under 10 are strictly prohibited from the front seat. **Seat Belts:** Mandatory for front-seat occupants; enforcement for rear-seat passengers is now standard in 2026. **Mobile Phones:** Any use of a handheld device whilst driving is a major violation, often caught by sophisticated facial-recognition cameras.

**Accident Protocol Minor Accidents (No Injuries)**

Check current regulation with your hire company. For minor "fender benders" where no one is injured, do not call the police to the scene. In Qatar, the current priority is to clear the roadway immediately to maintain the flow of traffic. **Contact the Hire Company:** As a visitor, you cannot use the Metrash app directly. Your first call must be to your rental agency. Major companies (such as Hertz or Budget) have dedicated teams who will register the accident for you via their corporate Metrash app access once you send them the photos and location. **Document:** Take at least four clear photos of each vehicle. Ensure at least one photo shows the damage in relation to the other car and another clearly displays the number plate. **Clear the Road:** Move the vehicles to a safe spot, such as the hard shoulder or a nearby parking area, to avoid obstructing traffic. **The Resident Advantage:** If the other party involved is a Qatari citizen or resident, they can register the accident on their **Metrash app** immediately. After confirming with your car hire company - you will simply provide the other driver with your passport details, visa number, and the rental company's registration information. **Police Station Visit:** If neither party can access the app (for example, two visitors with their own cars in a collision), you must both drive to the nearest **Traffic Department** station. The police will inspect the vehicles and issue the report there. **The SMS:** Once registered, both the driver at fault and the affected party will receive an SMS from the **Ministry of Interior (MOI)**. This digital report is essential for the hiring company and insurance providers to process repairs.

*Highway out of Doha*

### Major Accidents (Injuries or Fatalities)

In the event of a significant collision involving serious injury or death, the procedural landscape shifts from a simple administrative task to a formal criminal investigation. In Qatar, such incidents are treated with the utmost gravity by the **Ministry of Interior** (MOI). **Emergency Contact:** Immediately dial **999**. This central hub coordinates the **Hamad Medical Corporation** (HMC) ambulance service and the traffic police. The response is typically swift – HMC's fleet of modern ambulances is a constant, reassuring presence on Doha's arterial roads. **Scene Preservation:** Unlike minor "fender benders", you must **not** move the vehicles. The position of the cars is vital forensic evidence. Hazard lights should be activated, and if it is safe to do so, place a warning triangle 50 metres behind the site. **Medical Priority:** Provide what assistance you can, but do not move an injured person unless there is an immediate threat of fire or explosion. The HMC paramedics are highly trained; let them take the lead the moment they arrive. **Police Investigation:** A specialized unit from the **General Directorate of Traffic** will attend the scene. They will conduct a thorough investigation, including measurements and witness statements. As a visitor, you must provide your passport, entry visa, and international driving permit. **Ensure the hire company is notified immediately**, as they will need the police-generated case number to manage the vehicle's recovery. **The Metrash App:** While you cannot initiate the report for a major accident yourself, the police will eventually link the case to your records

**Legal Implications and Diya.** In the Arab World, and specifically under Qatari Law, the concept of **Diya** (Blood Money) is a critical pillar of the justice system. It serves as a financial compensation to the victim's family and is distinct from any criminal penalties. **Fixed Compensation:** As of 2026, the legal Diya for wrongful death is fixed at **QAR 200,000** per individual. This amount is standard regardless of the victim's nationality, gender, or religion. **Insurance Coverage:** Your mandatory visitor insurance or the rental car's third-party liability policy is legally obligated to cover this amount, provided you were not driving under the influence of alcohol or drugs, or without a valid licence. **Criminal Proceedings:** An accident involving a fatality or serious injury automatically triggers a court case. The public prosecutor will determine if negligence or a traffic violation (such as running a red light) occurred. It is highly advisable to seek legal counsel through your embassy if you are involved in such a case, as a travel ban may be placed on your passport until the matter is settled. **The "Golden Hour" of Documentation.** While the police handle the formal report, your own documentation remains your best defence: **Witnesses:** If bystanders stop to help, politely ask for their mobile numbers. **Dashcam:** If your rental vehicle is equipped with a dashcam – a growing trend in Qatar – ensure the footage is saved and mention its existence to the investigating officer. **Medical Reports:** Even if you feel unhurt, seek a check-up at a HMC Emergency Department.

*Karwa Taxi - Souq Waqif*

## TAXI SERVICES

The most recognisable vehicles on the road remain the turquoise Karwa taxis, operated by the state-owned Mowasalat. In 2026, these vehicles - often adorned with the image of the Arabian Oryx - represent the backbone of the city's point-to-point transit. Under Qatari law, all Karwa vehicles must be metered. If a driver refuses to engage the device, the passenger is entitled to a free ride; such firm regulations are the bedrock of the country's consumer protection.

The **Airport Taxi Kiosk** is signed at the end of the arrivals on the left side (east). Taxis may be flagged on the street in town , though in the midday heat – it's easy to use the Sila App or the Karwa Taxi App. For passengers with reduced mobility, specialised accessible taxis should be booked via the app or by calling +974 4458 8888. Contact to give at least two hours' notice for these bookings. Payment is handled seamlessly via cash, credit card, or the "Karwa Wallet".

Karwa Fares (2026): All Karwa taxis are metered. Trips originating from the airport carry a mandatory starting flag-fall of QAR 25.00. Day Rate (05:00 - 21:00hours):QAR1.60 per kilometre. Night Rate (21:00 - 05:00hours):QAR1.90 per kilometre (this rate also applies to trips outside Doha city limits).

### Ride-Hailing Apps

While Karwa remains the "on-demand" choice at the rank, app-based services offer upfront pricing and digital tracking. **Uber** is the primary international ride-hailing service in Qatar. For a journey from **Hamad International Airport** to **West Bay** or the **Sheraton**, expect to pay approximately **QAR 40 - QAR 60** for an UberX, and **QAR 65 - QAR 85** for an UberXL. **Careem:** Note that Careem ceased its ride-hailing operations in Qatar in early 2023, making **Uber** the sole international heavyweight in the sector. However Careem still provides delivery services. **Logistics:** Airport pickups for app-based rides are strictly regulated. After booking, follow the "Ride-share" signage to the **Short Term Car Park** (specifically the East Car Park area). Your app will designate a specific numbered pillar or zone for the meeting point.

**The Robo-Taxi (Level 4):** An addition to the fleet in 2026 is the driverless **Robo-Taxi**. Currently (on a limited period trial assessment basis) operating daily from 6 am to 4 am to select zones, such as **West Bay** from the **Airport** area, these electric Lexus RX450 vehicles equipped with advanced cameras and LiDAR are autonomous vehicles that can be requested via the Karwa app. They offer a glimpse of a future in which the "Sheikh of the road" may no longer need a human hand on the wheel – though there is currently a human assistant in the driver's seat! The service is limited to 2 passengers at the moment.

A Note on Fare Negotiation. Regardless of the service, one must never accept a "negotiated" price. A driver suggesting you "decide the fare" at the destination is a ruse as old as the desert sands; the eventual "decision" will invariably be by them and will exceed the metered or app-estimated rate. Always ensure the meter is active or the app fare is locked before the vehicle begins its journey.

## THE TRAM SYSTEMS

Doha's metro network is supported by three distinct tram systems, all integrated into the broader Sila identity to ensure a frictionless transition for commuters.

**Msheireb Tram** is a complimentary circular tram system operates on a 2 km loop. The fleet consists of hydrogen-electric vehicles, a silent and sustainable nod to the district's "smart city" ethos. The service includes nine stops including: **Sahat Al Nakheel** (The Date Palm Square), - serves as the connection point for the Metro. **Wadi Msheireb. Galleria** - the primary stop for **Souq Waqif** and **Heritage Quarter** - providing access to the **Msheireb Museums**.

The tram runs from 10:00 - 22:00 between Saturday and

Thursday, and on Fridays from 14:00 - 22:00. It is a sleek, efficient service that allows visitors to bypass the humid stroll between the historic Souq and the modern boutiques of Msheireb.

**Education City Tram**

The Education City Tram is a state-of-the-art, battery-powered network. It is a small illustration of Qatar's investment in sustainable urban mobility. This catenary-free system uses Siemens Avenio technology. It charges its super-capacitors at each station so there are no overhead wires. The network is fully integrated into the Sila app for journey planning, though it currently remains Free of Charge (FOC) for all passengers.

**The Network:** Yellow, Blue, and Green Lines. **The Yellow Line** is the main route for visitors, starting at Al Shaqab Metro Station (Gold Line Metro) and stopping outside the **Qatar National Library** (QNL). The tracks are lined with Sidra trees (Ziziphus spina-christi), the symbol of **Qatar Foundation**. **The Blue** and **Green Lines** serve the western and northern campus sectors. The Green Line crosses north of the Dukhan Highway via a dedicated underpass. It reaches Oxygen Park and the residential quarters. While lines are integrated, transitioning between the Blue and Green lines may require a brief walk across a landscaped car park. Operating Hours: Saturday to Thursday: 06:00 - 22:00 - Friday: 14:00 - 22:00

**Lusail Tram**

Located in the growing coastal city of Lusail, this light-rail system www.metrotram.qa/ is integrated with the Doha Metro. Commuters can interchange between the two networks at the Legtaifiya and Lusail QNB stations. While the network is designed for four lines, three are currently operational in 2026 - the Orange, Pink, and Turquoise lines. These serve the burgeoning residential and commercial hubs, including Marina South, Yacht Club, and Seef Lusail. Due to the district's occupancy, some stations remain closed or operate on restricted schedules; check the Sila App for the live status of the "Seef" coastal sections.

Fares and Operations: A single Lusail Tram journey is QAR2, with daily caps identical to the Metro. **TravelCard:** The standard Metro TravelCard is valid for all Lusail Tram journeys. Note that there are no "Gold Club" carriages on the tram. **Operating Hours:** Saturday - Thursday 05:00-01:30, Friday 14:00-01:30 (Saturday morning). On the Lusail Tram, some stations appear fully functional but the tram doors do not open because the surrounding towers are not yet used. It is a peculiar "sim-city" experience.

**BICYCLES & SCOOTERS**

While utilising a bicycle for a daily commute remains an outlier for many "ex-pats" in Doha - often deterred by the summer sun that feels like a physical weight upon the shoulders - leisure cycling has surged in popularity. For those unfamiliar with local road habits, it is prudent to ride with more experienced riders before riding solo on the expressways.

**Dedicated Cycling Routes**

Qatar has built many safe cycling paths with smooth surfaces. **The Olympic Cycling Track stretches** 33 km from Doha north to Al Khor. It starts near Doha Sports Park at GPS 25.378, 51.498. This route holds the Guinness World Record for the longest continuous cycle path. It features 29 underpasses and 5 bridges, so rides are uninterrupted by vehicles. The Olympic Cycling Track is being fitted with "mist-cooling" stations. On Tuesday and Wednesday evenings (October to June), the **Lusail International Circuit** opens for cyclists. Riders can use a 5.3 km loop without cars. On dedicated "Training Days" (usually Tuesday or Wednesday evenings), the circuit provides on-site rentals. This is the safest way to ride at high speeds under floodlights, avoiding the unpredictability of Doha's traffic. Website: www.lcsc.qa

**For easier rides**, **Al Bidda Park** and **Aspire Park** have shorter trails with landscaping and Sidra trees.

**Safety and Regulations (2026).** The Ministry of Interior (MoI) has tightened enforcement of cycling regulations to ensure the safety of all road users. In 2026, the following rules will be strictly applied: Helmet and reflective vests are required for visibility, especially at night. **Positioning:** Cyclists must use designated lanes or remain on the far-right side of the roadway. Riding in parallel is prohibited; cyclists must move in a single file. Bicycles must have fixed front and rear lights.

**Road Bike Hire Companies**

Rasen Sports. This is arguably the most professional outfit for serious cyclists. They offer well-maintained road bikes for hire from their showrooms. It is the ideal choice if you intend to venture onto the longer expressway routes or participate in community rides. **Rates:** Hourly: **QAR70** | Daily: **QAR170** | Weekly: **QAR450** **Website:**www.rasensports.com Berg Arabia is active in large parks such as Al Bidda and MIA Park. They offer fast road bikes for those who want more speed than a basic model provides. **Website:** www.bergarabia.com

The Tour of Qatar bike race ended in 2016. There may be talk of its return, but in 2026, the focus is on local community races and regional events.

### E-Scooters

For "last - mile" connectivity within the Sila network, on - demand E-scooters have become a common sight. Operated by companies such as Loop Mobility (a Qatari startup), Falcon Ride, and Fenix, these can be unlocked via their respective apps.

Usage Guidelines: **Central Business District (CBD):** Sidewalk riding is strictly prohibited downtown. You must use bicycle lanes or share the roadway with vehicles. **Parking:** Park scooters upright, away from pedestrian walkways and building entrances. Never block fire hydrants or bus stops, or you may be fined. **Age & Safety:** Riders must typically be 16 years or older. While the wind in your hair, even in the heat, is a delight, operators strongly encourage helmets.

### Paying for E-Scooters

The payment ecosystem for E-scooters (such as Loop Mobility, Falcon Ride, and Lime) is entirely digital, functioning through their respective smartphone applications. Account Setup: You must download the app and register with a valid mobile number and email. **Payment Method:** You link a **Credit or Debit card** (Visa, Mastercard) to the app. Most major services now also support **Apple Pay** or **Google Pay** for a faster checkout. **Loop and others** use a "Wallet" feature. Top up your account (e.g., QAR50) and ride costs will be deducted from your balance. **Pricing Structure:** Typically, there is a flat **Unlock Fee** (around QAR3) followed by a **Per-Minute Rate** (usually between **QAR0.50** and QAR1). Note on Parking: Always end your ride in a 'Green Zone,' as shown on the app map. If you end your ride in a restricted area, a recovery fee will be charged automatically. Avoid this extra fee by finishing in a permitted zone.

### Embassies & Travel Advice

Qatar is remarkably stable, but international relations and travel requirements can change, making your official government advice an important part of your visit planning. Diplomatic Missions. Most major nations maintain a diplomatic presence in Doha. These embassies are the ultimate authority for their respective citizens regarding passport renewals, legal assistance, or emergency support. **Directory of Foreign Embassies in Qatar:** https://hukoomi.gov.qa/en/embassies. **Qatar's Embassies Abroad:** https://www.mofa.gov.qa/en#The-World

**Official Travel Advisories.** Your government's travel advice can have significant legal and financial implications. Many travel insurance policies are rendered invalid if you travel to a region against the explicit advice (do not travel) of your home country's foreign ministry.

For the most current security, health, and entry assessments, consult the following portals; **United Kingdom (FCDO):** https://www.gov.uk/foreign-travel-advice/qatar. **United States (State Department):** https://travel.state.gov/content/travel/en/traveladvisories/traveladvisories/qatar-travel-advisory.html.

**Australia (Smartraveller):** https://www.smartraveller.gov.au/destinations/middle-east/qatar. **Germany (Auswärtiges Amt):** https://www.auswaertiges-amt.de/de/reiseundsicherheit/reise-und-sicherheitshinweise.

**Qatar Government Tourism Portal:** https://www.visitqatar.com

## HEALTH AND SAFETY CONSIDERATIONS

The response to the COVID-19 pandemic demonstrated Qatar's capacity for rapid digital mobilisation. While the specific Ehteraz app (https://www.ehteraz.gov.qa) and the dedicated MOPH COVID-19 portal (https://covid19.moph.gov.qa) are currently inactive, they remain a blueprint for how the state disseminates information during public health events. Should a similar situation arise, the Ministry of Public Health (https://www.moph.gov.qa) will be the primary source for mandatory health protocols and entry requirements.

**Travelling with Children**

Qataris are welcoming to children, so families travelling with young kids can expect a warm reception. People often go out of their way to make children feel comfortable, which helps make your trip enjoyable and easy. **Family-Friendly Infrastructure.** Many hotels and upscale restaurants are exceptionally well-equipped for children, though it's always advisable to ensure the equipment you need is available. **Dining:** High-chairs and tailored children's menus are standard in major establishments. However, always confirm availability when booking to avoid disappointment during peak hours. **Hotels:** Many resorts, particularly along the West Bay and Lusail coastlines, offer dedicated 'Kids' Clubs' and separate shaded pools. Notable examples for 2026 include **Banana Island** – with the Cool Mint Club aged 4-12 – and Peppermint Club (for teens) **Sheraton Grand** and **Waldorf Astoria Lusail**, both known for their extensive family facilities.

**Sun & Heat Safety.** The Qatari sun is intense, and children are more susceptible to heat exhaustion and dehydration. **The 10-to-4 Rule:** Aim to keep children indoors or in heavily shaded areas between **10:00 and 16:00 hours**, when UV levels are at their peak. **Hydration:** Make sure children drink water regularly, even if they do not say they are thirsty. It is a good idea to carry an insulated water bottle for each child. **Protection:** Use a broad-spectrum sunscreen with **SPF 50+ or higher**, reapplying every 2 hours. A wide-brimmed hat and UV-protective sunglasses are essential.

**Transport & Car Seats.** Driving in Qatar with children is subject to new regulations for 2026, which are likely similar to those in your home country. **The Law:** Children under **10 years old,** or those older than 10 but shorter than **145 cm** (height is key here), are legally prohibited from sitting in the front passenger seat. They must be secured in the rear using an age-appropriate restraint system (infant carrier, booster seat, etc.). **Car Rentals:** While rental agencies offer child seats, they are an "optional extra", and stocks can be depleted during busy periods. **You should book these in advance** and follow up 24 hours before arrival to ensure the correct seat (infant, toddler, or booster) is reserved. **Taxis & Apps:** Standard taxis are not legally required to carry car seats. If you are not bringing your own, use the **Uber** app's 'Car Seat' option (where available) or pre-book through a specialist family transfer service like **TaxiBambino** www.taxibambino.com to guarantee a vehicle equipped with certified restraints.

### THE OFFICIAL QATARI STANCE ABOUT VISITORS

**Clothing**. Qatar Tourism (https://www.visitqatar.com) explicitly states: *"Visitors (men as well as women) are expected to show respect for local culture by avoiding excessively revealing clothes in public. It is generally recommended for men and women to ensure their shoulders and knees are covered."* This is not a uniquely Middle

Eastern phenomenon; similar mandates exist in European enclaves like Monaco. In Qatar, however, the police have the legal standing to intervene if clothing is deemed indecent. The national campaign #Reflect_Your_Respect serves as a constant reminder of these community standards.

To avoid unwanted attention or intervention, aim for a more conservative clothing baseline than you might adopt elsewhere. While you will see individuals in shopping malls disregarding these 'suggestions', as a visitor, you lack the local understanding or social network that might mitigate a confrontation. **For Men:** Avoid shorts in public town settings unless engaged in sport. Opt for long trousers and shirts or T-shirts with sleeves. **For Women:** Avoid transparent fabrics, strappy or sleeveless tops, crop-tops, and low-cut necklines. Skirts or trousers must reach below the knee. Leggings should not be worn as a primary outer garment. **Text & Graphics:** Select clothing with neutral designs. Avoid Hebrew lettering or garments displaying 'I Love Dubai or Iran' - regional tensions can still make these choices awkward. Similarly, avoid sports jerseys sponsored by airlines from formerly boycotting nations (such as Emirates or Etihad). It is also prudent to avoid T-shirts featuring niche subculture imagery, such as Grime or Drill motifs, which may be misinterpreted.

**Contextual Clothing Requirements. Museums:** Most government-run institutions, such as the **Museum of Islamic Art** [PAGE 65], require a "modest" dress code, often leaning toward smart-casual. **Dining:** Smart-casual is the standard for better restaurants. Formal five-star hotel dining rooms may require a more tailored look; it is wise to verify the specific dress code when booking. **Beaches:** On public beaches, avoid revealing bikinis or 'Speedo' style swimwear. When not in the water, a loose 'cover-all' is the expected attire. Private hotel beaches are generally more relaxed, though modesty is still appreciated in common areas.

**Other considerations**

Fabric & Function. The Qatari climate - specifically the high humidity – should inform your choice of material. Sweat does not evaporate quickly in Doha. **Polycotton Blends:** An excellent choice; the cotton absorbs moisture while the synthetic fibre maintains the garment's structure.. **Technical Fabrics:** 'Breathable' or fast-drying fabrics used in high-end travel gear are ideal.. **Fit:** Loose-fitting, opaque clothing is superior for both thermal comfort and cultural compliance. **Footwear.** Doha's primary districts are well-paved and suitable for standard walking shoes. However, the stony desert interior requires more robust protection. **The Desert:** Sandals offer no protection against sharp stones, thorns, or the occasional bite from desert fauna. However, in purely sandy environments, closed shoes can become frustratingly heavy with grit. A high-quality light hiking shoe is often the best compromise for the "Autonomous Specialist" exploring the peninsula.

**Essential Provisions & Services.**

Qatar is a sophisticated retail environment where the "little things" are managed with high efficiency. For the international traveller in 2026, the availability of Western brands and professional medical services is a constant, ensuring you can travel light with confidence. **Shopping for Essentials.** Retailing is dominated by large-scale hypermarkets that stock a vast array of global brands for personal care. **Supermarket Chains: Carrefour, Lulu & Monoprix:** These giants provide the most familiar experience for European travellers. Monoprix is particularly noted for its premium organic selections and luxury toiletries. Lulu Hypermarket: A regional powerhouse with an immense range of British, American, and Asian foods. It is often the best source for specific brands of infant formula or niche dietary products. Additionally Marks & Spencer Located in major malls like Villaggio, provide clothing, toiletries and food staples. **Operating Hours**: Most supermarkets open by 08:00 and remain active until midnight or 01:00. Friday Note: While many branches now remain open throughout the day, smaller shops and some mall-based outlets will close between 11:00 and 12:30 hours for mid-day prayers. **Prices** for daily essentials are generally stable and comparable to those in the UK or Germany. Electronics and luxury goods can occasionally be cheaper due to lower tax structures, while fresh "Western" produce (like berries or specific cheeses) will reflect the cost of air freight.

**MEDICAL SERVICES & PHARMACEUTICALS**

Healthcare in Qatar is world-class, with a blend of government-run Hamad Medical Corporation (HMC) facilities and private hospitals. The Ministry of Public Health (MOPH) manages the system, while Hamad Medical Corporation (HMC) and Primary Health Care Corporation (PHCC) run state hospitals and clinics. According to Qatar's Planning and Statistical Authority (QPSA), there are over two dozen major hospitals and more than 3,000 beds.

This means about 890 people per bed, which is higher than the UK's 460 or the USA's 410, but still good by international standards.

Private clinics like **Al Emadi** www.alemadihospital.com.qa +974 4477 6444 or **The Cuban Hospital** (in Dukhan a government-to-government agreement) hamad.qa/The-Cuban-Hospital Key Contact: +974 4015 7777 offer high-quality outpatient care. For emergencies, the government-run **Hamad General Hospital** is the primary trauma centre hamad.qa/Hamad-General-Hospital Key Contact: +974 4439 4444.

**Personal Care & Childcare. Sanitary Products:** A comprehensive range of tampons and sanitary towels is available in all supermarkets and pharmacies. Major brands like Always and Kotex are ubiquitous. **Childcare:** Disposable nappies (Pampers, Huggies) and wet wipes are stocked everywhere. Pharmacies like **Boots** or **Kulud** carry specialised dermatological brands (such as Mustela or Cetaphil) for sensitive infant skin. **Toiletries:** Expect to find everything from high-street brands to luxury K-beauty products in stores like **Sephora** or **Gold Apple**.

**Pharmacies and Medication**

Pharmacies are widespread in Doha, and many open 24 hours. Staff usually speak English, and international franchises like Boots are common in malls. If you travel with chronic medication, the following should be observed: **Carry the original prescription** and a formal letter from your doctor, signed and officially stamped. Keep all medicine in its original pharmacy packaging, including the printed literature.

**Pharmacies:** Chains such as **Boots**, **Kulud**, and **Ebn Sina** are found in every mall and major residential street. **24-Hour Service:** Several branches of **Kulud Pharmacy** operate 24/7 across Doha. Prices are generally approved or set by the government – and are therefor uniform across the country. This price setting does not apply to vitamin supplements, cosmetics, non medicinal skin care and so on.

**Qatar enforces a zero-tolerance policy on narcotics and psychotropics. Codeine** is banned, as are some herbal supplements that are legal elsewhere. Prices for registered medicines are regulated by the government, ensuring consistency across all dispensaries. This price control does not apply to "non-medicinal" items like cosmetics or vitamins.

**Environmental Health: Sun and Water**

The sun is a key health concern in Qatar. Sunlight is stronger here than in London, even during spring or autumn. Use high-factor sunscreen and try to stay in the shade.

Tap water in Qatar comes from desalinated seawater. It is pure and demineralized when it leaves the plant, but it can pick up contaminants in pipelines or storage. Because it lacks natural electrolytes, it can affect your hydration, especially in the desert. The water is safe for washing and brushing your teeth, but it tastes different. Most people drink bottled water. If you are active outdoors, ask a professional about replacing electrolytes.

**Official Health Advice and Resources**

Always review the latest clinical advice from your respective government: **United Kingdom:** www.gov.uk/foreign-travel-advice/qatar/health; **Clinical Advice:** www.fitfortravel.nhs.uk; **United States:** wwwnc.cdc.gov/travel/destinations/traveler/none/qatar; **Germany:** The **Auswärtiges Amt** provides comprehensive updates at www.auswaertiges-amt.de, while the **Centrum für Reisemedizin (CRM)** offers detailed medical briefs at www.crm.de.

## SPECIAL NEEDS TRAVELLERS

Qatar's accessibility has had major infrastructure upgrades. However, travellers with special needs may notice differences between newer and older areas. Always check with your healthcare provider and specialist organizations for advice that fits your needs.

**Arrival and Transport** - Hamad International Airport leads in inclusivity. It joined the Hidden Disabilities Sunflower program, allowing travellers to discreetly request extra support at www.hdsunflower.com. Passengers with non-visible disabilities can collect a sunflower lanyard free of charge from the information desks at: the Check-in area (for departing passengers), the Lamp Bear area, or the ORCHARD (for transferring passengers). The airport's own special assistance page provides further details on how they integrate the program into the passenger journey: www.dohahamadairport.com/airport-guide/traveler-guide/special-assistance

**For moving around the city: The Doha Metro is the most accessible option.** All stations include lifts, floor markings for the visually impaired, and level access to trains. **Mowasalat (Public Buses):** The Mowasalat fleet features low-floor buses with designated seating and ramp access. **Karwa Taxis:** Accessible vehicles equipped with ramps and floor anchoring systems can be booked via the Karwa app.

**Cultural Sites and Museums** - Most major cultural landmarks now offer excellent facilities, including wide corridors and dedicated special needs toilets. **National Museum of Qatar [PAGE 60]:** Fully accessible with elevators and freight lifts. However, do note that some galleries feature unconventional, sloping floor surfaces that may be disorienting. **Museum of Islamic Art (MIA) [PAGE 65]:** Offers spacious elevators and gentle ramps. Wheelchairs are available on-site for visitors. **Msheireb Downtown Doha:** As a "smart city," this district is designed with inclusivity at its core. It features flat, shaded walkways and a tram system with level boarding. **Souq Waqif:** While much of the Souq is now wheelchair-friendly with adapted toilets and ramps at major entrances, the 'ancient' charm of some narrow, uneven side-alleys can still present a challenge. **Katara Cultural Village:** Highly accessible with flat waterfront promenades and free adapted golf carts to assist with movement between venues.

**Leisure and Sports** - **The Corniche:** The wide, flat paved surface makes this 7 km promenade ideal for wheelchairs and scooters. **Lusail Winter Wonderland:** The park is designed for easy accessibility; visitors with disabilities often receive free entry upon presenting a government-issued card. **Camel Racetracks:** Access for people with special needs is limited, and the ground surface is often uneven; facilities are sparse.

**Specialist Resources** - For up-to-date information, the **Accessible Qatar** app (www.accessibleqatar.com) is a great resource. It offers user reviews and checked accessibility data for hotels, malls, and tourist sites, using a simple traffic-light system. In Qatar, you can go from the modern, accessible Metro to an uneven alleyway within one city block.

## SAFETY IN GENERAL

Qatar is very safe for most visitors. Street crime, robberies, and assaults are rare. Still, petty theft and credit card fraud can happen, even if they are not often reported. Take the same care with your belongings, passport, and money as you would in any big city.

**Awareness of the Built Environment** - Qatar's infrastructure is modern and new, but some safety features like handrails or clear warnings for changes in floor level may be missing. Stay alert to your surroundings, especially in older areas or where construction is happening.

## DIGITAL CONDUCT AND PRIVACY

**Photography, video and Social Media:** Recent updates to the Cybercrime Law (Law No. 14/2014, specifically Article 8 bis added in August 2025) prohibit the filming or sharing of images of individuals in public without their express consent. This carries a penalty of up to one year in prison or a fine of QAR 100,000. Always ask for permission before photographing individuals, particularly Qatari women. A simple word to use is "mumkin" which means – "is it possible/may I" – of course a smile and "please" will often be understood.

Avoid photographing sensitive sites, including military installations, government buildings, and industrial plants and be cautious about around the airport due to national security concerns.

**Sensitive Incidents:** The Ministry of Interior has issued specific warnings against filming "ongoing field developments" – such as military movements, security drills or damage and destruction caused by third parties. Furthermore, the publication or electronic circulation of content deemed prejudicial to national interests or harming the public order – including the re-posting of third-party footage or adding commentary to that content (such as "ongoing field developments")– is strictly prohibited and subject to prosecution. Authorities monitor digital platforms closely.

Photographing victims of accidents or emergency response teams is a criminal offence under Article 333 of the Penal Code, which protects the sanctity of private life. Penal Code Art. 136 (bis) covers - spreading "false news" or biased rumours affecting national interest carries up to 10 years' prison and up to QAR 200,000 fine.

**Drones** (for non Qatari entities) are not permitted within Qatar and will be confiscated on immigration. A receipt might be issued, enabling them to be reclaimed when leaving at **Customs Disclosure Office** located in the Departures Hall (Level 2) before you check in for your flight. Check current regulations regarding this.

**State Institutions and Lèse-majesté:** Unlike the UK, where public commentary, of any sort, regarding the government or head of state is a common feature of civil life, in Qatar such discourse is strictly regulated. Qatar maintains strict protections for its institutions, symbols, and leadership. Under Article 134 of the Penal Code, notably strengthened by Law No. 14 of 2024 - an amendment to the original Penal Code of 2004, the dignity of His Highness the

Amir, the Deputy Amir, and the Al Thani ruling family is protected by law – broadly as crimes against internal state security. Any public or digital commentary perceived as an insult to the leadership or the state's highest symbols (flag etc) is met with significant legal consequences. For the visitor, the rule is simple: the state's highest offices are not subjects for public debate or digital critique. This statutory requirement extends to publishing or commenting on media (whether public or in social media direct messaging) regarding any issues or incidents that might be considered, within Qatar, to reflect unfavourably on the state.

All GCC States - and most Arab States have similar regulations to the above, though the GCC countries manage the application of them most effectively.

### Cultural Sensitivities and Local Laws

Qatar's legal system combines civil and Sharia law; consequently, certain actions considered commonplace elsewhere may result in fines, imprisonment, or deportation. It is prudent to consult your government's current travel advice for Qatar [PAGE 32, 37, 46, 343] for the most recent updates. **Public Conduct and Language:** Qatar maintains a zero-tolerance policy regarding public confrontation. The use of obscene language, insults, or offensive gestures – including those occurring during "road rage" incidents – constitutes a criminal offence. Under Qatari law, if a formal complaint is lodged, the police are statutorily required to investigate and respond. **Public Displays of Affection:** As a conservative society, Qatar expects a degree of decorum in public spaces. While authorities are generally tolerant of foreign visitors, significant public displays of affection between adults are considered inappropriate. Holding hands is typically ignored within international hotels or shopping malls, but excessive intimacy in public settings often leads to complaints and subsequent police intervention.

### Qatari Cultural Etiquette and Hospitality

The heart of Qatari culture is not found in its skyscrapers, but in its hospitality - a tradition rooted in the Bedouin values of generosity and protection for the traveller. For a visitor, understanding these social rhythms transforms a trip into a meaningful cultural exchange.

### The Spirit of the Majlis

The *Majlis* (literally "a place of sitting") is a cornerstone of Qatari social life. If you are invited into one, it is a significant gesture of trust and welcome. **The Ritual of Welcome:** Upon entering a home or Majlis, it is customary to remove your shoes. The room is usually scented with *Oud* or *Bukhoor* (incense – both are burnt to give off smoke), a sensory signal that guests are honoured. **Qahwa (Arabic Coffee):** You will be served traditional Arabic (not Turkish or Italian) coffee flavoured with cardamom and saffron, poured from a *Dallah* (pot) into a small *Finjaan* (cup). **Accept** and drink with your right hand at all times. **The Signal:** Your host will continue to refill your cup until you gently jiggle or tilt it from side to side, indicating you have had your fill. **Dates and Dining:** Coffee is almost always accompanied by dates. If you are invited to a meal, you may find yourself sharing from a large communal platter of *Machboos*. Using your right hand to eat is not just a tradition; it is a sign of respect for the shared meal.

**Greetings and Personal Space**

Qataris place a premium on courtesy and "social preamble" before commencing any business or serious discussion. **The Greeting:** The universal greeting is *As-Salaam Alaikum* ("Peace be upon you"), to which the reply is *Wa Alaikum As-Salaam*. **Physical Contact:** Between men, handshakes are common and often lengthy. However, when a man meets a woman, he should wait for her to extend her hand first. If she does not, a polite nod or placing the right hand over the heart is the traditional and respectful alternative. Equally a woman decides if she wants to shake a man's hand; a polite smile might be the alternative. However – if on important business and you, as a woman, are in a senior position a hand shake would be appropriate.

**Personal Space:** You may notice that Qataris stand slightly closer during conversations than Westerners do. Thoughtful Gestures - **Shukran:** A simple "Thank you" (*Shukran*) goes a long way. Qataris are proud of their language and appreciate the effort to use basic Arabic phrases. **The Right Side:** In Qatari etiquette, the right side is the "honoured" side. Whether entering an elevator or a doorway, it is polite to let the person on your right go first. **Modesty:** While the rules on dress are often seen as a restriction, they are locally viewed as a form of "dignified presentation." Dressing modestly is seen as a gesture of respect for the host country's values.

Like other Gulf states, Qatar remains a place where the car is the undisputed Sultan of the street. However, the Doha Metro and an efficient bus network make the city - particularly its coastal core - increasingly hospitable to pedestrians.

### General Security and Identification

You may notice a high level of active security in Qatar. Many shopping malls, 4&5* hotels, and government buildings employ airport-style screening or bag checks (a government initiative). For the frequent traveller to Doha, a suitcase sliding through a scanner has become as much a part of the hotel check-in ritual at as the offering of dates and gahwa. This has been in place since 2015. **Identification:** Under Qatari law, you must carry identification at all times. For visitors, a photocopy of your passport's photo page is usually sufficient for daily movement, but you should be prepared to produce the original if requested by the police.

### Alcohol And Drugs

In Qatar, the approach to alcohol and controlled substances is one of strictly managed access and zero tolerance for unauthorised use.

**Alcohol** is not banned, but its consumption is confined to specific, regulated environments. **Licensed Venues:** Alcohol is served in authorised locations, primarily high-end hotel bars, clubs, and select restaurants. Note that you may be required to show your original passport or Qatar ID to enter these venues, and the legal drinking age is 21. Residents with a valid Qatar ID and a minimum basic salary (typically **QAR3,000+**) may apply to the **Qatar Distribution Company (QDC) for a permit** to purchase alcohol and pork products for private consumption at home. Tourists and visitors are not eligible for this permit. **Import Restrictions:** You cannot bring alcohol into Qatar. Any alcohol found in your bags at Hamad International Airport will be confiscated. While **Qatar Duty Free** in the departures terminal sells alcohol, these purchases are strictly for consumption outside of the country and are provided in sealed, tamper-evident bags. **Public Conduct:** Drinking in public or being under the influence in a public space is a serious offence. Law enforcement maintains a zero-tolerance policy for drink-driving, which can attract heavy fines, deportation, or a prison term of up to three years.

**Drugs** Qatar enforces some of the world's most stringent drug laws. There is no distinction made between recreational use and more serious offences in terms of the rigour of prosecution. **Possession and Use:** The possession or use of prohibited drugs carries severe penalties, including lengthy imprisonment and major fines. **Trafficking:** The smuggling or trafficking of controlled substances is a capital offence. Under Qatari law, the death penalty may be sought and carried out for those convicted of drug trafficking. **Prescription Medication:** As noted in the **Health** section [PAGE 4,5], always ensure any necessary medications are in their original packaging with a stamped doctor's prescription to avoid being misidentified as prohibited substances.

### Pedestrian Safety

Doha is increasingly becoming more pedestrian-friendly, yet the 'right of way' is often a theoretical concept rather than a practical reality. **Walking Awareness:** When walking near roadsides, always face oncoming traffic to maintain awareness. Even at marked pedestrian crossings, never assume a vehicle will stop; wait for a clear gap or for the vehicle to come to a complete halt. **Feral Dogs:** On the outskirts of smaller settlements and industrial areas, you may encounter packs of feral dogs. While generally shy, they can be intimidating if you are on foot; it is best to avoid walking in these isolated areas after dark.

### Electrical Standards and Compatibility

**Electrical Power.** Qatar's electrical system is similar to the British standard, though there are a few local differences that experienced travellers might notice. Qatar uses a 240V supply at 50Hz. If you are coming from the UK, where the voltage is 230V (usually between 216V and 253V) at at 50Hz, your devices will work without a voltage converter. Travellers from North America encounter a different grid. The USA and Canada use 120V and 60Hz. Most modern 'switching' power supplies - like those for laptops or smartphones - are dual-voltage (100V-240V). Check your device for compatibility; if it is not rated up to 240V, using it in Qatar may cause damage.

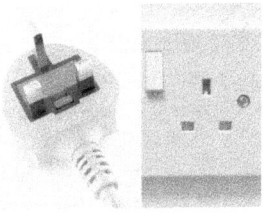

*British electrical plug and sockets*

Plug Types and Sockets. Type G (British style) rectangular 3-pin sockets are the standard in Qatar, but you might also come across two other types. Type D (The "Old British" Style): Found in older buildings, these feature three large round pins in a triangular pattern. Many small appliances are sold with or use 2-pin Type C or F plugs. These usually need an adaptor to fit Type G

## Media

Qatar's media landscape is unique. The country is home to one of the world's most influential, investigative global news networks, but local media is managed to support national stability and cultural values. This creates a system with a strong international presence and a carefully managed domestic message.

Because of the historically low national population numbers in Qatar local media has needed government support, either through grants or state advertising, enabling them to stay in business. This support has resulted in media whose output has usually matched the government interests and viewpoint. Even though official censorship ended in 1995, self-censorship is still common. Journalists (and others) avoid topics related to the ruling family, national security, and religion, as required by **Law No. 14 of 2014** and **Law No. 11 of 2025.**

Currently, five major Arabic dailies are active in 2026: Al Sharq, Al Watan, Al Raya, Al Arab, and Lusail (which focuses on the economy). Their combined daily print run is estimated at 65,000-75,000 copies. These publications are also the primary physical news source for the roughly 300,000 Egyptians and other Arabic-speaking expatriates. English-language readers are served by the Gulf Times, The Peninsula, and the Qatar Tribune. While thousands are delivered to villas and ministries, the true national conversation has shifted to encrypted digital platforms.

*Al Jazeera studio*

Al Jazeera Media Network is Qatar's most well-known cultural export. Since 1996, it has changed journalism in the Arab world by giving a voice to people often left out elsewhere. It is a private foundation for public benefit and was first funded by a former ruler of Qatar. The network is known for its "editorial duality": it reports aggressively on international news but avoids domestic Qatari politics. Recently, it has become more closely aligned with the state's goals. In late 2025, Sheikh Nasser Bin Faisal Al Thani from the ruling family became Director General. In 2026, Al Jazeera launched "The Core," an AI-powered news model that centralizes content management.

Broadcasting and Lifestyle Media - beyond news, the media landscape includes Qatar Television (a government operation) and Al Rayan TV, which is under the Private Engineering Office (reporting directly to the Amir's office) and focuses on national heritage. Radio remains popular, particularly Sout Al Khaleej and the Al Jazeera channels. For the Western expatriate community, lifestyle publications like Expat Woman Qatar and Time Out Doha provide essential guides to navigating the city's social silos. There are Asian papers - Malayala Manorama, Gulf Madhyamam are Malayalam Dailies also Pilipino Star Ngayon (Tagalog), Rajdhani (Nepalese) offer media for these communities. These are printed in Doha. Additionally there are glossy magazines flown in. All are overseen by the Qatari Ministry of Culture.

**Photography and Video**

Doha's West Bay skyline is a striking vista that becomes especially captivating at dusk. The optimal time for photography is as the skyscrapers' lights are illuminated until Astronomical Dusk. The Dhow Harbour and the Museum of Islamic Art Park offer the most iconic vantage points. While the National Museum is an example of architectural ingenuity, the general area around Museum of Islamic Art provides a versatile backdrop, allowing traditional dhows to be framed against the city's glass buildings.

For those drawn to heritage, Souq Waqif is a rich tapestry of texture and life - from the Falcon Souq to the sight of the Amiri Guard on horseback. If your lens is focused on exotic cars, The Pearl remains the premier destination, particularly on weekend afternoons. In the Souqs, though the camera is commonplace, a request for permission is a vital nod to the local concept of *Haya* - that persists even in the age of the smartphone as well as a legal safeguard.

*Horsemen Souq Waqif Doha*

However, capturing the vast Qatari interior can be challenging due to its monotone landscape, without great differences in elevation. For this, the golden hour at Khor Al Udaid [PAGE 105] or the west coast sunsets offer the best depth and contrast. Official Perspective: For the most current official guidance on photography and local customs, consult your foreign ministry: **UK FCDO:** www.gov.uk/foreign-travel-advice/qatar/local-laws-and-customs **US State Department:** travel.state.gov/qatar

### Legal Restrictions and Sensitive Sites

While Qatar has many great photo opportunities, there are firm boundaries you must respect. Any government building, palace, military installation, or security post is a strictly protected area. Photography is not merely discouraged at these sites - it is illegal. Violators may face arrest, detention, or prosecution under Qatari law. Similarly, following significant international scrutiny regarding construction labour, you should avoid photographing building sites. In 2026, many major projects remain under close official supervision, and cameras at these locations are often met with swift security intervention, which could include confiscation of equipment or legal action.

Privacy and the Law - Qatar's legal framework regarding privacy is exceptionally robust under **Cybercrime Law (No. 14/2014)** and was further strengthened by **Law No. 11 of 2025,** which amended the Anti-Cybercrime Law (adding Article 8 bis). **Consent is Mandatory:** It is an offence to capture, publish, or circulate photos or videos of individuals in public without their explicit consent. **Penalties:** Violating an individual's privacy via social media or electronic circulation of their image can result in criminal prosecution, with penalties of up to **one year in prison** and/or a fine of **QAR100,000**. **Practical Advice:** Avoid making anyone the focus of your shot without asking. Wide-angle shots in crowded areas like Souq Waqif or malls are usually tolerated, but the "right of focus" belongs to the subject. As of 2026, It is effectively prohibited for foreign tourists to bring drones into Qatar.

PUBLIC HOLIDAYS IN QATAR

Qatar's holiday calendar combines fixed Gregorian dates with Islamic lunar holidays that shift each year. Some are only "bank holidays." These mainly affect financial institutions. On state holidays, the government and many private offices close for several days.

Fixed and Annual Holidays - **January 1 - New Year's Day:** A holiday for banks and financial institutions only; government offices typically remain open. **Second Tuesday in February - National Sports Day:** A nationwide public holiday dedicated to promoting healthy lifestyles. For **2026**, this falls on **10 February**. **First Sunday in March - Bank Holiday:** Observed only by the Qatar Central

Bank and financial institutions. In **2026**, this falls on **1 March**.
**December 18 - Qatar National Day:** The primary national celebration marking the country's unification.

**The Islamic Calendar (Hijri)** is lunar, meaning dates shift approximately 10 to 12 days earlier each year in the Gregorian calendar. Official confirmation of the start of Ramadhan and the two Eid festivals always rests with the Moon Sighting Committee at the Ministry of Awqaf and Islamic Affairs. Their announcement - often made only a day in advance - is the final authority.

**Estimated Dates for Ramadhan**

During the holy month of Ramadhan, the country's rhythm changes significantly. Working hours are reduced, and public consumption of food or drink during daylight hours is strictly prohibited, as is smoking. **2027:** 8 February - 9 March - **2028:** 28 January - 26 February - **2029:** 16 January - 14 February.

**Estimated Dates for Eid Observances**

Eid celibrations are the longest holidays in the Qatari calendar. While the religious festival may last three days, when bridged with weekends and additional government days off, the actual closure for public sectors can span 7 to 11 days.

**2026**, Eid Al Adha may start on 27 May; in **2027**, Eid Al Fitr is on 9 March and Eid Al Adha on 16 May; in **2028**, Eid Al Fitr might be observed on 26 February and Eid Al Adha on 5 May; and in **2029**, the dates are 14 February for Eid Al Fitr and 24 April for Eid Al Adha.

*Parisa - Souq Waqif*

# ARRIVAL IN QATAR

- Lusail
- Katara
- The Pearl
- Westbay
- Education City
- Banana Island
- Souq Waqif
- OldDoha Port
- Aspire
- Hamad International Airport HIA
- Al Wakrah

**DOHA**

NORTH
6 KM

# CHAPTER 2
# WHERE TO GO
## AND WHAT TO SEE

Introduction and Practicalities
**Culture Vultures: A Half-Day in Doha**

Start at the Museum of Islamic Art (MIA), a large building by I.M. Pei, set on an artificial island and reached by an avenue lined with palm trees. The museum's windows look onto dhows in the harbour and the West Bay skyline.

*West Bay and Museum of Islamic Art*

From the MIA, a 1.5-kilometre stroll west along the Corniche brings you to Souq Waqif. Pause halfway at the Dhow Harbour; the scent of salt and seasoned teak from these traditional wooden vessels provides a sharp, sensory contrast to the city's glass towers. The Souq itself is a labyrinthine hive where the past refuses to be quieted. Here, you can refuel on anything from street-side *regag* bread to fine Persian cuisine.

If you have limited time in Doha, this route gives the best cultural experience. It is easy to use via Souq Waqif or Msheireb Metro stations.

Sitara of the Kaaba (the embroidered door cover) Makkah

## The Museum Marathon: A Full Day of Immersion

For those with a full day, the narrative of Qatar unfolds in a sequence of architectural marvels. Begin at the National Museum of Qatar, easily accessed via its eponymous Metro station. Opened in 2019, the building - a masterpiece by Jean Nouvel - mimics the 'desert rose' (*gypsum rosette*), a naturally occurring crystal formation. Inside, the experience is immersive, tracing the peninsula's journey from a pearl-diving past to its gas-driven present.

A 2-kilometre journey (either a brisk walk or a short taxi ride past the Mövenpick Hotel) leads you back to the Museum of Islamic Art for an afternoon exploration of its five floors of global treasures. After a late lunch in the shaded alleys of Souq Waqif, continue 800 metres west to the Msheireb Museums. These four restored heritage houses offer a poignant look at Doha's social evolution, including the sobering history of the domestic slave trade. Conclude your day by riding the complimentary Msheireb Tram to the Metro interchange for a seamless return.

Dhow "Wreck" - Katara Beach

### Dunes and Drama: From the Desert to Katara

To see the desert is to understand the soul of the peninsula. A full-day excursion begins with a drive south, where the expressways give way to the "singing sands." These powder-white dunes are spread like a carelessly tossed blanket across the landscape. Ensure you book a 4x4 excursion with a skilled driver to experience "dune bashing" - a heart-thumping ballet of steel and sand - before enjoying a quiet lunch by the inland sea of Khor Al Udaid.

On your return, have your tour operator drop you at Katara Cultural Village. Within a half-kilometre radius, you can explore the Postal Stamp Museum, the Al Gannas Society (dedicated to the art of falconry and the Saker Falcon, *Falco cherrug*), and an amphitheatre that blends Greek and Islamic styles. As the sun sets, Katara's restaurants come alive, and the nearby Metro station provides a simple exit strategy.

While independent exploration is rewarding, several established tour companies offer "Stopover Packages" that condense these experiences with expert narration. These services are particularly useful for those who prefer a structured itinerary with the benefit of a local guide's insight.

**Discover Qatar:** As the destination management arm of Qatar Airways, it offers exclusive "Transit Tours" for those with a minimum 6-hour layover. These are particularly useful for the **Khor Al Udaid** desert trips, as they handle the complex logistics of 4x4 vehicle swaps and ensure you return to Hamad International Airport in time for your connection.

**Website:** www.discoverqatar.qa

**Regency Holidays:** One of the most established names in the region, they provide specialised "Art and Architecture" tours. These often include prearranged, fast-track entry to the major museums and a guided walk through the **Falcon Souq**, where an expert explains the intricacies of avian healthcare at the adjacent Falcon Hospital.

**Website:** www.regencyholidays.com

**365 Adventures:** For the more active traveller, this company offers "Kayaking in the Al Thakira Mangroves" - home to the Grey Mangrove (*Avicenna marina*). This is a refreshing alternative to the city, often paired with a visit to the **Purple Island** and its ancient dye-production sites. It also has accommodation in western Qatar.
**Website:** www.365adventures.me

### Beach Day Passes and Island Escapes

Doha's coastline offers a spectrum of experiences, from high-octane luxury in West Bay to the understated simplicity of public zones. Most beachfront hotels offer day passes, though availability can be as temperamental as the winter shamal; it is always prudent to call ahead, especially during public holidays.

Costs typically range from QAR100 - QAR500 for full island resort access. Alternatively, the cultural enclave of Katara Beach (www.katara.net) offers a more modest option, with entry starting at QAR 25 on weekdays and QAR 50 on weekends for adults.

**Banana Island** Departure Details Both the Adventure Park and the Resort Day Pass packages include a luxury return boat transfer. These catamarans depart from the Al Shyoukh Terminal on the Corniche in downtown Doha, conveniently located near the Museum of Islamic Art. The crossing takes approximately 25 - 30 minutes, cutting through the turquoise waters of the Gulf with the city skyline receding behind you. Adventure Park Doha (Banana Island) A high - energy precinct designed for the restless traveller. It features zip lines, climbing walls, and "free fall" attractions that offer an adrenaline spike rather than a contemplative afternoon. **Website:**www.adventureparkdoha.com | **Phone:** +974 4040 5131 **Opening Hours:** Daily 10:00 - 20:00. **Entry Cost (2026):QAR 300** for adults (12+); **QAR 250** for children (5 - 11). This pass includes return boat transfers, pool and beach access, two hours of park attractions, and one zip line ride. Banana Island Resort Doha by Anantara (Resort Day Pass). This is the choice for those seeking the "Maldivian" experience. It offers an 800-metre private beach, a lagoon pool, and a surf pool, packaged as a contained island retreat. **Website:**doha.anantara.com | **Phone:** +974 4040 5050 **Opening Hours:** Daily 09:00 - 19:00. **Entry Cost (2026):QAR 350** (Weekdays) and **QAR 495** (Weekends & Public Holidays). These prices include the return boat transfers from Al Shyoukh Terminal and a credit of **QAR 200** (Weekdays) or **QAR 250** (Weekends) to spend at any of the resort's eight restaurants.

**Doha Beach Club** A vibrant, family - friendly destination in West Bay that bridges the gap between a private resort and a public beach. It has sports facilities, a dedicated ladies-only zone with all-female staff, and a casual "Street Food District". **Website:** discoverqatar.qa/beach-clubs | **Phone:** +974 5999 6122 **Opening Hours:** Daily 08:00 - 17:00 (Beach); the Beach House stays open until 22:30. **Entry Cost (2026):QAR 80** on weekdays; **QAR 100** on weekends. Entry is free for children under 16 (limited to two children per adult).

**Hilton Doha (West Bay)** A practical choice for combining a private beach with a well - monitored pool environment. It is particularly favoured by families for its straightforward access. **Website:**hilton.com | **Phone:** +974 4423 3333 **Opening Hours:**

Pool 07:00 - 19:00; Beach 07:00 - Sunset. **Entry Cost (2026):QAR100** (Sun - Thu); **QAR150** (Fri - Sat). Child rates (5-11) are QAR75.

**West Bay Beach** (WBB) A managed public beach zone that offers an outdoor cinema, volleyball courts, and a prayer room, making it more organised than the open public stretches. **Instagram:** @visitwestbaybeach **Opening Hours:** Daily 08:00 - 23:00. **Entry Cost (2026):QAR30** per person; children under 12 enter free.

**Four Seasons Hotel Doha** For refined luxury, the Four Seasons offers a premium day pass with access to five outdoor pools and a private beach, where service is as polished as the lobby marble. **Website:**fourseasons.com/doha | **Phone:** +974 4494 8888 **Opening Hours:** 06:00 - Sunset. **Entry Cost (2026):QAR295** (Sun - Thu, includes **QAR150** F&B credit); **QAR395** (Fri - Sat, includes **QAR175** F&B credit).

**Public Parks and general open spaces**

A green spine now runs from the Museum of Islamic Art through to The Pearl [PAGE 136]. The most expansive of these spaces is Al Bidda Park [PAGE 88], which offers vast underground parking and is served by the Al Bidda Metro station. For those preferring two wheels, cycles can be hired from Saikl [PAGE 88], located at the northern end of Hotel Park near the Sheraton. To the north of West Bay lies 5/6 Park. It is notable for its sprawling plant maze shaped like a map of Qatar and its collection of native flora, including the resilient Sidra (*Ziziphus spina-christi*). Further along the Red Line, Katara Cultural Village offers more than just its beach; the Katara Green Hills provide elevated walking trails with views over the amphitheatre, easily reached via the Katara Metro station. For a final coastal stretch, the Lusail Marina Promenade offers a wide, paved path that remains popular well into the humid evening hours. The evolution of Doha's outdoor spaces has been a triumph of engineering over the relentless humidity of the Gulf. For the modern visitor, the city is no longer a strictly seasonal destination; an array of cooling technologies has extended the "outdoor season" well into the warmer months.

Native Shade and Sustenance. While the high-tech grilles of Katara provide a modern solution, the city's parks still rely on the more traditional, biological cooling of the Sidra trees (*Ziziphus spina-christi*). This hardy species, synonymous with Qatari heritage, provides a dense canopy that has sheltered travellers for centuries. In spaces like Al Bidda Park [PAGE 88], the strategic planting of these trees creates "cool islands" where temperatures are noticeably lower than on the open asphalt.

The city's commitment to "humanising" its urban spaces is most evident in Msheireb Downtown Doha. Designed with traditional Qatari *sikkas* (alleys) that catch the breeze, it is the city's most walkable district, further supported by its own internal tram. Nearby, the Corniche Metro station provides access to several pocket gardens that offer respite from the asphalt. A common sight across the terraces of Msheireb Downtown and the waterfront cafes of The Pearl [PAGE 136] is the widespread use of high-pressure misting systems. These systems atomise water into ultra-fine droplets that evaporate before touching the skin, a process that can lower the immediate ambient temperature by several degrees. While effective for a casual lunch, they are merely the appetiser to the city's more ambitious climate-control projects.

21 High Street: The Extreme of Engineering. The most assertive example of this technology is found at 21 High Street within Katara Cultural Village. Here, the concept of the "outdoor" is redefined. The entire street is fitted with a sophisticated ground-cooling system that pumps chilled air through ornate bronze grilles, creating a stable, temperate environment even when the sun is at its zenith. This is not merely a comfort gimmick; it is a structural commitment to walkability. The system allows visitors to browse luxury boutiques and dine al fresco in conditions that feel more like a crisp Mediterranean afternoon than a desert noon. For more details on the specific retail and dining options available in this cool corridor, visit their website at www.21highst.net.

The main Corniche in Doha is eminently walkable, though in full sun, supported by Metro stations and bus routes that provide easy access. The park adjacent to the Museum of Islamic Art serves as an ideal terminus or starting point for a coastal stroll, offering several shaded coffee shops. A walk from Souq Waqif [PAGE 73] through to Msheireb [PAGE 83] offers a rich architectural narrative and a pleasant, slow-paced experience; one can also hop on the Msheireb Tram for a circular tour of the district. South of the capital, the beachfront at Al Wakrah [PAGE 100] is an excellent choice for a seaside wander. To the north, while the Lusail Boulevard remains somewhat underserved by street-level businesses, its wide vistas make it a quiet spot for a constitutional.

The midday heat is often the arbiter of distance. Many visitors choose to "mix and match" their journey, combining short walks with the Metro, Tram, or bus services to stay within the climate-controlled "bubble".

Doha offers a burgeoning bounty of sites, conveniently clustered for the curious traveller. This guide presents locations in a logical geographical sequence rather than by category. Please note that GPS coordinates serve as a general reference only - they are not intended for precise navigation, as local device variations and satellite signal shifts may affect accuracy.

**Health and Comfort**

When exploring Qatar, weigh your physical fitness against the prevailing heat and humidity before choosing to walk. Only you or a qualified medical advisor can determine what is suitable for your constitution. Ensure you carry a constant supply of drinking water; should you find yourself flagging in the humidity, electrolyte replacement may be essential to maintain your pace.

**Transport**

Public transport in Doha is a seamless and sophisticated system. For most visitors, the Metro, MetroLink buses, and trams provide all the connectivity required - unless the privacy of a taxi or limousine is preferred.

**Navigating the City**

The sites detailed below follow a path from the National Museum in the east, moving steadily westward. For instance, after departing the National Museum (*National Museum of Qatar*), a traveller heading towards Souq Waqif will encounter the Fish Market, followed by the Museum of Islamic Art and the Riwaq Gallery. This flow lets you follow the city's narrative or simply select the segments that pique your interest.

**Dining and Accommodation**

While dedicated sections for hotels and restaurants follow the main attractions, a few notable venues are mentioned in passing. A truly comprehensive list would be vast - and inevitably dated - but certain establishments are highlighted for their specific value or vantage point. Doha's culinary scene has matured significantly, now boasting three Michelin-starred establishments: IDAM within the

Museum of Islamic Art, Jamavar in the Sheraton Grand grounds, and Alba at Raffles Doha.

*National Museum*

### Ticketing and Entry

Qatar Museums currently offers a "Discover One Pass" for QAR 99, which provides access to four major museums over five days. If you prefer individual tickets, prices for non-residents have recently settled at QAR 50 for major sites, though some smaller galleries and heritage sites, such as Al Zubarah Fort, are currently free. Be aware that these prices are somewhat elastic and may rebound; it is always wise to enquire at the first ticket office you encounter. While booking via the official portal (https://qm.

org.qa/) is officially encouraged, it is generally only vital during the busy Eid holidays.

**The Doha Distinction: Authenticity over Franchising**

Doha has deliberately set itself apart rom its regional neighbours by eschewing what critics and art historians have dubbed the "McGuggenheim" or "McLouvre" model. These terms were coined by sceptics - and famously put to former Guggenheim director Thomas Krens - to describe the perceived "fast-museum" branding of culture, where Western museum "satellites" are imported wholesale into The Arabian Gulf. Critics such as Professor Andrew McClellan (author of *The Art Museum from Boullée to Bilbao*) have noted that while other cities focus on the "container" (the spectacular starchitect-designed shell) over the "content," Doha has built its narrative from within. By developing institutions around locally owned, bespoke collections rather than paying vast licensing fees for Western "brands," Qatar has avoided the franchise label. The result is a cultural landscape that feels authentic, whether as a history or a collection, albeit developed at a staggering sovereign cost.

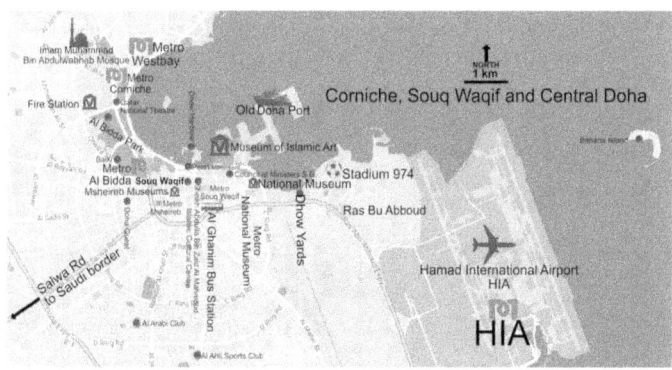

**MSHEIREB MUSEUMS**: BIN JELMOOD HOUSE - WITHIN THE heritage quarter of Msheireb Downtown, four restored family homes offer a poignant counterpoint to the city's shimmering towers. The most arresting is Bin Jelmood House. In a rare act of regional self-reflection, this museum - housed in a former slave trader's residence - traces the history of human bondage in the Indian Ocean world. It does not shy away from the historical reality of the trade, documenting the lives of East Africans and Baluchis who once powered the pearling fleets. By bridging the gap between historical manumission and modern-day labour issues, the museum acts as a sober, essential anchor for anyone seeking the truth behind the silk.

The Incubators: **Katara's Galleries** - Further north, the Katara Cultural Village acts as a sprawling incubator for this organic growth. Beyond its grand amphitheatre, the village is peppered with smaller, more intimate spaces: **Al Markhiya Gallery:** A premier venue for the "who's who" of the Arab modernist movement. **Katara Art Centre (KAC):** A hub for contemporary, cross-disciplinary projects that often challenge the status quo. **Qatar Museums Gallery, Katara:** A "pocket" gallery used for high-impact photography and community-focused exhibitions.

These venues offer a granular view of a local art scene that is being built, piece by piece, rather than bought off a Parisian shelf.

## CORNICHE AREA

### National Museum of Qatar

National Museum of Qatar: Navigating the "Rose"

*National Museum - Doha*

The National Museum of Qatar is a sprawling storyteller of the nation's soul. Opened in 2019, the building is a masterclass in avant-garde geometry, inspired by the "desert rose" - mineral crystals formed in saline sands. To the unromantic eye, the structure resembles a fleet of celestial frisbees frozen mid-collision. The Visitor Experience - The entrance is notably discreet, tucked beneath overlapping discs rather than on an obvious thoroughfare. Once inside the lobby (with a cash desk), an escalator ascends past the monumental silver sculpture *Motherland*. This represents a *battoulah* (a traditional Qatari face mask) and was created by Sheikh Hassan bin Mohammed Al Thani.

**The Gallery Experience** The interior is a realm of spacious displays, in rooms intentionally devoid of right angles or vertical walling. This offers the impression of standing on the deck of a dhow as it rocks in the sea. An immersive, multidimensional sound-and-video system ensures the experience is as visceral as it is visual. While the architecture is spectacular, it is also dominant; the galleries span 1,500m, and the immense scale can make the physical collection feel sparse at times.

*Weaving National Museum*

**Formation of Qatar:** The journey begins 700 million years ago. Meteorites and fossils are set against audio-visual backdrops depicting a prehistoric, shifting environment. **Natural Habitats:** The second gallery focuses on ecology. Taxidermied Arabian Oryx (*Oryx leucoryx*) and Dugongs (*Dugong dugon*) are presented in realistic settings. **Archaeology:** Displays span the Stone and Iron Ages through to the Islamic Period. The inclusion of modern archaeological finds alongside prehistoric pottery helps bridge the gap between the ancient and the extant. **The People of Qatar:** Galleries 4 and 5 focus on human history. The **Cirebon Wreck**, a 10th-century ship found off Java, illustrates early trade links. Built likely in the Straits of Malacca and carrying Chinese ceramics intended for Basra, it highlights Qatar's role as a link in a global chain. **Life on the Move:** Nomadic existence is detailed through the tools of the desert. Camels (*Camelus dromedarius*) are central here, with displays of tribal 'wasms' - branded marks of ownership and identity.

**The Pearl and the Palace Gallery 7** is dedicated to the pearling industry. The centrepiece is the Pearl Carpet of Baroda, commissioned by the Maharaja of Baroda in the 1860s to adorn the Prophet's Tomb in Medina. Auctioned in 2009 for USD5.5 million, its presence here gives a hint at the historic ties between the Gulf: once the source of the world's most decadent gems, and India where princely wealth acquired the pearls, and finally a buyer of its own history back from the global market. The final galleries chart the **'Modern Period'**, where the discovery of oil acted as a tectonic shift, catapulting a pearling community into a global financial powerhouse. Before departing, walk through the **Old Palace**. This early 20th-century structure became the original National Museum and the residence of Sheikh Abdullah bin Jassim Al Thani. It stands as a modest, earth-toned contrast to the high-concept concrete rose that now envelops it.

Facilities and Practicalities

The gift shop features a cavernous, cave-like ceiling constructed from 40,000 wooden pieces. For dining, Jiwan on the museum roof offers a sophisticated French interpretation of Qatari flavours, including Harees, a UNESCO-listed dish, while the Desert Rose Cafe offers lighter Middle Eastern fare. **GPS:** 25.287, 51.548 **Transport:** Metro Gold Line - National Museum Station. **Museum Hours:** Sat - Thu 09:00 - 19:00; Fri 13:30 - 19:00. (Last entry 18:30). **Cost:QAR50** for non-residents; Free for residents and students. **Contact:** +974 4452 5555 | infonmoq@qm.org.qa **Web:** nmoq.org.qa

**Fish Market**

Traditional Fish Landing & New Fish Market Doha's

relationship with the sea is most evident at its two distinct fish markets. For a glimpse of the city's traditional rhythm, visit the small open-air landing site on the eastern end of the Corniche. Here, in the crisp light of the early morning, small dhows pull alongside to land their catch directly onto the pavement. Activity resumes in the early evening, providing a salty, sensory contrast to the polished museum district nearby.

*West Bay from Old Doha Port*

For those seeking a more formal experience, the newly developed **Chabrat Al Mina** in the nearby Mina District (Old Doha Port) offers a modern take. Beneath a striking glass ceiling, rows of gleaming sea bass, kingfish, and local hamour are displayed on ice. You can purchase the catch of the day or dine at the adjacent restaurant, where the fish is prepared to order.

**Traditional Landing (Corniche): GPS:** 25.291, 51.548 **Street:** Al Corniche (East end) **Public Transport:** Metro Gold Line - National Museum Station (a 10-minute walk).

### Old Doha Port

The Old Doha Port is a purpose-built gateway to the city, featuring a sophisticated Grand Terminal (approx. GPS 25.304, 51.558) capable of accommodating the world's largest cruise vessels. It also serves as the mooring for the private yachts of the Amir of Qatar. Compared to the frenetic pace of ports in Abu Dhabi or Dubai, Doha offers a more measured and manageable experience.

**The Terminal and Transit** passengers have access to a small museum and a boutique aquarium. Facilities include currency exchange and ATMs (see the earlier section on banking). While cruise lines often provide shuttle services towards Souq Waqif, you should allow at up to an hour for immigration formalities and travel. For shorter hops within the port, golf buggies are frequently available. If you choose to walk to Souq Waqif, the distance is roughly 5km - a journey of about an hour. The National Museum and the Museum of Islamic Art are closer, though all these routes are entirely exposed to the sun; midday trekking is not for the faint-hearted.

The Mina District Much of the port is accessible to the public, particularly the Mina District (GPS 25.300, 51.552). This area is a vibrant, perhaps slightly 'Disneyfied' homage to Mediterranean coastal towns like Burano, with its pastel-painted buildings. It is a compelling alternative to Al Wakrah or even Souq Waqif for an evening stroll. **Dining:** The district now hosts over 50 eateries. A standout is **La Mesa** (+974 3999 4481), open from midday to 23:00. Located in the southern part of the village, it serves Latin American and Argentinian cuisine. It is worth requesting a window seat to observe the maritime activity. **Seafood:** The **Chabrat Al Mina** is a highlight - a beautifully designed fish market and restaurant. While the setting is superb, it is wise to check pricing and service expectations during peak hours. **Retail:** The village is peppered with supermarkets, souvenir shops, and essential facilities.

**Accommodation and Activities** - For those who prefer the sea breeze to the city centre, the Mina Hotel and Residences By The Torch (www.mina-hotel.com) offers heritage-style apartments and hotel rooms directly within the district. Water-based pursuits are plentiful. The Boxbay Boat Club (+974 3001 5911 | www.boxbayclub.com) is a primary contact for boat charters and marine training. During major events, a maritime transport service often operates, connecting the port to The Pearl and the Rixos Gulf Hotel. Logistics **Street:** Al Corniche (Old Doha Port branch). **Public Transport:** Bus 76 or 109. The nearest Metro is the **National Museum** (Gold Line), followed by a 20-minute walk or a short taxi ride. **Web:** odp.qa

**Reflective Flow Chandelier** (Al Hitmi Building) - Located in the glass atrium of the Al Hitmi Property Development building (often associated with the Council of Ministers Secretariat General on the west side of the Corniche). Designed by the Scottish artist Beau McClellan, the installation is known as Reflective Flow. The chandelier weighs approximately 18 tons and held the Guinness World Record for the largest chandelier upon its completion in 2010. **Access:** The building itself is not open to the public; however, the chandelier is housed within a seven-storey glass atrium and is clearly visible from the street, particularly after dusk when it is fully illuminated. **Rough GPS:** 25.291, 51.544 - **Street:** Al Corniche (West side, near the National Museum). **Public Transport:** Metro Gold Line - National Museum Station.

**Museum of Islamic Art (MIA)**

*Museum of Islamic Art*

The Museum of Islamic Art is a premier centre for the collection, display, and study of Islamic masterpieces spanning three continents. Since its opening in 2008 and a comprehensive 2022 refurbishment, it has served as Doha's cultural anchor. The five-storey structure sits on a bespoke man-made island, flanked by the Dhow Harbour to the west and a sprawling public park. **Architectural Vision** The architect I.M. Pei sought the essence of Islamic design in the *sabil* (ablution fountain) of Cairo's 9th-century Ibn Tulun Mosque. The resulting building is one of austere geometry, where shifting sunlight plays across sand-coloured facets. Visitors approach via an avenue of date palms that frames the museum like a modern citadel.

**Practicalities** The authorities request that all visitors dress conservatively (shoulders and knees covered). After entry, a **library** dedicated to Islamic Art sits to the right, housing a vast bilingual collection for on-site study. The museum adopts a traditional approach: objects are isolated in impeccably lit cases, allowing for a level of focus that larger, more cluttered institutions cannot match. While the collection may lack the sheer volume of some European counterparts, its curation is remarkable.

**Navigating the Galleries** The central atrium features an imperial-style staircase and a 45-metre-high window offering a cinematic view of the West Bay skyline. Permanent galleries are arranged in a horseshoe flow across Floors 2 and 3.

*Sabil - Ibn Tulun Mosque - Cairo*

**Floor 2** of the MIA in Doha serves as the historical anchor of the collection, charting the formidable birth and rapid spread of Islam. The reimagined galleries on this level function as an intellectual atlas – mapping a civilisation's expansion through its foundational focus on faith, stellar science, and the written word. Scientific Mastery: The **10th-Century Astrolabe**. Among the earliest scientific artefacts on display is a brass planispheric astrolabe signed by the astronomer Hamid ibn Al Khidr Al Khujandi. Crafted during the Buyid period in either Rayy or Baghdad and precisely dated to 374 AH (984–985 CE), this cast and engraved instrument is a masterpiece of metallurgical mastery. For the educated elite of the 10th century, this was the ultimate tool – a single device used to calculate prayer times, navigate vast landscapes, and read the turning of the night sky.

The Written Word: **Ferdowsi's Shahnameh** - The floor also houses spectacular folios from the *Shahnameh* (Book of Kings), the epic versification of the history and mythology of Greater Persia by Abu'l-Qasim Ferdowsi. MIA holds leaves from the renowned *Shahnameh of Shah Tahmasp*, produced in the Safavid royal workshops of Tabriz between 1525 and 1535 CE. This specific manuscript, which consumed the royal workshop's resources for over a decade, is a triumph of illumination. In these margins, the nib and the brush captured the mythic soul of the empire, actively drawing a reader's attention to the fluid boundary between artifice and reality.

The **Blue Quran** and Ceramic Innovation - The religious narrative is anchored by the famous *Blue Quran* from the 9th century, featuring stark gold Kufic script on rare indigo-dyed parchment. The MIA juxtaposes this medieval manuscript with a monumental contemporary piece, **Infinite Expression**, commissioned from the Afghan calligrapher Ali Baba Awrang – demonstrating that the region's calligraphic pulse remains entirely vital. Finally, the galleries explore the spread of early ceramic techniques, notably the 10th-century blue-and-white earthenware from Iraq. These vessels, often bearing bold Kufic inscriptions promising good fortune to the owner, mark the very first time cobalt blue met white opaque glaze. This was a monumental innovation in firing technique that would eventually travel along trade routes, heavily influencing later global ceramics.

*Indian Dagger and Scabbard - MIA*

**Floor 3** of the MIA broadens the visitor's journey into the later regional and imperial cultures of the Islamic world. Its galleries move through Ayyubid and Mamluk Syria and Egypt, featuring Mamluk glasswork produced between the 13th and 15th centuries CE, along with a **Mosque Lamp (around 1382–1399 BC)** from the Mamluk Sultan Al Malik Al Zahir Sayf Al Din *Barquq's mosque and madrasa complex* in Cairo – on it is written from the Sura of Light: "Allah is the Light of the heavens and the earth".From Ottoman Turkey are **Iznik pottery and tiles**, glazed using proprietary recipes and processes, with strong palace support for the workshops. Art from imperial Iran and Central Asia, manuscript arts, South Asia, arms and armour, and the maritime worlds of the Indian Ocean and Southeast Asia are a feature. Among the strongest themes at this level are courtly patronage and technical refinement, including a dagger with a pommel carved from pale green nephrite jade.

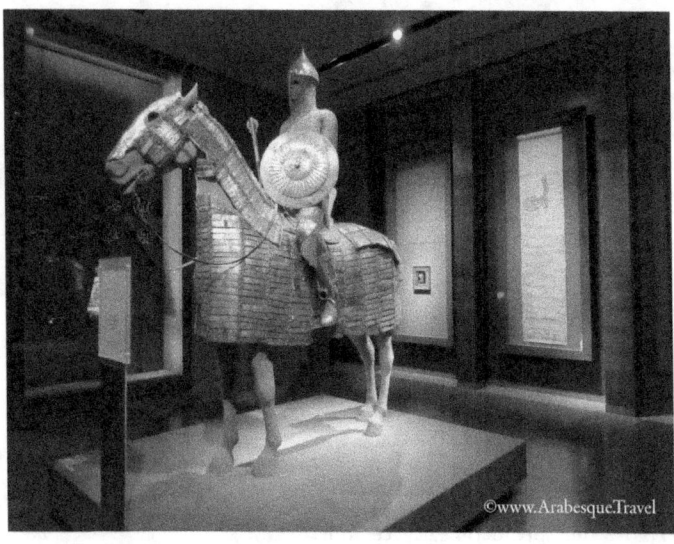

*Ottoman armour early 16thc*

**FLOOR 4 (TEMPORARY SPACE):** IN EARLY 2026, **"EMPIRE of Light: Visions and Voices of Afghanistan"** focused on a now-neglected core of the Islamic world. This floor also occasionally hosts concerts; check the Qatar Philharmonic Orchestra's schedule for upcoming performances.

**Fifth Floor dining** At the pinnacle of the museum's interior is

IDAM by Alain Ducasse. This One Michelin Star establishment fuses French *nouvelle cuisine* with Arabic influences. Philippe Starck's design, featuring white calligraphy on black carpets, provides a dramatic setting for sunset views from the 5th floor.

*Museum of Islamic Arts 7 (Seven)*

MIA Park and the Serra Sculpture The park wraps around the museum and is one of Doha's best locales for a twilight stroll. **7 by Richard Serra:** At the park's terminus stands an 80-foot steel sculpture titled *7*. This is made up of 7 pieces - representing Islamic spiritual geography: the seven heavens, the seven verses of the *Al Fatiha*, and the seven circumambulations of the Kaaba. Complimentary golf buggies run the 1km route from the museum entrance to the sculpture. **Activities:** The park hosts a popular weekend bazaar during the cooler months and features several cafes overlooking the water.

Acessing the MIA **GPS:** 25.295, 51.539 - **Transport:** Metro Gold Line - Souq Waqif Station (approx. 30 min walk). **Museum Hours:** Sat - Tue & Thu 09:00 - 19:00; Fri 13:30 - 19:00. **(Closed Wednesday). Cost:QAR50** for non-residents; Free for residents and students. **IDAM Hours:** 12:30 - 14:00 & 19:00 - 21:00. (Closed Fri & Sat; open during museum closure on Wed). www.mia.org.qa | + 974 4422 4444

*Walk Museum Islamic Art Park*

### Al Riwaq Gallery

A vast, 3,500-square-metre "white cube" space Riwaq Gallery is just southeast of the Museum of Islamic Art,. It serves as a flexible canvas for Qatar's most ambitious temporary exhibitions, often hosting major retrospectives or site-specific installations that require significant scale. The gallery has earned international acclaim for hosting some of the most significant solo shows in the region. In February 2026, "I. M. Pei: Life Is Architecture" was the first comprehensive retrospective of the architect who designed the adjacent Museum of Islamic Art. Looking ahead, Al Riwaq will be a primary venue for Rubaiya Qatar, the nation's new contemporary art quadrennial, which officially launches in November 2026 with the headline exhibition *Unruly Waters*.

The gallery's hours are now aligned with the broader Qatar Museums schedule, remaining open seven days a week. It is a useful addition to a visit to the MIA, providing a modern, often provocative contrast to the historical treasures next door. **Hours:** Sat - Thu 09:00 - 19:00; Fri 13:30 - 19:00. **Entry is at** the standard museum price (**QAR50** for non-residents), though some community exhibitions may be free. **Rough GPS:** 25.293, 51.543 **Street:** Al Corniche (Museum of Islamic Art grounds). **Public Transport:** Metro Gold Line - Souq Waqif Station. **Web:** qm.org.qa

### The Corniche

The Corniche is arguably Doha's most frequented 'attraction', its a scenic arterial route that stitches together the city's cultural highlights. Its crescent sweep encompasses the National Museum, Museum of Islamic Art, Dhow Harbour and Al Bidda Park, culminating in the neon-drenched silhouette of West Bay.

For a gourmet journey that bookends the 7km walk, consider a lunch at IDAM within the Museum of Islamic Art, followed by a stroll to dinner at Jamavar in the Sheraton Grand, via Souq Waqif. The walk takes approximately two hours at a leisurely pace, though the allure of Souq Waqif and Msheireb can easily double that time. Ensure you carry a bottle of water; while cafes are scattered along the route - particularly around the Souq - the Gulf sun remains a persistent companion. **GPS:** 25.291, 51.534 - **Public Transport: Gold Line:** Souq Waqif or National Museum. **Red & Green Lines:** Al Bidda (Interchange). **Red Line:** Corniche or West Bay QIC.

### Dhow Harbour and the West Bay Skyline

The Dhow Harbour is a drift of traditional wooden hulls

anchored against the steel-and-glass backdrop of the modern city. The public jetty offers an intimate vantage point to observe these vessels - many of which still serve as the workhorses for sunset excursions. The grandest, oldest dhows are typically Uru, handcrafted from teak in Beypore, Kerala; while the majority of the working fleet was built in Iran, and those featuring the most sophisticated navigation and finish are often the products of Sur, Oman. From this jetty, the view back towards the Museum of Islamic Art is peerless. It is also the departure point for the Anantara ferry to Banana Island Resort. The small islet in the harbour's centre, formerly known as Palm Tree Island, was a thriving resort until 2006. Today, it sits barren - a sun-bleached mound of sand that serves as a quiet reminder of an earlier, simpler era of Qatari tourism. **GPS:** 25.295, 51.535 **Public Transport:** Metro Gold Line - Souq Waqif Station.

*Dhows and Doha's SkyScrapers*

### The Pearl Monument

Located on the Corniche near the entrance to the Dhow Harbour, the Pearl Monument is an open oyster shell with a pearl at its heart creating a fountain that serves as a tribute to Qatar's maritime heritage. It is a useful landmark, standing in the shadow of the spiral minaret of the Sheikh Abdulla Bin Zaid Al Mahmoud Islamic Cultural Centre (Fanar).

A pedestrian subway is located here, providing a safe, air-conditioned passage beneath the Corniche road directly into the heart of Souq Waqif. **GPS:** 25.291, 51.534 - **Public Transport:** Metro Gold Line - Souq Waqif Station.

**Sheikh Abdulla Bin Zaid Al Mahmoud Islamic Cultural Centre (Al Fanar)**

*Pearl Monument and Al Fanar minaret*

Commonly known as Al Fanar (The Lighthouse), Sheikh Abdulla Bin Zaid Al Mahmoud Islamic Cultural Centre is a state initiative dedicated to explaining Qatari culture and the foundations of Islam to non-Arabic speakers.

*Vies over Fanar towards West Bay*

Its architecture is instantly recognisable: the singular, wedding-cake spiral minaret is a direct homage to the 9th-century Malwiya Minaret of the Great Mosque of Samarra in Iraq - showing the continuity of Islamic architectural heritage.

**Inside the Centre** The interior houses prayer rooms, lecture halls, and a library. It is an excellent resource for visitors seeking authoritative, rational dialogue on local customs, Arabic, and Islam. While the centre's mission is outreach (and indeed a quiet invitation), the location is welcoming and educational rather than overbearing.

**Exhibitions:** The newly opened **Values Hall** and Civilisation **Hall** use posters and VR films (available in seven languages) to trace the evolution of Islamic contributions to global knowledge and education. **Cultural Programs:** They offer "Coffee Mornings" for ladies and "Qatari Majlis" sessions for mixed groups, where you can learn about the nuances of dress codes, Ramadhan, and traditional Bedouin life. **Arabic Courses:** For the longer-term visitor, the centre is the premier location for Arabic language lessons tailored for non-native speakers. The building is at its most striking after sunset, when the spiral is bathed in a golden glow, making it a "must" for night photography. **Hours:** Sun - Thu 08:00 - 20:00; Fri & Sat 14:00 - 20:00. **Dress Code:** Modest attire is essential; shoulders and knees must be covered. Women can usually borrow an abaya at the entrance if required. Footwear must not be worn inside the building. **GPS:** 25.289, 51.536 - **Street:** Junction of Abdulla bin Jassim St and Hamad Al Kabir St, east of Souq Waqif. **Public Transport:** Metro Gold Line - Souq Waqif Station. **Contact:** +974 4444 7444 | binzaid@islam.gov.qa | www.binzaid.gov.qa

## SOUQ WAQIF

Souq Waqif is the undisputed "living room" of Doha. Spanning roughly 20 hectares, this labyrinthine market combines authentic heritage with the requirements of a modern capital. It is a sensory assault of spice, song, and commerce, and arguably the most vital stop for any visitor to Qatar. Its popular with locals and visitors - simple street dining is a key attraction.

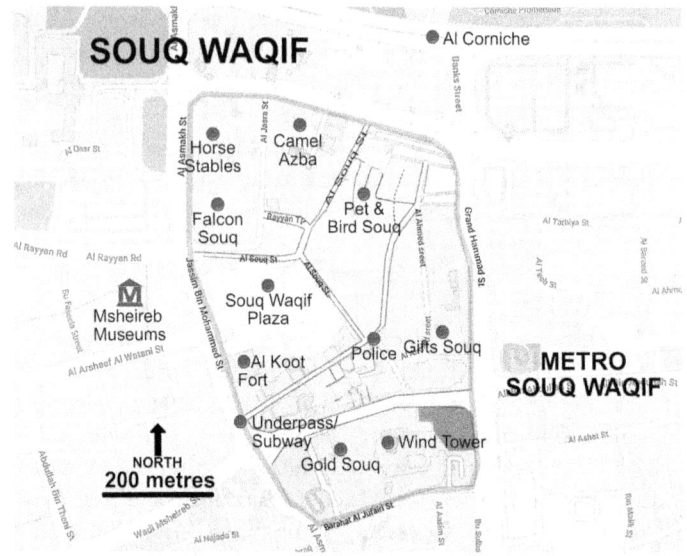

## History and the "Standing Market"

The souq's origins mirror those of Doha itself, dating back to the 1820s. It originally occupied the mouth of the Wadi Msheireb, where Bedouin would gather to trade wool and livestock for essential sea-bound goods. The name *Souq Waqif* translates to "The Standing Market." Historically, the wadi bed would flood during heavy rains or high tides, forcing vendors and customers to conduct their business while standing on the higher banks to avoid the encroaching water. While the oil boom of the 1970s saw a shift towards modern malls, the souq was saved by a catastrophic fire in 2003. This prompted a massive restoration project (2006-2008) led by Sheikh Hamad bin Khalifa Al Thani. Any structures built after 1950 were demolished, and the remaining heart of the souq was rebuilt using traditional coral stone, timber beams, and bamboo. A key element of the new souq is its multi-use: retail shops selling a mix of everyday necessities for the local population, and providing services like shoe repairs and souvenirs for visiting tourists. Cafes and restaurants encourage shoppers to linger; frequent entertainment events held in Souq Waqif Square and peripheral sites, including a cinema below the square, bring people in regularly. Security personnel, mounted on horses, add to the souq's picturesque appeal.

Finally, the souq's original residents have been replaced by guests of the various hotels.

*Souq Waqif - Dinner time*

## Navigating the Souq

The souq is largely pedestrianised and best accessed from Souq Waqif Metro and Souq Waqif Square to the south. Under the square is the underground car park and the **Novo Cinemas** (a luxury 7-star subterranean cinema).

**Southeast:** The **Golden Thumb** (*Le Pouce*) (GPS 25.286 ,51.532) by César Baldaccini. Nearby is the **Gold Souq**, where jewellery is sold by weight - expect 18k and 22k Gulf and Indian styles. Near is a small Police Station north of the Golden Thumb and a mass of restaurants along the street north of the Police Station - including Parisa. To the south of the square is an underground cinema and a street lined mainly with restaurants. **Northwest:** The main maze of narrow, shaded alleyways.

*Souq Waqif Falcon souq*

**Falcon Souq** Falcons and their Hospital are located on the eastern edge (GPS 25.288, 51.531) of Souq Waqif. This is a dedicated quarter for one of Qatar's national sports. Falcons (*Falco peregrinus*) sit on hooded perches in air-conditioned showrooms. They wear a *burka* (hood) to keep them calm; a souvenir hood makes for an evocative and lightweight gift for your family and friends - ask permission to take photographs. Just north is the Souq Waqif Falcon Hospital, a state-of-the-art medical facility dedicated solely to birds.

# WHERE TO GO

**ANIMALS OF THE SOUQ.** NORTH OF THE FALCONS ARE THE Amiri Stables, housing the Arabian horses used by the heritage police. Further north is the Camel Azba (pen), where these "ships of the desert" (can be seen up close. Nearby, the Pet and Bird Souq offers a more chaotic collection of parrots, rabbits, and exotic species.

*Camels in Souq Waqif - with West Bay as a backdrop*

## Besht Al Salem (بشت السالم)

The "Messi" Bisht. Football fans should seek out Besht Al Salem - the spelling is usually bisht. This is the tailor that supplied the gold-trimmed *bisht* (cloak) worn by Lionel Messi during the 2022 World Cup trophy presentation.

*"Messi" Bisht - Souq Waqif*

*Majlis Al Dama - Souq Waqif*

## Majlis Al Dama

Hidden in the northern passageways (GPS 25.288, 51.533) Majlis Al Dama is a government-funded café. It is dedicated to Al

Dama, a traditional board game similar to checkers. Elderly Qataris often gather here to play; the coffee shop is hushed and authentic, and you may find your tea or *regag* (thin bread) provided as a courtesy of the house.

To find Majlis Al Dama, look for the police station near the Golden Thumb; follow the small passage to the left (marked with a toilet sign), turn right at the end, and the shop is a few doors down. Inside, the tailors still work beneath a photograph of the iconic moment.

### Dining And Art

**Parisa** An opulent Persian restaurant with an interior of mirrors and hand-painted tiles that looks like it was "carved from a diamond." **Al Shurfa:** Offers a Levantine menu and a balcony with an unparalleled view of the Fanar spiral and the West Bay skyline. **Souq Waqif Art Centre:** GPS 25.286, 51.532 A beautiful courtyard space featuring local woodwork, calligraphy workshops, and galleries that are free to enter. Website / phone: swacqatar.net, 4417 6204 Opening hours: Daily 8 am-2 pm / 4 pm-10 pm - Entry cost: Free

*Al Najada Heritage House*

### Al Najada Wind Tower House

A few minutes' walk south of the Golden Thumb (Le Pouce)

brings you to the Al Najada Heritage House #15 (GPS 25.285, 51.533). This is an authentic wind tower house (*Barjeel*), an ingenious architectural survival stratigy of the pre-oil era. Wind towers, which originated in ancient Persia (Iran), were common along the Gulf coast. The tower rises above the roofline, open on four sides to "catch" the prevailing breeze from any direction. Internal cross-walls then funnel the air down into the living quarters below. In the most sophisticated versions, jars of water or damp matting were placed at the base of the shaft to provide evaporative cooling - a primitive yet effective precursor to modern air conditioning. While the house in Souq Al Najada is occasionally closed for official maintenance, it is now frequently used by Qatar Museums for satellite exhibitions, such as the recent previews of the *Art Mill Museum*. **Rough GPS:** 25.285, 51.533 - **Street:** Intersection of Grand Hamad Street and Ali bin Abdullah Street. - **Public Transport:** Metro Gold/Red/Green Lines - Msheireb Station (5-minute walk).

Arabian Horse show Souq Waqif Square- Souq Waqif is behind the stands

**Souq Waqif Square** - is a frequent venue for entertainment and activities. These might be aimed at families and children - or cultural events. The events are busiest in the afternoon and evenings, especially at the weekend. Typically there are free, or at low cost.

**Souq General Information Hours:** Most shops 10:00-12:30 & 16:00-22:00 (many shops will have longer hours). Restaurants stay open from early until midnight. **Transport: Souq Waqif Metro** (Gold Line) is the most convenient; **Msheireb** (Interchange) is a 10-minute walk to the west. Negotiation is expected for handicrafts and textiles; expect to bargain for a 10-20% discount. Gold is fixed by daily market weight, though the "workmanship fee" might be nudged a fraction.

### Al Koot Fort (Doha Fort)

Dominating the southwest corner of the Souq is Al Koot Fort (GPS 25.287, 51.530), a stark white sentinel in the desert sun. Originally built by the Ottomans in 1880 as a police post to protect merchants from thieves, it was later used as a jail before being rebuilt in 1927 by Sheikh Abdullah bin Jassim Al Thani.

While many visitors simply enjoy the fort as a striking backdrop for photography, the interior has been converted into a museum showcasing traditional Qatari handicrafts, fishing equipment, and historical photographs. Though its regular opening can be inconsistent, it is currently accessible by appointment (+974 4442 4143) and often hosts cultural events, such as the *Tasweer* photo festivals. Tivoli hotels (www.tivolihotels.com/en/souq-waqif-doha) have several boutique hotels and some of the better restaurants in Souq Waqif.

### Dar Al Kutub Al Qatariya

*Al Koot Fort - Souq Waqif*

The Qatari House of Books, lies to the southeast of Souq Waqif, the oldest public library in the Gulf region. Established in 1962, this building represents the "dawn of the digital age" in Qatar. Following a comprehensive restoration completed in early 2025, the library has been reimagined as both a research hub and a "museum of the book." Unlike the hyper-modern Qatar National Library in Education City, Dar Al Kutub is a traditional, old fashioned library It is a quiet sanctuary for those seeking a deeper, text-based understanding of the region. **The Collection:** It houses over 1,200 rare manuscripts, including historical texts on astronomy, mathematics, and medicine, as well as

WHERE TO GO 83

a good archive of early 20th-century Gulf newspapers. **The Architecture:** The renovation has preserved its mid-century character while adding a modern reception hall and an outdoor "Iqraa Plaza" for literary events. Information **GPS:** 25.282, 51.5401 **Hours:** Generally Sun - Thu 08:00 - 20:00 (Check locally for Saturday morning hours). **Entry:** Free for visitors and researchers. **Public Transport:** Metro Gold Line - Souq Waqif Station (approx. 8-minute walk southeast). **Web:** daralkutub.qa

MSHEIREB

**Msheireb Museums**

The Msheireb Museums provide a profound, intimate counterpoint to the city's grand architectural statements. Set within four restored heritage houses, they document the social and economic evolution of Qatar. Designed by Ralph Appelbaum Associates, the restoration is a masterclass in "adaptive reuse," preserving the traditional coral stone and timber while housing state-of-the-art interactive exhibits. The museums are less than 200m west of the Souq Waqif square (opposite the underground car park entrance) and make an easy add-on to a visit to Souq Waqif. The buildings are close together on Al Arshef Al Watani St.

**Radwani House** The smallest and perhaps most evocative of the four, Radwani House offers a glimpse into the domestic rhythm of a Qatari family before the era of air conditioning. Occupied until 1971, the house serves as a visible history for the city's transformation; it now stands in the shadow of the massive Qatar National Archive, a silent witness to the speed of Doha's growth. Look for the traditional "majlis" areas where the affluent Radwani family would receive guests, illustrating the transition from communal courtyard living to modern privacy.

**Company House** Set in what was once the headquarters for Qatar's first oil company, this museum tells the story of the pioneering "oil men" who laid the foundations of the nation's current wealth. In 2026, the courtyard hosts Hosh Msheireb, a boutique heritage experience featuring storytelling sessions and a "reading corner" that brings the history of the petroleum era to life for younger generations.

*Company House*

**BIN JELMOOD HOUSE** THIS MUSEUM IS PROBABLY UNIQUE in the Arab world, for its exploration of the history of slavery. There are others in West Africa, Zanzibar, Liverpool, Nantes (France), Bermuda and USA. It addresses the "untold story" of the African and Asian individuals whose labour built the early Gulf. A Journey to the Heart of Life: This high-tech laboratory-exhibition inside Bin Jelmood House is a unique collaboration between the museum and Sidra Medicine. It is free to enter and offers an interactive look at how DNA mapping validates the historical migration stories told in the house. While the exhibit serves as a recruitment hub for Qatar's national genome project, providing free sequencing and clinical consultations for residents, it offers every visitor a fascinating look at the "science of identity."

*Bin Jelmood House*

**Mohammed Bin Jassim House** The house of the founder of modern Qatar's son stands on the very ground it addresses. It documents the transition of Msheireb from a bustling residential district to a derelict quarter, and finally to the world's most sustainable urban heart. The "Echoes of Memory" installation, which uses digital projections to recreate the sights and sounds of the old "Kahraba Street" (Electricity Street), the first in Doha to be lit by a generator.

**M7: The Creative Engine**

Just a short walk from the heritage houses is M7, Qatar's epicentre for design, fashion, and tech. While the museums look back, M7 looks forward. In early February 2026, M7 hosted the inaugural edition of Art Basel Qatar. This landmark event, the first of its kind in the Middle East, featured 87 galleries from 31 countries. It solidified M7's status as a global hub for the "art of cultural commerce." Throughout the spring (April - June 2026), M7 serves as the primary venue for the Design Doha Biennial. Highlights include the *Arab Design Now* exhibition, which showcases contemporary Middle Eastern furniture and industrial design that balances traditional materiality with modern sustainability. Information **Museum Hours:** Mon - Sat 09:00 - 17:00; Fri 15:00 - 21:00. **(Closed Sunday). M7 Hours:** Sat - Thu 11:00 - 21:00; Fri 15:30 - 21:00. **Cost:** Entry to Msheireb Museums is **Free** (registration required); M7 exhibition prices vary by show. **Transport:** Metro Msheireb (Interchange for Red, Green, and Gold lines).

### Msheireb Tram and Barahat Square

*Msheireb Tram*

While exploring the district, take advantage of the complimentary Msheireb Tram. This high-tech, hydrogen-powered service operates on a 2km loop with nine stops, including a station right outside the heritage museums. Enjoy a silent, air-conditioned reprieve and an 18-minute ride through the district's architectural highlights.

The tram passes the Harrods Café in the Baraha zone. Reflecting Qatar's global financial connections, the Harrods brand and its London flagship are owned by the Qatar Investment Authority (QIA). This café acts as a local ambassador for the Knightsbridge institution, serving a sophisticated menu inspired by its British roots. **Tram Hours:** Sat - Thu 09:00 - 12:00 & 16:00 - 21:00; Fri 16:00 - 21:00. (Trams run roughly every 6 minutes). **Cost:** The tram is free for all visitors.

*Barahat Msheireb*

**Barahat Msheireb** - The district's centrepiece is Barahat Msheireb, the largest open-air covered square in the Middle East. It is a masterpiece of environmental engineering: A massive, retractable membrane roof can be closed to provide total shade during the fierce midday sun or opened at night to let heat escape into the desert sky. The square utilises "cool pools" - localised areas of radiant cooling in the floor and cooled-air vents - to maintain a comfortable temperature even when the city swelters.

**Msheireb Galleria** - Bordering the square is the Msheireb Galleria, a boutique shopping destination that anchors the district's retail experience. It features the Smart Msheireb Monoprix, the first of its kind in Qatar to offer a "Shop & Go" contactless service. The Galleria is conveniently located near the Msheireb Metro Station (the central hub for the Red, Gold, and Green lines), making it the most accessible entry point for those arriving by rail.

## THE DOHA GRAND PARK: AL BIDDA, AL RUMAILA, AND WADI AL SAIL

Looking beyond Msheireb, the amalgamation of Al Bidda, Al Rumaila, and Wadi Al Sail Parks forms the expansive 'Doha Grand Park' 25.298, 51.516. This green lung of the capital covers 1.745 million sqm (approximately 1.7sq km) - making it larger than London's Hyde Park. Beneath the manicured lawns of Al Bidda lies the original 18th-century settlement. Ground-penetrating radar surveys have revealed the foundations of the old town, its mosques, and a rectangular fort, which were demolished in the 1960s. Near the natural rock outcrops, you will find the Al Bidda Tower. This is a 2005 reconstruction of a 16th-century watchtower, originally used to monitor pearl-diving dhows and defend against maritime incursions. A cherished relic from the original 1990s park, this rainbow-like structure remains a premier spot for photographers capturing the West Bay skyline at sunset. Unusually for Qatar's public spaces, Al Bidda was the first park in the country to allow leashed dogs, a nod to the city's changing social fabric.

**Flora and Fauna** The park's landscaping is not merely aesthetic; it is a botanical sanctuary. The iconic Sidra (*Ziziphus spina-christi*) provides shade alongside the drought-resistant Ghaf (*Prosopis cineraria*) and the native Samr (*Acacia tortilis*). These trees offer a haven for the migratory Hoopoe (*Upupa epops*) and various desert butterflies that flit between the formal gardens of Al Rumaila. The park features a sophisticated water feature, multiple cafes, and a children's maze at 25.303, 51.514. For the active visitor, there are professional tennis courts, an outdoor gym, and a sprawling 850-seat amphitheatre for cultural events. Specific zones must be pre-booked via the Al Bidda Park app or website. Fees are typically QAR50 for a four-hour slot. Cash is not accepted - payments are strictly by card. **Parking:** A massive underground facility provides space for 6,000 vehicles, accessible from the Al Corniche (southbound) and Uhud Street.

**Saikl Bike** is a Qatari-owned bike rental service and is a fixture of the city's recreational scene, particularly within the manicured surroundings of the Sheraton Hotel Park and the broader Al Bidda Park area. **Services and Pricing** Bicycles are available for adults and children, with a diverse fleet that includes standard two-wheelers, three-wheelers, and larger four-seater family bikes. **Adults:** QAR35 for one hour - QAR60 for two hours. **Children:** QAR25 for one hour - QAR45 for two hours. **Family Bikes:** Prices range from QAR50 to QAR60 per hour, depending on the size. **Inclusions:** Rental fees include a helmet. **Repairs:** A bike repair service is available for those using their own equipment who may require a "tune-up" or brake adjustment. **Hours**: 15:00 - midnight daily (often extending to 02:00 during weekends or peak season). Rough **GPS**: 25.298, 51.513 - Location: Off Al Bidda Street (West of the Al Corniche) - Al Bidda Park area. Branch: Sheraton Hotel Park (Hotel Park Doha). **Public Transport**: Accessible via the Al Bidda Metro Station (Red and Green Lines) or Corniche Metro Station (Red Line) for the Sheraton branch. **Contacts**: +974 5028 0404 Email: info@saiklbike.com Website: www.saiklqtr.com

*Imam Muhammad ibn Abd al-Wahhab Mosque*

## IMAM MOHAMMED BIN ABDULWAHHAB MOSQUE

Constructed on a prominent limestone ridge in the Al Jebailat district, this is the largest mosque in Qatar. It serves as a stark, architectural focus for the nation's religious identity. Named after the 18th-century theologian from Najd, the mosque was inaugurated in 2011. Its design is a contemporary interpretation of the traditional Qatari mosque - austere, functional, and devoid of the flamboyant ornamentation often found in other regions of the Arab World.

The structure features 93 domes: 65 crowning the main building and 28 covering the *sahn* (courtyard). These are not merely decorative but serve as a historic nod to the multi-domed mosques of Makkah and Al Madinah. Inside, the sheer scale is sobering; the men's prayer hall alone covers 7,400sqm, while the entire complex can accommodate 30,000 worshippers. The Library's Treasure: The on-site library is not just for scholars; it contains over 30,000 volumes, including rare English translations of Islamic jurisprudence, offering a quiet space for the "Pattern Seeker" to study.

**Visiting** For the non-Muslim visitor, the experience is one of quiet observation. Children under 8 are not permitted inside the prayer halls. **Dress Code:** Men must wear long trousers and long-sleeved shirts (avoiding clothing with text). Women must be covered so that only the face, hands, and feet are visible; the mosque provides returnable **Abayas** (*clothing*) and headscarves. **Photography:** Mobile phone photography is permitted in the main areas, but strictly forbidden in the ladies' prayer rooms or during active prayer times. **The Panorama:** The mosque sits on a "low hill", which is actually a natural outcrop of the **Doha Formation** (limestone). Shortly before the *Maghrib* (sunset) prayer, the mosque's facade glows with a warm amber light, while the glass towers of West Bay start being lit up. Practical Information **Operating Hours:** Open to non-Muslims 08:00 - 11:00 (except Friday). Outside of these hours, entry is less certain and never permitted during the five daily prayer times. **Rough GPS:** 25.318, 51.507 **Location:** Junction of Khalifa Street and Al Istiqlal Street - Al Jebailat. **Public Transport:** Red Line Metro to West Bay, followed by the Metrolink M107 bus (note: the bus does not operate on Fridays). Use the north exit of the station. **Entry**

**Charge:** No Charge. **Contacts:** +974 4470 0000 - binzaid@islam.gov.qa - www.binzaid.gov.qa

### The Qatar National Theatre

The Qatar National Theatre, inaugurated in 1982, remains a primary venue for the performing arts in Doha. Its architecture is stark, and functional as was the city's early modern development. With its accessible location on the Al Corniche and a well-designed interior, it offers an intimate yet professional venue for theatrical productions, concerts, and cultural seminars. The auditorium is noted for its excellent acoustics and comfortable tiered seating. While the facility is a pillar of the local arts scene, it notably lacks a dedicated, standalone website. Visitors seeking information on upcoming performances typically rely on local English-language newspapers, the Ministry of Culture's social media channels, or physical signage at the venue. •Operating Hours: Subject to performance schedules. •Entry Charge: Varies according to the specific event. •**Rough GPS**: 25.305, 51.516 •Street: Off Al Corniche - Al Masrah Park area. •Public Transport: Accessible via the **Metro Red Line - Corniche Station**. From the station, it is a short walk through the Al Masrah Park. •Contacts: +974 4483 6118

### Khalifa International Tennis and Squash Complex

The Khalifa International Tennis and Squash Complex is the premier venue for racket sports in Qatar. Opened in 1992, it was the start of Qatar's sporting ambitions. The facility features over 20 outdoor hard courts, with the majestic centre court providing seating for 7,000 spectators. It is the permanent home of the Qatar ExxonMobil Open (ATP) and the Qatar TotalEnergies Open (WTA), attracting the world's elite players to Doha's winter sun. Beyond the professional circuit, the complex is a public resource. Courts are available for private booking through the Qatar Tennis Federation (QTF), subject to availability (STA). The venue also houses a high-performance squash centre, reflecting the region's historical dominance in the sport.

### Fire Station: Artist in Residence

Situated just west of the Al Corniche, the Fire Station is a compelling overview of Qatar's rapid cultural evolution. Originally built in 1982 as the Civil Defence headquarters, the building was decommissioned in 2012 and reopened in 2014 as a premier contemporary art hub. The iconic honeycomb-patterned tower remains, though it now serves as a beacon for the city's creative community rather than a lookout for smoke. At its core, the facility is an incubator. The "Artist in Residence" programme supports approximately 20 artists annually, providing them with private studio space and a professional platform to "finish" their residencies with a public exhibition. The galleries host a rotating schedule of world-class exhibitions that often bridge the gap between regional talent and international movements. The complex includes Cass Art (+974 4452 5625), the first Middle Eastern branch of the renowned British art supplier. It is a well-stocked haven for professionals and amateurs alike, retailing everything from high-grade pigments to architectural drafting tools.

**Operating Hours**: Saturday - Thursday 09:00 - 19:00; Friday 13:30 - 19:00. Entry Charge: No charge for residents of Qatar (with QID). For non-residents, a fee of approximately **QAR50** is usually charged for major exhibitions. Always check current guidelines at qm.org.qa. Rough **GPS**: 25.303, 51.507 •Street: Junction of Mohammed Bin Thani Street and Al Istiqlal Street - Al Bidda Park area. •Public Transport: Accessible via the **Metro Red Line - Corniche Station**. It is approximately a 1,500m walk through the park; a taxi is recommended in high summer. Contacts: +974 4422 4222 - contact@firestation.org.qa - www.firestation.org.qa

**Qatar Bowling Centre**

The Qatar Bowling Centre (QBC) is the definitive home of the sport in Doha. Managed by the Qatar Bowling Federation, it serves as the official training ground for the Qatar National Bowling Team - a squad with a formidable international reputation, including multiple World Championship titles and Asian Games gold medals. It has 32 synthetic lanes equipped with Brunswick automatic scoring and pin setters. Beyond bowling, the centre is a social hub for billiards, snooker, table tennis, and mini-football. Operating **Hours**: Sunday - Wednesday: 10:00 - 00:00 (Midnight) - Thursday: 10:00 - 01:00 - Friday: 08:00 - 18:00 (Leagues only); 18:00 - 01:00 (Open to all) - Saturday: 10:00 - 00:00 (Midnight) - Entry Charge: Games start from QAR8 - QAR12 per person (prices fluctuate based on the day and "happy hour" timings). Shoe rental is typically included in the per-game price. Rough **GPS**: 25.292, 51.516 - Street: Off Al Khaleej Street (near the Mannai Roundabout) - Musheireb/Al Corniche area. Public Transport: Accessible via the Al Bidda Metro Station (Red and Green Lines). It is a short walk from the station. Contacts:

+974 4432 9178 - qatarbowlingcenter@gmail.com - www.qatarbowlingcenter.com

**Hotel Park**

Located at the northern apex of the Al Corniche, Hotel Park is a sophisticated green lung situated directly in front of the iconic Sheraton Grand Doha Resort & Convention Hotel - the 'Pyramid of the Gulf'. This 80,000sqm space is a clever architectural synecdoche for Doha's urban ingenuity; it is effectively one of the world's largest roof gardens, concealing a massive four-storey underground parking facility beneath its manicured lawns and water features.

While the park serves as a practical link between the West Bay financial district and the sea, its design is far from utilitarian. It offers a series of "pleasure gardens" with varying topographies, including man-made hills that provide some of the best unobstructed views of the city's skyline. The strategic placement of trees and the use of cascading water features create a localised micro-climate. On a still day, the temperature within the park's shaded avenues can be up to 10°C cooler than the exposed asphalt of the surrounding West Bay streets. Parking Fees: Approximately QAR5 per hour after the initial five-minute grace period. Rough GPS: 25.320, 51.534 - Location: At the intersection of Al Corniche Street and Al Funduq Street - West Bay. Public Transport: Accessible via the Metro Red Line (West Bay Station), followed by a 10-minute walk. Website:www.hotelparkdoha.com

WEST BAY

West Bay is a towering glass forest of skyscrapers on a prominent peninsula in Doha's Bay. This district is an architectural reminder of Qatar's rapid transition from a pearl-diving economy to a global energy giant; as recently as the 1980s, this entire area was merely an expanse of sand and shallow tidal flats. While it serves primarily as a commercial and diplomatic hub, the skyline itself is the attraction.

Architectural Highlights - **Doha Tower (Burj Qatar):** Designed by Jean Nouvel, this 238m tower is a modern interpretation of the traditional Islamic *mashrabiya* (screen). Its intricate butterfly-patterned cladding serves as a functional sunshade. Notably, the building lacks a central core, utilising a diagrid structural system to maximise internal space. **Tornado Tower:** Known for its distinctive hourglass shape, this tower features an exterior lighting system capable of displaying 35,000 patterns, mimicking the kinetic energy of lightning. **Palm Towers:** A pair of hexagonal buildings that recreate the form of the **Date Palm** in glass and steel - a nod to the most vital tree of the Arabian Peninsula.

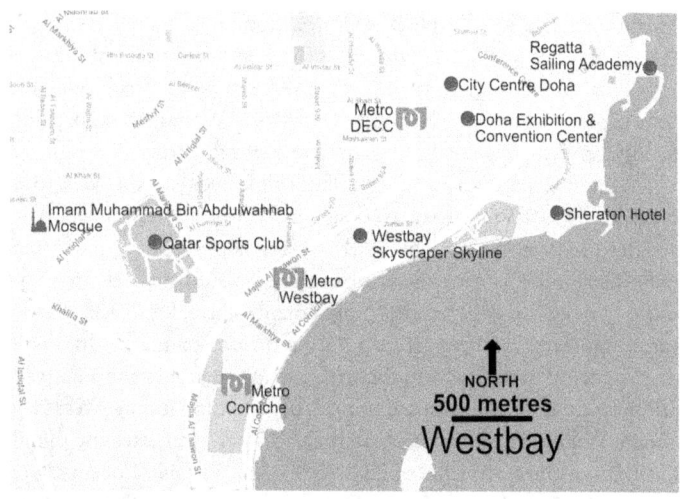

**Qatar Sports Club: Suheim Bin Hamad Stadium**

This complex is the home of Qatar Sports Club, one of the nation's oldest and most successful multi-sport institutions (formerly known as Al Istiqlal). The stadium is a premier venue for the Qatar Stars League and is equally renowned for hosting world-class track and field events, including the Diamond League. The stadium's running track is widely considered one of the fastest in the Middle East due to its specific synthetic composition and the protection from crosswinds provided by the surrounding West Bay towers. Practical Information **Typical Hours:** 08:00 - 22:00 (subject to match schedules). **Rough GPS:** 25.317, 51.514 - **Street:** Junction of Al Istiqlal Street and Al Markhiya Street - Al Dafna. **Public Transport:** Accessible via the Metro Red Line (Corniche Station), followed by a 1,500m walk or a short taxi ride. **Contacts:** +974 4483 1777 - info@qatarsc.com - www.qatarsc.com

**City Centre Doha**

City Centre Doha is perhaps the most practical mall for visitors. Opened in 2001, it was the first "mega-mall" in Qatar. Unlike the newer, more sprawling suburban malls, its vertical design and central

West Bay location make it a highly efficient "one-stop shop" for tourists. The mall's Green Court recently underwent a massive 3,400sqm expansion to house **Inflata Park**, Qatar's largest indoor inflatable adventure zone, featuring space-themed galactic obstacles. **Anchor Stores:** It houses a massive Carrefour hypermarket and the British favourite, Debenhams. The mall is strategically linked to three international hotels, allowing guests to walk directly from their rooms into the retail floors. Practical Information - **Typical Hours:** 10:00 - 00:00; Friday 15:00 - 01:00. **Rough GPS:** 25.326, 51.530 - **Street:** Conference Centre, Omar Al Mukhtar - West Bay. **Public Transport:** Metro Red Line to Doha Exhibition and Convention Centre (DECC) Station. **Contacts:** +974 4493 3355 - info@citycenterdoha.com - www.citycenterdoha.com

### Doha Exhibition & Convention Centre (DECC)

The DECC is the primary venue for international trade fairs and exhibitions. Its most striking feature is the "floating blade" roof, a massive steel structure that appears to hover over the glass foyer, offering panoramic views of the skyscrapers. The facility can be configured into five independent halls or opened into a single, cavernous space of 35,000sqm - one of the largest pillar-less exhibition halls in the world. Practical Information - **Parking:** The complex sits atop a 2,800-capacity underground car park, which is remarkably affordable for central West Bay (approx. QAR3 per hour for the first 4 hours). **Typical Hours:** As per event schedule. **Rough GPS:** 25.323, 51.529 **Street:** Conference Centre Street, Omar Al Mukhtar - West Bay. **Public Transport:** Metro Red Line to DECC Station. **Contacts:** +974 4033 1111 - info@decc.qa - www.decc.qa

### Landmark Mall

Located to the north-west of the city centre, Landmark Mall offers a more traditional aesthetic, with its exterior inspired by a classic Qatari fort, complete with stylised turrets. It is a favourite for long-term residents and those seeking a quieter, single-storey shopping experience away from the West Bay crowds. **Regional Buying:** The Carrefour here is noted for its "local first" policy; it is an excellent place to find Qatari-grown tomatoes and regional dates that are often bypassed by the more internationalised supermarkets. **Circus Land:** The mall houses an indoor amusement park themed like a traditional travelling circus, featuring one of the few permanent indoor carousels in the country. Practical Information - **Typical Hours:** 09:00 - 22:00. **Rough GPS:** 25.334, 51.467 **Street:**

Doha Expressway / Al Markhiya Street - Al Duhail. **Public Transport:** Bus routes 100 or 101. **Contacts:** +974 4487 5222 - info@landmarkdoha.com - www.landmarkdoha.com

## DOHA SOUTH AND EAST: SPORTS AND LOW-COST SHOPPING

Doha's south and east offer a stark, industrial contrast to the glass forests of West Bay. This is a region of functional utility, characterised by sprawling townships and world-class sporting arenas that rise like ziggurats above flat, arid plains.

### Dragon Mart and China Mall

Situated in the southwest, Dragon Mart is a sprawling, warehouse-style marketplace that serves as a vital market for East Asian trade in the Gulf. While the user might find the interior layout resembles a labyrinth of narrow alleyways, it is a focused hub for "pile it high - sell it cheap" commerce. From intricate building materials to the latest electronics, it is the city's primary destination for those seeking utility over luxury. Inside, the sheer variety of goods is overwhelming; one can find everything from industrial-grade power tools to delicate silk fabrics within a few metres of each other. **Bargaining:** Unlike in the high-end malls of West Bay, it's an unspoken rule here. If you are buying in bulk, a "discount" is almost always a possibility. Practical Information - **Typical Hours:** 10:00 - 22:00 (Individual shops vary). **Rough GPS:** 25.194, 51.455 **Location:** Junction of Industrial Area Road and East Industrial Street - Industrial Area. **Public Transport:** Metro Link or Bus T610 from West Bay. (Note: Bus routes were recently renumbered; check the Mowasalat app for the most current 'T' or 'R' prefixes.

### Asian Town

Directly south of Dragon Mart, across the highway, lies Asian Town. This leisure district is designed to cater to the vast expatriate community from the Indian Subcontinent. It is a vibrant, bustling zone that offers a sense of home for thousands, featuring affordable dining that is arguably the most authentic in the country.

**Cricket Heritage:** The **Asian Town Cricket Stadium** (also known as West End Park) is the first international-standard cricket venue in Qatar. It has a capacity of 13,000 and serves as the official "home ground" for the Afghanistan National Cricket Team for their international Test matches. **Cinema Culture:** The four cinemas here often screen the latest blockbusters from Bollywood and the South Indian film industries, frequently featuring midnight premieres that attract thousands of spectators. Practical Information **Rough GPS:** 25.189, 51.461 **Public Transport:** Bus T603 from Msheireb Metro Station.

### Al Arabi Sports Club

Al Arabi is one of Qatar's most storied multi-sport institutions, affectionately known by fans as "The Dream Team." Their home, the Grand Hamad Stadium, is a multi-purpose arena that was a key venue during the 2006 Asian Games.

**Sports Diversity:** While football is the crown jewel, the club is a powerhouse in volleyball and basketball. The surrounding grounds are often shaded by **Date Palms** (*Phoenix dactylifera*), providing a brief respite from the sun for visitors to the public swimming pool. Practical Information - **Typical Hours:** 08:00 - 22:00 **Rough GPS:** 25.259, 51.519 **Contacts:** +974 4467 3666 - www.alarabi.qa

### Al Thumama Stadium

Rising from the desert like a pristine white *gahfiya* (a traditional woven cap) dropped onto the floor, this 40,000-seat stadium (now being reduced to 20,000 as a legacy move) is a masterclass in cultural architecture. The stadium's design is more than aesthetic; the circular shape and the "woven" exterior allow for highly efficient natural ventilation. In the post-World Cup era, the upper tiers are being replaced by a boutique hotel and a branch of the world-renowned Aspetar sports clinic. Practical Information - **Rough GPS:** 25.235, 51.531 **Public Transport:** Bus M126 from Free Zone Metro Station.

### Qatar Racing Club (QRC)

For those with a penchant for speed, the QRC is the premier destination for drag racing and "drifting" in the region. Located near the edge of the industrial zone, it hosts the Arabian Drag Racing League during the winter months. On a Thursday night, the air is thick with the smell of high-octane fuel and the roar of massive engines - it is a sensory overload that contrasts sharply with the quietude of Doha's museums. Practical Information - **Typical Hours:** Events usually start from 18:00 (October - April). **Rough GPS:** 25.175, 51.481 **Contacts:** +974 4028 6000 - www.qrc.qa

### Al Ahli Sports Club

Founded in 1950 as Al Najah, Al Ahli is the oldest sports club in Qatar, earning it the nickname "Al Ameed" (The Brigadier). Their home, the Hamad Bin Khalifa Stadium, is a relatively intimate venue with a capacity of 12,000. **Historical Milestone:** In 1973, the legendary Pelé played a friendly match at the Doha Sports Stadium against a Qatari selection led by Al Ahli, a moment still spoken of with reverence in local sporting circles. Practical Information - **Typical Hours:** 08:00 - 22:00 **Rough GPS:** 25.252, 51.534 **Public Transport:** Bus T609 from Al Gharafa or Metro Link services from Oqba Bin Nafie station. **Contacts:** +974 4032 7777 - www.al-ahliclub.com

## AL WAKRAH AND SOUTHEAST QATAR

### Al Janoub Stadium, Al Wakrah

Inaugurated in 2019, Al Janoub Stadium was designed by the late Dame Zaha Hadid. The stadium's sweeping, aerodynamically fluid form is inspired by the hulls of the traditional dhow, the wooden vessels that once dominated the Gulf's pearl-diving industry. While the stadium held 40,000 spectators during the 2022 World Cup, in its 2026 legacy mode, the capacity has been reduced to 20,000 seats. The removed upper-tier seats have been donated to developing nations to support sporting infrastructure. It now serves as the permanent home of Al Wakrah Sports Club. **The Cooling Sails:** The stadium features a retractable roof resembling a sail that can close in 30 minutes. This, combined with an innovative under-seat cooling system, allows the pitch to be used even during the height of the Qatari summer. **Legacy Park:** The precinct surrounding the stadium has been transformed into a massive public park. It features a community market, an 800m cycling track, and a 1km running track. **The "Upside Down" Roof:** To appreciate the architectural intent, view the stadium from the ground; the roof beams are intentionally visible and designed to echo the interior timber ribs of a dhow's hull. Practical Information - **Rough GPS:** 25.159, 51.575 **Street:** Khat Al Wakrah Road - Al Wakrah. **Public Transport:** The closest Metro station is Al Wakrah (Red Line). From here, the **MetroLink M127** bus provides a direct service to the stadium.

WHERE TO GO 99

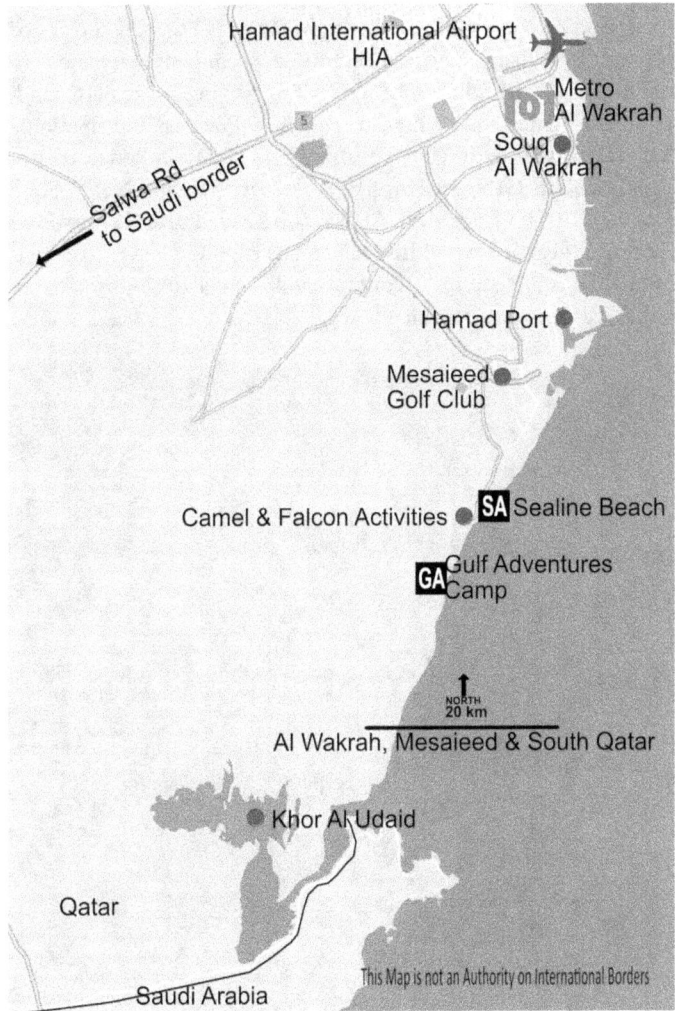

**Gulf Youth Bicycle**

Established in 1985, Gulf Youth Bicycle is one of the oldest and most trusted bicycle retailers in the country. Located in the low-rise, heritage-inspired Barwa Village, it is a major supplier of everything from children's first bikes to high-performance e-scooters. It probably has the largest selection of entry-level and intermediate bicycles in Doha, making it a "go-to" for families. **Barwa Village**

**Design:** The shop is situated within Barwa Village, an integrated community where the architecture is a contemporary nod to traditional Qatari village planning - low-rise buildings with sand-coloured facades and stylised battlements. Practical Information - **Typical Hours:** Saturday - Thursday 09:00 - 21:00; Friday 16:30 - 22:00. **Rough GPS:** 25.214, 51.580 **Street:** Building No. 9, Shop No. 13, Barwa Village - off Al Wakrah Road. **Public Transport:** Accessible via the **MetroLink M126** bus from the Ras Abu Fontas Metro Station (Red Line). **Contacts:** +974 4455 1092 - info@qatar-bicycle.com - www.qatar-bicycle.com

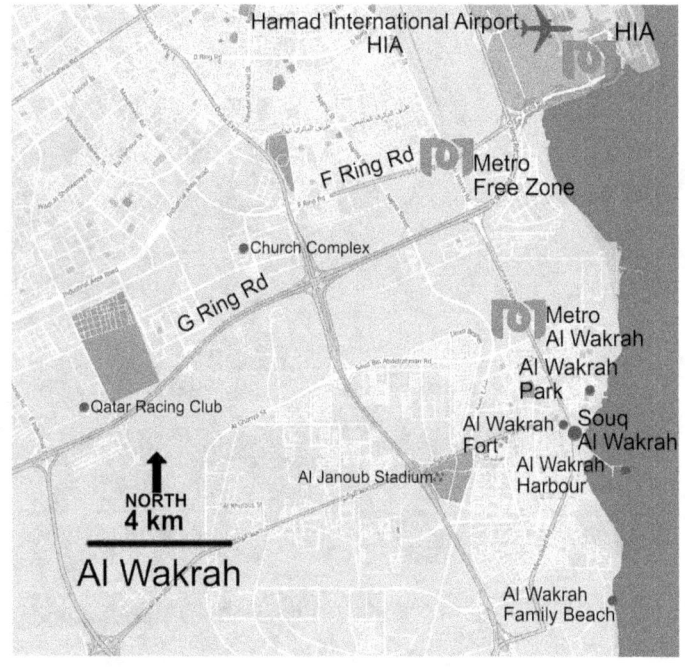

### Souq Al Wakrah

Souq Al Wakrah is a heritage-inspired coastal development situated 19km south of Doha's Souq Waqif. A drive between these two architectural siblings typically takes 30 minutes, while the journey to Hamad International Airport is less than 15 minutes. Upon arrival, golf-style buggies operate during the busier evening hours to ferry visitors from the parking areas into the heart of the souq.

*Souq Al Wakrah*

Designed as a residential village rather than a purely commercial market, Souq Al Wakrah serves as a serene memory of Qatar's maritime past. Its narrow alleyways and "homes" function as boutique retail outlets and restaurants. Unlike its busier Doha counterpart, the entire area here is tranquil, making it a "calm before the storm" for those seeking a slower pace. South of the heritage area is the small port, which usually has dozens of Dhows tied up. Offshore, there might be authentic sailing Dhows at anchor. The jetty is 1,200m long, creating a good evening walk from the beach area. **The "Bird's Nest":** The name Al Wakrah is derived from the Arabic *wakar*, meaning "bird's nest." This refers to the nearby low hills, which historically hosted numerous avian nests.

**Souq Al Wakrah Hotel Qatar by Tivoli** is not a single building but a collection of former heritage houses. It lacks a traditional central lobby, requiring guests to walk through the public alleyways to reach their rooms - a literal immersion into the local fabric. **The Living Museum:** The seafront promenade is an ideal spot to feel the **Sea Breeze** - a natural air conditioner that can be 2°C - 3°C cooler than the inland desert. Look for the **Grey Heron** (*Ardea cinerea*), often seen standing motionless on the rocky shore at low tide. **Marine Commerce:** A small, functional fish market operates daily. For the freshest catch, arrival before 07:00 is essential.**Dining and the Waterfront** - A concentrated strip of restaurants at approx. GPS 25.169, 51.610 offers a diverse palette of Middle Eastern and international cuisines. **Seafood:** A dedicated seafood restaurant is positioned 100m north of the main strip. **Budget Options:** Lower-cost seafood and local eateries are clustered at the southern end near the car park and fish souq.

Al Waqrah sea front

**The Dhow Harbour:** To the south, the small port shelters dozens of traditional wooden dhows. An evening walk along the 1,200m jetty offers a spectacular view of authentic sailing dhows at anchor, silhouetted against the moonlit Gulf.

### Al Wakrah Park and the North Beach

Located 500m north of the souq, this park provides essential greenery. The adjacent beach extends 1km northward and is a popular swimming spot for bachelor groups. **Ecology:** The seabed near the northern edge is characterised by the presence of the **Grey Mangrove** (*Avicennia marina*). The ground here can be muddy; water shoes are recommended to navigate the submerged roots safely. Note that there are no lifeguards or safety facilities on this specific stretch.

### Sheikh Abdulrahman bin Jassim Fort

Commonly known as Al Wakrah Fort, this structure was likely built in the early 20th century on the site of an earlier fortification. It served as the seat of power during Sheikh Abdulrahman's tenure as governor. The fort features reduced corner towers and internal modifications. While usually closed to the public, the imposing wooden gates are a photographer's delight. **Rough GPS:** 25.172, 51.606

### Al Wakrah Family Beach

Located 5km south of the main souq, this beach is strictly reserved for women and families. Unaccompanied men are prohibited and liable to arrest; they are instead directed to Al Wakrah Park. The water is exceptionally shallow; swimming requires a significant trek out to sea. However, the undulating sandy seabed creates low-tide "tidal trap" pools that capture small fish and crustaceans, providing natural interest for children. **Facilities:** Toilets are available, though maintenance can be sporadic. There is no public transport to this location. Practical Information - **Typical Hours:** Shops: 10:00 - 12:00 and 16:00 - 22:00. Restaurants: 10:00 - 22:00. **Entry Charge:** Free. **Rough GPS (Souq):** 25.173, 51.609 **Public Transport:** MetroLink M127 or Karwa Bus has several local intra-Wakrah services

*Camp Khor Udaid*

## SOUTHEAST QATAR KHOR AL UDAID

### Camel and Falcon Activities

Arabia finds its most evocative expression in the silhouette of a dromedary against the dunes. These single-humped beasts, are native to the peninsula and remain a powerful image of Bedouin resilience. Opposite the Sealine Beach Resort, and continuing south toward the Sarab Camp (+974 6657 3448), visitors will find casual stations for camel rides and falconry displays. **The Saker Falcon:** The handlers at Sealine often feature the **Saker Falcon** (*Falco cherrug*), a species that can reach diving speeds of 300km/h. In Qatari culture, the falcon is not a pet but a highly respected family member, often possessing its own passport for international travel.

**Sarab Camp:** Located approximately 500m from the shoreline, this 'glamping' destination blends modern comfort with a traditional tented aesthetic. It offers a rare opportunity to sleep under the desert stars without sacrificing amenities like air conditioning and ensuite bathrooms. **Negotiation Tip:** If you wish to photograph a falcon on your arm without a full ride or display, a fee of QAR20-QAR30 is usually sufficient. Practical Information- **Typical Hours:** Activities are probably best from 15:00 until sunset, as the temperature drops. During the summer months, midday rides are avoided to protect both the animals and the riders from the extreme heat. **Cost:** Negotiating the charge is part of the experience; a short ride typically costs between QAR50 and QAR75. For those venturing further to the permanent campsites near Khor Al Udaid, camels are often available on-site, though it is prudent to confirm this at the time of booking. **Rough GPS:** 24.862, 51.512 **Public Transport:** There is no public transport to this area; a 4x4 vehicle is recommended for exploring beyond the paved road, though the camel stations are accessible by standard car. **Contacts:** Sarab Camp: +974 4446 5600 (General) or +974 6657 3448 (Operational).

### Khor Al Udaid (The Inland Sea)

In Qatar's extreme southeast lies Khor Al Udaid (also spelt Khor Al Adaid), a remarkable dune field that cascades into the sea. A *khor* is a creek or lagoon; appearing almost entirely landlocked, this body of water is known globally as "The Inland Sea". It is one of the few places on earth where the deep desert dunes cascade directly into the tidal waters of the sea. The sand here is exceptionally pale, composed of powdered coral and sea shells, creating white dunes known locally as *naqiyat* (meaning 'pure'). The lagoon is not truly enclosed but is fed by a narrow, deep channel from the Arabian Gulf. This area forms part of the ancient estuary of the Wadi Sahba, a prehistoric river that once carried water from the central Arabian plateau into the sea.

Camel rides - *Khor Al Udaid*

Designated as a nature reserve in 2007, the area covers approximately 1833sq km. It is currently on the UNESCO World Heritage Tentative List due to its unique "interdune" sabkha flats and diverse ecosystem. **The Desert Rose:** In the undisturbed **Sabkha** (*salt flats*), one may find the 'Desert Rose'. This is a complex crystal cluster of **Gypsum** (*Calcium sulphate dihydrate*), formed through evaporation in the arid soil. These fragile, sand-embedded "petals" served as the primary architectural inspiration for the National Museum of Qatar. **Singing Sands:** On the steeper slopes of isolated **Barchan** (*crescent-shaped*) dunes, a curious acoustic phenomenon occurs. When the surface sand collapses - often triggered by the wind or a footfall - the friction between grains creates a low-frequency hum or "song" that can be felt as a physical vibration through the feet. **Fauna:** The waters are a sanctuary for the **Dugong** (*Dugong dugon*), while the shores play host to the migratory **Greater Flamingo** (*Phoenicopterus roseus*) and the **Osprey** (*Pandion haliaetus*).

**Navigation and the Frontier** The journey to Khor Al Udaid is an exercise in both skill and adventurous driving. The sand is notoriously soft and powdery, requiring a 4x4 vehicle and tyre deflation to increase the "footprint" on the surface. It is a recreational theatre where dozens of vehicles often gather for "dune bashing," yet the landscape remains formidable; careless driving frequently leaves vehicles "bogged down" in the soft base. The southern shore of the khor marks the border with Saudi Arabia, a boundary formally agreed upon in November 2021. While the line is not physically demarcated in the water, visitors should exercise caution. To avoid potential arrest or being classified as an illegal immigrant in Saudi Arabia, it is advised not to step onto the southern shore. If swimming, remain close to the northern (Qatari) coastline and always carry identification (suitably protected).

*Khor Al Udaid - Sun, Sea and Sand and the adventure to enjoy it*

**Typical Hours:** Best visited at sunrise or mid-afternoon to avoid the peak heat. **Entry Charge:** No gate fee, but guided tours (highly recommended for the inexperienced) vary in cost. **Rough GPS:** 24.615, 51.365 **Access:** No public transport. Access is via a 4x4 vehicle, ideally 2 vehicles, both with very experienced drivers. **Gulf Adventures Camp Beach Camp** - On the edge of relatively shallow seas and powdery white sand dunes, this camp near Khor Al Udaid is run by Gulf Adventures. It offers a getaway from Doha - ideal if you don't like self-catering camping. The set-up allows dozens of people to enjoy the combination of sun, sea and sand, with camels on call. The only missing ingredient in the Instagram-perfect setting is a few coconut palms. There are several alternative beach camps run by other companies around Khor Al Udaid. **Operating Hours:** Primarily evening and overnight stays (check specific tour departure times). **Rough GPS:** 24.805, 51.491 **Location:** East Coast, south of Mesaieed - Khawr Al Udaid area. **Public Transport:** None; access is typically via a pre-arranged 4x4 tour or private off-road vehicles. **Contacts:** +974 4436 1461

(Office) or +974 4422 1888 (Bookings) - info@gulfadventures.com - www.gulf-adventures.com

### Jebel Nakhsh (Khashm Al Nakhsh)

Rising like a jagged tooth from the flat, stony plains of southern Qatar, Jebel Nakhsh (also known as Khashm Al Nakhsh) is a prominent landmark in an otherwise horizontal landscape. This 33km-long ridge, composed of the Early Miocene Dam Formation, reaches an elevation of approximately 90m - 100m. It is a geological graveyard of the time when this arid plateau was a thriving, shallow marine paradise. **The Dugong Cemetery:** The area is a world-class palaeontological treasure house. While it has long been known for fossilised oysters (*Ostrea latimarginata*) and benthic foraminifera (*Borelis melo melo*), significant 2025 research has highlighted the nearby Al Maszhabiya bonebed. This site contains the densest collection of fossil sea cows ever discovered, including a new species: *Salwasiren qatarensis*. These 21-million-year-old "sea cows" still possessed hind limbs, a feature lost by their modern descendants. **The Selenite Slabs:** The middle layer of the ridge is exceptionally rich in **Gypsum** (*Calcium sulphate dihydrate*). Visitors can find massive, translucent selenite crystals, some over a metre long, glinting in the sun like discarded shards of glass. **Stromatolites:** This is one of the few locations in the region where one can observe **Stromatolites** (*layered sedimentary formations created by cyanobacteria*), providing a rare window into the microbial life of the Miocene epoch. Practical Information - **Rough GPS:** 24.875, 50.907 **Street:** West of the Salwa Road (near the Abu Samra border post) - Salwa. **Public Transport:** No public transportThe site is situated approximately 1km from the main road. The terrain is soft and stony; a 4x4 vehicle is essential to avoid becoming "marooned" in the loose surface sands.

### Al Mashabiya and Al Eraiq Reserves

The Al Mashabiya and Al Eraiq Reserves are vital for Qatar's commitment to rewilding its arid interior. Located in the southwestern corner of the peninsula, near the Saudi Arabian border, these protected areas serve as a sanctuary for the nation's most iconic and endangered species. Al Mashabiya Reserve Established in 1997 and covering 54 sq km, Al Mashabiya is primarily an animal-breeding and reintroduction facility. It was conceived as a "safe zone" for the Arabian Oryx (*Oryx leucoryx*), known locally as *Al Wadhihi* due to its stark white coat. By 2026, the reserve continues to play a pivotal role in the national strategy to repopulate the desert with native ungulates. Beyond the Oryx, the reserve is a breeding ground for the **Sand Gazelle** (*Gazella marica*), also known as the *Al Reem* gazelle. These animals are perfectly adapted to the shifting sand sheets and gravel plains of the south.

**Al Eraiq Reserve** Established by decree in 2006, Al Eraiq was specifically designated to protect the region's fragile vegetation from the pressures of overgrazing. It acts as a botanical buffer for the breeding programmes in Al Mashabiya. **Vegetation and Shade:** The reserve is dominated by the **Samr** (*Acacia tortilis*) and the **Salam** (*Acacia ehrenbergiana*). These trees are the skeletal giants of the Qatari desert, providing vital nesting sites for birds and shade for the **Arabian Hare** (*Lepus arabicus*). Look closely at the mounds of earth near the *Acacia* roots for the **Spiny-tailed Lizard** (*Uromastyx aegyptia*), known locally as the *Dhub*. These prehistoric-looking reptiles are often seen basking in the sun before retreating into their deep, subterranean burrows.**Restricted Access:** Unlike Doha's public parks, these reserves are functioning conservation sites. They are **not officially open to the general public** for casual tourism, a measure taken to minimise human disturbance to the breeding animals. **Rough GPS:** 24.837, 50.876

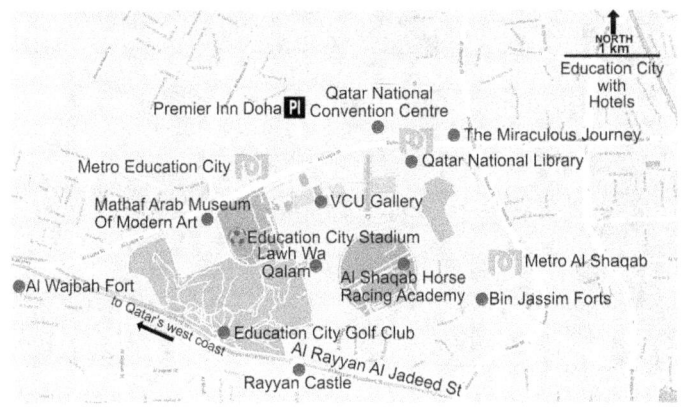

## EDUCATION CITY AND RAYYAN

British Council Qatar The British Council Qatar is a premier educational and cultural institution that serves as a semi-government conduit for British cultural diplomacy and services. Established in 1972, it connects the local community with the United Kingdom's expertise in English language learning, creative industries, and international examinations. Beyond its role in English language teaching, it acts as the official hub for IELTS and various UK professional qualifications. The centre is an active participant in Qatar's cultural calendar, often facilitating partnerships in the arts and science sectors. It sits just 660m from the Joaan Metro Station (Gold Line), a short 10-minute walk that bypasses the dense Al Sadd traffic. **Digital Integration:** The council has recently expanded its digital footprint in Qatar, offering "IELTS Online" and extensive virtual library resources, allowing students to engage with British literature from anywhere in the country. Practical Information - **Operating Hours:** * Sunday - Wednesday: 08:00 - 20:00 Thursday and Saturday: 09:00 - 17:00 Monday: Closed from 13:30 - 14:30 Friday: Closed **Rough GPS:** 25.280, 51.490 **Street:** 99 Al Sadd Street (Zone 38, Street 343, Building 99) - Al Sadd. **Public Transport:** Gold Line Metro to Joaan Station. **Contacts:** +974 800 5501 (Toll-free) or +974 4419 6494 - general.enquiries@qa.britishcouncil.org - www.britishcouncil.qa

*Education City from Qatar Foundation*

### The Miraculous Journey

Commissioned by Sheikha Al Mayassa bint Hamad bin Khalifa Al Thani (sister of the Amir), "The Miraculous Journey" is an ambitious series of 14 monumental bronze sculptures by the British artist Damien Hirst. Positioned prominently outside the Sidra Medicine hospital in Education City, these works provide a visceral, cutaway narrative of human development (*Homo sapiens*) from conception to birth. The installation, rising from a reflecting pool, reportedly cost USD20 million and collectively weigh 216 tonnes, took three years to cast. Originally revealed in 2013, the statues were almost immediately shrouded in protective covers, officially attributed to the ongoing construction of the hospital, though viewed by many as a "cooling - off" period following a social media outcry regarding the graphic nature of the work. On a still morning, the water provides a perfect mirror, doubling the height of the already massive figures and creating a serene, albeit provocative, corridor. Location GPS 25.320971, 51.444736

**Qatar National Convention Centre (QNCC)**

The Qatar National Convention Centre (QNCC) is a gargantuan structure that serves as a premier venue for regional and international events. Opened in 2011, its most striking feature is the organic, tree-like structure supporting the cantilevered roof. These steel "limbs" represent the Sidra (*Ziziphus spina-christi*), the national tree of Qatar, which historically served as a place of learning and congregation in the desert.

The facility is a titan of architecture, encompassing nine exhibition halls, ten performance spaces, and 52 meeting rooms. It is a world-class venue for everything from high-stakes governmental board meetings to large-scale entertainment concerts. **The Giant Spider:** The foyer is famously home to **'Maman'**, a monumental bronze sculpture of a spider by the French-American artist Louise Bourgeois. Standing over 9m tall, the spider carries a sac containing 32 marble eggs. The artist intended it as an ode to her mother, symbolising strength, protection, and the industrious nature of a weaver. While the building hosts massive trade fairs, it also provides an intimate setting for the **Qatar Philharmonic Orchestra**. Concerts are frequently held in the smaller, acoustically superior halls; detailed schedules and ticketing can be found via qatarphilharmonicorchestra.org. Practical Information - **Rough GPS:** 25.321, 51.437 **Street:** Al Luqta Street / Dukhan Highway - Education City. **Public Transport:** Exceptionally well-connected via the **Metro Green Line** (Qatar National Library Station) and the **Education City Tram Green Line**. **Parking:** The centre provides a multi-storey car park for 2,800 vehicles, connected to the main building by an air-conditioned walkway. **Contacts:** +974 4470 7000 - sales@qncc.qa - www.qncc.qa

*Qatar National Library*

### QATAR NATIONAL LIBRARY (QNL)

The Qatar National Library is a monumental, ultramodern commitment to Qatar's "knowledge economy." Designed by the renowned Dutch architect Rem Koolhaas (OMA), the 42,000sqm building serves a triple function: it is a central public library, a university research facility, and the state's historical repository. Departing from the traditional, dimly lit aesthetic of historic archives, the QNL is conceived as a single, vast room. Its "folded" concrete corners create a diamond-shaped profile, while the interior is flooded with natural light diffused through a wavy, corrugated glass facade. The Excavated Archive: At the heart of the library lies the Heritage Library, which is sunk 6m into the ground. Clad in beige travertine to resemble an archaeological dig, it houses rare manuscripts and maps related to Arab-Islamic civilisation. The first book placed here was a 15th-century Quran manuscript by Her Highness Sheikha Moza bint Nasser. Under the marble floors is a sophisticated book delivery system utilising Radio Frequency Identification (RFID) technology. When a borrower returns a book at the ground-level receptacle, it is whisked away via a conveyor belt to the sorting area in the basement, reaching its destination in less

WHERE TO GO 113

than two minutes. Practical Information - Operating Hours: * Saturday – Thursday: 08.00 – 20.00 Friday: 16.00 – 20.00 - Rough GPS: 25.318 , 51.441 Location: Education City, Al Luqta Street, Al Rayyan. Public Transport: * Tram: The Education City Tram (Yellow Line) serves the library directly. Metro Station: Qatar National Library Station (Green Line). Website: https://www.qnl.qa/

*Lawh Wa Qalam*

### Lawh Wa Qalam (The Tablet and the Pen)

Opened in November 2025, Lawh Wa Qalam is the world's first institution dedicated exclusively to the life and legacy of Maqbool Fida Husain (1915 - 2011), the "Picasso of India." He spent his final, prolific years as a Qatari citizen, and this museum serves as the definitive repository of that final chapter. The name *Lawh Wa Qalam* (The Tablet and the Pen) refers to the tools of traditional Islamic scholarship and the artist's own transition toward monumental calligraphy in his final decade. Practical Information - **Operating Hours:** * Saturday - Sunday, Tuesday - Thursday: 10:00

- 17:00 Friday: 13:30 - 19:30 Closed: Mondays and National Holidays **Entry Charge:** Free for all visitors. **Rough GPS:** 25.309, 51.431 **Location:** Opposite the Qatar National Convention Centre (QNCC) - Education City. **Public Transport:** Accessible via the **Education City Tram Green Line** (Station: Lawh Wa Qalam) or a short walk from the **Qatar National Library Metro Station** (Green Line). **Website:** www.lawhwaqalam.org.qa

**The Media Majlis at Northwestern University in Qatar**

The Media Majlis is the first museum of its kind in the Arab world, serving to illustrate the region's complex and evolving relationship with journalism, communication, and digital narratives. Housed within the Northwestern University in Qatar (NU - Q) building - an architectural marvel designed by Antoine Predock - the museum moves beyond static displays. It uses a striking, multi-screen 'media skin' facade and highly interactive internal technology to explore how stories are constructed, contested, and consumed across the Global South. Practical Information - **Operating Hours:** Sunday - Thursday: 10:00 - 20:00. Closed Friday and Saturday. **Entry Charge:** Free. **Rough GPS:** 25.316, 51.446 **Location:** Northwestern University in Qatar, Al Shabab Street - Education City. **Public Transport:** Accessible via the **Education City Tram Yellow Line** (Station: NU - Q). It is also a 10-minute walk from the **Al Shaqab Metro Station** (Gold Line). **Contacts:** +974 4454 5000 - mediamajlis@northwestern.edu - mediamajlis.northwestern.edu

**VCUarts Qatar Gallery**

The Gallery at VCUarts Qatar was established in 1998 in the inaugural branch campus of Education City, the Virginia Commonwealth University School of the Arts. The gallery is housed within a building designed by the renowned Mexican architect Ricardo Legorreta, characterised by its minimalist geometric forms and its use of "Legorreta Purple" and ochre to play with the sharp desert light. Many works first exhibited here are later acquired by the Mathaf: Arab Museum of Modern Art, marking the gallery as a critical starting point for the region's modern masters. Practical Information - **Operating Hours:** Sunday - Thursday: 10:00 - 17:00. Closed Friday and Saturday. **Entry Charge:** Free. **Rough GPS:** 25.314, 51.434 **Street:** South of Al Luqta Street - Education City. **Public Transport:** Highly accessible via the **Education City Tram Green Line** (Station: VCUarts Qatar). Alternatively, it is a 10-minute walk from the Qatar National Library Metro Station (Green

Line). Use the **Sila** app for real-time tram synchronisation. **Contacts:** +974 4402 0555 - gallery.qatar.vcu.edu - gallery@qatar.vcu.edu

### Education City Stadium

Inaugurated in 2020, the Education City Stadium is located within the nation's "academic quarter." The stadium's most striking feature is its facade - a tessellated pattern of triangles that form complex, diamond-like geometrical shapes. These panels appear to change colour as the sun moves across the sky, a phenomenon that has earned the venue the nickname "The Diamond in the Desert."

While it held 40,000 spectators during the 2022 World Cup, in its 2026 legacy mode, capacity will be reduced to 20,000. Practical Information - **Typical Hours:** Accessible during match days and scheduled events; the surrounding precinct is open daily for public exercise. **Entry Charge:** Subject to event ticketing. **Rough GPS:** 25.311, 51.426 **Street:** Al Rayyan Al Jadeed Street - Education City. **Public Transport:** * **Metro:** Green Line to **Education City Station**. It is a 600m walk from the station to the stadium entrance. Yellow and Blue Lines are adjacent to the stadium. **Tram:** Use the **Education City Tram Green Line** for a direct drop-off at the stadium. **Sila App:** Use the Sila app for real-time synchronisation between the Metro and Tram schedules. **Contacts:** +974 5082 6700

### Al Shaqab

Al Shaqab is much more than a world-class equestrian centre. Founded in 1992 on the historic site where the Battle of Al Shaqab took place in 1893 - a pivotal victory in the nation's struggle for independence - the facility is dedicated to the preservation and promotion of the Arabian Horse. The academy is a titan of the equestrian world, focusing on three pillars: excellence in breeding, veterinary medicine, and athletic competition. While it is famed for dressage and show jumping, the stabling facilities are perhaps the most sophisticated on the planet, providing a temperature-controlled environment for some of the world's most expensive Thoroughbreds and Arabian stallions.

Practical Information Al Shaqab **Typical Hours:** Events as per schedule. Regular working hours: 07:30 - 15:30 (Sunday - Thursday). **Tours:** Must be booked in advance; check for the "Behind the Scenes" experience. **Rough GPS:** 25.306, 51.440 **Street:** Al Shaqab Street - Al Shaqab area. **Public Transport:** Accessible via the **Metro Green Line** (Al Shaqab Station) or the

**Education City Tram Yellow Line**. Bus 526 also serves the area. **Contacts:** +974 4454 1992 - alshaqabtours@qf.org.qa - www.alshaqab.com

*Horse Dressage*

Qatar Endurance Village **Events:** Primarily Saturdays, starting in the cool of the early morning (often 04:00 or 05:00). **Rough GPS:** 24.967, 51.506 **Location:** Mesaieed, south of Doha. **Access:** No public transport; 4x4 vehicle required for off-road viewing.
**Education City Golf Club**

Designed by the two-time Masters champion José María Olazábal, the Education City Golf Club is one of Qatar's "oasis in the desert" philosophy transformed into a golf course. Opened in 2019, the facility is a global sustainability pioneer and holds GEO Certification. It has a 100% non-potable water system, primarily Treated Sewage Effluent (TSE), to maintain its lush fairways amidst the arid landscape. The club features 33 holes across three distinct layouts. The final hole offers a dramatic view of the Education City Stadium (the 'Diamond in the Desert'), providing a striking visual link between two of Qatar's premier sporting landmarks. **Public Access:** The club offers various membership tiers (Full, Midweek, and Junior), and it is fully open to the public. Green fees for visitors typically range from QAR410 in the summer to QAR890 during the peak winter season.

Practical Information - **Operating Hours:** 06:00 - 20:00 (Last tee time typically 19:30 for floodlit courses). **Entry Charge:** Visitors are welcome; green fees apply. Membership is optional for regular players. **Rough GPS:** 25.303, 51.422 **Street:** Al Rayyan Al Jadeed Street (Gate 2) - Education City. **Public Transport:** Accessible via the **Education City Tram** or **Bus 616** from the **Al Shaqab Metro Station** (Gold Line). The service is fully integrated into the **Sila** app for real-time journey planning. **Contacts:** +974 7773 7973 - info@ecgolf.com - www.ecgolf.com

### Mathaf: Arab Museum of Modern Art

Mathaf - which simply translates from Arabic as 'museum' - serves as a vital cultural ledger of the Arab world's modern and contemporary evolution. Occupying a repurposed 1970s girls' school building in Education City, the institution was inaugurated in 2010 to house one of the world's most comprehensive collections of Arab art. The collection was founded by Sheikh Hassan bin Mohamed bin Ali Al Thani, a pioneering collector and artist in his own right, whose monumental sculpture *Motherland* is a centrepiece at the National Museum of Qatar. Mathaf is currently entering a transformative phase, with an expansion scheduled across 2026 and 2027 to accommodate its growing role as a global research hub. Practical Information - **Operating Hours:** * Saturday - Wednesday: 09:00 - 19:00 Thursday: 09:00 - 21:00 Friday: 13:30 - 19:00 *Closed on Mondays.* **Entry Charge:** * Free for Qatar residents (with QID) and students (with ID). QAR50 for non-residents. *Tickets must be booked online in advance via qm.org.qa.* **Rough**

**GPS:** 25.310, 51.419 **Street:** Al Luqta Street, via Gate 1 Entrance (accessible also from Al Rayyan Al Jadeed Street) - Education City. **Public Transport:** * **Tram:** Use the **Sila** app to coordinate the Education City Tram (Green and Blue Lines), which stops within a 600m walk of the museum. **Metro:** The Blue Line is adjacent - From the Green Line Metro stations, it is approximately a 1.5km (15-minute) walk. **Contacts:** +974 4452 5555 / +974 4402 8855 - mathaf_info@qma.org.qa - mathaf.org.qa

### Education City Tram

The Education City Tram is a state-of-the-art, battery-powered transit system showing Qatar's investment in sustainable urban mobility. This catenary-free network is fully integrated into Sila, the national public transport brand that unifies Qatar's metro, bus, and taxi services into a single coordinated system. While the tram remains Free of Charge (FOC), it is a key component of the Sila multimodal network, enabling seamless journey planning via the Sila app. The Network: Yellow, Blue, and Green Lines. The tram network is designed to link the diverse academic and cultural landmarks of Education City with the broader Doha Metro system. **The Yellow Tram Line** originates at the **Al Shaqab Metro Station (Gold Line)**. It travels north, passing 300m south of the Qatar National Library Metro station (Green Line), and stops directly outside the **Qatar National Library (QNL)**. **The Blue & Green Tram Lines:** In the western sector, the Yellow Line connects with the Blue and Green Lines. The **Green Line** is notable for crossing north of the Dukhan Highway via a dedicated underpass to reach residential quarters and Oxygen Park. **The Link:** While the lines are integrated, transitioning between the Blue and Green lines may require a brief walk across a landscaped car park. The system utilises Siemens Avenio technology, charging its super-capacitors at each station. The tracks are frequently flanked by the **Sidra** (*Ziziphus spina-christi*), the resilient tree that serves as the emblem for the Qatar Foundation Practical Information - **Operating Hours:** 06:00 - 22:00 (Saturday - Thursday); 14:00 - 22:00 (Friday). **Entry Charge:** Free of Charge (FOC). **Rough GPS:** 25.311, 51.442 (Al Shaqab Tram Hub). **Public Transport:** Directly accessible via the Al Shaqab Metro Station (Gold Line). Use the Sila app for real-time arrival data.

### Bin Jassim Forts

To the east of Al Shaqab, two fenced enclosures stand as architectural siblings in the Al Rayyan landscape. These structures, known collectively as the Bin Jassim Forts, date from the early 20th century and are named for a son of the founder of modern Qatar, Sheikh Jassim Bin Mohammed Al Thani. Although the heavy wooden gates remain closed to visitors, the forts serve as a reminder of the regional transition from tribal fortifications to a settled state. The limestone battlements are a frequent haunt for the Common Myna, an opportunistic bird that thrives in the shaded corners of the outer walls.

Practical Information - **Status:** Currently not open to the public. **Rough GPS:** 25.305, 51.449 **Street:** Al Athar Street - Al Rayyan. **Public Transport:** Accessible via Bus 526 from the Al Shaqab Metro Station (Green Line). I recommend using the **Sila** app to coordinate the bus connection with the metro schedule.

**Rayyan Castle (Sheikh Ali Bin Abdullah Fort)**

A five-minute drive southwest of the Bin Jassim Forts is Rayyan Castle also known as the Sheikh Ali Bin Abdullah Fort. This was the fortified residence of the Amir who ruled from 1949 to 1960. The enclosure is defined by a massive wall, 180m in length on each side, which secures several internal buildings, including a central mosque. A secondary fortified structure sits to the north of the main complex. A notable architectural highlight is the roofline above the entrance door; it features intricate detailing in the colour and form of the serrations found on the Qatari flag. Practical Information - **Status:** Currently not open to the public. **Rough GPS:** 25.301, 51.431 **Street:** Al Rayyan Al Jadeed Street - Al Rayyan. **Public Transport:** Bus 526 from the Al Shaqab Metro Station (Green Line).

**Al Wajbah Fort**

About 15km west of Doha. Constructed in the late 19th century, It is one of the oldest forts in the country. The structure follows a traditional courtyard design, with various rooms opening onto a central limestone expanse, defended by four watchtowers - three rectangular and one cylindrical. While the fort has had a recent restoration, it is currently closed to the public.

This site is the location of the historic **Battle of Al Wajbah** in March 1893. Under the command of Sheikh Jassim Bin Mohammed Al Thani, Qatari forces achieved a decisive victory over a numerically superior Ottoman army. This event is a cornerstone of national history, as it effectively secured Qatar's autonomy from Ottoman rule. The fort was strategically positioned near a vital *rawda* (a fertile depression) and ancient wells, which allowed it to sustain a garrison during the sweltering summer months. ***The fort is situated directly east of Al Wajbah Palace, a high-security official residence.*** Visitors must be extremely cautious; photography of any adjacent government buildings or palace gates is strictly prohibited and heavily monitored. Adhere to all "No Photography" signage to avoid legal complications. Practical Information - **Typical Hours:** Currently not open to the public; exterior viewing only. **Entry Charge:** not open **Rough GPS:** 25.302, 51.393 **Street:** South of Dukhan Road - Al Wajbah. **Public Transport:** Accessible via Bus 512 from the Education City Metro Station (Green Line). Note that the bus stop is approximately 2km from the fort. **Contacts:** +974 4402 8888 (Qatar Museums General Enquiries).

*Horse Stables Doha*

### The Qatar Racing and Equestrian Club

Located in Al Rayyan this serves as a centre of Qatar's horse racing culture. Officially established in 1975, the club manages a world-class facility that includes a 1,800m turf track and a 1,400m sand track. It is a major venue for both Thoroughbred and Purebred Arabian horse racing, hosting a competitive season that typically runs from late October through May. Races includes **HH The Amir Sword Festival:** Held annually in late February, this three-day festival is the most prestigious event on the Qatari racing calendar. It draws top-tier international horses and riders, culminating in the "Amir Sword" race, a high-value competition that is a significant social and sporting highlight. The main grandstand can accommodate 1,400 visitors and offers excellent views of the tracks, parade ring, and winners' enclosure. General admission to the races is usually low-cost, making the experience accessible to families and tourists. **Stabling and Training:** The complex features extensive, state-of-the-art stables for hundreds of horses, along with a specialised veterinary clinic, a horse swimming pool, and a horseshoeing section. These facilities make it one of the most advanced horse training centres in the Middle East.

Practical Information - **Operating Hours:** Races are generally held on Wednesday and Thursday evenings during the season (October-May); training occurs daily in the early morning. **Dress Code:** While smart casual dress is acceptable for regular race days, formal attire is required for major festivals. For the Amir Sword Festival, visitors should follow modest guidelines (shoulders covered and skirts or dresses falling at or below the knee). **Rough GPS:** 25.278, 51.428 **Location:** Furousiya Street, Muaither. It is located approximately 10km south of the Al Shaqab equestrian area. **Public Transport:** Accessible via Bus 701 from the Al Shaqab Metro Station (Green Line). You can use the **Sila** app to coordinate the arrival of the bus with your metro journey. **Contacts:** +974 4419 7722 | info@qrec.gov.qa | qrec.gov.qa

ASPIRE

**Aspire Park**

Aspire Park is a sprawling 88-hectare emerald in the heart of Doha's Baaya district. Established in 2003 to complement the massive sports infrastructure of the 2006 Asian Games, it has matured into the city's premier green sanctuary. While Doha's city parks feel manicured and artificial, Aspire Park offers a sense of rolling topography. It has the only lake in Qatar, a 3.37-hectare man-made body of water that serves as a vital refuge for resident and migratory waterfowl.

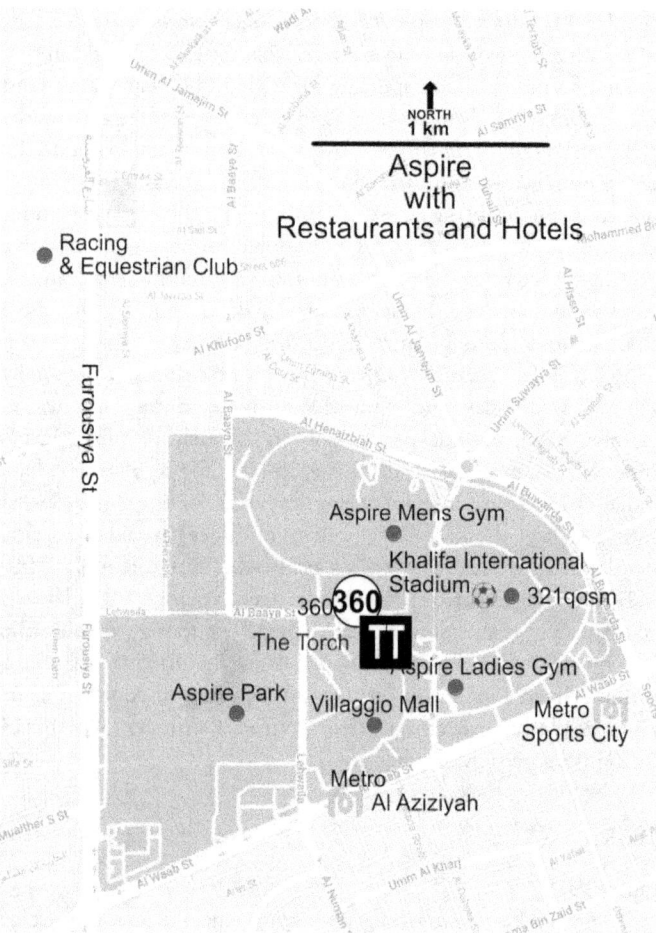

Practicalities **Jogging Tracks**: The park is a magnet for the fitness-conscious. There is a **1.6km rubberised track** for easy impact, while a longer **3km outer loop** provides a more scenic route for serious runners. **Entry Policy**: The park is officially designated for **"families only"**. This shows broader Qatari effort to maintain a safe, quiet environment for domestic groups. Single males may find entry restricted by security guards, though those in dedicated sports attire are usually permitted for exercise. **Facilities**: Free Wi-Fi is available throughout, a modern convenience in an ancient-feeling landscape. Small lakeside cafés provide refreshments, but for a more substantial meal, the park is flanked by the **Villaggio** and **Hyatt Plaza** malls. Typical Hours 08:00 - 22:00 (Park gates are open 24/7) **GPS** 25.260, 51.436 **Location** Baaya / Aspire Zone **Entry Cost** Free **Website / Phone** aspiresports.qa / 4413 8188 **Public Transport** Gold Line Metro (Al Aziziyah) / Green Line Metro (Al Shaqab); Bus 701; **Aspire Academy**

Situated at the northern perimeter of the Aspire Zone, the Aspire Academy is a $2.8 billion statement of developing the Gulf's elite athletic talent. It is widely regarded as one of the most advanced sports hothouses on the planet. The Academy's centrepiece is the Aspire Dome (the world's largest indoor sports dome), designed by the renowned French architect Roger Taillibert (the visionary behind the Parc des Princes in Paris and the Montreal Olympic Stadium). The dome houses an Olympic-sized swimming pool and a diving tank, which serve as the primary venue for international competitions, including the World Aquatics Championships. The Academy has 7 outdoor football pitches and one full-sized indoor pitch. Champions trained here include Mutaz Essa Barshim: Akram Afif: Abdulla Al Tamimi. Essential Information - **Typical Hours** 07:30 - 20:30 (Saturday - Thursday) **GPS** 25.267, 51.442 **Location** Al Hunaizibiya Street, Northern Aspire Zone **Website** aspire.qa **Access** Primarily an elite training facility, public access is usually limited to pre-booked tours or during international sporting events hosted at the Dome.

**The Khalifa International Stadium**

The veteran of the Peninsula's sporting landscape Khalifa International Stadium was originally inaugurated in 1976 to host the 4th Arabian Gulf Cup. The new canopy uses 4,000 tonnes of steel and is covered in PTFE (Polytetrafluoroethylene) panels, designed to work in tandem with the stadium's revolutionary cooling system which was the first stadium globally to deploy large-scale outdoor cooling. Chilled water is piped from a dedicated energy centre located 1km away, trying to maintain a pitch-side temperature of 26°C regardless of the external desert heat. Essential Information - **Typical Hours** as per match **GPS** 25.264, 51.447 **Location** Al Waab Street - Baaya / Aspire Zone **Public Transport** Metro Gold Line (Sports City Station) **Nearby Hotel** The Torch Doha (300m high, built for the 2006 Asian Games)

**3-2-1 Qatar Olympic and Sports Museum (QOSM)**

A global heavyweight in the museum circuit, QOSM is a

masterclass in interactive storytelling. Designed by the Spanish architect Joan Sibina, the museum explores the origins of sport, tracing the transition from survival skills to organised competition. It manages to contextualise Western "Olympic" history alongside the traditional sports of the East and the Arab World. A Global History of Sport (Gallery 2) **The 1888 FA Cup Final Ball**: This historic leather artefact, sourced from cattle (*Bos taurus*), is found in this gallery rather than the Hall of Athletes, as it represents the birth of the professional game. **The 1857 Sheffield FC Rulebook**: As the world's oldest football club, these original rulebooks are housed here to illustrate the codification of the modern sport. **The Activation Zone**: A massive interactive space where visitors can test their own physical literacy. It uses advanced sports science technology to provide a profile of your own athletic potential.

The Hall of Athletes (Gallery 4) the heart of the modern collection, profiling 90 trailblazers. **Michael Schumacher (German)**: This gallery holds the most space-consuming and visually arresting exhibit: the **Ferrari F1-2000** car. Besides it, you will find his signed **2006 racing suit**. **Mohammed Ali (American)**: His signed left boxing glove from the **1960 Rome Olympics** is a central highlight here. **Steffi Graf (German)**: Her racquet from the **1999 French Open** - the year she famously defeated Monica Seles - is featured in her dedicated display. **Michael Jordan (American)**: A signed **Chicago Bulls** No. 23 jersey represents the "Dream Team" era. **Chris Boardman (British)**: His **1992 Olympic Gold** bicycle, a marvel of carbon fibre engineering, is showcased as a pinnacle of British cycling history. **Babe Ruth (American)**: A signed bat, crafted from Northern White Ash, is from the "Golden Age" of baseball.

Essential Information - **Typical Hours** Sat - Thu: 09:00 - 19:00; Fri: 13:30 - 19:00 (Note: Closed Tuesdays) **GPS** 25.263, 51.448 **Location** Khalifa International Stadium, Aspire Zone **Entry Cost** QAR50 (Non-residents); Free for residents and children under 16 **Tickets** Must be booked in advance at qm.org.qa/tickets**Website** 321qosm.org.qa As with all Qatar Museums (QM) sites, a standard of "modest dress" is expected. This typically means covering shoulders and knees. It is a quiet mark of respect in a nation that values its traditional sensibilities. Limited p**hotography**: Permitted for personal use, though flash and equipment like tripods or "selfie sticks" are strictly prohibited to ensure a smooth flow of visitors.

**Planning**: Allow at least two to three hours to fully appreciate the galleries. If visiting on a Friday, note the later opening time of 13:30 to accommodate the Jumu'ah prayer.

### Aspire Active Ladies Gym

Within the Aspire Zone the Aspire Active Ladies Gym is dedicated exclusively to women. It serves as a social and health hub, bridging the gap between elite sports infrastructure and community well-being. The facility is housed in a purpose-built complex that maintains the high architectural and functional standards seen throughout the surrounding Sports City. **Facilities and Programmes Aquatics**: The centre features a premier indoor swimming pool used for both "Open Swim" sessions and structured aquatic fitness. Programmes include **Aqua Aerobics** and **Aqua HIIT**, designed for low-impact, high-resistance training particularly suited to the local climate and **Fitness Suites**. Essential Information - **Typical Hours** 07:00 - 20:00 (Saturday - Thursday); Closed Fridays **GPS** 25.261, 51.447 **Location** Junction of Al Waab Street and Aspire Park Road **Contact** +974 4413 6430 **Website** aspireactiveqa.com **Public Transport** Gold Line Metro (Sports City or Al Aziziyah) **Entry and Membership Cost**: Membership typically starts at 3 months QAR3,080 though to 1 year QAR5,940 **Visitor Access**: While primarily a membership-based club, short-term visitors can often enquire about "Class Passes" if they wish to maintain their routine while in Doha.

### Villaggio Mall

Located in the Baaya district, southeast, in the Aspire Zone, Villaggio Mall mimics Venice with indoor canals and a ceiling painted like a Mediterranean sky. An indoor version of The Pearl district of Doha. The Venetian Experience is achieved through its indoor canal, which runs through the centre of the retail space; a short gondola ride is QAR15. **Gondolania** is the mall's extensive indoor leisure wing, designed as a sanctuary for families during the height of the summer heat. **The Ice Rink**: An Olympic-sized ice rink is a central feature, with sessions starting from QAR35 **High-Octane Leisure**: The area includes an indoor **roller coaster**, 10-pin bowling, and a **Go-Kart** track, with Go-Karting starting at QAR70 per person. **Laser Games**: Tactical laser tag sessions, available from QAR40.00.

*Villaggio Mall*

The mall hosts a broad spectrum of outlets, from well-established brands like **Carrefour** and **Virgin MegaStore** to upscale boutiques and a multi-screen cinema, highlighted by an IMAX theatre – though as audiences often treat the screening room like a living room an additional soundscape is often present. **Cost**: Cinema tickets for the cinema typically start at QAR75 per person, which is slightly lower than European cinema prices. **Typical Mall**

**Hours** 09:00 - 22:00 (Daily); Fri: Closed 11:00 - 12:30 for prayer **GPS**
25.259, 51.445 **Location** Junction of Al Waab St and Aspire Park Rd - Baaya / Aspire **Public Transport** Gold Line Metro (Al Aziziyah Station) **Mall Contact** +974 4422 7400 / villaggioqatar.com **Gondolania** Contact +974 4403 9800 / gondolania.com **Cinema** Contact info@cinemaqatar.com

### Ali Bin Hamad Al Attiyah Arena

is a multi-purpose indoor venue for international indoor sports. Located in the Fereej Al Soudan district, north-east of the main Aspire Zone, the arena was completed in a record 18 months to serve as a primary venue for the 24th World Men's Handball Championship in 2015. While it is the spiritual home of Qatari Handball, the arena's versatility is its primary strength. It is the home ground for Al Sadd SC, the nation's most decorated multi-sport club. The interior can be rapidly reconfigured to host: **Badminton and Basketball**: Utilising a high-grade sprung timber floor. **Spaces** designed for international boxing and wrestling events feature a retractable seating system that accommodates up to 5,500 spectators and fosters an engaging, intimate sports arena. Essential Information - **Typical Hours** Subject to event schedules **GPS** 25.270, 51.490 Al Nadi Street - Fereej Al Soudan **Entry Cost** Varies by event QAR20 - QAR200 typically **Contact** +974 4032 5529 **Website** abha-arena.com **Public Transport** Gold Line Metro (Al Sudan Station)

### Al Sadd Sports Club

Al Sadd Sports Club is the most decorated and dominant force in Qatari athletics. Founded in 1969 by four students who refused to join existing teams, preferring to forge their own path, the club has grown from a local neighbourhood side into an international powerhouse. It is the only Qatari club to have won the AFC Champions League twice (1989 and 2011). Jassim Bin Hamad Stadium is the club's home ground, a boutique stadium that while smaller than the World Cup "behemoths," it offers one of the most intimate and high-pressure experiences in the Gulf. The complex is a true multi-sport hub, featuring a world-class indoor swimming centre located immediately adjacent to the main stadium. Essential Information- **Typical Hours** 08:00 - 22:00 (Daily) **GPS** 25.266, 51.483 **Location** Off Al Nadi Street - Fereej Al Soudan **Public Transport** Gold Line Metro (Al Sudan Station) **Contact** +974 4444 8080 Website al-saddclub.com

### Central Market area

Leaving behind the world of recreation and elite sport, Doha's Central Market is a testament to the city's relentless outward crawl. The original markets stretch south for 2km along Wholesale Market Rd, beginning at the junction with Salwa Rd. At the northern anchor sits the "Omani" Souq, a pocket of trade named for the Omani merchants who arrived in the 1950s to establish a foothold in the Qatari capital. Moving south, the market's sensory profile shifts rapidly. The air thickens with the earthy sweetness of the Dates and the briny tang of the fish stalls. The row continues with a sequence of establishments dedicated to flora and fauna: **Livestock:** Sheep, goats, and the Dromedary Camel. **Avian:** A dedicated market for birds. **Plants**: The Doha Municipal plant nursery and a separate slaughterhouse. Location - **Rough GPS:** 25.248, 51.476 **Street:** Junction of Wholesale Market St and Salwa Rd - Abu Hamour (Bu Hamour) **Public Transport:** Bus 604 from Msheireb Bus Station **Typical Hours:** 07:00 - 21:00 daily

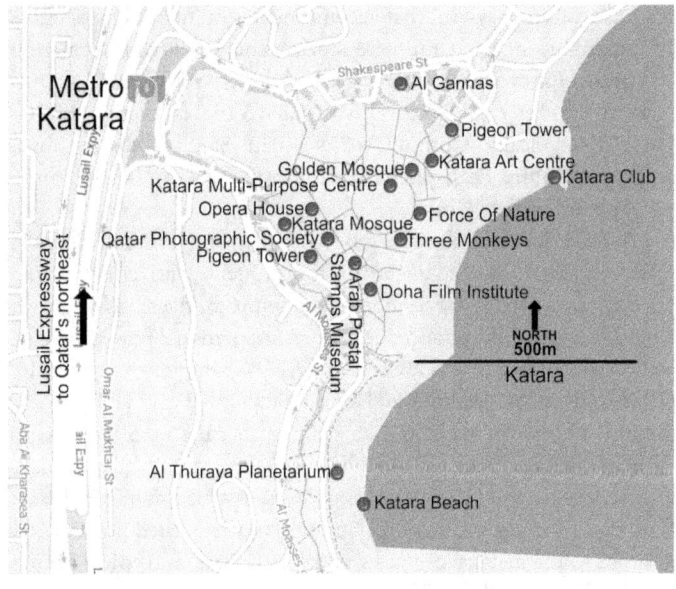

*21 High St Katara*

## KATARA

### KATARA CULTURAL VILLAGE

Katara is a sprawling cultural hub 10km north of the Doha Corniche. While it mimics the thin, winding alleyways of a traditional Arab town to provide shade, it is intersected by a grand, Haussmann-style boulevard that feels more like a polished Parisian quartier than an Arabian Gulf outpost. An overview is in the website https://katara.net/en/

## 21 High St

The Entry & **21 High St** From the Katara Metro station, a grand boulevard leads east. This is 21 High St. Located within the Katara Cultural Village in Doha, 21 High Street serves as a focal point for luxury retail and refined gastronomy. Often referred to as "The Village's Jewel," it represents a bold architectural attempt to reclaim the outdoors from the intense Peninsula heat. The outdoor cooling technology is the street's most significant feature. While the ambient desert temperature may soar, the street maintains a micro-climate through a series of "outdoor air conditioning" vents. Chilled air is distributed through a network of ornate bronze grilles embedded in the pavement and walls. This system reduces the temperature by approximately 10°C to 15°C compared to the surrounding areas, making al fresco dining viable for much of the year.

*OliOli Katara*

The street is paved with Pietra Serena sandstone - a grey-blue volcanic rock traditionally used in the palaces of Florence. The anchor of the street is Galeries Lafayette, a 14,500 square metre department store. Its glass dome and intricate interiors mirror the Parisian original, offering three floors of high fashion, jewellery, and cosmetics. The promenade features specialised outlets such as **Graff** and **Cartier**, alongside niche perfumeries and high-end accessory brands. 21 High Street is home to several notable eateries, including **Joe's Café** (with a mix of fast food and more interesting dishes) and **959 Real Food** with an international flavour. The cooling system ensures that diners can sit outside even when the Sun is at its zenith, enjoying views of the Katara hills.

### Museum & Heritage
### OliOli

North of the boulevard is OliOli, Doha's Children's Museum. Encased in a striking geometric gift box shell, it offers a tactile playground for those aged 1 to 16. Pre-booking is essential. Prices range from QAR45 to QAR135. **Website** www.olioli.qa

*Street Cafes Katara*

### Al Gannas

Al Gannas (The Hunter), is the headquarters for Qatar's falconry and Saluki hunting traditions. The building is famously shaped like a falcon's hood, known locally as a *burka* or in Britain a rufter. The association holds the annual **Marmi Festival** in January near Mesaieed (approx. GPS 24.894, 51.465) - do not attempt to find this without contacting Al Gannas first. It is a spectacle of speed, focusing on the hunting of the Houbara Bustard and racing pigeons (*Columba livia domestica*). **GPS:** 25.362, 51.527 **Contact:** Main Office Line: +974 4408 1303 This is the "Reception" desk for the society). **WhatsApp**: +974 5544 0554 www.instagram.com/algannas_qa/

### Street Cafes Katara.

Below the Pigeon Towers, near Al Gannas, is a selection of takeaway street cafes (no seating). They are a cheap alternative to some of the superb restaurants in Katara.

### The Pigeon Towers

Overlooking the street cafes near Al Gannas are the towering, perforated cylinders of the Pigeon Towers. While these modern versions are largely ornamental, they are architectural echoes of the ancient towers found across the Fertile Crescent and the Nile Delta. Traditionally, these were "guano factories," designed to harvest nitrogen-rich fertiliser or to provide a steady supply of birds for the kitchen. In Katara, they house pristine white doves, serving as a silent, fluttering frieze against the sky.

**Opera House** - This is a traditional-looking Opera House that wouldn't look out of place in Milan or Paris. The building is the home of the Qatar Philharmonic Orchestra qatarphilharmonicorchestra.org, which held its 0rst performance in October 2008. As with so much in Qatar, the Orchestra's performances are focused on the new. They support rising new Arab performers and composers with performances in Qatar and worldwide. Performances are principally during the winter, including classical western and other culture's concerts.

*Pigeon Towers Katara*

Typical hours - as per performance Entry charge - as per event Rough GPS - 25.360, 51.525 - Contacts - +974 4454 8185

### The Heart of Katara

Moving clockwise toward the sea:

**Katara Club,**

For an easy to get to spa and fitness centre on the northern beach, Katara Club is an option. While the ambience is as smooth as silk, the culinary offerings occasionally stumble. **Hours:** Sun - Thurs 06:00 - 22:00; Fri & Sat 09:00 - 21:00. **GPS:** 25.361, 51.529

**Katara Art Centre (KAC)**

The village's "art incubator" is the Katara Art Centre. It functions as a grassroots hub for workshops and contemporary retail. **GPS:** 25.361, 51.528 | dohakac.com

**Katara Traditional Dhow Museum**

Here at Katara Traditional Dhow Museum there is a compact but authoritative look at the maritime machinery that built Qatar - pearling, fishing, and trade. With a few model boats, and some associated materials, the museum itself relies on being an interpretive gallery. **Hours:** Daily 07:00 - 22:00. Entry is free.

**The Amphitheatre**

A Greco-Roman theatre-in-the-round with a capacity of 5,000 is at the heart of Katara. It was inaugurated in 2011 with a concert by the Greek composer **Vangelis**. The design balances classical European geometry with Islamic motifs. **GPS:** 25.360, 51.526

**Katara Public Art & Specialised Museums**

**The Force of Nature:** A bronze and steel hurricane tribute by **Lorenzo Quinn**, showing Mother Nature hurling the world in a sling. (GPS: 25.359, 51.527). **Gandhi's Three Monkeys:** A satirical military installation by **Subodh Gupta**, fashioned from cooking utensils. (GPS: 25.359, 51.527).

*Force of Nature Katara*

*Qatar Photography Centre*

**Arab Postal Stamps Museum:** A philatelic journey through 22 countries. It is a quiet study of how young nations project their identity. (GPS: 25.359, 51.525). **Al Thuraya Planetarium:** Often missed by tourists, this high-tech dome offers astronomical shows and digital exhibits. It is named after the Pleiades star cluster, a vital navigational marker for ancient Arab mariners. **Qatar Photography Centre** - https://www.instagram.com/qpc.qa/ rough GPS 25.359, 51.525 (east of Katara Mosque) holds occasional workshops and regular exhibitions.

**The Golden Mosque,**

Tucked north of the amphitheatre, the Golden Mosque, is sheathed in shimmering golden tiles. While the exterior, is simple yet extraordinary, the interior is somewhat more traditional, with a more grounded, metallic palette. It is

*Golden Mosque interior Katara*

a space defined by Subdued Lustre rather than overt brilliance. Generally not open for non-Muslims **GPS:** 25.360, 51.526

**Katara Mosque**

Southwest of the amphitheatre stands the Katara Mosque. This is a masterpiece by Zeynep Fadillioglu, the first woman to design a mosque in the Islamic world. While the Iznik-style tilework is Turkish, the overall silhouette leans toward the Iraqi tradition. The interior was finished by restorers from Istanbul's **Dolmabahce Palace**. Open between 08:30 and 11:30 (often the quietest period before tour groups arrive). Between 13:30 and 15:00 Between 16:00 and 17:00 (Friday its best not to visit as prayers are often extended). Before entering ask "Mumkin a shoof" (may I look). There is a small visitor centre with information. The mosque sometimes offers guides. **Dress Code:** Men must wear long trousers and long-sleeved shirts (avoiding clothing with text). Women must be covered so that only the face, hands, and feet are visible. Footwear must not be worn inside the mosque.

**Pigeon Towers**

East of the mosque are three traditional pigeon towers, comparable to those in Katara's northern area. The number of white pigeons must be keeping the mosque's cleaning crew perpetually busy.

**The Katara Hills**

The grassy elevations to the north and south of the entrance are the Katara Hills. These are manicured wilderness areas with running tracks and artificial waterfalls. The hills to the north are home to the ultra-exclusive **Chedi Katara Hotel** and the **Katara Hills Doha** villas. They offer a quiet vantage point to watch the city's skyline

# WHERE TO GO

ignite at dusk with some also having views over the canal into The Pearl.

*Katara Mosque*

Practicalities for Katara - **Transport:** Metro Red Line (Katara Station). **Activities:** The beach offers jet skis, dhow rides, and kayaking (entry fees apply). **Website:** katara.net

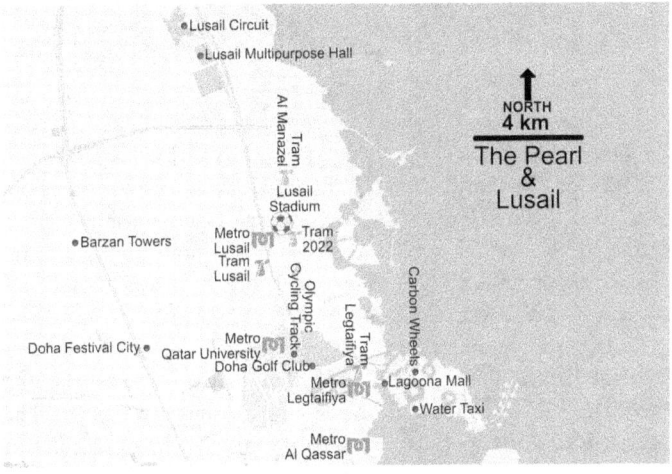

## THE PEARL

The Pearl is a man-made marvel of reclaimed land, rising from the seabed like a shimmering mirage of the "Arabian Riviera". Spread across nearly four million square metres, this archipelago of artificial islands is built over Qatar's historical pearl diving beds - where the pearl oyster (*Pinctada radiata*) once provided the lifeblood of the nation's economy. Today, it is a polished enclave of Mediterranean-style marinas, pastel-hued townhouses, and high-rise luxury, including offshore palaces of the Qatari royal family.

*The Pearl - Konevi*

### Doha Golf Club

West of The Pearl is Doha Golf Club, looking south towards the West Bay skyline. It's a 72 - par, 18-hole championship course. Designed by Peter Harradine, the course is famous for its "desert" character, punctuated by eight strategically placed lakes and abundant indigenous flora. While the club maintains an air of exclusivity, the restaurant remains open to non-members. About - **Typical Hours:** 06:00 - 21:00 daily. **Rough GPS:** 25.380, 51.505. **Street:** Located off Al Jamia St, West Bay. **Public Transport:** The **Metro Red Line** to Qatar University station is the most efficient route, followed by a short taxi ride to the clubhouse gates. **Contact:** +974 4496 0777 | info@dohagolfclub.com | www.dohagolfclub.com

WHERE TO GO 137

*Murano glass sculptures The Pearl*

**Porto Arabia & Public Art**

Porto Arabia is the cosmopolitan heart of the island, a massive circular lagoon fringed by a 2.5km promenade known as La Croisette. This is the premier spot for a sophisticated stroll - or *flânerie* - among the sleek hulls of international yachts. As you walk, look for the intricate public art. A major hub of **Murano glass sculptures** sits at the entrance to the marina (GPS 25.378, 51.538), featuring delicate, hand-blown forms that capture the desert light. Further along the promenade (GPS 25.377, 51.537), you will find more glass installations that serve as modern beacons against the turquoise water. **The Pearl Fountain:** Located near the boardwalk, this features holographic effects and lasers every hour from 18:00, adding a touch of digital magic to the maritime setting. Getting There: Take the Red Line Metro to Legtaifiya, then board the M110 MetroLink bus, which loops through the island.

**Luxury Retreats at The Pearl**

Four Seasons Resort and Residences at The Pearl-Qatar. For a day of relaxation, this resort offers a secluded beach and pool experience. It is a tranquil pocket of calm away from the bustling retail strips. **Entry (2026):** Sun - Thurs QAR295 (includes QAR150 food credit); Fri - Sat QAR395 (includes QAR175 food credit). Ladies' Day on Mondays is QAR400, with QAR100 redeemable. **Contact:** +974 4144 3000 | fourseasons.com/thepearlqatar

*Marina The Pearl*

### Alhosh Gallery

Tucked within the island's Porto Arabia, Alhosh Gallery is a beacon for contemporary Qatari and regional art. It often hosts artist-in-residence programmes, making it a living space rather than a static vault. **Hours:** Sat - Thurs 10:00 - 22:00; Friday 15:00 - 22:00. **Contact:** +974 5999 0910 | alhosh.qa

### The Water Taxi

To see The Pearl as it was intended - from the water - board the public Water Taxi. While walking is often faster, the boat provides a perspective reminiscent of a desert Venice. **The Experience:** The taxi cruises the enclosed bay of Porto Arabia. For a more evocative trip, book the **Qanat Quartier** route, which glides through Venetian-style canals and under arched bridges. **Public Service:** 14:00 - 00:00. Tickets are QAR25 for a gate-to-gate hop. **Private Hire:** QAR200+ for 20 minutes (advance booking required). **GPS:** 25.364, 51.541 (Main gate/Ticket office). **Contact:** +974 4409 5279 | ronauticame.com

### Lagoona Mall & The ZigZag Towers

Located just across the bridge in the West Bay Lagoon area (GPS 25.376, 51.525), Lagoona Mall acts as a gateway to The Pearl. This is not just a shopping destination but an architectural landmark.

Rising above the mall are the twin towers known as the ZigZag Towers they are one of the largest zigzag structures in the world. Their leaning, wavy silhouette is a challenge for window cleaners. **Hours:** 10:00 - 22:00 (Fri 14:00 - 00:00). **Contact:** +974 4433 5555 | lagoonamall.com

*Doha Bus and ZigZag Towers*

## LUSAIL AND NORTHEAST DOHA

Lusail is Qatar's first "smart city," a multi-billion dollar urban development rising north of Doha. The name is derived from Al Wusail (*Juncus rigidus*), a sea rush or tall, rigid grass that was once prevalent in the area. Today, the landscape is defined by bold architecture and world-class sporting infrastructure.

**Qetaifan Island North & Azure Beach**

Located on the northern reaches of Lusail, Qetaifan Island North is the city's dedicated entertainment hub. Azure Beach offers an alternative to public beach it has infinity pool and curated DJ sets. **Hours:** Daily 10:00 - 19:00 (Check local media for evening events/nightlife hours). **Entry:** QAR 200 for adults (typically includes sunbed, towel, and a redeemable food and beverage credit). Note that this venue is primarily focused on an adult audience (18+). **Web:**azurebeachdoha.com | +974 4009 7777 **GPS:** 25.435, 51.528

**Meryal Waterpark**

home to the Icon Tower, an 85-metre structure that holds the Guinness World Record for the tallest water slide in the world,

Meryal Waterpark is Qatar's largest waterpark. The park features 36 water slides and its own private beach. **GPS:** 25.431, 51.529

**Katara Towers**

The iconic crescent-shaped building at the edge of the Lusail skyline is Katara Towers. It houses the Fairmont and Raffles hotels. The design is a literal architectural representation of the crossed scimitars on Qatar's national emblem. There are function halls and dining options within the same building. **GPS:** 25.385, 51.525

*Katara Towers*

**Lusail Boulevard**

Stretching from the stadium to the sea, Lusail Boulevard is the city's answer to the Champs-Élysées. Despite the architectural ambition of the Boulevard, the area often feels like a scale model waiting for its inhabitants, with a stillness not found in Katara or Souq Waqif. The repetitive glass facades and vast, sun-bleached pavements offer vista that are impressive in a photograph.

# WHERE TO GO

*Tram Lusail*

Currently acting more as a moving viewing gallery than a vital transit link, the **Lusail Tram**, does offer a cool, efficient reprieve from the heat. The boulevard is a car-free zone during major sports events at the nearby stadium . From the metro station its just over 2kms walk, to the sea – passing underneath a vast hanging sculpture of a **Whale Shark**, just over 2 times life size.

**Sporting Icons in Lusail**
**Lusail Stadium**
Designed by Foster & Partners, Lusail Stadium is an 80,000-seat vessel-shaped stadium that was the centrepiece of the 2022 World Cup. Its golden facade is inspired by the *fanar* lantern and traditional bowls used across the Arab world. **Access:** It is a 700m walk from the Lusail Metro (Red Line). During major events, shuttle buses bridge this gap during games. **GPS:** 25.421, 51.492

A long distance **Cycle Route** runs from near Doha Sports Park GPS 25.378, 51.498 - north through Lusail to near Al Bayt Stadium, Al Khor GPS 25.654, 51.495 (about 32km one way).

*Cycling through Lusail*

*Whale Shark Lusail*

## Lusail Multipurpose Sports Arena

hosts handball, volleyball, and entertainment spectacles like the WWE is the 15,000-seat indoor venue, Lusail Multipurpose Sports Arena. **Public Art:** On the northwest exterior, look for **The Challenge 2015** by Iraqi artist **Ahmed Al Bahrani**. This monumental sculpture features five giant bronze hands reaching for a basketball. Al Bahrani is also the artist behind the *Flag of Glory* at the National Museum of Qatar. **GPS:** 25.482, 51.462

**Qatar Shooting and Archery Association.**

Located south of the arena, Qatar Shooting and Archery Association is a world-class facility hosting international competitions and is open to the public for practice. **GPS:** 25.481, 51.460 | qatarshooting.qa

**Lusail International Circuit**

The home of Qatar's motorsport, Lusail International Circuit is a 5.38km floodlit track is a staple for MotoGP and Formula 1. The circuit is renowned for its smooth asphalt and high-speed corners, all illuminated by a stadium-grade lighting system that makes night racing a cinematic experience. **F1 2026:** The Qatar Grand Prix is scheduled for **27 - 29 November 2026**. **Arrive and Drive:** For visitors without a personal vehicle, the circuit offers "Experience Days." These are structured sessions in which a specialised car is provided. The flat fee includes a professional instructor, fuel, and track insurance.

*Lusail International Circuit Vinod Thadhani*

You can typically choose from high-performance machinery such as the **Porsche 911 GT3**, the skeletal **KTM X-Bow** (*KTM Sportcar GmbH*), or even a **Formula 4** single-seater. Expect to pay between **QAR 2,500** and **QAR 3,500** for a session lasting approximately 30 to 60 minutes. **Lusail Karting** is an accessible "arrive and drive" option available at the adjacent karting track. For **QAR 125**, you receive a 15-minute session in a world-class kart, with all safety gear provided. **GPS** 25.488, 51.449 **Web:** lcsc.qa

### Doha Festival City

Doha Festival City is one of Qatar's premier shopping and entertainment destinations. Managed by the Al Futtaim Group, distinct from the Majid Al Futtaim "City Centre" brands, it offers a polished, professional retail environment. The complex is home to over 500 stores, including the nation's only IKEA, alongside high-street stalwarts such as Next, Old Navy, and Debenhams, as well as the luxury department store Harvey Nichols. **Snow Dunes** is an indoor frost-filled park is an icy escape in the heart of the desert. The temperature is maintained at a constant -4°C, with real snow produced by state-of-the-art guns. It is themed around an ancient Arabian castle. **Hours:** 10:00 - 22:00 (Sat - Wed); 10:00 - 00:00 (Thu - Fri). **Entry:** Regular passes start at **QAR 149**, with unlimited options at **QAR 199**. **Web:** snowdunes.qa **Vox Cinema** is 19-screen multiplex offering the latest English, Arabic, and Hindi releases. The cinema features 4DX technology, incorporating motion seats, wind, and scent, as well as a high-end theatre for a luxury dining experience. While ticket prices are competitive, screenings are subject to local censorship. **Standard tickets** start at QAR45, 4DX at QAR130, and THEATRE at QAR175. Web:qat.voxcinemas.com

Practicalities - **Typical Hours:** 10:00 - 22:00 Sat - Wed; 10:00 - 23:00 Thu; 10:00 - 11:30 & 13:00 - 00:00 Fri. (Closed for Friday prayers between **11:30 - 13:00**). **Public Transport:** Take the Metro Red Line to **Lusail QNB Station**. From there, board the free **Metrolink** feeder bus (**M145** or **M146**) directly to the mall. Alternatively, take **Bus 517** or **701**. **GPS:** 25.385, 51.442 **Street:** Al Shamal Road (Junction of Al Daayen). **Contact:** +974 4035 4444 | dohafestivalcity.com

*Barzan Towers*

**Barzan Towers**

The Barzan Towers are a pair of watchtowers built in the late 19th and early 20th centuries. Constructed from local lime rubble and coral stone, and built under the direction of Sheikh Mohammed bin Jassim Al Thani, these 16-metre-high structures monitored the *rawda* (a depression where rainwater collects) and provided early warning of approaching ships. As well as their defensive role, the towers served as a celestial observatory to help determine the Islamic calendar. A small mosque remains on the site, with a distinctive exterior staircase to its roof. A staircase to a mosque's roof dates from the time of the Prophet Mohammed, to enable the call to prayer from an elevated location. Historically, this mosque also served as a *madrassa*, where local children were taught the Quran. Visitor Information - **Typical Hours:** Sat - Thu 08:30 - 12:30; Fri 15:00 - 18:00. **Entry Cost:** Free. **Public Transport:** Take the Green Line Metro to **Al Shaqab Station**, then board **Bus L528**, which connects directly to the Umm Salal Mohammed area. It is approximately a 1,200-metre walk from the nearest bus stop to the towers. **GPS:** 25.418, 51.413 **Contact:** +974 4470 1531 | qm.org.qa

**Darb Al Saai**

In Umm Salal Mohammed, northwest of the Barzan Towers, Darb Al Saai is a permanent 150,000-square-metre venue dedicated to celebrating Qatar's heritage. The name translates to "The Path of the Messenger," a reference to the couriers who once delivered the Amir's messages across the desert. Known as a hub for **Qatar National Day** festivities (10 - 20 December), it increasingly hosts major cultural events throughout the year, including Eid celebrations and Ramadhan heritage programmes. The venue includes a dedicated maritime zone called *Al Bidda*, which features a museum documenting Qatar's relationship with the sea, complete with traditional pearl-diving equipment and sea heritage games.

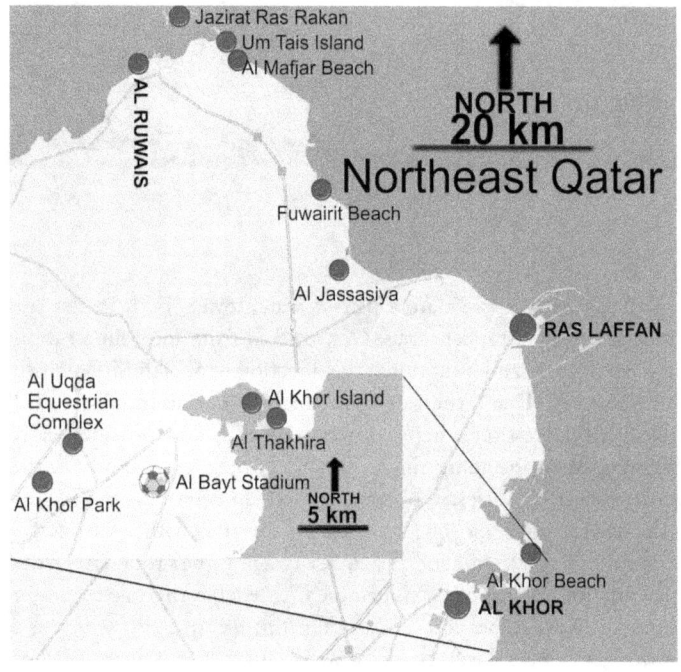

AL KHOR

**Al Bayt Stadium**

Al Bayt Stadium is a monumental tribute to Qatari hospitality, designed to resemble a *bayt al sha'ar* - the traditional black-and-white striped tent of the nomadic Bedouin. Located in Al Khor, approximately 50km north of Doha, this 60,000-seat venue hosted the 2022 World Cup opening ceremony. GPS 25.652, 51.486 Typically on match days a bus shuttle service (usually S950) operates from Lusail QNB Metro Station (the bus station is to the west) – the journey time is about 30 minutes. Other departure points might be added. All such services are free for match ticket holders. An alternative on other days – to the stadium and Al Khor in general is R702 (hourly departure) from Lusail bus station (west of the Metro station) with normal bus fares.

*Al Bayt Stadium*

### Al Bayt Park

The stadium is surrounded by a sprawling green oasis the size of 30 football pitches. It is a destination in its own right for families and fitness enthusiasts. The park has a 4.4km running track and a 3.4km cycling loop. An artificial lake offers boat rentals and is surrounded by trees sponsored by members of the Qatari community. Look for the "floating" palm trees set on concrete bases within the water. **Food & Beverage:** Numerous small cafes and snack stations are peppered throughout the grounds, providing refreshments for picnicking visitors. While Al Khor has few hotels, the Tio Sea Resort is 7km from the stadium. Public Transport see the options for Al Bayt Stadium. GPS: 25.652, 51.484 Approximately 49km from central Doha via the Al Khor Coastal Road.

### Al Khor Family Park and Zoo

Approximately 55km north of Doha, this 24-hectare destination is one of Qatar's oldest and most popular municipal parks. It had a significant renovation between 2010 & 2016 and a maintenance operation in 2020 to become a premier family-oriented leisure hub, featuring landscapes with 42 species of trees and shrubs. The park primarily functions as a family park; however, on Tuesdays, it is reserved exclusively for women and children. The facility combines botanical beauty with a diverse mini-zoo and a large walk-in aviary. The zoo houses 315 animals across 49 species. Highlights include the **Arabian Oryx** (*Oryx leucoryx*), the **Reticulated Giraffe** (*Giraffe camelopardalis reticulata*), and the **White Rhinoceros** (*Ceratotherium simum*). The primate section features **Chimpanzees** (*Pan troglodytes*) and **Olive Baboons** (*Papio anubis*).

**Amenities:** A miniature battery-operated train (QAR 5.00) traverses the grounds. The park also includes a 1,200-square-metre museum, a mosque for 360 worshippers, and a large artificial lake with waterfalls. **Ticketing:** Entry is QAR15 for adults and QAR10 for children under 10. Tickets must be purchased in advance through the **Oun app** (www.mm.gov.qa ) or at select **Al Meera** branches (Airport, Hyatt Plaza, and Gulf Mall) to avoid disappointment at the gate. Typical Hours: Park 08:00 - 22:00; Zoo 08:00 - 18:00 Rough **GPS**: 25.649, 51.420 Public Transport: No direct Metro link bus R701 (not especially convenient in Doha as its from the Industrial area).

### Panda House

Located adjacent to Al Khor Park (though requiring a separate ticket and entrance), the Panda House is a custom-built, ultra-luxurious sanctuary. It was opened in 2022 to house two Giant Pandas (*Ailuropoda melanoleuca*), Suhail (the male) and Thuraya (the female) are named after two of the brightest stars in the Arabian sky and gifted by China to commemorate Qatar's hosting of the FIFA World Cup. Their diet consists almost exclusively of bamboo, with 1,000kg airlifted weekly from China. Access is strictly via timed entry booked through the **Oun app (www.mm.gov.qa)** Tickets are **QAR 50** for adults and **QAR 25** for children under 14. Tickets are non-refundable and valid only for the specific day and time slot selected. Typical Hours: 09:00 - 17:00 (Daily) Rough GPS. 25.652, 51.425 Contact: +974 3342 7954

### Al Uqda Equestrian Complex

On the northern fringes of Al Khor, the Al Uqda Equestrian Complex is a premier multipurpose venue that serves as a vital site for Qatar's equine fans. Al Uqda offers a more intimate, rural atmosphere compared to Al Shaqab or Rayyan's **Equestrian Club**. Al Uqda has a grass racecourse, jumping arena, and a riding school. Typically the racing season lasts from mid October to mid April. Al

Uqda hosts over 20 meeting during this period. Spectators can witness purebred Arabians and thoroughbreds competing under floodlights during the winter months. As of **early 2026**, the complex is undergoing a significant "Phase 4" expansion. This **QAR290million** (approx. $80 million) project includes the construction of a new 5,000-square-metre grandstand and a new 1,000-metre straight track – check about it being open. Visitor Information Open primarily during scheduled events. Racing typically commences in the late afternoon (around 15:30) to avoid the midday heat. Generally free entry for public seating at races, though VIP or hospitality packages are available for major meetings. There is currently no direct public transport to the site. A private vehicle or taxi is essential for the journey from Doha. **GPS:** 25.672, 51.438 - off the **Al Shamal Road** corridor, north of Al Khor. **Contact:** +974 4482 5708 | info@qrec.gov.qa | qrec.gov.qa

### Al Thakhira Mangroves

The Al Thakhira Mangroves (also spelt Al Dakhera) represent the largest and oldest area of mangroves in Qatar. This coastal fringe is a resilient green bastion against the hyper-saline waters of the Gulf. The primary species here is the Grey Mangrove (*Avicennia marina*), known locally as *Qurum*..

The area is an ornithological crossroads, supporting over 130 bird species. Look for the **Greater Flamingo** (*Phoenicopterus roseus*) in the winter months, alongside curlews and reef herons. On land, you may encounter the **Spiny-tailed Lizard** (*Uromastyx aegyptia microlepis*), known locally as the *Dhab*, or the elusive **Hooded Malpolon** (*Malpolon moilensis*), a "false cobra" that mimics a lethal stance when threatened. A good way to experience the forest's interior is by kayak.

*Mangroves northeast Qatar*

Several operators run guided tours through the narrow channels during high tide (see PAGE 187). GPS: 25.748, 51.540 Public Transport: Take Bus 722 from Lusail Bus Station to Al Thakhira, followed by a 2km walk to the water's edge.

*Bin Bin Ghannam Island walkway*

## BIN GHANNAM ISLAND (PURPLE ISLAND)

Bin Ghannam Island, popularly known as Purple Island, is an alternative destination to see mangroves.

A raised wooden walkway allows visitors to cross the wetlands and mangroves without disturbing the delicate mudflats. The "Purple" in its title is a historical reference to the island's ancient industry. During the second millennium BC, the island was a major site for the production of red-purple dye extracted from the **Murex Snail** (*Hexaplex kuesterianus*). Thousands of crushed shells still litter the island's limestone ridges - a silent reminder of a luxury trade that once supplied the elite of the Mediterranean and Mesopotamia: A small, discreet bird watching hide is located along the walkway, offering a shaded vantage point to observe migratory waders without being seen. The wooden walkway leads through the mangroves and onto a path on the rocky island. This is a limestone formation with water and wind-eroded bluffs. Open 24 hours though daylight visits recommended. There is no cost to entry and no facilities - it is strictly "leave no trace." GPS: 25.686, 51.554 Public Transport none.

### Al Farkiah Beach

Al Farkiah Beach offers a fenced, family-friendly beach area, east of Tio Sea Resort. It features over 50 shaded areas, barbecue pits, and play zones for children. Sunday and Wednesday are typically reserved for women and children only. Access is generally free, though it is one of the busiest spots in the northern region on Fridays. Public Transport: There is no public transport to these coastal areas; a 4x4 vehicle is strongly recommended for the northern tracks to avoid becoming mired in the *sabkha* (salt flats). Rough GPS: 25.679, 51.539

*Bin Ghannam Island*

**Torba Farm**

Nestled in the Umm Qarn area near Al Khor, Torba Farm has been a pioneer of regenerative agriculture. Established in the early 1980s and now managed by twins Mohammed and Fatma Al Khater, it was the first farm in Qatar to implement a full permaculture model - an integrated system of design that mimics the resilience of natural ecosystems. Currently the farm would benefit from a more organised and effective vegetation and infrastructure care schedule. The farm is open primarily during the winter months (typically November to April) when the desert climate allows the gardens to flourish. **Opening Hours (Winter):** Sun - Wed 06:00 - 22:00; Thu - Sat 08:00 - 00:00. **Entry Cost:** Adults QAR75; Children QAR50. Children under 3 years enter free of charge. Workshops and farm-to-table dining experiences carry additional fees. **Dining:** The on-site cafe serves a seasonal menu featuring ingredients harvested daily, including 100% gluten-free and dairy-free options. **GPS:** 25.576, 51.309 **Public Transport:** There is no direct public transport to the farm; a private vehicle is essential. It is approximately a 40-minute drive north of Doha. **Contact:** www.torbafarm.qa +974 3116 6707 (WhatsApp)

**North Sedra Farm**

Locateed in Al Ghuwayriyah, approximately 75km north of Doha, North Sedra Farm is a seasonal agritourism destination. The farm is a pioneer of the "pick-your-own" (PYO) in Qatar. During the winter season, visitors can fill baskets with seasonal produce, including strawberries and fresh vegetables. A diverse collection of animals inhabits the farm's mini zoo. The Arabian Oryx (*Oryx leucoryx*), with its striking ivory coat and rapier-like horns, is joined by the Common Ostrich (*Struthio camelus*) (both these species are re-introductions to Qatar) and the Dromedary Camel (Camelus dromedarius). The concept is good, but would benefit from more attention to details. Visitor Information - **Winter Season (October - April):** Friday and Saturday, 12:30 pm - 20:00 pm. **Entry Cost:** QAR20 per person (Children under 2 years are free). Some activities, such as animal feeding and boat rides, incur additional small charges. **Public Transport:** There is no direct public transport to this area; a private vehicle is essential. **Rough GPS:** 25.985, 51.298 **Contact:** +974 6665 0388 | northsedra.qa

NORTHERN QATAR

### Al Jassasiya Rock Art Site

Al Jassasiya is Qatar's most significant open-air petroglyph site. While carvings appear at over a dozen coastal sites, this limestone ridge has the highest concentration, with almost 900 petroglyphs on 12 low outcrops. The site was first reported internationally in 1957 by Danish archaeologist Peter Glob and systematically recorded in 1974. In December 2019, its international status grew when it was inscribed on the ICESCO (Islamic World Educational, Scientific and Cultural Organization ) Heritage List. The name Al Jassasiya means "The Searchers" or "The Hill" - a fitting title for a ridge likely used as a lookout for vessels.

These carvings offer a visual representation of a maritime culture deeply dependent on the sea. Images of boats are common, Boat carvings appear, most from a bird's-eye view - like insect skeletons with oars stretching out as centipede legs. **Cupules** are the most common motifs, consisting of small circular depressions arranged in rows, rosettes, or double-parallel lines. The double rows of seven holes are widely believed to be boards for Al Haloosa or Al Huwaila - local variants of the ancient board game Mancala. This suggests the site was a place of social gathering where a game was played while watching the horizon. Maritime themes dominate, but rare carvings show the Common Ostrich - now

*Al Jassasiya Rock Art*

extinct locally in the wild alongside scorpions, human figures, and *wasms* (tribal marks).

The carvings' age is debated. Dhow styles - rudder details - suggest a 10th–16th-century origin. However, the 2012 scientific dating of calcium oxalate layers found a younger age around AD1790; around the time of Al Zubarah. Soft limestone erodes quickly in the north wind (*Shamal*), so older carvings may have vanished.

Visitor Information - **Opening Hours:** Sat - Thu 09:00 - 17:00; Fri 12:30 - 17:00. **Entry Cost:** Free. **Preparation:** There is no shade or water on site. Visit at sunrise or sunset for the best view; low light reveals carvings that midday glare hides. **GPS:** 25.952, 51.406 **Location:** East of the Al Shamal Road (Route 1), near Al Jassasiya Beach. **Public Transport:** None serves this area. A private vehicle is required.

### Fuwairit Beach

Fuwairit Beach is a natural coastline in northern Qatar, known for its fine sand and turquoise waters. Popular for kitesurfing, its northwesterly winds suit both enthusiasts and experts. Access is via the Al Shamal Road (Exit 79) and a short off-road track. The coastline here is defined by a significant sand spit that extends into the sea - a vital sanctuary for the Hawksbill Turtle (*Eretmochelys imbricata*). This spit acts as the nation's primary marine nursery; approximately 30% of Qatar's hawksbill nests are found on this single stretch of shore. **Seasonal Closure:** The beach is closed annually from **1 April to 31 July** to protect nesting turtles. Dates may vary by official decree. Plan your visit outside this period. During closure, the area is fenced and patrolled by the Ministry of Environment and Climate Change. **The Khor:** A silted *khor* (creek) lines the landward side of the beach, where hardy mangroves (*Avicennia marina*) offer a stark green contrast to the sun-bleached limestone ruins and abandoned houses nearby. The sand at Fuwairit consists of finely crushed seashells and coral, which stays cooler underfoot than the inland desert's quartz-heavy sand. **GPS**: 26.059, 51.354. Public Transport: There is no public transport to this location. Visitors must arrive by private vehicle.

### Fuwairit Kite Beach

South of the main beach area is Fuwairit Kite Beach (FKB) is a resort popular for kitesurfing , blending coastal adventure with upscale hospitality, the resort also offers padel tennis, beach volleyball, and a gymnasium. **Day Pass:** For visitors not staying overnight, a Day Pass is available for **QAR 300.00**. This fee includes access to the pool and sports facilities, with **QAR 200 credited** toward food and beverages at "The Rider" restaurant. **Hours:** The beach and resort facilities are open to day guests from **10:00 to 17:00** daily. **Contact:** +974 4030 1555 | 3990 2420 | fkb.qa Web: fuwairitkitebeach.tapestrycollection.com

### Al Mafjar

Leaving Fuwairit behind, Al Mafjar is abandoned settlement; its name translates roughly as "The Place of the Explosion." Today, it is colloquially known as "Old Ruins Beach", where the remains of stone houses are all that remains of a fishing community. On 24 February 2026, Al Mafjar was inscribed on the **ICESCO Heritage List for** its "Outstanding Universal Value." Currently it is fenced off, and undergoing restoration. The Sand Spit: A dramatic sand spit extends from the village towards the sea, offering a surreal landscape during low tide. It is a prime location for observing the Greater Flamingo (Phoenicopterus roseus) and other migratory waders.

Visitor Information -not currently accessible **GPS:** 26.136, 51.301

### Umm Tais National Park

Umm Tais (meaning 'Mother of the Male Goat') is a low-lying island and sand bar just off Qatar's tip. Today it is separated from the mainland at Al Mafjar, by a shallow channel wadable at low tide. It has been protected as a national park since 2006. The island's geography demonstrates ongoing coastal changes. Its terrain, close to sea level, is regularly reshaped by winter storms and tidal surges, which alter the arrangement of sand bars over time. A large area of Grey Mangrove (*Avicennia marina*) dominates the shoreline. These trees act as the island's skeletal system, their tangled roots trapping sediment and providing a sheltered nursery for juvenile fish and shrimp. The beaches of Umm Tais are a critical nesting site for the **Hawksbill Turtle** (*Eretmochelys imbricata*) between April and July. Visitor Information - This is a remote destination with no shade, freshwater, or mobile phone signal in places. Visit with a high-clearance 4x4 and pay attention to tides to avoid being stranded. Umm Tais is best explored as part of a guided eco-tour or kayaking expedition. **Entry Cost:** Free. **Typical Hours:** Daylight hours only are recommended for navigation and safety. **Public**

**Transport:** None. The journey from Doha takes approximately 90 minutes. **GPS:** 26.156, 51.276

Flamingo

### Jazirat Ras Rakan (Island)

Jazirat Ras Rakan is the true northernmost point of the Qatar peninsula. This low-lying, T-shaped islet is a slender, sand-swept finger pointing toward the heart of the Arabian Gulf. Approximately 3.2km in length from east to west, the island is extremely narrow, characterised by a fragile landscape of sand, tufts of hardy salt-grass, and small clusters of mangroves on its southern flank. Opposite Zulal Wellness Resort, the islet is separated from the mainland by a channel roughly less than 3km wide. This waterway is not passable for dhows or larger motorboats due to its extreme shallowness, but at low tides it offers a unique experience for the determined walker – guided by a knowledgeable guide. Underwater is seagrass (*Halophila stipulacea*). providing a critical nursery for juvenile fish and a primary grazing ground for the **Hawksbill Turtle**. Wading to the island requires "strategic timing" with the tide. Ensure you have sturdy water shoes to protect against sharp coral and stonefish. There is no shade or freshwater on the island; it is an environment only for hardy plants and animals. Best Time to Visit: Early morning at low tide offers the best light for photography and the safest walking conditions. Public Transport: There is no public transport to the shore. The nearest town is Al Ruwais, located about 4km to the southeast. **GPS**: 26.178, 51.226 Distance: Approximately 110km from Doha via the Al Shamal Road (Route 1).

**Zulal Wellness Resort;** Situated on the mainland opposite the island of Jazirat Ras Rakan Zulal is a wellness destination. It provides a stark architectural contrast to the wildness of Ras Rakan, its a modern reimagination of the traditional Qatari villages, which have now disappeared. The resort offers a curated "Island Walk" for guests, allowing for a guided exploration of Jazirat Ras Rakan ecosystems.

### Al Ruwais

The northern tip of Qatar offers an unhurried contrast to Doha's vertical ambition. Here, the town of Al Ruwais serves as a gateway to the west and northwest coastlines of Qatar. Southwest of Al Ruwais the tarmac roads bypass the abandoned villages, which means in all cases it's several kilometres to the coast . It is critical for the visitor to note that the maritime borders with Bahrain (and Saudi Arabia) are strictly monitored. In early 2026, GCC security coordination reached a new peak with the Arabian Gulf Security 4 exercises at Zekreet, underscoring the high-tech surveillance of these waters.

**Al Ruwais Town** offers petrol stations and local restaurants, try **Istanbul Garden** +97444730630 with a good takeaway option (is quite small inside) off the main road leading to the western coast. serving as the final staging point before exploring the more remote western coast. **GPS**: 26.127, 51.208

### Al Ruwais Beach

This modest shore has clear water covering a shallow and rocky bottom, making it unsuitable for traditional swimming or sunbathing, quite apart from cultural issues.. It is, however, an excellent location for "coastal flânerie" - to observe the traditional dhows and the local birdlife that frequents the shallows. **GPS:** 26.143, 51.217 **Location:** Accessible via Al Kasooma Street.

### Al Mina Market (The Irani Souq)

Within Al Ruwais Port, this market is a modern iteration of the ancient trade routes that linked Qatar to Persia. Known as the Irani Souq, it is a single-storey building that houses a vibrant, if somewhat temporary, bazaar. The market can be a treasure trove of Iranian exports. Look for Persian carpets, hand-knotted and brought directly across the Gulf by commercial dhows. Here is saffron (*Crocus sativus*), dried fruits and Iranian honey. Visitor Information - **Typical Hours:** 08:00 - 18:00 (Sun - Wed); 08:00 - 20:00 (Thu - Sat). **GPS:** 26.139, 51.206 **Location:** Al Ruwais Port **Public Transport:** Bus E801 (Lusail Bus Station)

# QATAR

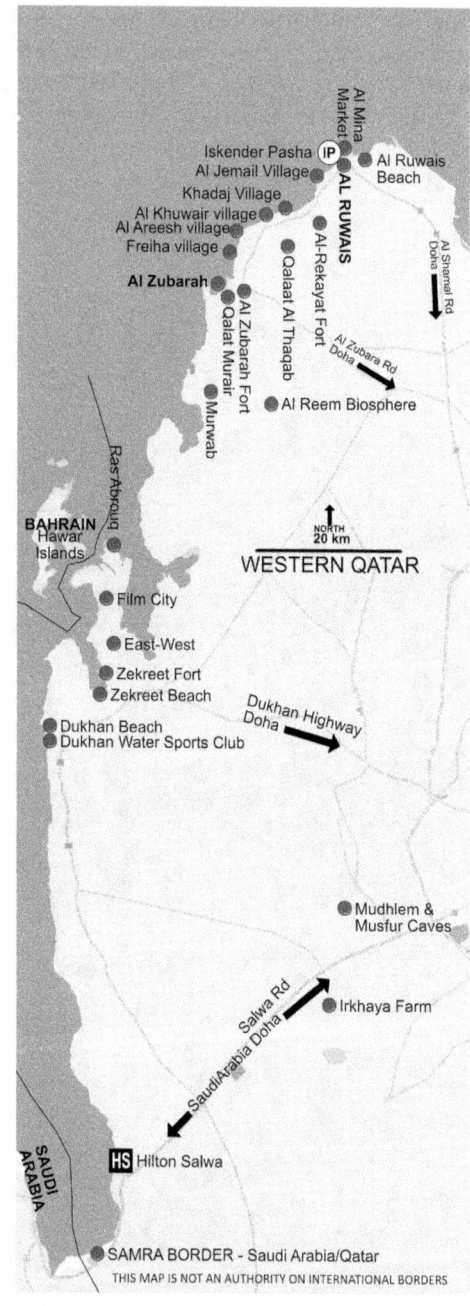

# GHOST VILLAGES OF WESTERN QATAR

Stretching down a 30km corridor south of Al Ruwais, this western coast of Qatar has the remains of a series of skeletal settlements that were at the hub of Qatar's pre-oil life. These sites range from the fortified remnants of 18th-century "pirate" outposts to a UNESCO World Heritage Site. The landscape here is a bleak, sun-scoured expanse where the vegetation is sparse, and the slight limestone ridges offer the only relief from the horizon.

Unspectacular in their physical scale, these villages are a poignant reminder of the endurance needed by the Qatari people before the hydrocarbon era.

There are no retail outlets or services within these ruins. It is essential to carry an ample supply of drinking water and some snacks – or a picnic, perhaps from Istanbul Garden. The ground alternates between powdery dust, damp, saline mud and gravels. Wear sturdy, closed-toe shoes that you are prepared to see heavily soiled; sandals will let in all the debris from the sites – that might include all sorts of bugs and bighting animals. Facing west across the Gulf, the villages are without any tree shade, finishing a trip around sunset is good for photography and reflection – though an unlit drive back much of the way to Doha will be needed. A 4x4 vehicle is strongly recommended. While some tracks are visible, the "sabkha" (salt flats) can be treacherous for standard vehicles, particularly after rare rainfall. Individually, they offer little reward for a drive across Qatar, but together they offer a great insight into the scale of life in Qatar decades or hundreds of years ago. There is no bus service here.

**Warning:** Entering the territorial waters of Bahrain or Saudi illegally is a serious offence that typically results in immediate arrest and detention. Ensure any boat charters or coastal explorations stay well within Qatari waters.

### Al Jemail Village

Al Jemail (often spelt Al Jamil) is roughly 8km southwest of Al Ruwais. This was abandoned in the mid-20th century as the population migrated toward the modern amenities of Doha and Al Khor. The architecture is a study in local materials: walls are constructed from a rugged mix of limestone and fossil coral stone, bound by a mud-and-gypsum mortar. In the less dilapidated houses, there are still sections of the traditional roofing systems visible. These consist of *danchal* (mangrove or teak wood) beams imported from East Africa or India, overlaid with *basgijl* (woven bamboo matting) and finished with a thick layer of compressed mud.

Al Jemail Mosque

The most complete structure in the village is the mosque. This has been restored, using traditional materials. Its minaret remains standing, featuring a small doorway to provide access to an election for the *muezzin* to deliver the call to prayer across the windswept shore. The village sits above the high-water mark. At low tide, The Gulf retreats to reveal a vast, shimmering expanse of sand and tidal flats - a perfect opportunity for a coastal walk. The final few hundred metres to the village are via a rough, unpaved track. A 4x4 helps with ground clearance. Wear sturdy, closed-toe shoes; the ruins are filled with rubble, and the tidal flats can be muddy. Open 24 hours (Sunrise or sunset is highly recommended for the best photographic light). Entry Cost: Free. GPS: 26.094, 51.152 Public Transport: None.

**Al Maskar: The Inter-tidal Fish Traps**

Stretching from Al Jemail south toward Al Zubarah, the shallow coastal waters are crisscrossed by innumerable low stone walls. These are *Al Maskar* - traditional inter-tidal fish traps. These U-shaped or semi-circular walls were built from beach rock and coral. As the tide receded, fish were trapped in the apex of the trap, where they could be easily collected by hand or with nets. Some traps used a woven basket, fixed to the apex, to collect the fish. Therse reliable, low-energy ways of capturing protein was the primary reason these settlements flourished in such a parched landscape. The *Al Maskar* represents a sophisticated human adaptation to the Gulf's tidal rhythms.

**Al Ruwaida Archaeological Site**

Al Ruwaida Archaeological Site is one of the most extensive and historically significant settlements on Qatar's northwest coast. Extending over 2.5km of the beach between Al Zubarah and Al Ruwais, this 90-hectare site offers a glimpse into a larger settlement that thrived before the rise of Zubarah. The name is a diminutive of the Arabic word *rawda*, signifying a "fertile depression" - a fitting title for a location where the water table is high enough to have once supported green gardens and crops. The heart of the settlement is a multi-period fort that is significantly larger than its contemporaries in the region. This suggests that Al Ruwaida had gown to become the principal settlement in the area. The fort underwent three distinct phases, at one point being massively enlarged to eight times its original size, before being reduced in size. It features a unique solid corner tower, rather than a hollow one, likely built as a cannon platform. The construction is believed to be based on an original 16th-century Portuguese fortification, by Dr Andrew Petersen. The fort is where a Portuguese map of The Gulf depicts "Sidade de Catar' in a similar location. Excavations have unearthed a wealth of international trade goods, including fine 18th-century Chinese porcelain and red-and-blue glazed ceramics from Safavid Iran.

Because the coastal waters are exceptionally shallow, the inhabitants engineered a shipping channel through the seabed to allow large dhows to approach the shore. Archaeologists have identified a workshop containing iron rivets and large quantities of bitumen - a substance used to waterproof the hulls of dhows - indicating a thriving boat-repair industry. While many villages were abandoned due to tribal shifts, Al Ruwaida's decline in the 1770s is attributed to a devastating plague epidemic known as "Persian Plague" of 1772–1773. This swept down from Baghdad, into The Gulf leaving the urban settlement a n abandoned relic of coral and limestone. The rise of Zubarah dates from the decline of Al Ruwaida. Visitor Information **Opening Hours:** Sat - Thu 09:00 - 17:00; Fri 12:30 - 17:00 (the site is fenced). **Entry Cost:** Free.**GPS:** 26.084, 51.147 **Public Transport:** None . **Contact:** qm.org.qa

### Khadaj Village

Khadaj is the smallest and most understated of the abandoned settlements on the northwest coast. While its larger neighbours, Al Jemail and Al Khuwayr, were thriving maritime hubs, Khadaj was a minimalist outpost - a "micro-settlement" of what seems to be 4 or 5 houses probably was inhabited by a single extended family or a small splinter group of the Al Kubaisi tribe. Visitor Information - The final 2km of the approach is via a rough, unpaved track that can be punishing on a standard car. A 4x4 is highly recommended to navigate the loose stones and occasional soft sand. Open 24 hours; Entry Cost: Free. GPS: 26.081, 51.112 ; Public Transport: None.

### Al Khuwair Village (Khor Hassan)

The abandoned village of Al Khuwair (historically known as Khor Hassan, meaning "Beautiful Inlet") sits on the edge of a desolate stretch of the northwest coast. In the late 18th and early 19th centuries, this was the formidable base of Rahmah ibn Jabir Al Jalahimi (c. 1760 - 1826). Described, perhaps unfairly, by British authorities as a ruthless pirate, he is perhaps the most enduring "style icon" of the era; after losing an eye in battle, his use of an eye-patch reportedly established the quintessential pirate aesthetic. His body was a patchwork of wounds and lost body parts, but still, he commanded his forces effectively.

Rahmah bin Jabir Al Jalahimi was a complex political figure who navigated the volatile tribal loyalties of the Gulf. Originally a partner with the Al Khalifa sheikhs, he became their sworn enemy after feeling excluded from the spoils following their occupation of Bahrain. He strategically cooperated with the Al Saud in central Arabia, who were then extending their influence over the eastern coast of Arabia. Later, he was supporting the Al Said rulers of Oman and, remarkably, the East India Company. Despite attacking British shipping, he often avoided direct military conflict with the British Empire through "strategic diplomacy."

His death in 1826 was as dramatic as his life. During a fierce naval battle against his sister's son (a Khalifa sheikh) and the Bahraini fleet, Rahmah - realising defeat was imminent - took his youngest son in his arms and ordered his ship, the *Al Ghatrusha*, to be blown up. The resulting explosion destroyed his vessel and the principal Bahraini ship, a final act of "explosive defiance" that cemented his legend.

### Architectural Remains

The village's location was chosen for its natural defences; the surrounding sandbanks and coral reefs protected the "pirate lair" from sea-borne assaults. Most of the remaining ruins date from the late 19th and early 20th centuries, reflecting a community of the Al Kubaisi (الكبيسي) tribe who survived through pearling and fishing. The most prominent structure is the ruined mosque, whose minaret remains the tallest point in the village. It features an internal staircase accessed via a small doorway, once used for the call to prayer. The houses are constructed from the standard regional mix of coral stone and limestone. Many still feature the remains of *danchal* (mangrove wood) beams and *basgijl* (woven bamboo) ceilings. Lacking its own freshwater, the village was tethered to the wells at Al Thaqab, located approximately 5km to the southeast.

Visitor Information - The terrain is predominantly Sabkha (salt flats). It is essential to stay on the established tracks; even a light rainfall can turn the fine, powdery soil into a treacherous trap that can mire a 4x4. Look for the 5 radio masts that dominate the horizon near the tarmac road. No shops or services exist within the village. The nearest petrol and food supplies are in Al Ruwais, roughly 10km to the north. GPS: 26.068, 51.083 Public Transport: None.

### Al Areesh Village

Al Areesh is one of the larger abandoned settlements on the northwest coast, once a thriving community of the Al Kabesi tribe. The name Al Areesh derived from and Arabic term for "a shelter made from date palm tree leaves" - a reference to the verdant shade that once defined this coastal outpost before the groundwater turned brackish and the residents departed.

**Historical Conflict:** The village has a storied military past. In July 1937, it was occupied by the forces of **Sheikh Abdullah bin Jassim Al Thani** during a significant regional conflict. The settlement was a strategic piece on the era's geopolitical chessboard, caught in the friction between the mainland authorities and the **Al Naim tribe of Zubarah.**

**The Architecture:** Most of the housing dates from the late 19th century to the mid-20th century. The ruins, like most of these villages, uses coral stone and limestone held together by mud-and-gypsum mortar. Most roofs have succumbed to rain damage, which rots and collpses the roof supports. The mosque's minaret is comparable to others along the coast; it encloses and internal staircase once used by the muezzin to summon the faithful. On the eastern edge of the village stands a more modern structure that served as the local school. This building represents the final chapter of the village's life, reflecting the shift toward formal education, while the improved economy drew the population towards Doha, or oil facilities. West of the main ruins, the cemetery is a quiet expanse of simple stone markers. In accordance with local custom, the graves are unadorned, serving as an egalitarian marker of past lives.

**Navigation and Surroundings** The village is situated near the Sabkhat Al Areesh, a salt flat at sea level; rain and high tides create a sticky trap. The high salinity means the landscape is dominated by halophytic flora such as the Shrubby Horsetail (*Ephedra foliata*) and Sea Lavender (*Limonium axillare*). **Hours:** Open 24 hours. There is a partially open fence around the village – a restoration effort may be made as in Al Mafjar. **Entry Cost:** Free. **Access:** Located near a Coast Guard station. The final 2km is a rough, unpaved track where a 4x4 is necessary to avoid the biting edges of the limestone. **GPS:** 26.051, 51.057 **Public Transport: none**

### Al Thagab Fort

Situated 11km northeast of Al Zubarah, Al Thagab Fort was sentinel over one of the few reliable water sources in the northern peninsula. The name "Thaqab" translates to "the water that collects at the bottom of the valley after rain." Historically, this fort was the primary refuge for the inhabitants of the nearby fishing villages of Al Ruwais and Al Khuwayr during times of regional instability. The structure is a classic example of 19th-century Qatari defensive architecture, built from rough blocks of coral and limestone bound, as with the housing, by a mud-and-gypsum mortar. The fort follows a rectangular ground plan, though it uniquely features three circular towers at the corners and a single rectangular tower - a design that allowed for a wide field of fire across the surrounding *rawdha* (depression).

Restoration in 2003 has resulted in an interior contains several small, vaulted rooms that likely served as living quarters and storage for dates. In 2015, a modern floral-shaped monument was constructed adjacent to the fort, an artistic reference to the historical importance of the deep wells that the fort was commissioned to protect. To the west of the fort lies the original 35-foot-deep hand-dug well. While the agricultural potential of the area has diminished due to groundwater salinity, the well remains a vital historical marker of Qatar's pre-oil water heritage.

Adjacent to the fort is a small farm, with accommodation https://365adventures.me/.

Access requires a 4x4 vehicle. The soil in this region is exceptionally fine and powdery - known locally as *sabkha* - which can lose all traction if even slightly dampened by rain. It is essential to remain on the established tracks. Fort **Typical Hours:** Open 24 hours (Daylight visits are recommended for safety). **Entry Cost:** Free. **GPS:** 26.033, 51.117 **Public Transport:** There is no public transport to this location; it is best visited as part of a northern desert loop that includes Al Rekayat and Al Zubarah.

### Al Rekayat Fort

Like a sun-bleached sentinel Al Rekayat Fort looks over the limestone plains of northwest Qatar. The name "Rekayat" is derived from the Arabic word for water-wells; referring to the vital freshwater sources the structure was commissioned to protect. Built in the 19th century, it secured the lifeblood of the nearby settlement against both the elements and regional instability. **Architecture and Design:** The fort follows a rectangular plan (approximately 22m by 38m) and is unique for its tower configuration. While most Qatari forts favour uniform towers, Al Rekayat features three rectangular corner towers and a single cylindrical tower at the southwest corner. The walls, only three metres high, are constructed from marine limestone and coral, originally bound with mud mortar.

**Restoration:** The structure underwent a significant conservation project between October 2020 and September 2021. Excavations within the central courtyard revealed a *madbasa* - a traditional date press used to extract *dibs* (date syrup). This industrial detail highlights the fort's role as a communal storehouse and refuge during the winter harvest. Despite its 19th-century construction, an Islamic coin dating to the Abbasid period (749-846 AD) was discovered during the 1988 excavations. While the coin predates the masonry, its presence suggests that the wells have been a focal point of human activity for over a millennium. This 150-year-old fort now utilises solar-powered outdoor lighting along with traditional building materials - such as *danjal* wood beams and *basgijl* (woven bamboo) - to maintain its historical integrity for the 2026 visitor.

**Typical Hours:** Saturday-Thursday 09:00-17:00; Friday 12:30-17:00. **Entry Cost:** Free. **Public Transport:** none. **GPS:** 26.051, 51.130 **Contact:** qm.org.qa

**Freiha Archaeological Site**

Approximately 4km north of Al Zubarah Fort, Freiha is one of the oldest abandoned settlements on the northwest coast of Qatar. Archaeological evidence provided by the University of Copenhagen dates ceramic finds here to the 16th century – a period that aligns with the initial Portuguese maritime incursions into the Gulf. The site's historical significance is further cemented by the German explorer Carsten Niebuhr, who, sailing under the Danish flag, documented the settlement during his 1765 expedition; it remains a permanent fixture on his seminal map of the region. Remarkably, Freiha survived the plague, unlike Al Ruwaida, and also outlived Al Zubarah; each town was originally a settlement of a distinct tribe. Freiha eventually faded due to the collapse of the pearling industry, a reduction of the aquifer that supplied its water, and the consolidation of power in Doha.

Visitor Information - Freiha offers a comparable experience to the settlements to its north, though unlike several others, it does have the remains of a fort. Footwear: The ground is exceptionally dusty and, near the shore, can be deceptively damp. Wear sturdy, closed-toe shoes.•GPS: 26.014, 51.040

East of Freiha and opposite Al Zubarah visitor centre, Ain Mohammed, itself originally a small settlement, has 24 units of simple accommodation. An added bonus is that if offers heritage activities and Qatari style food. GPS 26.005, 51.054 www.ainmohammed.com/ +974 77600011.

Before arriving at Zubarah – some modern sculptures "Shadows Travelling on the Sea of the Day" by the Danish artist Olafur Eliassonare to the west of the road.

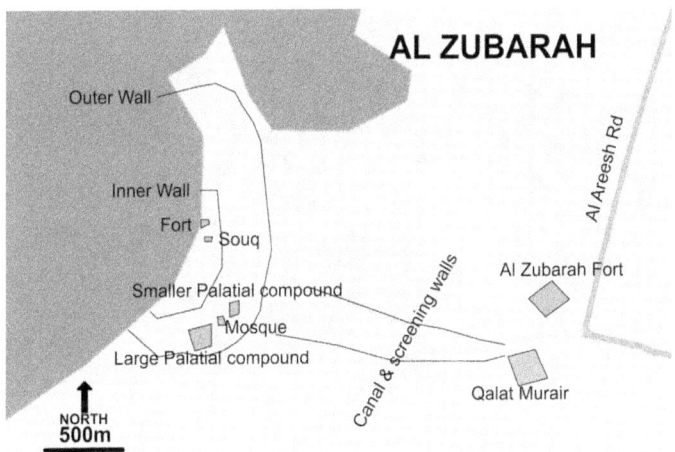

## AL ZUBARAH

### Al Zubarah World Heritage Site Visitor Centre

Deliberately set away, 4km north of Al Zubarah archaeological site, the visitor centre offers an excellent overview of what can be seen, along with the site's history. Exhibition rooms outline the history of the 18th-century pearling economy, the Utub tribal migrations from central Arabia to Kuwait, Qatar and Bahrain, and the ongoing archaeological excavations. There is a dedicated space focusing on the terrestrial and marine ecology of the surrounding Al Reem UNESCO Man and Biosphere Reserve.

Critical for visitors it is the logistical starting point, providing essential shade, parking, and digital guides before visitors navigate the exposed tracks to the actual ruins. Hours 09:00 to 17:00 Saturday to Thursday, 12:30 to 17:00 PM on Fridays. A shuttle bus services runs from the centre to the Al Zubarah fort and archaeological area. Currently access is free (previously it was QAR35.) GPS 26.005, 51.053

Al Zubarah is Qatar's premier archaeological treasure and its first UNESCO World Heritage Site (inscribed in 2013). This 61-hectare walled coastal town was once a thriving pearling and global trading hub, flourishing in the late 18th and early 19th centuries before its abandonment in the early 20th century.

### Al Zubarah Fort

This small mid-20thc military fort was built in a pivotal period in Qatar's history. It was errected in 1938 as a response to Bahrain's building of an outpost on the Hawar Islands to the southwest. The fort is a single-story, with three circular towers and a fourth square tower. The military use of the fort continued until 1986 Arranged against the exterior wall are the interior rooms – all of which open onto the courtyard. Climb up the rear left tower for a "tactical overview" of the desert plains and the town's skeletal footprint.. Inside the rooms have displays about the history of the site. Outside, some relatively ordinary buildings have a museum about Al Zubarah. Exhibits include explanations about pearling. A rusting ship's canon, and perhaps a couple of camels complete the scene. As this fort symbolises Qatar's history, periodic unique events are held here - some may close the building. For more information, see the Al Zubarah section below.

### Qalat Murair

Built in around 1768, the largely invisible remains of Qalat Murair fort is 300m southwest of Al Zubarah Fort. The Qalat Murair fort was approximately 160m on each four sides. The fort, which is contemporary to Al Zubarah town, protected the numerous shallow water wells around it. Around Qalat Murair fort were several courtyard houses and a mosque. Qalat Murair was destroyed in the 1960s, a period when Al Zubarah Fort was improved, and a rough track was made to the peninsula of Ras Ushairiq to Al Zubarah's west. The material of the fort may have been used for the construction of Al Zubarah Fort. GPS - 25.974, 51.043

### Al Zubarah Town

The abandoned town of Al Zubarah is a walled 61-hectare site stretching 1.5 km along a shallow bay. The larger UNESCO area extends beyond the town and fort and includes sea shallows and a hinterland. Visitors see a partially excavated 200-year-old town in a beach setting. The white sand comes from coral, with rocky outcrops and, offshore, several intertidal fish traps known as 'al maskar.' The University of Copenhagen has conducted excavations here.

Several species of land mammals can be found near Al Zubarah, including dromedaries and, very occasionally, sand gazelles. Foxes can also be found. Dugongs feed on seagrass, and common bottlenose dolphins hunt for fish in the sea.

Many birds can be found throughout the year, including the Socotra Cormorant, which might be seen on Umm Jatila Island off the north of Al Zubarah. Osprey might be seen hunting for fish in the lagoon. In winter, Greater Flamingos gather on the mudflats. Reptiles, including Uromastyx aegyptia, Yellow Spotted Agama and Sand Vipers, are found inland. In the sea, other reptiles are found, including Green Turtle and Hawksbill Turtles.

South of the fort and archaeological site lies a 1.8 km canal – which was replaced by walls or barriers. This canal is believed to have served Qalat Al Murair, the ruined fort located south of Al Zubarah Fort, on the southern side of the road. Much of the southern area outside the town's walls is Sabkha, which will be wet and, in places, slippery after rain or very high tide.

The site of Al Zubarah, as a settlement, probably dates to around 1766, with the arrival of the Al Khalifa sheikhs, who originally lived in Kuwait between 1716 and 1732. Towards the end of the 18th century, the Al Khalifa turned their focus to Bahrain, while the Al Saud family of central modern Saudi Arabia gained increasing control over the general region of eastern Arabia. In 1811, the town was attacked by the Al Said rulers of Oman. Some rebuilding of Al Zubarah took place in the mid-1820s, but by then, settlements in the general region of modern Doha were becoming increasingly important. Between 1820 and around the mid 1860s a pearling community occupied the smaller inner town. The size of the individual houses, and the quality of the construction was less than in the original town. The conflict between Bahrain and Qatar diminished Al Zubarah's importance as a settlement and increased it as a symbol of control. By 1908, it was reported to be abandoned. The fort of Al Zubarah was a final statement of control by the Al Thani rulers of Qatar, when it was completed in 1938. UNESCO listing was made in 2013.

Elevated boardwalks run through the excavated residential areas, protecting the archaeology and giving visitors a better perspective.

Al Zubarah has two town walls. The inner wall, about 1km in length and with 11 towers, dates to after the massive naval bombardment in 1811 ordered by Sayyid Sa'id bin Sultan of Oman, which left the town largely burned to the ground. The latter population occupied a smaller footprint. The original outer wall was presumably much higher than its current height. Generally, it's now about 0.5 to 1 meters wide and about 2.5km long, with 22 towers.

A 'northern house' stands in Al Zubarah's north and is believed to be a merchant's house. Originally a two-storey building with numerous rooms and several staircases, this design was typical: private family accommodations were on the upper floor and public rooms and warehousing on the ground level. After a possible attack on the town by Oman, the house appears to have been repurposed on a smaller footprint.

The souq is next to the beach. This meant that goods could be loaded and unloaded from boats without a long walk to the buildings. Dates were stored here, and trade as far away as Japan took place, as shown by Arita porcelain (Hizen ware) from the late 17th and 18th centuries. Whether this trade was direct or, more probably, indirect is unknown.

Excavations Al Zubarah

Just northwest of the souq stands a small fort, overlooking deeper water to its southwest, possibly an open harbour. Between this fort and the Ras Ushairiq peninsula to the west, British warships likely sank many dhows in 1895; these vessels were thought to have massed for an attack on Bahrain. In the north of the town, another mosque may exist. Farther north, the outer town wall extends about 50m into the sea, forming a barrier against ships grounding on the shallow offshore reefs in northern Al Zubarah.

The walk continues south toward the 'palatial compounds' in southeast Al Zubarah. These fortified compounds are square; the larger stands against the southern outer wall. Measuring over 100m per side, with a tower at each corner, it was almost self-contained, featuring date fruit stores and a hammam. The walls were plastered with typical Arabic decorative features, also showing Persian and Indian influences. A smaller fortified compound, also called a palatial compound, sits northeast of the larger one, measuring only 60m per side with square corner towers. Between the two compounds stood a mosque that collapsed in 1965; photos taken before its collapse show its columns and arches.

A residential area surrounds the palatial compound. Unlike older Arab towns, this area has a grid-like street layout perpendicular to the outer wall. The settlement appears planned, with most housing of the courtyard type.

Although Al Zubarah is a UNESCO site and its fort is an iconic Qatari structure, the area is not touristy. It is possible you could be the only visitor there.

Rough GPS: 25.977, 51.029. Located on the Al Shamal Road northwest of Doha. No public transport available.

Under Qatar's Law of Antiquities, it is a criminal offence to excavate, remove antiquities, or damage any historical site without Qatar Museums' permission.

Visitor Information (2026 Update) **Entry Cost:** Free for residents and visitors (as of early 2026). A complimentary ticket is provided for visitor tracking. **Hours:** Saturday-Thursday 09:00-17:00; Friday 12:30-17:00. **Important:** The final entry to the archaeological site is at **15:30**. The visit to the Al Zubarah Archaeological Town remains a managed experience that involves a specific transition from the Fort to the town ruins. In early 2026, the protocol for visiting is as follows: The Shuttle and Access You cannot drive your own vehicle into the 61-hectare town site. Instead, the Al Zubarah World Heritage Site Visitor Centre (GPS 25.977, 51.046) serves as the base of operations and the Visitor Centre – check here in case changes have been made. A dedicated shuttle bus departs from here to transport visitors into the Al Zubarah site.

Once you arrive at the town ruins, you explore via a recently constructed elevated walkway (boardwalk). This protects the fragile archaeological layers, which are mostly composed of soft limestone and coral, from foot traffic.

The Guided vs Self-Guided Experience. The "guided" nature of the visit has become more streamlined. Qatar Museums frequently offers free guided tours departing from the Visitor Centre. These are highly recommended as the guides explain the "invisible" history of the covered-up excavations and the significance of the walling heights. While guided tours are encouraged, visitors are often permitted to walk the 2km boardwalk loop independently during standard operating hours, provided they arrive before the cut-off. The last shuttle to the town ruins typically departs at 15:30. This ensures visitors have enough time to complete the loop before the site officially closes and the sun sets over the Gulf. The town loop is approximately 2km and takes about 45-60 minutes in full sun. Save the Fort interior for after the town visit, as the Fort stays open until

17:00, whereas the town access closes by 15:30. The southern areas are primarily Sabkha (salt flats); stay on the marked tracks, as the ground becomes dangerously slippery when damp. **GPS:** 25.977, 51.046 (Fort) | 25.977, 51.029 (Town Ruins) **Public Transport:** There is no practical public transport.

*Courtyard House Zubarah*

## Al Reem Biosphere Reserve and Rawdat Al Numan
The Al Reem Biosphere Reserve is Qatar's largest protected area,

covering approximately 10% of the nation's landmass. This vast, sun-scoured expanse in the northwest stretches from the heritage landscapes of Al Zubarah in the north, east towards Al Ghuwayriyah, and southwest to the dramatic mesas of Zekreet.

The reserve is a geological mosaic, featuring limestone cliffs, mesas, and gravel plains that give way to coastal sabkhas (salt flats) and shallow marine waters. In early 2026, the reserve remains a critical "living laboratory" where human development and ecological preservation attempt a delicate balance. Despite its desolate appearance, the area contains oil and gas infrastructure, traditional villages, and the recently opened "Our Habitas Ras Abrouq" - an eco-luxury resort that highlights the region's shift toward "strategic tourism." A central feature of the reserve is the Rawda (plural *Rawdat*), a term translating to "meadow that occurs after rain." These natural depressions collect runoff and fine sediment, creating pockets of life in an otherwise arid plateau.

**Rawdat Al Numan:** This is the reserve's most verdant inland sector. It is characterised by scattered stands of the Thorn Acacia (*Acacia ehrenbergiana*) - locally known as Salam - and Sidra trees (*Ziziphus spina-christi*). To combat the "environmental friction" caused by off-road driving and overgrazing, the Ministry of Environment and Climate Change has fenced off over 70 rawdas as of 2026. These enclosures allow the soil to recover and the native flora to flourish without the pressure of camel grazing.

**Fauna of the Reserve.** The terrestrial and marine ecosystems support a wide diversity of species: The High Ground: The Sand Gazelle (Gazella marica) and the Arabian Oryx (Oryx leucoryx) are the focal points of reintroduction programmes within the reserve. You may also encounter the Egyptian Spiny-tailed Lizard (Uromastyx aegyptia), a prehistoric-looking reptile that acts as a sentinel of the rocky wadis. The shallow seagrass beds of the western coast are a vital nursery for the Dugong (Dugong dugon). The coastal mudflats attract migratory birds, including the Greater Flamingo (Phoenicopterus roseus), which gathers in pink-hued clusters during the winter months.

Visitor Information - Al Reem is an environment for the "autonomous specialist" traveller. It offers a sense of profound isolation, particularly during the transition from day to night when the limestone mesas of Zekreet glow with an ochre light. There is no shade or freshwater available within the wilder parts of the reserve.

Visitors must be entirely self-sufficient. A 4x4 vehicle is mandatory for any excursion off the primary tarmac roads; the "sabkha" can appear solid while hiding a treacherous, damp interior that can mire an ill-equipped vehicle. **GPS:** 25.860, 51.080 (Rawdat Al Numan area) **Public Transport:** None.

### Ras Abrouq Peninsula

The Ras Abrouq peninsula is a windswept finger of land on Qatar's west coast, where the desert meets the sea. Its marked by a series of low limestone cliffs and turquoise shallows. The landscape is defined by "geological theatre" and, increasingly, a focus for "strategic tourism" that blends luxury with environmental stewardship. The peninsula is a rich repository of prehistoric human activity. Some limestone mesas are scattered with Neolithic flint tools and debitage (waste flakes from tool production). These hunters may have used the high ground as a vantage point to track game across the plains below. Excavations have uncovered fragments of Ubaid pottery (*Earthenware*) dating to the 5th and 4th millennia BC. Originating from southern Mesopotamia (modern-day Iraq), these ceramics are a testament to an ancient, sophisticated maritime trade network that linked the peninsula to the wider world over 7,000 years ago.

At the peninsula's northernmost tip sits a modern coastguard station. From the shoreline here, the proximity of Bahraini waters is startlingly clear - the international maritime border is a mere few hundred metres offshore. Entering Bahraini waters means that a person then becomes an illegal immigrant.

**East - West / West - East (Richard Serra).** Deep within the Abrouq Nature Reserve, the landscape is interrupted by four massive, vertical steel plates. This is the installation East-West/West-East by the late American sculptor Richard Serra (1938-2024), who also created the "7" sculpture at Doha's Museum of Islamic Art Park. The steel plates, each standing over 14m tall, are perfectly aligned along a desert corridor spanning over 1km. Despite their modern, industrial origin, they are at home in their bleak environment. Serra intended for the work to be interactive, though this has led to some visiting "kilroys" leaving graffiti on the steel. Qatar Museums periodically removes the signs of this activity, restoring their stark monolithic purity.

**Yardangs and Stone Huts** The area is famous for its Yardangs - mushroom-shaped limestone formations sculpted by the persistent *Shamal* winds at ground level.. These natural structures create a surreal, almost extraterrestrial tableau. Scattered across the mesas are small, primitive stone huts. While their origins are debated, they are believed to have served as temporary shelters for fishermen or as prehistoric burial cairns, blending seamlessly into the weathered white limestone.

### Film City (Ras Abrouq)

Film City is a 3,000sqm creation built in 2000 as a Qatari village set for a TV series. Against the stark Ras Abrouq landscape, its mud walls and thatched roofing evoke traditional Gulf architecture, possibly inspiring Doha's Souq Waqif. A stone's throw from the village gates lies a small, verdant oasis. This pocket of green is a frequent haunt for the Arabian Oryx (*Oryx leucoryx*), the Sand Gazelle (*Gazella marica*), and the Common Ostrich (*Struthio camelus*). While these animals may appear tame, they are roaming wild within the biosphere reserve and are not pets. Visitors, particularly those with children, should maintain a respectful "strategic distance" to avoid startling them. Visitor Information - A 4x4 is ideal to give better ground clearance. Entrance is controlled by Our Habitas Ras Abrouq Resort its suggested to contact this hotel for specific information on the day you want to visit. **Entry Cost:** QAR50 Entry may be denied without prior permission or during closures as determined by reserve management. The site **GPS:** 25.578, 50.847. **Public Transport:** None.

*Yardangs Zekreet*

By early 2026, the character of Ras Abrouq has shifted toward "low-density luxury." The northern reaches of the peninsula are now restricted due to the **Our Habitas Ras Abrouq Resort** www.ourhabitas.com/ras-abrouq, a somewhat congested villa-style property that serves as a base for premium eco-tourism. This development, along with the Brouq Desert Experience (a seasonal "activation") – it's intended to be a premium experience, often with a less than premium delivery. Surprisingly non-native Sika Deer (from East Asia) have been introduced here.

### Zekreet Fort

Northwest of the modern village of Zekreet lie the ruins of Zekreet Fort, a structure that once served as a "strategic anchor" on the western coast. Probably constructed in the first decade of the 19th century, it is likely entangled with the history of the naval tactician Rahmah ibn Jabir Al Jalahimi. Like the grander town of Al Zubarah, the fort appears to have fallen into disuse following the regional conflicts of 1811. In 1974, the site was surveyed by the archaeologist Beatrice de Cardi, who pioneered archaeology in The Gulf region. Her team's work provided the first modern documentary evidence of its historical significance. The fort follows a standard Qatari defensive with three circular corner towers and a single square tower, a configuration that allowed for a full 360-degree field of fire over the surrounding gravel plains. Traces of rooms are visible abutting the interior walls, indicating that the structure was not merely a military outpost but a communal refuge.

Today, little remains of the original masonry except for the modern consolidation of the walling, which provides a clear "skeletal footprint" of the original 19th-century layout only a few layers high. A small, simple mosque complex sits near the fort. This is from the early 20$^{th}$ century and today is a restored structure.

There are no facilities on-site. Although the drive through Zekreet village is brief, the terrain can be dusty; ensure you have water with you. From the Dukhan Highway (Route 30), take the exit north toward Zekreet. Drive through the village onto a dirt-track road; the fort is located approximately 500m north of the settlement. **Typical Hours:** 09:00-17:00 Saturday – Thursday and 12:30-17:00 Friday – however in practice there is nothing to stop a visit 24 hours a day. **Entry Cost:** Free. **GPS:** 25.490, 50.844 **Public Transport:** None.

### Zekreet Beach

Zekreet Beach is a shallow, sheltered lagoon situated on the western edge of the peninsula. This half-moon bay is defined by its calm, turquoise waters and a sense of coastal solitude that appeals to those seeking an unscripted encounter with the Gulf. The beach is bordered by the unique yardangs, which stand like stone sentinels guarding the bay.

*Socotra Cormorant*

In the winter months, you may spot the Socotra Cormorant (*Phalacrocorax nigrogularis*) diving in the shallows for a silver-scaled snack. There is Kitsurfing here https://saltykites.com/, in a less busy location than at Fuwairit. At low tide, the lagoon retreats significantly, exposing vast flats of damp sand and sea-grass. It is a striking sight, but one that requires a careful eye on the return of the tide to avoid being cut off. There are no retail outlets or petrol stations at the beach; the nearest services are in Zekreet village, which offers only basic provisions. **GPS:** 25.471, 50.849 **Public Transport:** None. The beach is a 90-minute drive from Doha via the Dukhan Highway (Route 30).

### Dukhan Beach and Water Sports Club

**Dukhan Beach** is near the industrial heart of western Qatar, yet its coastline offers some of the most accessible and family-friendly beaches on the leeward side of the peninsula. Unlike the rugged, 4x4-dependent tracks of Ras Abrouq, the shore here is served by tarmac roads, providing an easy way to get from the desert highway to the water's edge. The public beach at Dukhan is a well-maintained stretch of coast, easily identified by its cluster of Date Palms and permanent shade shelters. It is a popular retreat for those seeking a tranquil sunset over the Gulf. The main beach area is just the beginning; several kilometres of public shoreline extend both north and south, offering varying degrees of privacy. This is one of the few sites on Qatar's west coast where a saloon is all that's needed, as the beach sits adjacent to the Dukhan Corniche.

**The Dukhan Water Sports Club**, is a long-standing institution that serves as a social hub for the local industrial community. The club is a "maritime oasis" equipped with a swimming pool, jet ski rentals, and direct sea access for various sailing activities. Its a private membership club primarily for employees of Qatar Energy and associated companies.

Visitor Information - Beach is open 24 hours. **Entry Cost:** Public beach is Free; Club is Membership/Invitation only. Follow the Dukhan Highway (Route 30) to its western terminus. The beach is accessible via the Dukhan Corniche. **GPS (Public Beach):** 25.414, 50.759 **Public Transport:** This area (to the town only) is accessible by public bus. **Buses R707 and R727** operate from the Industrial Area Bus Station directly to Dukhan, and 708 and 709 from Education City via Mall of Qatar .

CENTRAL QATAR

**Retaj Salwa Resort & Spa**

Situated near the Rawdat Rashid interchange, approximately 45 minutes southwest of Doha, the Retaj Salwa Resort & Spa is a sprawling, low-rise resort with gardens, offering 168 rooms and villas. The resort's identity is is linked to its extensive water features. It boasts a massive 4,000 sqm outdoor swimming pool and a private "lazy river" and a comprehensive spa offering traditional and modern treatments.

The resort is a convenient base for observing the local fauna attracted to the nearby Abu Nakhla wetlands. These lagoons, formed by treated water, have become an accidental paradise for migratory birds. **GPS:** 25.156, 51.289 **Public Transport:** None. **Contact:** +974 4428 6000 | retajsalwaresort.com

**Heenat Salma**

in central Ash Shahaniyah, Heenat Salma is a 50-hectare multidisciplinary project. Transformed from a conventional plot in 2018 by the Caravane Earth Foundation, the farm operates as a permaculture centre of excellence. The farm cultivates over 30 varieties of crops, including lemons (*Citrus limon*) as well as a plantation of more than 1,500 date palms (*Phoenix dactylifera*). Visitors can engage with goats (*Capra hircus*) and sheep (*Ovis aries*), through milking and feeding activities that illustrate the relationship between animals and soil fertility. Immersive sessions are available in traditional crafts, including wood carving, wheel-thrown pottery, and the creation of herbal bundles and incense. Overnight guests are hosted in tents positioned around a central courtyard with a communal fire. Visitor Information - **Opening Hours:** Winter season; daily 08:00 - 22:00. **Entry Cost:** Farm tours are priced between QAR 50 and QAR 570 per person, with additional costs for wellness sessions, workshops, and overnight lodging. The farm is approximately a 45-minute drive from Doha. **GPS:** 25.398, 51.260 **Contact:** +974 5096 0007 | heenatsalma.earth

### Dahl Al Misfir and Dahl Al Mudhlim

Qatar's largest and deepest accessible natural cave is **Dahl Al Misfir**, also known as Musfur Cave. Its actually a sinkhole, plunging approximately 40 metres into the central limestone plateau, it is on of the odd corners of the peninsula's geology. The 'cave' was formed hundreds of thousands of years ago by the dissolution of gypsum and limestone layers, creating a chamber that remains significantly cooler than the surface. The cave is renowned for its fibrous gypsum deposits, which can occasionally emit a faint, otherworldly phosphorescent glow in the darkness. Reaching the bottom requires navigating a steep, potentially dangerous scree slope; the terrain is loose rocks and fine dust, making sturdy footwear essential. **Accessibility:** Located near the Mekainis Interchange off Salwa Road (GPS: 25.174, 51.211), the site is enclosed by a protective fence to manage visitor entry, though no official entry fee is currently required.

**Dahl Al Mudhlim** is a smaller, less-frequented sinkhole located approximately 6km south of Dahl Al Misfir. It is part of a larger network of karst features and potential sinkholes that dot the Mekainis region. While smaller than its neighbour, it offers a similar glimpse into the "subterranean plumbing" of the desert landscape. The site is located roughly at GPS 25.123, 51.228, near the Mekainis Interchange. Like much of the surrounding desert, there is no public transport access.

The sinkholes have a potentially hazardous scree slope leading to its base. Although the area is fenced off for safety and conservation, the site remains a point of interest for experienced desert travellers.

### Al Karana bird watching

A green enclave within the arid central plateau the the bird watch spot of Al Karana. This 4 km² site represents a masterclass in ecological reclamation; once a dumping ground for industrial waste, it was thoroughly remediated in 2020 to create a series of four artificial lagoons, part of the adjacent sewage plant. It offers a shimmering contrast to the surrounding gravel desert, where treated water now sustains a thriving avian population along the African-Eurasian Flyway. The lagoons are a critical stopover for over 50 species, most notably the **Greater Flamingo** (*Phoenicopterus roseus*), which gathers in pink-hued clusters during winter. Birdwatchers frequently record the **Osprey** (*Pandion haliaetus*),

**Purple Heron** (*Ardea purpurea*), and **Water Pipit** (*Anthus spinoletta*), alongside resident breeders such as the **Black-winged Stilt** (*Himantopus himantopus*) and **Little Grebe** (*Tachybaptus ruficollis*). The lagoons are accessible via a standard saloon car, located approximately 60 kilometres southwest of Doha. Qatar is using its treated wastewater for urban landscaping and roadside irrigation through an integrated national pipeline network. Consequently, water levels at managed sites like **Al Karana** fluctuate by design, with significant drops during the peak summer months when the city's greenery needs more irrigation.

**Visitor Facilities:** None Practical Information: - **GPS:** 24.985, 51.044 **Opening Hours:** Open 24 hours (Daylight visits are recommended)

## Mall of Qatar and The Grand Zone

On the Dukhan Highway, west of Doha is the Mall of Qatar, a vast retail and lifestyle destination housing nearly 500 outlets. By early 2026, the mall had evolved beyond a simple shopping centre into a comprehensive "lifestyle precinct" known as The Grand Zone. The mall features the **Welcome Park** at its main entrance, showcasing the world's first "sky fountain." High-end dining is available in the luxury precinct, including six signature restaurants with retractable roofs for al fresco dining during cooler months. **Al Rayyan Hotel Doha:** For those seeking an overnight stay, the Al Rayyan Hotel Doha, Curio Collection by Hilton, is attached directly to the mall. It offers 201 rooms and high-end wellness facilities, including three outdoor pools.

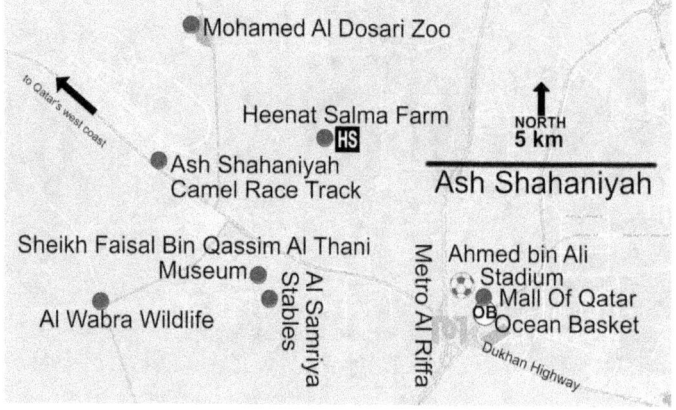

The mall is uniquely integrated with **Sherborne Qatar**, a flagship British school (ages 3-18) located within the Grand Zone. This provides a rare urban mix of education and commerce. Note that the **Sherborne Qatar Preparatory School** is located approximately 4km to the east in **Bani Hajer**.

## Ahmad bin Ali Stadium (Al Rayyan)

The Ahmad bin Ali Stadium, colloquially known as the Al Rayyan Stadium, stands as the "gateway to the desert" on the western edge of the metropolitan area. Inaugurated on Qatar National Day in 2020, its glowing "Naqish" facade features intricate patterns reflecting Qatari culture. A key venue for the 2022 FIFA World Cup, the stadium's capacity reached approximately 45,000 during the tournament. In early 2026, the venue continues its legacy by hosting matches for the **2025 FIFA Arab Cup** and as the home ground for **Al Rayyan SC** and **Al Kharitiyath SC**.

Visitor Information The area is exceptionally well-served by public transport. The **Al Riffa - Mall of Qatar Station** is the western terminus of the **Green Line Metro**, with a direct pedestrian bridge connecting the station to the mall. **Opening Hours (Mall):** Generally 10:00 - 22:00 (Sundays - Wednesdays) and 10:00 - 24:00 (Thursdays - Saturdays). **Entry Cost:** Free access to the mall - the stadium may be free or a small charge **GPS:** 25.330, 51.341 **Public Transport:** Green Line Metro (Al Riffa Station).

### Ash Shahaniyah Camel Race Track

Between November and March, the Ash Shahaniyah Camel Race Track offers a compelling glimpse into a sport that is a cornerstone of part of Qatari identity. Supported extensively by the government, camel racing is more than a pastime; it is almost a closed-loop within Qatar's economy and certainly cultural pillar. The most prestigious events see the camel's competing for significant rewards, including the coveted "Golden Sword" presented by the Amir.

*Robot Jockeys on racing Camels*

The facility features five tracks of varying lengths. In a modern twist on tradition, the camels are steered by small robot jockeys rather than human riders. The real drama, however, often unfolds on the parallel car tracks. There, trainers pursue their camels in 4x4 vehicles with a focused intensity, shouting tactical encouragement to their mechanical jockeys and camels via walkie-talkies – presumably both a fluent in Arabic. The start line is located to the right of the entrance road. Because the oval tracks cover several kilometres, spectators can watch the initial charge before heading to the grandstand on the left to witness the finish. Entry to the grandstand is at no charge. High-profile races often draw senior members of the ruling family and significant crowds – dress at least smart casual. The morning and afternoon light provide exceptional opportunities to photo the "dust and speed" of the event.

**Logistics:** There are toilets in the grandstand, major events will usually have extra facilities. There are small cafes and supermarket close to the grandstand. In the general area of the racetracks (especially against the highway) there are innumerable camel pens (azab) where camels are stabled. Early mornings and late afternoons is the time when they are exercised – most of the handlers are from Bangladesh, Pakistan, and Sudan.

Visitor Information - Races and training sessions typically occur in the early mornings or late afternoons. For specific race schedules, visit www.hejen.qa **GPS:** 25.402, 51.205 **Public Transport:** Take the **Green Line Metro** to **Al Riffa Station**, then use **Buses R708 or R709**.

### Sheikh Faisal Bin Qassim Al Thani Museum

The cabinet of curiosities collected by Sheikh Faisal Bin Qassim Al Thani, was opened in 1998. This private institution houses a colossal collection that spans millions of years - from Jurassic fossils to the motorised marvels of the 20th century. For the visitor, the museum is arranged entirely on a single floor, stretching over 200m. This horizontal layout allows for a seamless, if somewhat overwhelming, transition between the dozen themed halls that showcase over 40,000 artefacts. A dedicated hall houses a fleet of some 400 roadworthy classic cars, motorcycles, and steam-powered vehicles, making it among the largest in the world. These include the earliest mechanical transport used in Qatar; there are rumours that there are another 600 vehicles owned by Sheikh Faisal. A significant highlight is the complete interior of an authentic 19th-century

Damascene house, reassembled to simulate a living residence. The galleries house thousands of unique pieces, including rare manuscripts, a dedicated Quran room, an expansive weaponry section and over 700 hand-woven carpets, enough to blanket a stadium, alongside coins and currency from across four continents.

*Sheikh Faisal Bin Qassim Al Thani Museum*

Outside is the **Leaning Mosque of Qatar** with a 27-metre-tall minaret and a main body that both incline at a striking 20-degree angle.

**Al Samriya Estate**

The museum sits within the wider Al Samriya Estate, allowing a cultural visit to be combined with an encounter with the local environment. The estate includes a dedicated reserve for the Arabian Oryx (Oryx leucoryx), which can be viewed as part of the visitor experience.

Museum Visitor Information - **Opening Hours:** Mon - Thu 09:00 - 17:00; Fri 14:00 - 19:00; Sat 10:00 - 18:00 (Closed Sundays). **Entry Cost:** QAR50 for adults. Guided tours are available for an additional QAR25. **GPS:** 25.351, 51.262 **Website** www.fbqmuseum.org

**Public Transport:** Take the **Green Line Metro** to **Al Riffa Station**, followed by **Bus 708 or 709**.

*Leaning Mosque of Qatar*

### Al Samriya Riding School,

A British Horse Society (BHS) approved equestrian centre, Al Samriya Riding School is located within the Al Samriya Estate, near the Sheikh Faisal Bin Qassim Al Thani Museum. The school offers a structured learning environment that emphasises both riding technique and comprehensive horse care. Training is available for all ages and skill levels. Beyond the arenas, the school offers expansive trail rides that wind through the estate's farm and the Oryx reserve

Visitor Information - **Lesson Windows:** Typically 07:00 - 11:00 and 13:00 - 15:00 daily (subject to seasonal adjustment and booking). **Cost:** Lessons start from approximately QAR 185 for group sessions; private lessons and specialised workshops vary. **Location:** Off the Dukhan Highway, Ash Shahaniyah (near the Al Samriya Estate). **GPS:** 25.351, 51.262

**Public Transport:** Accessible via **Buses R708 and R709** from the **Al Riffa - Mall of Qatar Station** (Green Line Metro) – taxi for final leg. **Contact:** +974 4490 2359 alsamriyaestate.com/riding

### Mohamed Al Dosari Zoo and Game Reserve

The Mohamed Al Dosari Zoo is a private facility that offers a glimpse into an older, less refined era of animal display. Set in the manner of a mid-20th-century menagerie, the zoo is a popular local destination for weekend picnics and barbecues. The collection includes the **Arabian Oryx** (*Oryx leucoryx*), the **Arabian Wolf** (*Canis lupus arabs*), and several **Cheetahs** (*Acinonyx jubatus*), alongside a variety of birds and reptiles.There is a small museum housing maritime and cultural artefacts, though these are secondary to the animal displays. Visitor Information -

**Hours:** Daily 07:00 - 19:00 (Closing times often fluctuate with sunset). **Entry Cost:** QAR10 It is advisable to have small change available. **Navigation:** Located off the Dukhan Highway, take the exit immediately before the Ash Shahaniyah Camel Race Track. The final approach is well-signposted but dusty. **GPS:** 25.440, 51.224 **Public Transport:** None. **Contact:** +974 4490 8785 | AlDosariZoo@Hotmail.com

SERVICE PROVIDERS - TOURS, EVENTS

**Tour Providers**

A terrific way to see the city is by taking an air tour around Doha - they do have restrictions on the airspace they can fly in, so some places are off-limits. If you have a choice of times - sunset is a magical option - when the lights start coming on over West Bay. **Qatar Flying Club** (www.qatarflyingclub.net) offers short fixed-wing flights. The well-established **Gulf Helicopters** (www.gulfhelicopters.com) provides helicopter flights and photo tours. In all cases, booking several days in advance is suggested. Some experiences are private to you - others are usually shared with other passengers. Transport to the place of departure is your responsibility - it may be in the central area of Qatar at Um Al Shkot Airfield (Al Khor Airfield), Ash Shafallahiyah 25.696 51.361 (60km from central Doha). **Asfary www.asfary.com** +974 5543 4313.offers several flying experiences, including Hot Air Balloon (with a small basket rather than a large one), Paragliding, Gyrocopter with a pilot, Helicopter, and small Plane. There are some weight restrictions on Paragliding and the Gyrocopter. Check for any extra flying restrictions if there are security alerts in Qatar.

Several companies offer game fishing as a private activity (not a group program). Qatar's game fishing is an excellent way to enjoy cooler sea temperatures and, usually, not too rough seas. Equipment and bait are supplied; you need to bring your passport. You have a chance of catching sea bass, tuna, or hamour (grouper). Much of the fishing from Doha is between Banana Island and off Al Wakrah. The start may be from the Dhow Harbour off the Corniche. Dhow cruises are available from **Arabian Adventures** www.arabianadventuresqatar.com (possibly Qatar's oldest tour operator), which also offers a complete range of tours - typically, you will join other people. Private yacht tours are also a possibility.

Seas are calmer in the morning; however, for sea tours that are simply for sightseeing or leisure, a good time is dusk, when you can take in the city lights of West Bay. **Dhow Harbour** Rough GPS - 25.295, 51.533 Street - Dhow Harbour off Corniche - Dhow Harbour /Public Transport - Bus 76, 777 Metro Gold Line Souq Waqif

**Blue Pearl** offers a range of land and sea activities suitable for all ages. Kite Surfing, Stand Up Paddleboarding (SUP), Kayaking, Fat-biking in Doha and around the city, and wilderness camping and other eco-activities. Rough GPS - 25.369, 51.548 Street - off Lusail Expressway - The Pearl No public transport - Contacts - +974 6660 2830 hello@bluepearlexperience.com www.bluepearlexperience.com

**National Cruise** - Cruises in a traditional dhow around the bay at Doha. Cruises can include meals; on some dhows, a table-dining experience is offered. An option is an evening cruise that takes in the lights of the skyscrapers on West Bay. Other tour companies are available. Private cruises are also available. National Cruise also deals through agents - and has various departure points - ask for details. Head Office Rough GPS - 25.297, 51.550 Street - access road to the Ol Port Cruise Terminals (they have relocated here from the Dhow Harbour on the Corniche) Dhow Harbour off Corniche - Dhow Harbour /Public Transport - Bus 76, 777 Metro Gold Line Souq Waqif - Contacts - +974 6600 0926 or +974 7799 9666 sales@nationalcruise.com www.nationalcruise.com/

**Doha Bus** - Group Bus tours throughout Qatar - a 24 hop-on hop-off operation, including Souq Waqif (look for the Kiosk on Bank St, etc.). If you have two or more people in your party, it's worth comparing the cost of private tours by other companies. A different type of bus venture is offered as a 4x4 vehicle into the sand dunes south of Doha. Rough GPS - 25.314, 51.5213 Street - Burj Al Mana, Corniche, West Bay (relocated from Doha Expressway) Contacts - +974 4442 2444 hello@dohabus.com www.dohabus.com

**Arabian Adventures** offers a complete range of inbound tourism services and is possibly the oldest inbound tour operator in Qatar. From a morning at the races to full-day city tours or an overnight in their camp, it's possible to pick & mix from their offering. Rough GPS 25.283, 51.532 Al Asmakh St, Doha, Qatar

+974 55534233 info@arabianadventures.com.qa https://arabianadventures.com.qa/ www.arabianadventuresqatar.com/

**Falcon Tours** - City Tour, Desert Safari, Dhow and Game Fishing, Yacht - Rough GPS - 25.200, 51.469 Street - Street 964, Umm Seneem, Doha, Qatar Contacts - +974 3144 0129 info@falcontoursqatar.com www.falcontoursqatar.net (www.falcontoursqatar.com)

**Golden Adventures Qatar** - City Tours, Tours to northern & western Qatar, Desert Safari Typical hours and cost - as per request Rough GPS - 25.299,51.418 Street - off Al Shafi Street - Contacts - +974 3111 0484 info@goldenadventuresqatar.com www.goldenadventuresqatar.com

**Qatar Inbound Tours** - Tours throughout Qatar, including Desert Safari, with optional overnights in the desert and Dhow trips. Rough GPS - 25.269,51.515 Street - Ali bin Abi Talib St / Rawabi St Contacts - +974 7734 1200 info@inboundtoursqatar.com www.inboundtoursqatar.com

**Qatar International Tours** (was Qatar International Adventures) - City tours, Desert Safari, Dhow Cruise, Game Fishing, Helicopter. In mid-summer, Whale Sharks appear off the Qatari coast - ask if trips to search them out are possible, Rough GPS - 25.270, 51.517 Street - 1st Floor, Office # 7, 16 Al Rawabi St - Rawdat Al Khail (Ali bin Abi Talib - off C Ring Road) Public Transport - Bus 602 from Msheireb Bus Station Contacts - +974 4455 3954 info@qittour.com https://qittour.com/ /

**Q-Explorer** - A range of programs in Qatar; essentially, Q-Explorer offers most of what Qatar can provide, including a variety of City Tours, Desert Safaris, Kayaking, Scuba, and Sea Excursions. Rough GPS - 25.318, 51.528 Street - Doha Tower, Al Corniche - West Bay Public Transport - Metro Red Line West Bay - Contacts - +974 4472 5146 info@q-explorer.com www.q-explorer.com

Qatari companies tend to relocate their offices surprisingly often, not for any ulterior motive but simply because it's a normal practice in Qatar & the rest of the Gulf. Rents, which typically are a single year contract, can fluctuate considerably from year to year, both up and down. If a business is a tenant, it often makes financial sense to relocate. If you want to visit an office, always check the location before the visit. Also, company name changes may happen - this is likely to fit with the extremely bureaucratic government regulations.

**Regular Events In Qatar**

## January

**Marmi Festival (Qatar International Falcons and Hunting Festival)**

Location: Sabkhat Marmi, Sealine. GPS 24.862, 51.510

What it offers: A near month-long festival celebrating Qatar's rich falconry heritage. It is a cornerstone of the nation's cultural calendar, featuring numerous competitions showcasing the skill of birds and falconers, heritage displays, and educational programmes about this traditional sport.

*Al Gannas Katara*

Do not attempt to locate the site without exact details from Al Gannas based in Katara. Contact: Main Office Line: +974 4408 1303 (This is the "Reception" desk for the society). •Official WhatsApp: +974 5544 0554 Alternative Support: +974 4408 1490 www.instagram.com/algannas_qa/

## February

Qatar Total Energies Open Location: Khalifa International Tennis and Squash Complex, Doha, GPS 25.312, 51.516. A prestigious WTA 1000 women's tennis tournament that annually attracts the world's top-ranked female players for a week of elite competition. The ATP Men's event usually follows.

Al Adaid Desert Challenge Location: Starts near Sealine and finishes at the 'Inland Sea' of Khor Al Adaid. A gruelling, internationally recognised endurance event for mountain bikers and trail runners. Participants race across the stunning desert landscape to reach the unique inland sea, a UNESCO-recognised natural reserve. Website: qatarcyclistscenter.com Race Management Portal: z-adventures.org Email: qrs@z-adventures.org Telephone: +974 5033 8622 https://www.instagram.com/aladaid.qa/

Al Shaqab International Equestrian Competition Location: Al Shaqab, Education City, Doha. GPS 25.310, 51.442 As part of the prestigious Commercial Bank "CHI AL SHAQAB" Presented by Longines, this is a world-class equestrian event. It is one of only five CHI ('Concours Hippique International') events in the world and the only one in the region, featuring top-tier international competitions in show jumping, dressage, and para-dressage.

**March**

HH The Amir's Sword Equestrian Festival This takes place in February (though Ramadhan does alter the timing). Location: Qatar Racing and Equestrian Club (QREC), Al Rayyan. 25.278, 51.428 What it offers: This is Qatar's premier horse racing event, culminating in the prestigious race for H.H. The Amir's Sword. The festival attracts elite international and local jockeys competing for a staggering USD10 million prize pool. The ambiance is a blend of high-stakes sport (no betting) and traditional hospitality. While the horse racing takes place at the Al Rayyan turf and sand tracks, the festival's showjumping arm is staged at the Al Shaqab arena. The Al Rayyan grandstand is compact, providing an intimate view of the finishing straight, with temporary seating added to accommodate the surge of spectators. The event is accessible to the public via ticketed entry through https://qrec.gov.qa/ Ticket Prices: While some zones are free, premium grandstand seating is typically priced modestly (approx. QAR50.00), though for 2026, many community-focused zones are open-access to encourage a family-friendly location. VIP tickets may be available.

HH The Amir's Sword Camel Racing Festival Location: Al Shahaniya Camel Racetrack. GPS 25.403, 51.205 The final is either late February or early March. Considered the pinnacle of the camel racing season in Qatar, this festival draws participants from across the Gulf. It features high-stakes races with valuable prizes, including the coveted Golden Sword, celebrating a core part of Gulf heritage.

MotoGP (Qatar Airways Grand Prix of Qatar): at Lusail International Circuit. This is a massive draw for international racing fans.

**May**

Amir Cup Final (Football) Location: Varies, often held at one of Qatar's new major stadiums like Khalifa International Stadium or Al Janoub Stadium. The final match of Qatar's most prestigious knockout football tournament. The event is a major highlight of the domestic sporting calendar, known for its passionate crowds and festive celebration, often including a grand pre-match ceremony.

Doha International Book Fair Location: Doha Exhibition and Convention Centre (DECC) GPS 25.322, 51.530 A major cultural event that brings together hundreds of publishing houses from around the world. It's a celebration of literature, offering a vast selection of books, author meet-and-greets, workshops, and cultural seminars for all ages.

### September

S'hail - Katara International Hunting and Falcons Exhibition Location: Katara Cultural Village, Doha. A premier exhibition for hunting and falconry enthusiasts. It showcases the latest hunting equipment, falconry gear, and outdoor supplies. The event also features falcon auctions, art displays, and activities that honour this deeply rooted aspect of Qatari culture. https://s-hail.qa/

s-hail@katara.net

### October / November

Qatar International Boat Show Location: Old Doha Port GPS 25.298, 51.552 What it offers: A luxury event showcasing the latest in the marine industry. Visitors can view a wide range of boats, from small vessels to superyachts, and explore marine-related accessories and technologies in a vibrant, waterfront setting. https://boatshowqatar.com/

### November

Formula 1 Qatar Grand Prix Location: Lusail International Circuit. What it offers: A thrilling weekend of high-speed motorsport as Qatar hosts a round of the FIA Formula One World Championship. The event attracts global attention and features the world's best drivers competing under the circuit's impressive floodlights, accompanied by fan zones and entertainment. www.formula1.com/en/racing/2026/qatar / www.lcsc.qa

### December

Qatar National Day Location: Celebrated nationwide, with the main parade on the Doha Corniche on 18 December. What it offers: The country's foremost national celebration, marking Qatar's unification. The day is filled with patriotic events, including a grand military parade, spectacular air shows, dazzling fireworks, and extensive cultural festivities at venues like Darb Al Saai.

**Variable Dates** (Often Spring/Winter)

Souq Waqif and Souq Al Wakrah Festivals Location: Souq Waqif in Doha and Souq Al Wakrah. What it offers: These historic markets host various festivals throughout the year, most notably the Spring Festival. These events bring the souqs to life with street performances, cultural displays, family entertainment, traditional food stalls, and a vibrant, festive atmosphere that attracts locals and tourists alike. The specific timing can vary, but they are a regular and popular fixture.

## CHAPTER 3
# HOTELS AND RESTAURANTS
## OPTIONS TO CONSIDER

**R**estaurants are grouped geographically. They are chosen to offer a reasonable meal, at their price, in that location, not to suggest any comparison with those in other locations. For example, in Al Ruwais (northern Qatar), Iskender Pasha is included; however, in Doha, other restaurants would squeeze it out. While Parisa might be included as a destination in any city.

In midsummer, or perhaps in Ramadhan, some better restaurants may close for a month or so. Business is down as higher-paid residents of Doha fly out for the period, and tourists & business people may not be visiting in hot weather. This closure allows the restaurants to give staff their holiday to match, so do check.

In Souq Waqif, a wide choice of restaurants will, in general, offer reasonable quality for the price & style. The government is likely the owner of the property where you will eat (they own the entire core and manage it through the Private Engineering Office), and they expect visitors to have a good meal, whatever the price. A similar situation in which the government or state-owned organisations own an area is found at Al Wakrah, Katara Cultural Village, Msheireb Downtown, and, to a slightly lesser extent, Lusail.

There is an excellent offering of restaurants in good hotels and standalone restaurants in Doha. So, if you do prefer a more traditional international dining experience, as found in a Western city, choose a restaurant in a better hotel or in Souq Waqif, Katara & The Pearl.

Increasingly, mid to high-end dining options use QR-Code

menus - a local SIM card with internet credit will help, though most will offer free wi-fi.

Restaurants in this book might be entirely local in appeal, or they may be 'tourist restaurants' - irrespective, they are worth considering. In many cases, local restaurants (by which I mean relatively simple, designed to appeal to the general population) offer freshly cooked food, often made to order.

They may be busy with **Talabat** www.talabat.com/qatar or **Snoonu** https://snoonu.com/ delivery drivers - your food may be fresher as a result of this additional volume. Within Talabat is the Talabat Mart for quick, but limited, supermarket deliveries. Snoonu offers a wider range of non-food delivery services, though it does not have the same reach within the restaurant market. While both services may be able to deliver to a hotel, have the delivery driver meet you by the main entrance to receive your fine-dining or local Karak tea as some hotels do have entrance restrictions. The Talabat app can also be used if you are dining at a restaurant for a general overview of the menu and very vocal reviews from actual customers.

Often these local restaurants have incredibly authentic cuisine, such as Pakistani, Turkish, and southern Indian – there customer base is from those countries. Unfortunately general hygiene may not be as high as McDonald's or 5* hotels, and service may be haphazard, if not seeming unhelpful or rude. After all, they do not have layers of management and head offices to lay down consistent or perhaps appropriate standards. However, away from tourist areas, the lower-cost options cater to the local population and absolutely depend on them returning day after day, so the combination of food, service, and price needs to work. As eating out is the norm for low-income non-national workers who may live in small dorm type bedrooms in vast areas of accommodation such as Mukaynis Compound at Barwa. They will have restricted access to communal kitchens, only unappealing company-provided meals which are delivered from distant kitchens, the potential customer base for in town restaurants is therefore is large, though their average client spend per head is low.

Consider how your stomach reacts when eating in new environments. For locals, a restaurant may be absolutely fine; for a visitor unused to the new range of bacteria, an upset stomach might result. This consideration would also apply to visitors to your own favourite dining option. Also, in small cafes, take note of how the payment/ordering/food service works. It might be that you pay at a till, then present the paper receipt to the food preparer and wait to receive your food. If you do not follow the restaurant's system, your food will never even be prepared.

**Hotels** are also listed geographically. Here, the intention is simply to show some choices and illustrate the range available in Qatar - and that not all are designed for Sheikhs. These hotels listings do not give an exhaustive critique. If you use a booking site or even a hotel's own website, you will see the very latest opinions of clients.

One very common issue with hotels in Doha is a lack of car parking - it's worth checking this if you intend to rely on your own hire car.

Again, as with restaurants properties in Souq Waqif, Al Wakrah, Katara Cultural Village, Msheireb Downtown, and, to a slightly lesser extent, Lusail will have a landlord who is either the government itself or a state-owned organisation.

The area from Msheireb - through Souq Waqif to the National Museum offers a broad selection of hotels at many price points. The advantage of this area is that you have Metro stations, such as Msheireb, Souq Waqif, and the National Museum, to use for transport. Around Msheireb and Souq Waqif - Park Hyatt and Al Najada Doha are worth looking at. A disadvantage of the hotels may be that they don't have have a beach, though there are some which do.

The star rating for hotels in Doha may be at odds with the actual experience received - luxury facilities and service worldwide have improved dramatically - and a 5* graded 15 years ago may fall short today. Hotel prices vary seasonally, and you may have a loyalty card with an international chain that can decide where you stay. The brand name 'international' hotels offer the most consistent service.

# HOTELS AND RESTAURANTS

Service may be patchy at the lower end of the price range, especially in hotels not part of an international group. In these hotels that are more than a few years old, the lack of maintenance starts to change their quality. In these lower-cost hotels, a change of manager also makes an immediate difference. With hotels, it's unlikely you will need to book well in advance if all you want is a room at a price point, except at peak periods like Eid & Christmas. The only exception is when you want a specific hotel.

It's quite possible that if you ask at the hotel front desk for a room, the rate through a booking site will be cheaper, or vice versa; choosing to book at the last moment does give the option to find out & perhaps negotiate - at the risk of not having any room available in a particular hotel. Inbound tourism has increased a lot since the World Cup (one of its purposes was achieved) - room occupancy % has risen to 72%. As this is an annual average, the rate in winter will likely be about 10% higher. In winter, consider booking in advance to get your preferred hotel room.

- (BI) Azraq
- (BI) Al Nahham Restaurant
- (BI) Q Lounge & Restaurant
- (BI) Riva
- (PP) Pak Pakwan
- (SB) Saravana Bhavan
- (SR) SMAT Restaurant
  - (XX) *RESTAURANTS*
  - (XX) *HOTELS*
- (AW) Alwadi Hotel
- (AW) Banana Island (Shangri-La Hotel)
- (CH) Century Hotel
- (FS) Fraser Suites Doha
- (GQ) Grand Qatar Palace Hotel
- (JH) Jouri Hotel
- (KH) Kingsgate Hotel
- (RE) Ramada Encore
- (SM) Saray Musheireb
- (SV) Sharq Village & Spa
- (TT) The Town Hotel
- (TH) Tourist Hotel

Major 5* hotels (& some others) and their restaurants will usually have alcohol available (the minimum age to drink alcohol in Qatar is 21 years old. An ID is often needed); Ramadhan does affect alcohol availability as the government reviews core Qatari values; elsewhere, alcohol is not available.

All hotels and restaurants rely on staff who work on contracts of a couple of years in Qatar, though some may stay longer. The result is that the hotels might struggle to maintain consistent standards amid staff churn. This is compounded by staff who may not have Arabic or English to a standard appropriate to the job, so misunderstandings might be common.

RESTAURANTS

Restaurants are rated by the dollar price (charges will be in QAR) of a typical lower-cost meal for a single person in that restaurant. Alcohol, which is available in some more expensive places, will add considerably to the cost.
   USD 1-4 *
   USD 5-9 **
   USD 9-13 ***
   USD 13-19 ****
   USD 19-25 *****
   USD 25 + ******

**CORNICHE, SOUQ WAQIF & CENTRAL DOHA**

   **IDAM** is a Michelin 1 Star restaurant within the Museum of Islamic Art. It offers contemporary French-Mediterranean cuisine with a touch of Arabian influence. After the World Cup was awarded to Qatar in 2010, IDAM may well have been opened in 2013 to ensure Doha would get that star for the for the World Cup - and 11 years after the restaurant's opening, a Michelin star was awarded in December 2024 - unfortunately, a couple of years late - but you can enjoy it.

   Typical cost range -***** Rough GPS 25.295, 51.538 Street - Eastern end of Al Corniche - Al Corniche Public Transport - Metro Gold Line Souq Waqif Typical hours 12:30-14:00 PM/19:00-21:00 (closed Fri & Sat - but open Wednesday)Contacts -https://idam.com+974 4422 4488

   **Bandar Aden** - Authentic, in all respects, with Yemeni food, meat and rice-based. The service is very patchy, and cleanliness is not ideal; however, the food is freshly prepared. Extremely popular. They must be getting something right. Ask for cutlery, or go Yemeni style: choose a meal on the floor indoors and use your right hand.

   Typical cost range - ** Rough GPS - 25.290, 51.533 Street - Abdullah Bin Jassim St, Public Transport - Metro Gold Line Souq Waqif Typical hours - 08:00-23:00 (Friday 12:30-23:00) - Contacts -

+974 44375503 / bandaraden@yahoo.com / http://www.bandaraden.com/

*Police horsemen - Souq Waqif*

**Shujaa Restaurant** - Small, and inexpensive; share a table with others - some patrons may have been eating here for over 50 years - it's that old. The food is loosely Lebanese in style. Meat-based dishes are available in the evening. This is a stone's throw away from the luxury of Parisa and just south of the more expensive Al Shurfa. Anticipate a rushed service that may not reach Basil Fawlty's style, but you might want to add some patience to your menu.

Typical cost range - ** Rough GPS - 25.289, 51.533 - Street - near Corniche in Souq Waqif Public Transport - Metro Gold Line Souq Waqif Typical hours - 16:00-midnight - Contacts - +974 5586 7895

**Al Shurfa Arabic Restaurant** - One of the more interesting views in Doha from this restaurant's upper-floor balcony, overlooking the Corniche and great after sunset. Middle Eastern food is paired with Arabic games and water pipes (also known as hookah/hubbly bubbly/, or shisha). One of two restaurants within the small Al Jumrok Hotel (Souq Waqif Boutique Hotels by Tivoli) - service can be lower than you'd like.

Typical cost range - *** Rough GPS - 25.289, 51.533 Street - off Al Corniche Public Transport - Metro Gold Line Souq Waqif Typical hours - 12:00-23:00 - Contacts - +974 4433 6666 / res.vswq@tivolihotels.com / www.tivolihotels.com/en/souq-waqif-al-jomrok-boutique-hotel

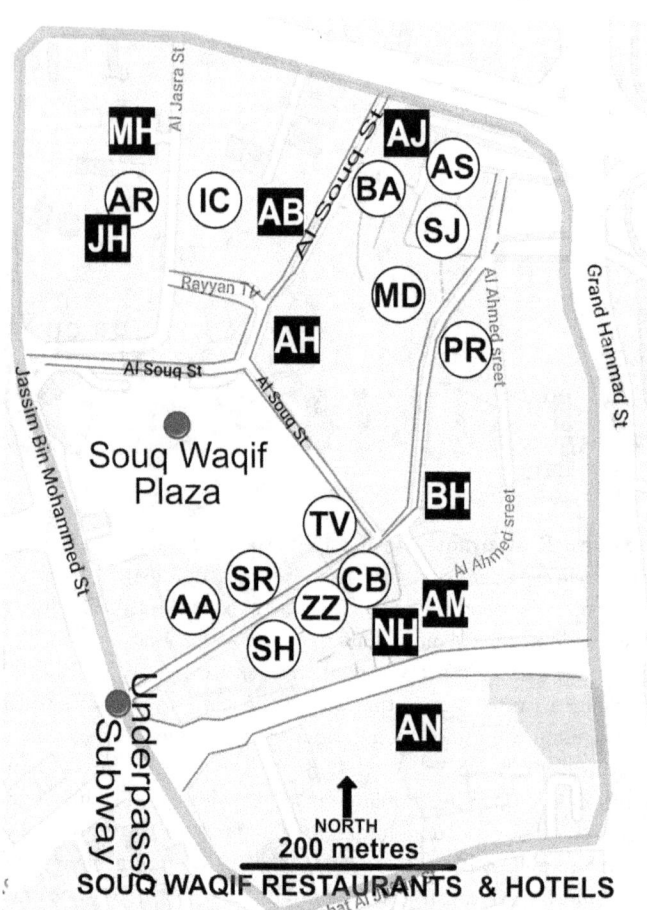

# HOTELS AND RESTAURANTS

- AA Al Adhamiyah
- SH Abu Shariha
- AS Al Shurfa
- AR Argan
- BA Bandar Aden
- CB Coffee Bean & Tea Leaf
- IC Icons Coffee
- MD Majlis Al Dama
- PR Parisa
- SR Saida Restraunt
- SJ Shujaa Restaurant
- TV The Village
- ZZ Zaatar w Zeit
- AB Al Bidda
- JH Al Jasra
- AJ Al Jomrok
- AM Al Mirqab
- AN Al Najada
- AH Arumaila
- BH Bismillah
- MH Musheireb
- NH Najd

**THE VILLAGE** - STYLISH DINING IN ONE OF THREE restaurant options here, just west of the Golden Thumb in Souq Waqif. Choose from Arabic, Iranian or Turkish cuisines. The other branch on the Salwa Rd (25.265308, 51.498197) is comparable - but not quite as attractively decorated.

Typical cost range - ***** Rough GPS - 25.287, 51.533 Street - Al Souq St Public Transport - Metro Gold Line Souq Waqif Typical hours - 08:00-23:30 - Contacts - +974 4411 1243 / www.thevillageqatar.com

**Argan** - This opulent restaurant in a modern Moroccan style offers an update on Moroccan cuisine, with a few international dishes thrown in. It's inside the Al Jasra Hotel, illustrating that the Tivoli group does have a remarkably good dining choice in Souq Waqif.

Typical cost range - ****** Rough GPS - 25.289, 51.531 Street - Al Jasra St, Doha, Qatar Public Transport - Metro Gold Line Souq Waqif Typical hours - 13:00-23:00 - Contacts - +974 4433 6872 / www.tivolihotels.com/en/souq-waqif-al-jasra-boutique-hotel/restaurants

**Parisa** is a destination in itself, with decor inspired by the Golestan Palace in Tehran, a UNESCO site. The Persian food is good, with reasonable service and, usually, light live music in the background. This is dining as an experience. Souq Waqif (also at Sharq Village).

Typical cost range - \*\*\*\*\*\* Rough GPS - 25.288, 51.533 Street - Inside Souq Waqif Public Transport - Metro Gold Line Souq Waqif Typical hours - 13:00 - 16:00/18:00-22:30 Contacts - +974 4441 1494 / dining.sharq@ritzcarlton.com / http://www.ritzcarlton.com/en/hotels/qatar/sharq-village/dining/parisa-souq-waqif

*Parisia*

**Jamavar**. This is a classic Indian-style experience, and since its opening in April 2021, it has excelled in its offerings, earning a Michelin 1 Star. Unusually for a haute cuisine Indian restaurant, it successfully features a range of pan-Indian flavours in its non-vegetarian menu. It's hoped you will feel as if you are dining in the Viceroy's House in New Delhi.

Typical cost ***** Rough GPS 25.318, 51.536 Sheraton Hotel grounds - Corniche. Typical Hours 12:30-16:00 / 19:00-midnight. Contacts +97444854535 https://jamavarrestaurants.com/indian-restaurant-doha/

**Saravanaa Bhavan** is a very well-established vegetarian restaurant (a major franchise from India). The food is authentically South Indian, with its presentation reflecting that. There are other branches in Doha.

Typical cost range - * Rough GPS - 25.283, 51.537 Street - Ras Abu Abboud St Public Transport - Metro Gold Line Souq Waqif or Red Line Al Doha Al Jadeda. Typical hours - 07:00-15:00/17:30-23:00 Friday 07:00-11:30 12:30-23:00 - Contacts - +974 4443 5557

**Al Adhamiyah** - This popular restaurant, south of Souq Waqif, serves meat-and-rice dishes in an Iraqi-style. Have one of their great fruit juices. It's possible to dine indoors or outside. The interior is exceptionally atmospheric, especially upstairs, with extensive use of a 'mashrabiya' style decoration. The service reflects how busy they are, and it's relatively low-cost.

Typical cost range - ** Rough GPS - 25.286, 51.532 Street - Ali Bin Abdullah St, Doha, Qatar Public Transport - Metro Gold Line Souq Waqif Typical hours - 12:30-midnight (Midnight) - Contacts - +974 4432 4326

**Lamazani Grill** - Busy, excellent value Persian-style kebab restaurant. The location and decor may not have the appeal of some other options, but a 30-minute walk from Souq Waqif does have its rewards (there are a few branches; all are comparable).

Typical cost range - *** Rough GPS - 25.280, 51.537 Street - Khaybar Rd off Ras Abu Abboud St Public Transport - Metro Gold Line Souq Waqif. Typical hours - 12:00-01:00 - Contacts - +974 4441 4554/ info@lamazani.com / www.lamazani.com

**Al Nahham Restaurant** at Banana Island Resort - Offering Lebanese / Gulf style Arabic food with indoor or outdoor dining overlooking the sea. The prices are generally justified by a premium experience.

**Azraq** at Banana Island - With various cuisines and an international buffet offering a wide selection of a typical Gulf-style main dining restaurant, though slightly skewed towards seafood. Choice of indoor or outdoor dining.

**Q Lounge & Restaurant** at Banana Island - Overlooking a pool, beach, sea and, in the distance, Qatar Airways taking off and landing at HIA, the Asian / Indian style food is also good.

**Riva** at Banana Island - A Mediterranean-themed restaurant with a remarkably good mix of taste and service.

Typical cost range of these Banana Island Anantara dining outlets - ****** Rough GPS - 25.295, 51.646 Street - Banana Island Public Transport - Metro Gold Line Souq Waqif & Ferry from Dhow Harbour 25.292135, 51.534429 Typical hours vary according to outlet - 13:00-17:00 / 19:00 - 17:00 - Contacts - +974 4040 5116 / fbreservations.adoh@anantara.com / www.anantara.com/en/banana-island-doha/

**Afghan Brothers** (one of seven branches; all are comparable) - Very Good value for Afghan (& Pakistani) food - meat-and-rice-based dishes veering to a Qatari style. Might only have spoons; ask for a knife and fork, or use hands. Takeaways are also available, as are assorted Afghan sweets.

Typical cost range - * Rough GPS - 25.273, 51.496 Street - Al Mirqab al Jadeed St Public Transport - Metro Joaan Metro 1km over busy rd. Typical hours - 07:00-01:00 - Contacts - +974 4488 8556 / Alnasr@afghanbrothers.com / www.afghanbrothers.com

**Layali** in Old Doha Port - A reasonable Lebanese restaurant; the food and port-side setting make this a worthwhile option.

Typical cost range - *** Rough GPS - 25.303, 51.549 Old Doha Port Typical hours -12:00-23:00 (Fri from 13:00-23:30) - Contacts - +974 4490 9517 / layali@adaragroup.co / www.layalirestaurantqatar.com/

**Pak Pakwan Restaurant** - This is a busy, small local restaurant with good Pakistani food. Fair-value grilled meats and curries are served with rice dishes and, usually, quick service.

Typical cost range - ** Rough GPS - 25.286, 51.523 Street - Al Diwan St Public Transport - Metro Msheireb (Hub) Typical hours - 11:30-23:30 (Friday 12:30-23:30) - Contacts - +974 3382 2399

**Turkey Central Restaurant** - A large, simple restaurant where you probably will be sharing a table with other diners. This is a well-established Turkish restaurant geared to high turnover business, especially with takeaways. It offers excellent value food, as does its nearby twin.

Typical cost range - ** Rough GPS - 25.274, 51.496 Street - Al

Mirqab Al Jadeed St Public Transport - Metro Gold Line Joaan
Typical hours - 09:30-01:30 - Contacts - +974 4443 2927

**SMAT Restaurant** - A contemporary version of Qatari & Gulf food, with lightly spiced meat and rice, most especially Harees, the wheat and meat dish, though it offers much more than that. The restaurant's location is good on the eastern Corniche, overlooking a small park and, beyond that, the sea. Well worth a meal if you have visited the National Museum or the Museum of Islamic Art.

Typical cost range - **** Rough GPS - 25.289, 51.547 Street - East Corniche Public Transport - Gold Line National Museum Typical hours - 08:00-midnight - Contacts - +974 4410 6600

**Saasna** focuses on "pure" Qatari cuisine, presenting traditional dishes in a refined, minimalist setting. The restaurant Saasna is a tribute to the late Ahmed Al Meer (often addressed as Sheikha Ahmed), a woman who famously bore her grandfather's name. Her seminal 2000 book, The Art of Qatari Cooking, serves as the menu's blueprint. Today, the vision is managed by her daughter, Sheikha Al Meer - who has vastly improved the service over the last few years.

Typical cost range ****- Rough GPS 25.286, 51.526 +97455197131 Typical Hours 08:00-22:30 Barahat Musheireb

## AL WAKRAH

**Danat Al Bahar** +974 7770 7085 & Samamij +974 5999 9061. These two small fish restaurants are next to each other near the car park area of Souq Al Wakrah (a few minutes west of the sea). They are so similar that they may well be operated by the same management (Danat Al Bahar also has a branch in Souq Waqif overlooking the eastern car park). These are popular in the evening and offer a good selection of seafood (fish sold by weight). The area they are in has a number of other options, so have a look before you decide where to eat.

Typical cost range *** Hours - 13:00-01:00 daily. Rough GPS - 25.170, 51.608

**Zaman Al Khair Restaurant** is a well-established Lebanese/Syrian restaurant known for quality mezze, main courses, and fresh juices. Located along the route to the Inland Sea, the restaurant offers both dine-in and takeaway options.

Typical cost range - *** Rough GPS - 25.186, 51.600 Street - Al Wakrah Main St Public Transport - MetroLink from Al Wakrah Typical hours - 08:00-midnight - Contacts - +974 4498 6111 / info@zamanalkhairrest.com / www.zamanalkhairrest.com

**Al Maskr Seafood** is a rustic-style restaurant featuring a distressed interior. The dishes are presented with a refined touch, like those of a domestic meal prepared by an expert chef. Situated just west of the seafront, it does not have direct sea views.

Typical cost range - *** Rough GPS - 25.172, 51.610 Street - off Al Wakrah Main St Public Transport - MetroLink from Red Line Metro Al Wakrah Typical hours - 11:00 - 23:00 Contacts - +974 4414 3057

## WEST BAY

The W Doha hotel does have some excellent restaurant options - these illustrate the depth of options offered throughout Doha.

**Spice Market** (W Doha) offers an Asian-themed menu in the W Hotel, served in a room with subdued lighting. The restaurant is popular, and the staff are attentive and helpful.

**La Spiga by Paper Moon** (W Doha) - A small Italian restaurant with a wine bar inside the W Hotel, located on Diplomatic Street in West Bay. The décor is less Italian than anonymous, while the surrounding skyscrapers may not suit all tastes.

# HOTELS AND RESTAURANTS

**Market by Jean-Georges** (W Doha) features a straightforward European design matched by the similarly styled cuisine. The menu ranges from the British Isles to Lebanon and Japan, offering a wide selection.

**Wahm** (W Doha) offers live music and a fashionable bar for drinks in the W Hotel in Doha.

**W Café** (W Doha), set in the W Hotel, offers an alternative coffee shop experience comparable in price to Starbucks.

Rough GPS - 25.328, 51.530 - W Doha - Street - Diplomatic St Public Transport - Bus 57, 74, 76, 777 Metro Doha Exhibition and Convention Centre (DECC). Location in Qatar - West Bay- Contacts - +974 4453 5000 / wdoha.reservations@whotels.com / www.marriott.com/hotels/travel/dohwh-w-doha/

**Applebee's** (Chain) - Part of the Applebee Franchise, one of several branches in Doha. American-style beef ribs and dine-in fast food options. Predictable food quality and efficient service.

Typical cost range - **** Rough GPS - 25.326, 51.530 Street - Conference Centre Public Transport - Red Line Metro Doha Exhibition and Convention Center (DECC) Typical hours - 12:00-23:00 - Contacts - +974 4493 4880 / contact form / www.applebeesme.com/qatar/

**Olive Oil** Rotana City Centre (all-day dining breakfast/lunch/dinner) offers a buffet in the Rotana Hotel. It is conveniently located for both the Conference Centre and City Centre Mall, with a menu reflecting standard Gulf International cuisine.

Typical cost range - **** Rough GPS - 25.324, 51.533 Street - Diplomatic St / Conference Centre St Public Transport - Metro Red Line Doha Exhibition & Conference Centre (DECC) Typical hours - 06:00-10:30/12:30-15:00/18:30-22:30 (Friday & Saturday - not open for lunch) - Contacts - +974 4445 8727 / Contact Form / www.rotana.com

**Trader Vic's** (Hilton) - Part of the established chain of Polynesian-themed restaurants - it's been in the region for almost 40 years. Frequent theme nights add to the appeal. They have a dress code to gain entry.

Typical cost range - ***** Rough GPS - 25.327, 51.541 Street - Diplomatic St Public Transport - Metro Doha Exhibition and Convention Center (DECC) Typical hours - 13:00 - 02:00midnight - Contacts - +974 4423 3118 / www.tradervicsdoha.com/

**RESTAURANTS**

- (RI) Royal Istanbul Restaurant
- (WD) La Spiga By Paper Moon
- (WD) Market By Jean-Georges
- (WD) Spice Market
- (WD) W Café
- (WD) Wahm
- (AB) Applebee's
- (RC) Olive Oil
- (RC) Teatro
- (RC) Boston's
- (TV) Trader Vic's
- (AH) Al Hubara
- (MC) Ipanema
- (MC) Sridan
- (MC) Shanghai Club
- (NR) Nobu
- (ZR) Zengo

**HOTELS**

- **ME** Marriott Executive Apartments
- **WD** W Doha
- **KR** Kempinski Residences & Suites
- **CH** The Curve Hotel
- **VH** voco
- **FS** Four Seasons Hotel
- **SG** Sheraton Grand Doha Resort

# HOTELS AND RESTAURANTS

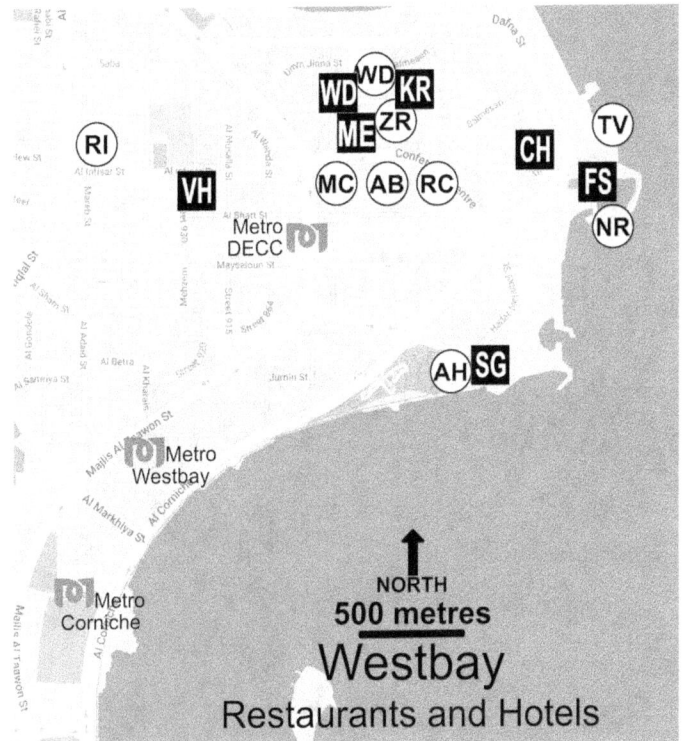

**Al Hubara Restaurant** IS A WELL-ESTABLISHED VENUE in the public atrium of the Sheraton, serving generally good international-style food.

Typical cost range - \*\*\*\*\*\* Rough GPS - 25.318, 51.536 Street - Al Corniche Sheraton Public Transport - Metro Red Line Doha Exhibition & Conference Centre (DECC) Typical hours - Breakfast Buffet: 06:00 AM - 11:00 AM Lunch Buffet: 12:00 PM - 15:30 PM / Dinner Buffet: 19:00 PM - 23:30 PM / Friday Brunch: 12:30 PM -16:00 PM - Contacts - +97444853000 / F&Breservations.doha@sheraton.com / www.alhubararestaurant.com

*Breakfast W Doha Hotel*

**Nobu** offers notable views from its location just off the beach, with expansive vistas over West Bay. This premium Japanese restaurant specialises in seafood; however, service and food may not always justify the pricing. Dress code applies, and window seats are recommended.

Typical cost range - \*\*\*\*\*\* Rough GPS - 25.323, 51.541 Street - Diplomatic St (Four Seasons Marina) Public Transport - Metro Red Line Doha Exhibition & Conference Centre (DECC) Typical hours - 18:00-01:00 (Friday 12:30-16:00) - Contacts - +974 4494 8600 / contact form / www.fourseasons.com/doha/dining/restaurants/nobu_doha/

## THE PEARL AND KATARA

**La Mar Doha** by Gastón Acurio, one of several Peruvian restaurants in Doha, is the flavour of the year. La Mar - lacks the pizazz of Tono - but more than makes up for it with the menu.

Typical Cost range \*\*\*\*\* Rough GPS25.349, 51.530 south of Al Khafji St (Street 61) Typical hours 18:00-11:30 (Fri & Say 12:30-23:30) Contacts +97444844098 https://lamarcebicheria.com/doha/

**L'wzaar Seafood** is a seafront restaurant in Katara, offering a broad seafood menu including Sushi and Fish & Chips, with views overlooking the sea. Outdoor seating is ideal in cooler weather, especially in the afternoon as the sun sets behind the building; at other times, window seats are suggested.

Typical cost range - \*\*\*\* Rough GPS - 25.358, 51.526 Street - off Al Moasses St/Lusail Highway Public Transport - Metro Red Line Katara Typical hours - midday - 23:00 Contacts - +974 4408 0710 / info@lwzaar.com / www.lwzaar.com/

**Bayt El Talleh** is located on a hillside in Katara, offering views over Katara Cultural Village. This set-menu restaurant is set in a spacious stone villa designed to evoke a Lebanese country home, complete with domestic animals.

Typical cost range - \*\*\*\* +97450101777 Rough GPS 25.363, 51.523 Katara Hills Metro Red Line (Katara Station).

**Sukar Pasha** is a Turkish restaurant located directly on an extension of Katara beach, offering both indoor and, in less humid weather, outdoor seating. The prime location contrasts with service and food quality, which can be inconsistent given the premium pricing.

Typical cost range - \*\*\*\* Rough GPS - 25.357, 51.527 Street - off Lusail Expressway Public Transport - Metro Red Line Katara

Typical hours - 09:00 - 01:00 (Fri 09:-11:00-13:00-01:00) Contacts - +974 4408 2000 / info@sukarpasha.qa. / http://sukarpasha.qa

**Al Sufra** excels in Lebanese cuisine and wine, with attentive service and a relaxed, subtly designed Arabic-inspired setting.

Typical cost range - ***** Rough GPS - 25.376, 51.549 Street - Marsa Malaz Kempinski, Pearl Boulevard Public Transport - No public transport Typical hours - 12:30-midnight - Contacts - +974 4035 5011 / restaurants.marsamalaz@kempinski.com / www.kempinski.com/en/doha/marsa-malaz-kempinski-the-pearl-doha/dining/restaurants/al-sufra/

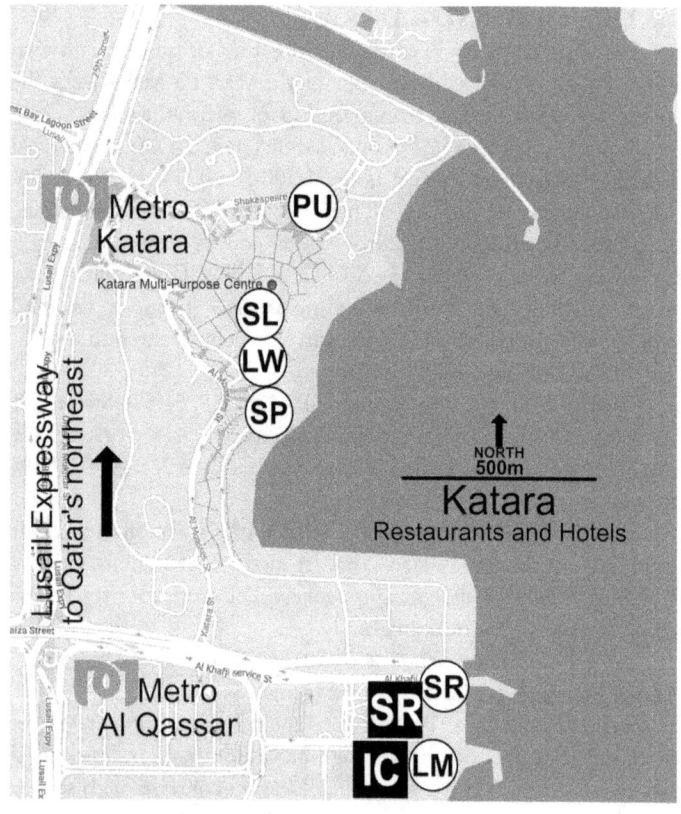

**Saffron Lounge** provides elegant surroundings and features quality North Indian cuisine. The presence of the three monkeys outside makes the location easy to identify.

Typical cost range - ***** www.saffronlounge.net Rough GPS - 25.359, 51.526 Street - off Lusail Express (next to Katara Hall) Public Transport - Metro Red Line Katara Typical hours - 12:00-22:00 (Friday 13:00-23:00) - Contacts - +974 4408 0808

**Tono** impresses with its interiors, The Pearl's scenery, and acclaimed Peruvian cuisine.

Typical Cost range ***** Rough GPS25.370, 51.540 Street La Croisette, Off Piazza Arabia Typical Hours 16:00-midnight +97430010145 https://linktr.ee/TONOQatar

**Yasmine Palace** is an opulent complex in The Pearl, housing four distinct dining areas, including a café-style venue. The Arabian Nights-inspired concept features Levant cuisine. Despite the less convenient location, the food, ambience, and service are noteworthy.

Typical cost range - ***** Rough GPS - 25.365, 51.543 Street - Porto Arabia Drive The Pearl Public Transport - No public transport Typical hours - 07:00-midnight - Contacts - +974 7711 1504 yasminepalace.com/

**Hakkasan** (St. Regis Doha) is among the most premium dining options in Doha, with sophisticated decor and ambience highlighting high-quality Chinese cuisine styled to mirror the interior. As an established restaurant, it has refined its offerings over time. Note the restrictive door policy, particularly for children under 11; reservations are recommended.

Typical cost range - ****** Rough GPS - 25.350, 51.529 Street - east of Lusail Highway Public Transport - Red Line Metro Al Qassar Typical hours - 19:00-23:30 (also weekends 13:00-16:00) wine bar (18:00-01:00) - Contacts - +974 4446 0170 / reservation.hakkasan@stregis.com / www.hakkasan.com/locations/hakkasan-doha/

**Morimoto** (Mondrian Doha) is a stylish Japanese restaurant in the Mondrian Hotel at The Pearl, offering food and service that align with its price point.

Typical cost range - ****** Rough GPS - 25.377, 51.523 Street - Pearl Boulevard/ Lusail Expressway Public Transport - Red Line Metro Legtaifiya & MetroLink Typical hours - 18:00-23:30 (Closed Sunday) - Contacts - +974 4045 5999 / Wineanddine-mondriandoha@sbe.com / www.morganshotelgroup.com/mondrian/mondrian-doha/

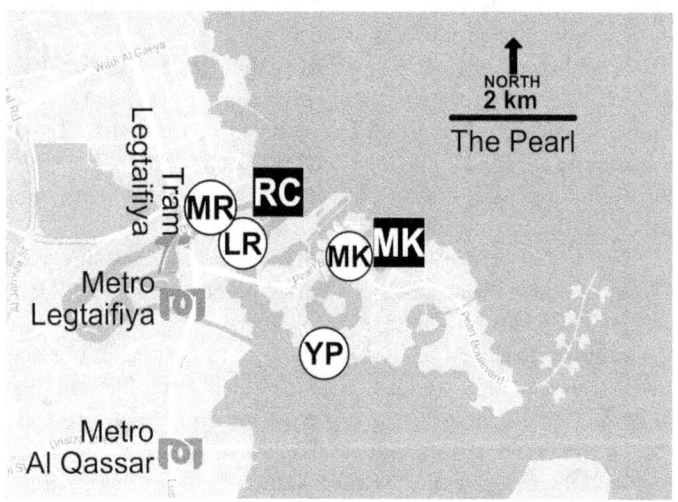

**Nozomi** (Marsa Malaz Kempinski) - With a view over the man-made lagoon around Marsa Malaz Kempinski, Nozomi is an excellent Japanese restaurant in a premium hotel. The food and service meet expectations, but the interior and exterior don't.

Typical cost range - \*\*\*\*\*\* Rough GPS - 25.377, 51.549 Street - Pearl Boulevard/ Lusail Expressway No public transport Typical hours - 19:00-23:00 (Thurs & Friday also 12:00-15:30) - Contacts - +974 4035 5089 / info@nozomidoha.com / http://www.nozomi-doha.com/

**Bibo** (Marsa Malaz Kempinski) - Overlooking the lagoon of Marsa Malaz Kempinski, this is a taste of Spain in Doha - it's superseded the popular Toro Toro .

Typical cost range - \*\*\*\*\*\* Rough GPS - 25.377, 51.549 Street - The Pearl Boulevard No public transport Typical hours - 18:00-01:00 (Friday & Saturday 12:30-01:00) - Contacts - +97431000373 https://grupodanigarcia.com/bibo/

**Vine** (St Regis) - An elegant restaurant with a spacious interior and options to dine outside. This is one of the better all-day dining options in Doha. Vine serves an international menu, though it also hosts themed evenings throughout the week.

Typical cost range - \*\*\*\*\*\* Rough GPS - 25.350, 51.529 Street - off Lusail Highway Public Transport - No public transport Typical hours - 06:00-11:00/18:00-23:00 and Friday (12:30-16:00) -

Contacts - +974 4446 0105 / dining.reservations@stregis.com / www.vinedoha.com/

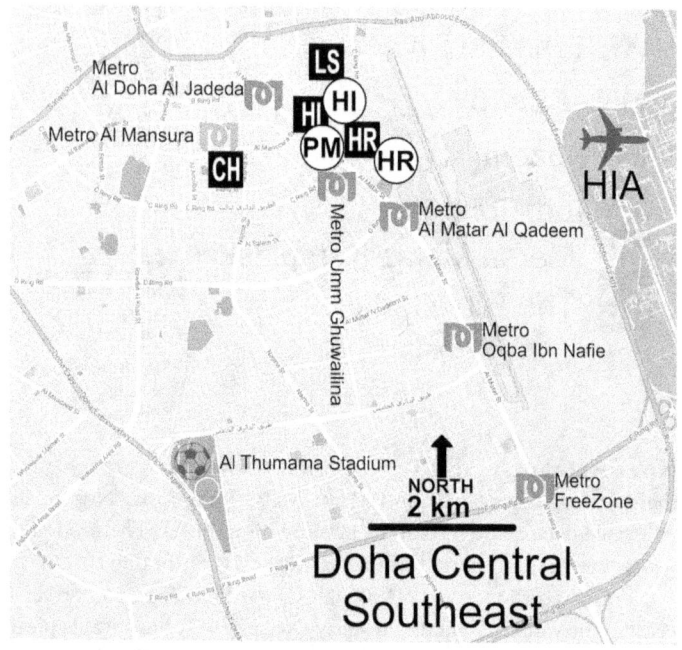

## DOHA SOUTH & EAST

**The Cellar** - This is now a Hyatt Regency Oryx managed property. With a good range of drinks, this Spanish-themed restaurant is a welcome change from the plethora of Middle Eastern and Indian sub-continent cuisines throughout Doha.

Typical cost range - *** Rough GPS - 25.268, 51.554 Street - Al Nahda School St / C Ring Rd. Public Transport - Metro Red Line Umm Ghuwailina Typical hours - 12:00-02:00 - Contacts - +974 4402 3454 / Contact Form / www.hyattrestaurants.com/en/dining/qatar/doha/spanish-restaurant-in-hamad-International-airport-the-cellar

**Al Nafourah Garden** - A change from a Rotana to Hyatt Regency Oryx management, but still a very good courtyard dining experience. Not the widest choice of food in this Lebanese restaurant, but what is there offers a delightful selection. The water pipes add to the experience.

Typical cost range - **** Rough GPS - 25.268, 51.554 Street - Al Matar St Public Transport Red Line Metro Umm Ghuwailina Typical hours - 12:00-02:00 - Contacts - +974 4402 3333 / www.hyattrestaurants.com/en/dining/qatar/doha/lebanese-restaurant-in-doha-s-business-district-al-nafourah-garden

**Paper Moon** (1st Floor Jaidah Square Complex) - A comfortable modern style restaurant with the possibility of indoor or outdoor tables. This may be the nicest overall experience in an Italian restaurant in Doha.

Typical cost range - ***** Rough GPS - 25.273, 51.545 Street - Umm Ghuwailina St / Al Matar St Public Transport - Metro Red Line Umm Ghuwailina Typical hours - 11:30 - 22:45 - Contacts - +974 4016 6000 / info@papermoondoha.com / www.papermoondoha.com/

(HR) Al Nafourah Garden
(HR) Jazz Club
(HR) The Cellar
(PM) Paper Moon
(HI) Stock Burger Co
[LS] Al Liwan Suites
[CH] Holiday Inn
[HI] Hyatt Regency
[HR] Chairman Hotel

## EDUCATION CITY AND DOHA WEST

**Saj Boutique** - Fast-food Arabic-style with the staple Shawarma (flat pitta-type bread with meat or falafel filling), nicely cooked and presented. Though famous for its takeaway food, the restaurant is well laid out.

Typical cost range - * Rough GPS - 25.267, 51.479 Jassim bin Hamad Stadium Metro Gold Line Gold Line Al Sudan Typical hours - 07:00-00:30 - Contacts - +974 4444 0078

**Al Sultan Restaurant** - Al Saad - Good value, though with a tired decor, Lebanese restaurant (one of two in a chain) with a good selection of Fruit Juices.

Typical cost range - ** Rough GPS - 25.274, 51.505 Street - Al

Mirqab Al Jadeed Public Transport - Metro Gold Line Al Saad Typical hours - 08:00-midnight - Contacts - +974 4441 1865 / info@al-sultanrestaurant.com / www.al-sultanrestaurant.com/

**Beirut Restaurant** (With Branches) - Simple, well-established, low-cost, popular Lebanese restaurant.

Typical cost range - ** Rough GPS - 25.285, 51.509 Street - Al Jazeera St Public Transport - Metro Gold Line Al Saad Typical hours - 04:30-23:00 Contacts - +974 4435 5258 / info@beirutrest.com / www.beirutrest.com/

**Summer Land** (Qatar Petroleum Service Station) - Turkish & Syrian style restaurant offering low-priced food. This is one of the larger of many restaurants on this petrol station forecourt. It offers dine-in and takeaway. There must be a dozen other choices on the same petrol station forecourt, making it an ideal stop for a takeaway meal.

Typical cost range - ** Rough GPS - 25.350, 51.457 Street - Doha Expressway (Al Shamal Road) /Al Khafji St No Public Transport Typical hours - 08:00-02:00 - Contacts - +974 4444 2056

**Atrium Café & Terrace** - With live piano music and light international food in a spacious atrium of the Millennium Hotel - this is a good choice for a quick meal if in the area.

Typical cost range - **** Rough GPS - 25.284, 51.496Street - Al Manara St, Jawaan St, Public Transport - Metro Gold Line Joaan Typical hours - 07:00-23:30 - Contacts - +974 4 424 7777 / info.mdoh@millenniumhotels.com / www.millenniumhotels.com/en/doha/millennium-hotel-doha/atrium/

**c.mondo** (previously c.taste)(Centro Capital Hotel) In Al Jazeera St - A limited but well-produced international menu from this modern, well-run all-day restaurant in the Centro Hotel.

Typical cost range - **** Rough GPS - 25.284, 51.512 Street - Al Jazeera St Public Transport - Metro Gold Line Al Sadd - 1km away Typical hours - 06:00-10:30 12:30-15:00 18:0022:30 - Contacts: +974 4455 5000 / centro.capitaldoha@rotana.com / www.rotana.com/centrohotels/qatar/doha/centrocapitaldoha/dining

**Di Capri Ristorante** (La Cigale Hotel) - Vivid ambience with a hint of the late 1950s modern Italy. The food lives up to the promise.

Typical cost range - **** Rough GPS - 25.280, 51.508 Street -, C Ring Rd /Suhaim Bin Hamad Street Public Transport - Metro Gold Line Al Sadd Typical hours - 11:30-15:00 / 07:00 - 23:00 - Contacts -

+97144288840 / info@lacigalehotel.com / http://www.lacigalehotel.com/sub_category.phpintCategoryId=4

**Ocean Basket** (Mall of Qatar) - Seafood as fast food. A reasonable choice if visiting the Mall of Qatar or Villaggio Mall

Typical cost range - \*\*\*\* Rough GPS - 25.324, 51.350 Street - Dukhan Highway / National Day Ceremonial Road (a complicated junction) No Public Transport - Typical hours - 11:00-23:00 (Friday 01:00-23:00) - Contacts - +974 4490 2944 / www.qatar.oceanbasket.com/

**Shebestan Palace Restaurant** is an extremely well-established Persian restaurant with a subdued, classic, and spacious interior. The food and service are less polished than in other Persian restaurants in Doha, though at an appreciably lower price.

Typical cost range - \*\*\*\* Rough GPS - 25.281, 51.504 Street - Al Saad St Public Transport - Metro Gold Line Al Saad Typical hours - 12:00-midnight - Contacts - +974 4432 1555

**Harees Jaddaty** This offers traditional Qatari food from a small, simple local restaurant. It specialises in takeaway (or home delivery). For dine-in, it's unfortunately well away from tourist areas.

Typical cost range \*\* Rough GPS 25.241, 51.456 Street - Salwa Rd 24 hours daily. www.hareesjaddaty.com

**Seasonal Tastes** (Westin Hotel) - An International restaurant with nightly themed food nights.

Typical cost range - \*\*\*\*\*\* Rough GPS - 25.275, 51.514 Street - Salwa Rd Public Transport - Metro Gold Line Bin Mahmoud Typical hours - 06:30-11:00 12:30-15:00 18:30-23:00 - Contacts - +974 4492 1555 / dining.doha@westin.com / www.seasonaltastesdoha.com/

**Three Sixty (360)** Torch Doha - Mediterranean & Seafood restaurant (no alcohol) set on the 47th floor of The Torch. The food is good, but what makes this an outstanding restaurant is the revolving view. This is best enjoyed from just before sunset (arrive early to catch the skyscraper lights coming on in West Bay). The other restaurants in The Torch are also good, but the revolving restaurant does make it especially worth the trip. The 360-degree journey your table will make is around 90minutes - possibly a hint to finish your meal when you have deja vu. Very Smart Casual, or suit & dress.

Typical cost range - \*\*\*\*\*\* Rough GPS - 25.262, 51.445 Street - off Al Waab Street, Al Buwairda St Public Transport - Metro Gold

Line Sport City Typical hours - 12:00-15:00 / 19:00-23:00 - Contacts - +974 4446 5600 / reservation@thetorchdoha.com / www.thetorchdoha.com.qa

The Torch

HOTELS AND RESTAURANTS 223

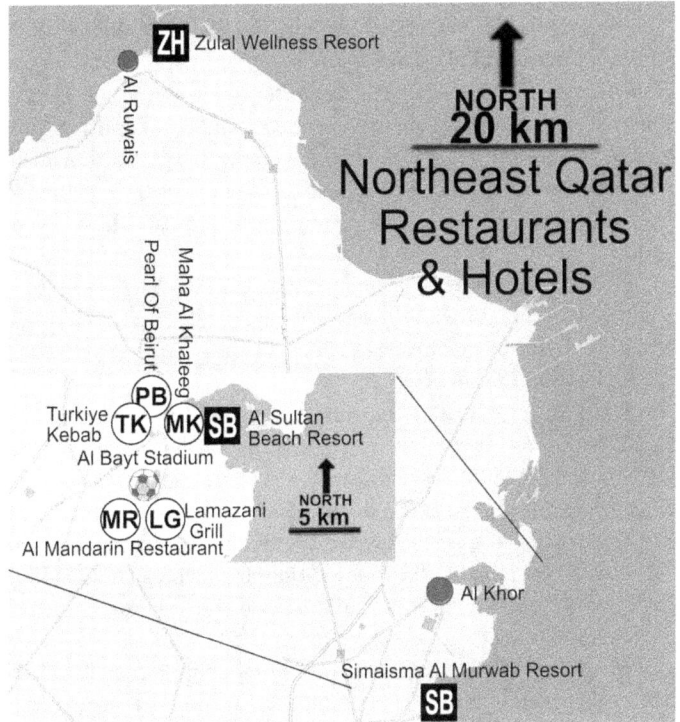

## NORTHEAST QATAR

**Maha Al Khaleeg** (it was Miknas Cafeteria) - A low-cost restaurant opposite the harbour in Al Khor, with Indian food, especially with a south Indian flavour. Outside seating is available.

Typical cost range - * Rough GPS - 25.686, 51.514 Street - Al Khor Coastal Rd / Al Khor Town Rd No Public Transport - Typical hours 24 hours - Contacts - +974 500 60179

**Pearl Of Beirut Restaurant** - Straightforward restaurant - moved from its seaside original location. As the name suggests, it started as a Lebanese-style restaurant, but since the move, it's more international Asian. The food is good value, and the new restaurant is cleaner than the original.

Typical cost range - * Rough GPS - 25.675, 51.500 Street - Al Khor Coastal Rd (a long way from the sea) No Public Transport Typical hours - 07:00-midnight (Friday closed for midday prayers)- Contacts - +974 4472 0123

## DUKHAN & WEST COAST, CENTRAL QATAR, AL RUWAIS & NORTH COAST

**Iskender Pasha** - About as far north as you can get in Qatar. This inexpensive restaurant serves simple Turkish and Mediterranean food. Ask if they have Iskender kebab, a dish named after its inventor, Iskender Efendi. Several other restaurants (including Tea Time) are on the same street; compare these if you wish.

Typical cost range - * Rough GPS - 26.126, 51.204 Street - Madinat Al Shamal Rd / Al Ghayra Rd Public Transport - Typical hours - 09:00-23:00 - Contacts - +974 3357 4304

## VARIOUS LOCATIONS

**Tea Time** - A Qatari franchise that is Gulf-wide. Spiced tea "Karak" – a word that means strong - but is usually spiced - (in the UK, Masala, the Hindi word for spice, is the equivalent), with a wide range of spice options, is the theme. The snack food isn't quite as good as the tea, but this is an excellent alternative to a burger.

Typical cost range - * - various locations (13+) in Qatar including Souq Waqif 25.287, 51.533 Typical hours - 24 Hours - web - teatime.qa/

**Wrap It** - In the food court of several shopping malls (Gulf Mall, Landmark, etc.) - The Gulf's most popular snack, the Shawarma, is branded here as Wrap-it. A shawarma in the Gulf is a pitta/Lebanese-style bread, split open and stuffed. Here, you can individually select the filling, a Subway-style way of getting precisely what you want.

Typical cost range - * - various locations Typical hours - 09:00-23:30 (or as in specific food court opening hours)

Of course, you will find the usual franchises McDonald's, Starbucks and many more - all over Doha.

HOTELS

Hotels are stared by the dollar price (charges will be in QAR) of their cheapest room, out of their main peak season (Christmas and major events). In those periods booking well in advance is suggested.

USD 0-60 *
USD 61-90 **
USD 91-125 ***
USD 126-190 ****

USD 191-250 *****
USD 251+ ******

## CORNICHE, SOUQ WAQIF & CENTRAL DOHA

This area has an excellent range of hotels. It's also a very popular area for leisure visitors. For a straightforward short-stay (a few nights) tourism, hotels within walking distance of Msheireb's Metro are ideal. The reason is that the Metro station serves 3 metro lines - one of which, the Red Line, serves the airport. South of the Metro station is the Karwa bus station - with a good range of bus routes & the MetroLink on the road to its south. It's also worth looking east from Msheireb, as it includes the Souq Waqif and National Museum Metro stations.

**Century Hotel** - Spacious rooms and potentially good facilities in a convenient location. The hotel opened in 2010 and is already slipping in maintenance & housekeeping - ask to see your room before checking in. A choice of 3 dining options. It's well located for the National and Islamic Art museums & with good access to the National Museum Metro (Gold Line).

Number of rooms - 215.Typical cost range - * Rough GPS - 25.286, 51.547 Street - Sheraouh St Public Transport - National Museum Metro Location in Qatar - Al Hitmi- Contacts - +974 4445 5111 / info@centuryhoteldoha.com / www.centuryhoteldoha.com

**Fraser Suites Doha** - Nice rooms of various sizes; many from the 10th floor & above have sea views. Choice of dining, gym, spa and rooftop pool with great views. The Museum of Islamic Art, the National Museum, and the Corniche are close, and Souq Al Waqif is just over a kilometre away. The hotel may not be a 5* hotel in terms of superlative facilities - but it succeeds in providing an excellent, predictable stay in Doha - worth considering.

Number of rooms: 138 apartments (several hotels are close by). Typical cost range - *** Rough GPS - 25.290, 51.544 Street - Al Meena St near Corniche Public Transport - Metro Gold Line National Museum Location in Qatar - Al Mirqab- Contacts - +974 442 43443 / sales.doha@frasershospitality.com / www.doha.frasershospitality.com

**Jouri Hotel** - With a warm, welcoming theme and excellent service, this hotel, managed by the Murwab Hotel Group and part of Katara Hospitality, a Qatari government group. Other hotels within the group include The Avenue. The facilities are suitable for a short stay, with 3 restaurants, a small gym, and a spa. Well located for the

National and Islamic Art museums & with reasonable access to the National Museum Metro (Gold Line). There is room to improve overall standards.

Number of rooms - 136 Typical cost range - ** Rough GPS - 25.287, 51.545 Street - Muthaf St Public Transport - National Museum Metro Location in Qatar - Al Hitmi- Contacts - +974 4004 1000 / info@jouridoha.com / www.jourihotel.com/

**Tourist Hotel** - A budget hotel with inexpensive Middle Eastern-style decor. Small gym and simple restaurant. Highly convenient to the National Museum and close to the Museum of Islamic Art, and less than 2km from Souq Waqif,

Number of rooms - 120 Typical cost range - * Rough GPS - 25.287, 51.547 Street - Al Aaliya St Public Transport Metro Gold Line National Museum Location in Qatar - Al Hitmi- Contacts - +974 4432 1321 / contact form / www.touristhoteldoha.com

**Kingsgate Hotel** - Modern, functional, and colourful - a lower cost brand of the Millennium Hotels chain - open since 2011. A small pool and gym with reasonable facilities for the price. The key bonus is the proximity to Souq Waqif (600 metres), the Gold Souq, and the Museum of Islamic Art or the National Museum, which is a kilometre away. It's also directly opposite the Gold Line Souq Waqif Metro – less than 300m. The downside is that it lacks consistent service standards & housekeeping needs a boost - another plus is the value.

Number of rooms - 140. Typical cost range - * Rough GPS - 25.286, 51.538 Street - Ali bin Abdullah (Al Mirqab Roundabout) Public Transport - Metro Gold Line Souq Waqif Location in Qatar - Old Al Ghanim- Contacts - +974 4408 5555 / reservations.kg-doh@millenniumhotels.com / www.millenniumhotels.com/en/doha/kingsgate-hotel-doha/

**Ramada Encore by Wyndham** - Simple, bright decor giving a sense of space in relatively compact rooms. Small pool, gym, restaurant. About 1 kilometre to Souq Waqif and Msheireb Museums. There are several equivalent hotels adjacent, though without the branding.

Number of rooms - 111 Typical cost range - * Rough GPS - 25.280, 51.530 Street - Al Areeq St Public Transport - Metro Msheireb (Hub) Location in Qatar - Msheireb- Contacts - +974 4444 3444 / info@ramadaencoredoha.com / www.ramadaencoredoha.com

**The Town Hotel Doha** is a low-cost hotel with service and standards that work hard to match. Single restaurant; small rooftop pool (often closed). About 1km to Souq Waqif and Msheireb Museums. There are several similar hotels adjacent.

Number of rooms - 120 Typical cost range - * Rough GPS - 25.280, 51.530 Street - Al Areeq Public Transport Metro Msheireb (Hub). Location in Qatar - Msheireb- Contacts - +974 4410 7100 / reservations@thetownhotelqatar.com / www.thetownhotelqatar.com

**Saray Musherieb Deluxe Hotel Residence** is just outside the main Msheireb Area. It is close to the Metro- Comfortable, though using domestic fittings for kitchens. Rooms in muted earth tones encourage sleep. Small pool, gym, sauna. The hotel opened in 2013 and has undergone some renovations since 2022, including updated rooms.

Number of rooms - 216 Typical cost range - ** Rough GPS - 25.283, 51.522 Street - Al Meyyah Street/Al Adhwaa St Public Transport - Bus, Salwa Rd (100m) Location in Qatar - Msheireb- Contacts - +974 4015 0555 / contact form / www.saraymshereb-hotel.online/

**Al Najada Doha Hotel** by Tivoli - A fresh, spacious property focusing on service and ambience. Well-appointed hotel with a range of facilities, a short walk from Souq Waqif, museums and Corniche. Straightforward access to transport. Next door is a former apartment hotel - compare rooms to see which is better for you.

Number of rooms - 151 Typical cost range - **** Rough GPS - 25.285, 51.534 Street - Barahat Al Jufairi Street, Grand Hamed St Public Transport - Metro Gold Line Souq Waqif Location in Qatar - Msheireb- Contacts - (+974) 4470 4444 / alnajada@tivolihotels.com / www.tivolihotels.com/en/al-najada-tivoli

**Alwadi Hotel** - Subdued interiors create a relaxing stay; it excels in its excellent location for leisure and business, and in its service and attention to detail. 3 restaurants and lots more in nearby areas. Some upper-floor rooms have superb views. South-west of Souq Waqif.

Number of rooms - 213 Typical cost range - **** Rough GPS - 25.286, 51.531 Street - Wadi Msheireb St. Public Transport - Souq Waqif Metro Msheireb Tram Location in Qatar - Msheireb- Contacts - +974 4009 9999 / Reservations.alwadihotel@accor.com / all.accor.com/hotel/8395/index.en.shtml

**Sharq Village & Spa**, Ritz-Carlton. Opulent Arabesque style with a series of low-rise buildings set like pleasure pavilions in a manicured environment. Choice of restaurants, including incredibly scenic outdoor options, pools, a gym, and a 250m beach. Near National Museum & Museum of Islamic Art, Dhow yard and along the Corniche to Souq Waqif and more of Doha's sights.

Number of rooms - 174 . Typical cost range - ***** Rough GPS - 25.284, 51.557Street - Corniche Public Transport - Metro Gold Line National Museum Location in Qatar - Al Corniche- Contacts - +974 4425 6666 / sharq.leads@ritzcarlton.com / www.ritzcarlton.com/en/hotels/qatar/sharq-village .

**Rixos Gulf Hotel** - this opened in 2022. Though from 2017, the Turkish brand Rixos itself became part of Accor Hotels, it has so far focused on Turkey & the Gulf. This is a relatively large hotel, set on a small beach. Overall, this provides an excellent experience - though at busy times the facilities cannot cope with the number of guests.

Number of rooms 350 Typical cost range - *****  Rough GPS 25.286, 51.563 Street - Corniche Public Transport - Metro Gold Line National Museum Location in Qatar - Al Corniche Contacts +974 4429 8888 https://www.rixos.com/en

**Souq Waqif Boutique Hotels** - Tivoli is a collection of 9 individual properties in central Doha. The style is restrained but opulent. Most of these hotels are small and might share some facilities, after a short walk, say from one hotel to another, for breakfast. Surrounded by Souq Waqif and close to Qatar's leading museums.

Typical cost range - ***** Rough GPS - 25.289, 51.532Street - Al Souq St Public Transport - Metro Gold Line Souq Waqif Location in Qatar - Souq Waqif - Contacts - +974 4433 6666 / / www.tivolihotels.com/en/qatar/souq-waqif-doha

**The Westin Doha Hotel & Spa** - Modern exterior matches the interior. Spa, gym, and fitness, along with sheltered gardens. Several good restaurants - southwest of the town centre

Number of rooms - 364Typical cost range - **** Rough GPS - 25.275, 51.514Street - Salwa Rd Public Transport - Bus 31, 32, 33.34, 137, 136, 301 Location in Qatar - Fereej Bin Mahmoud- Contacts - +974 4492 1555 / reservations.doha@westin.com/ www.marriott.com/hotels/travel/dohwi-the-westin-doha-hotel-and-spa/

**Banana Island Resort Doha** by Anantara - A stylish resort with access, by boat, to Doha's attractions, giving a real sense of being on an island getaway. This is a small, 25-hectare island about 1/2 hour boat ride from Doha's Dhow Harbour. A private 600m beach with 9 dining options (some included under suggested restaurants). A Surf Pool, main Pool, and Bowling Alley supply a range of activities. Open views to Doha and across to the Airport, with a welcome lack of noise.

Number of rooms - 141 Rooms Typical cost range - ****** Rough GPS - 25.295, 51.646Street - In Doha Bay Public Transport - Metro Gold Line Souq Waqif & Ferry from Dhow Harbour 25.292135, 51.534429 Location in Qatar - Banana Island Doha Bay- Contacts - +974 4040 5050 / doha@anantara.com / www.anantara.com/en/banana-island-doha

**WEST BAY**

**Marriott Executive Apartments** - A 24-story tower offering a central location. Remarkably, it seems to suffer from the problems that non-branded hotels have with housekeeping & maintenance. Just off the Corniche in West Bay, close to DECC and City Centre Mall

Number of rooms - 254Typical cost range - *** Rough GPS - 25.328, 51.530Street - 'Diplomatic Area Doha, Qatar Diplomatic St' Public Transport - Bus 74, 777 Metro Doha Exhibition and Convention Center (DECC). Location in Qatar - West Bay- Contacts - +974 4497 1111 / contact form / www.marriott.com/hotels/fact-sheet/travel/dohec-marriott-executive-apartments-city-center-doha/

**The Curve Hotel** - Excellent value for the location, though the large number of rooms would benefit from more restaurants and facilities. Roof Top pool, gym, and a few dining options. The DECC and City Centre Mall, along with the modern sights in West Bay, add to the hotel's appeal.

Number of rooms - 600 Typical cost range - *** Rough GPS - 25.326, 51.538Street - Diplomatic St Public Transport - Metro Doha Exhibition and Convention Center (DECC) Location in Qatar - West Bay- Contacts - +974 400 78888 / reservation@ezdancurve.qa / www.ezdancurve.qa/

**Voco Doha West Bay Suites** Doha. As you would expect from the chain (it's an IHG Hotel), the rooms offer clean, fresh options for a business traveller. A rooftop pool, gym, and a couple of restaurants are part of the facilities. A modern hotel with a good range of facilities. Close to the DECC and City Centre Mall.

Number of rooms - 396 rooms (one of Doha's largest hotels) on 46 floors. Typical cost range - **** Rough GPS - 25.325, 51.522 Street - Al Intisar St Public Transport - Metro Doha Exhibition and Convention Center (DECC). Location in Qatar - West Bay - Contacts - +974 4495 5000 / https://www.ihg.com/voco/

**Intercontinental (Beach & Spa) Doha** Hotel - This is an attractive, relatively low-rise hotel with a beach protected by Al Safliya Island. A mix of hotel and adjacent apartments on a 400m beachfront. With 10 dining outlets, several pools and a very stylish interior. Relatively close to Katara - a 3km walk is possible along the coast with a slight detour around Magical Festival Village

Number of rooms – 375 Typical cost range - **** Rough GPS - 25.348, 51.528Street - East of the Lusail Expressway, on Onaiza St Public Transport - Red Line Metro Al Qassar Location in Qatar - West Bay- Contacts - +974 4484 4444 www.ihg.com/intercontinental/hotels/us/en/doha

**W Doha** - Modern, fresh with a version of the eclectic W style. Choice of dining options, pools and gym. So many greeters that it can be overwhelming. Ask for rooms on the middle floors of the tower - they are quieter. The DECC and City Centre Mall, along with the modern sights in West Bay, are nearby.

Number of rooms - 442Typical cost range - **** Rough GPS - 25.328, 51.530Street - Diplomatic St Public Transport - Bus 57, 74, 76, 777 Metro Doha Exhibition and Convention Center (DECC). Location in Qatar - West Bay- Contacts - +974 4453 5000 / wdoha.reservations@whotels.com / www.marriott.com/hotels/travel/dohwh-w-doha/

W Doha lobby

**Four Seasons Hotel Doha** - Restrained and opulent - the style is welcoming and hints at the Arab world. A restricted beach and views are the facilities of this hotel. The hotel's height provides sea views from many rooms. A small marina and a Nobu restaurant complete the marine theme; there are 8 other dining venues. The DECC and City Centre Mall, along with the modern sights in West Bay, are nearby.

Number of rooms - 232 Typical cost range - ***** Rough GPS - 25.325, 51.539Street - Diplomatic St Public Transport - Metro Doha Exhibition and Convention Center (DECC). Location in Qatar - West Bay- Contacts - +974 4494 8888 / contact form / www.fourseasons.com/doha/

**Kempinski Residences & Suites** - The tallest hotel in West Bay (until the next one) offers a luxurious stay, with most suites offering sea views. The style is modern and simple. All you could expect from an upmarket hotel, plus unexpected facilities such as a boardroom - for the company on the move! Just off the Corniche in West Bay, close to DECC and City Centre Mall

Number of rooms - 368 on 60 floors Typical cost range - ***** Rough GPS - 25.328, 51.531 Street - Diplomatic Area Public Transport - Metro Doha Exhibition and Convention Center (DECC). West Bay- Contacts -+974 4405 3333 / reservations.doha@kempinski.com / www.kempinski.com/en/doha/residences/

**Sheraton Grand Doha Resort & Convention** - This is a very well-established, exceptionally well-located hotel (it's doubtless overall the best-located property in Doha). It's probably focused on the business traveller, but it is still an excellent leisure choice. Beach, pools, gym, racquet courts and more - with what must be the best pub in town. Check out the 'whale shark fountain' in the park to the west. The DECC and City Centre Mall are close.

Number of rooms - 371 Typical cost range - ***** Rough GPS - 25.318, 51.536 Street - Al Corniche Public Transport Metro Red Line Doha Exhibition & Conference Centre (DECC) Location in Qatar - West Bay Al Corniche- Contacts - +974 4485 4444 / sheraton.doha@Sheraton.com / www.marriott.com/hotels/travel/dohsi-sheraton-grand-doha-resort-and-convention-hotel/

**The St. Regis Doha** - Clean, fresh, slightly Arabic in feel. The grounds, though, are smaller than the number of rooms would suggest. Over 10 dining choices, a small beach, pool, gym and all the little touches you would hope for at the cost. a modern mix of buildings and close to Katara - a less than 3km walk is possible along the coast with a slight detour around Magical Festival Village

Number of rooms - 336 Typical cost range - ****** Rough GPS - 25.350, 51.529Street - East of the Lusail Expressway, on Onaiza St Public Transport - No public transport Location in Qatar - West Bay/The Pearl- Contacts - +974 4446 0000 / doha.reservations@stregis.com/ www.marriott.com/hotels/travel/dohxr-the-st-regis-doha

## THE PEARL AND KATARA

**Chedi Katara Hotel** looks like a Mughal palace - set on an expansive beach ,immediately next to Katara, this is a sprawling low-rise property with 5 options to dine in. While the spa is a highlight in the hotel, its proximity to Katara might be a key reason to stay.

59 Rooms & 32 villas Typical cost ***** appx GPS 25.363, 51.529 Shakespeare St Katara Contacts chedikatara@ghmhotels.com+97441447777 www.ghmhotels.com

**Marsa Malaz Kempinski** - One of the better hotels in Doha (there is a fair amount of competition), set on a man-made island in a man-made lagoon. The hotel aims to supply a genuine 5* service to its guests; it includes a Butler service. The hotel encourages guests to linger with 11 dining options, a small private beach, and tennis courts. A short drive from Katara and the other modern developments of The Pearl and West Bay.

Number of rooms - 281 Typical cost range - ***** Rough GPS - 25.376, 51.547Street - Pearl Boulevard Public Transport - No public transport Location in Qatar - The Pearl- Contacts - +974 4035 5555 / reservations.marsamalaz@kempinski.com / www.kempinski.com/en/doha/marsa-malaz-kempinski-the-pearl-doha/

**The Ritz-Carlton** - This well-established hotel offers amazingly comfortable luxury rooms. It lacks the opulent style of the Ritz-Carlton's Sharq Village Hotel. Overlooking the sea with grounds, pools and access to a man-made beach and marina. Convenient for Katara's cultural mix and West Bay's business area.

Number of rooms - 374Typical cost range - ***** Rough GPS - 25.380, 51.532Street - off Lusail Expressway Public Transport - No public transport Location in Qatar - The Pearl- Contacts - +974 4484 8000 / doha.reservations@ritzcarlton.com / www.ritzcarlton.com/en/hotels/qatar/doha

## DOHA SOUTH AND EAST

**Al Liwan Suites** - An older style accommodation with spacious, slightly dated rooms. As an established hotel (20 years old), it offers a non-pretentious place to stay that gives excellent value. Options for 3 meal locations; the best is the rooftop with Frangipani and a take on an old Qatari house. Small pool, gym, airport transfer, this is an older area in Doha (relatively speaking) that offers interest and reasonably easy access to tourist areas and the airport.

Number of rooms - 84 rooms/suites Typical cost range - * Rough GPS - 25.275, 51.547Street - Umm Ghuwailina St Public Transport - Metro Red Line Al Jadeda Location in Qatar - Umm Ghuwailina- Contacts - +974 44242888 / mohsen.khattab@alliwansuites.com.qa / www.alliwansuites.com.qa/

**Chairman Hotel** - With comfortable furnishings and spacious rooms, the hotel offers reasonable value. A single dining choice. In one of the older areas of Doha.

Number of rooms - 68Typical cost range - * Rough GPS - 25.269, 51.538Street - Najma St Public Transport - Al Mansoura Metro, Location in Qatar - Najma- Contacts - +974 4426 0444 / reservations@chairmenhotel.com / www.chairmenhotel.com/

**Holiday Inn Doha** - The Business Park - Modern, with a range of facilities expected from a Holiday Inn, including a pool and gym. There are three dining options, convenient to the Airport and transport to other areas. Request quiet rooms. Next to this is another IGH hotel - the Crown Plaza with 378 rooms. Both offer comparable standards.

Number of rooms - 307Typical cost range - * Rough GPS - 25.273, 51.543 Street - Al Matar St Public Transport - Metro Al Doha Al Jadeda Location in Qatar - Najma- Contacts - +974 4031 3333- holidayinndoha@ihg.com / www.ihg.com/holidayinn/

### DOHA CENTRAL SOUTHEAST

**La Villa Suites** - Very old-fashioned rooms with a small kitchenette. Rooms are furnished differently - look at yours before checking in. The maintenance and housekeeping are poor, making the hotel worth considering only at a favourable price. A single dining choice.

Number of rooms - Typical cost range - * Rough GPS - 25.271, 51.539Street - Ibn Firnas St Public Transport - Al Mansoura Metro and MetroLink buses Location in Qatar - Najma- Contacts - / info@lavillahospitality.com / lavillahospitality.com/

**Strato Hotel by Warwick** - Comfortably furnished, though with patchy service. Consider this hotel if you have early-morning or late-night flights, or a short stay. Rooftop pool, gym, sauna, and a couple of dining options. Convenient for the Airport, the National Museum and the Museum of Islamic Art.

Number of rooms - 97 Typical cost range - * Rough GPS - 25.269, 51.552 Street - C Ring Rd / Al Matar St Public Transport - Metro Red Line Umm Ghuwailina Location in Qatar - Umm Ghuwailina- Contacts - +974 4041 4444 / info.stratohotel@warwickhotels.com / warwickhotels.com/strato-hotel/

**Al Madina Suites** - This has a slightly older look offset by spacious rooms and comfortable facilities. Buffet-style restaurant and gym. The hotel is located in an older area of Doha (around 30 years old), less than 2km from Souq Al Waqif and Corniche.

Number of rooms - 40 small suites with a small kitchenette. Typical cost range - ** Rough GPS - 25.276, 51.534 Street - Al Nada Street Public Transport - Red Line Metro Al Jadeda Station Location in Qatar - Al Mansoura- Contacts - +974 4431 8800 / info@almadinasuites.com / www.almadinasuites.com/

**Holiday Villa Hotel & Residence** - A very distinctive hotel architecture: an oval building enclosing a courtyard that, in turn, encloses an 11-story tower - in total, over 700 rooms and apartments (the largest number in Qatar). Though an Asian chain, the service standards are generally lower than those of many other international chains. This is offset by a reasonable value-for-money otherwise. Five restaurants, a pool and a gym. There is a wide range of room options, each with different decor; ask to see before checking in. Close to local car rentals, though far from Corniche and other tourist areas. A large public park is opposite the entrance.

Number of rooms - 750 rooms in a large complex. Typical cost range - ** Rough GPS - 25.265, 51.525 Street - Rawdat Al Khail St / C Ring Road No Public Transport Location in Qatar - Al Mansoura- Contacts - +974 4408 4888 / info@holidayvilladoha.com / www.holidayvilladoha.com

**Hyatt Regency Oryx** - A former Rotana Hotel - it is a modern, functional hotel with a gym, pool, spa, and several restaurants. Probably, its convenience to the airport is a key point in choosing it. The area immediately next to the hotel has a number of plots that look ripe for development - and if started, this may impact the sound in rooms.

Number of rooms - 400 Typical cost range - *** Rough GPS - 25.268, 51.554 Street - off Al Matar St Public Transport - Metro Red

Line Umm Ghuwailina Location in Qatar - Umm Ghuwailina- Contacts - +974 4402 3333 / contact form / www.hyatt.com/en-US/hotel/qatar/hyatt-regency-oryx-doha/dohrd

## AL WAKRAH, MESAIEED & SOUTH QATAR

**Souq Al Wakra Hotel** Tivoli - South of Doha on a public beach in a leisure area. A charming hotel, in a modern reimagined village setting. With no more than two floors set around a series of courtyards. The rooms are compact, with a uniform style rather than an individualistic one. In general, the hotel lives up to its high government classification. The low density and courtyard style mean that you are unlikely to feel you are in anything other than a private home. A choice of 5 restaurants, including Mahaadeg, with views of the Gulf.

Number of rooms - 101 Typical cost range - **** Rough GPS - 25.174, 51.610 Street - Al Loulou St Public Transport - Al Wakrah Metro & MetroLink bus Location in Qatar - Al Wakrah- Contacts - +974 4428 7888 / souqalwakra@tivolihotels.com / www.tivolihotels.com/en/souq-al-wakra-tivoli

**Sealine Beach**, A Murwab Resort - Low-rise property, with only 35 rooms in the main building- this is a chalet & villa property. Owned by a Qatar government organisation, though not run by a brand-name chain, unlike several others in Doha. This is one of the more established hotels in Qatar. Pool, gym, spa, and a 1.3km long sandy beach - partially shared by a simple hotel to the south. Not far from the sand dunes and inland sea.

Number of rooms - 95 Units Typical cost range - ***** Rough GPS - 24.862, 51.514 Street - Sealine Beach Rd Public Transport - No public transport Location in Qatar - Khawr Al Udaid / Mesaieed- Contacts - +974 4021 4000 / info@sealinebeachqatar.com / www.sealinebeachqatar.com/

## EDUCATION CITY & DOHA WEST

**Asherij Hotel** offers limited services, a small gym and a coffee shop. Larger suites have a small kitchenette. Rooms have different decorations - ask to see what's available. A mix of residential and business appeal, this is just inside the C Ring Rd and about a 2.5km walk (if you want) to the Corniche.

Number of rooms - 100 Typical cost range - * Rough GPS - 25.282, 51.508 Street - Al Quds St /Majda St Public Transport - Gold Line Metro Al Saad Location in Qatar - Fereej Bin Mahmoud-

Contacts - +974 440 828 28 / info@asherijhotel.com / www.asherijhotel.com/

**Premier Inn Doha Education City**. The hotel offers outstanding value with comfortable, simply furnished rooms. This modern accommodation could be a good choice for a business person. A small pool, gym and restaurant add to the appeal. The hotel does offer a complimentary shuttle into town. This area is principally the educational focus of Doha, about 10km west of the Corniche. In the general area are the new Qatar National Convention Centre, National Library, Mataf Arab Museum of Modern Art and Shaqab Equestrian Stables

Number of rooms - 219 Typical cost range - * Rough GPS - 25.322, 51.430 Street - east of Garafat Al Rayyan Rd Public Transport - Metro Green Line Education City - 800m walk or Grey Tram Line Location in Qatar - Education City- Contacts - +974 4007 8333 / reservations.dec@mena.premierinn.com / global.premierinn.com/en/hotel/doha-education-city

**Qatar Youth Hostels Association** - A relatively simple accommodation offering, though far from basic. Its focus is on students or similar, and it offers a very patchy service. A basic coffee shop and do-it-yourself laundry.

Number of rooms - 40 Typical cost range - * Rough GPS - 25.317, 51.464 Street - Jawaan St Public Transport - +974 4421 7157 info@hi-qatar.com https://hi-qatar.com/ Public Transport Joaan.

*Premier Inn Doha Education City*

**Centro Capital Doha** - Simple, clean rooms create a modern look. All-day dining, with a bar, A small rooftop pool & gym, and 2 good restaurants. A newer area of Doha - about a 2km walk from the Corniche

Number of rooms - 229 Typical cost range - ** Rough GPS - 25.284, 51.512 Street - Al Jazeera St Public Transport Metro Gold Line Al Sadd - 1km away Location in Qatar - Fereej Bin Mahmoud- Contacts - +97444555000 / Contact Form / www.rotana.com/centrohotels/qatar/doha/centrocapitaldoha

**Zubarah Boutique Hotel Doha** - A small hotel with a small Spa and three small dining options. Mainly in a mix of residential and small business areas. It could do with refurbishment.

Number of rooms - 45 Typical cost range - ** Rough GPS - 25.270, 51.518 Street - Al Rawabi St No Public Transport - Location in Qatar - Rawdat Al Khail- Contacts - +974 4447 0000 / info@zubarah.com / www.zubarahhotels.com/

**The Torch Doha** - The most distinctive hotel in Doha, opened for the Asian Games. Rooms are simple in appearance, yet modern and opulent. The restaurants are unique and all worth a visit, especially 360. There are no grounds. Eight dining options, a gym and a remarkably small swimming pool. Nearby are sports stadiums and Villaggio Mall. It's, unfortunately, well out of the city centre. Torch Hospitality operates 3 other very different properties: Al Aziziyah Boutique Hotel, Mina Hotel & Residences, and 21 High Street Residence.

Number of rooms: 163 rooms across 51 floors, spanning 300 meters in height. Typical cost range - **** Rough GPS - 25.262, 51.445 Street - off Al Waab Street, Al Buwairda St Public Transport - Metro Gold Line Sport City Location in Qatar - Baaya / Aspire- Contacts - +974 4446 5600 / reservation@thetorchdoha.com / www.thetorchdoha.com.qa

**The Westin Doha Hotel & Spa** - Modern exterior matches the interior. Spa, gym and fitness, along with sheltered gardens. Several good restaurants - southwest of the city centre

Number of rooms - 364 Typical cost range - **** Rough GPS - 25.275, 51.514 Street - Salwa Rd Public Transport - Bus 31, 32, 33.34, 137, 136, 301 Location in Qatar - Fereej Bin Mahmoud- Contacts - +974 4492 1555 / No email / www.marriott.com/hotels/travel/dohwi-the-westin-doha-hotel-and-spa/

**NORTHEAST QATAR**

**Tio Sea Resort** (was Al Sultan Beach Resort) - Quirky hotel with a pool on a beach. A premium price compared to 5* hotels in Doha for this hotel's more modest offering. Along with the beach (and a mangrove swamp), a pool is the key asset - a basic restaurant provides food. The staff are helpful.

Number of rooms - 187 Typical cost range - **** Rough GPS - 25.685, 51.522 Street - Corniche Al Khor Public Transport Bus 702 & 722 from Lusail Location in Qatar - Al Khor - Contacts - ++974 4041 7111 www.tiosearesort.com/

**Simaisma Al Murwab Resort** - A property of villas set well back from but with access to the sea. Owned by a company of the Qatari government. Pool, gym, tennis, and beach. Opportunities for scuba diving

Number of rooms: 52; all villas offer up to 4 bedrooms. Typical cost range - ****** Rough GPS - 25.584, 51.488 Street - off Al Khor Coastal Rd Public Transport - No public transport Location in Qatar - Sumaysimah- Contacts - +974 4479 9555 / info@simaisma.com / www.simaisma.com/

## DUKHAN & WEST COAST, CENTRAL QATAR, AL RUWAIS & NORTH COAST

Zulal Wellness Resort - A newish upmarket hotel, managed by Thailand's Chiva-Som, on Qatar's northern tip. Opposite the hotel are two islands, and a few kilometres away is the town of Al Ruwais.

Number of rooms - 120 Typical cost range - ***** Rough GPS - 26.155, 51.242 Street - Public Transport - none - Location in Qatar - Al Ruwais- Contacts - +974 4008 4999 / info@msheireb.com / www.msheireb.com/zulal-wellness-resort/

**Hilton Salwa** - One of Qatar's newest hotels. Set on an expansive beach of 3+km in a location where it can only appeal as a resort property. With over 20 dining options to support 360 accommodation units (villas, suites, etc.), there's an option for everyone. A key attraction is a water adventure park.

Number of rooms 361, Typical cost range - **** Rough GPS 24.848 ,50.857 Public Transport - none - Location in Qatar - Salwa Road, southwest coast - Contacts +974 4423 6666 www.hilton.com

# CHAPTER 4
# BACKGROUND
## AND WHAT TO SEE

The State of Qatar occupies a limestone peninsula extending approximately 160 km into the Arabian Gulf from the east coast of the Arabian Peninsula. It shares its only land border with Saudi Arabia to the south. The coastline, stretching over 560 km, frames a landscape of low-lying rocky desert. Notable topography includes the Jebel Fuwairit outcrops in the north-east and the massive "singing" sand dunes of Khor Al Udaid (the Inland Sea) in the south-east – a rare geological phenomenon where the sea encroaches deep into the heart of the desert. The total land area is approximately 11,627 sq. km.

**Flag: in 'Qatar Maroon'**

*Qatar Flag*

The national flag (nationally refered to as *Al Adaam*) is white and 'Qatar Maroon', separated by a vertical serrated edge of nine white points. These points signify Qatar as the ninth member of the 'reconciled Emirates' following the 1916 Anglo-Qatari Treaty. The unique maroon hue is historically linked to the ancient purple dye industry on Bin Ghannam Island (Purple Island). This dye was extracted from the *Murex* sea snail (*Hexaplex kuesterianus*); the intense heat of the desert sun fermented the dye to a distinct deep red-violet rather than the brighter Tyrian purple found elsewhere.

### Economy & Wealth

Qatar remains one of the world's wealthiest nations per capita, driven by the North Field – the world's largest non-associated natural gas field. While oil remains a factor, the nation's transition to a global Liquefied Natural Gas (LNG) powerhouse provides a fiscal horizon stretching well into the next century. This wealth has funded a rapid "top-down" urban transformation, shifting the focal point from pearling dhows to the skyscrapers of West Bay in less than three generations.

### Population & Language

As of February 2026, the population is approximately 3,173,500, resulting in a density of 273 persons per sq. km. The demographic is highly urbanised, with the vast majority residing in the capital, Doha (*Ad Dawhah*).

**Language:** Arabic is the official language. English serves as the *lingua franca* of commerce. Due to the diverse workforce, Hindi, Urdu, and Bengali are ubiquitous in daily life.

### Governance & Religion

The State is a hereditary monarchy ruled by the **Al Thani** family. The Amir (head of state) appoints the government, and Islam is the state religion, providing the framework for the country's legal and social traditions.

### Logistics & Practicalities

**Currency:** The Qatari Riyal (**QAR**) is pegged to the US Dollar at a fixed rate of **$1 = QAR 3.64** (it is often rounded in casual text to **QAR 3.65**, but the official peg is **QAR 3.64**). One Riyal is divided into 100 Dirhams.

**Internet & Phone:** Internet domain is .qa. Country phone code +974 - there are no fixed line area codes - mobile numbers are 7 digits - starting 3,5,6,7

**Climate:** A desert climate characterised by extreme humidity and heat from May to September. The "window" for cultural travel is November to February, when temperatures are mild.

**Work Hours:** * **Government:** 07:00 – 14:00.
**Private Sector:** Often split-shift (08:00 – 12:00 and 16:00 – 20:00) or straight-shift (08:00 – 17:00).
**Retail:** Malls typically operate 10:00 – 22:00. On Fridays, businesses close for the midday *Jumu'ah* prayer, reopening around 14:00. Smaller, non mall shops might close 12:30-16:00.

∽

# Geography

On the eastern coast of the Arabian Peninsula, Qatar, a peninsula itself, is one of the world's smallest states at 11,627 square kilometres (sq. km). It stretches about 190 km from south to north and has a maximum width of 90 km from east to west. The country includes several offshore islands, such as Halul (some 97 km northeast of Doha), Al Ashat (60 km south of Doha), and Fasht Ad Dibal (northwest of Al Ruwais in northern Qatar).

Qatar geologically is part of the Arabian Shelf, the eastern sedimentary areas of the Arabian Plate that are moving north and being subducted under the Iranian/Eurasian plates. The geology of Qatar includes gravel and sandstone of the Hofuf Formation, deposited by rivers over the last 1.5 million years. The Hofuf Formation lies over the Dam Formation of the Miocene Period (approximately 23-2.6 million years ago). This formation is composed of clay and limestone and is found mainly in southwestern Qatar. Below the Dam Formation is the Dammam Formation, much of which is chalky limestone and dolomite. The Dammam Formation, created during the Middle Eocene (48-38 million years ago), extends over most of Qatar. It is a karst limestone environment featuring sinkholes and caves, which are thought to have developed over the past 560,000 years. Typical sinkholes can be found off Salwa Road, to the northwest and southeast of the Rawdat Rashid Interchange (GPS 25.172, 51.327). These sinkholes and caves, often collecting water run-off, are locally called *dahl*. Below the Dammam Formation is the Rus Formation, a chalky limestone and marl/clay also formed during the Middle Eocene.

Key structural elements within Qatar's rock formations are anticlines: rock strata that have been forced into a convex (upward and then downward) arch. This was enabled by the movement of ancient, deep-seated Hormuz Salt deposits rising towards the surface. It is here, in the upper part of the arch, where suitable 'capping' rock is found, that Qatar's wealth - its oil and gas - is trapped. The primary anticlines include the Qatar Arch, which extends from the south of the country into Iran; in its northeast, the vast North Gas Field is located primarily within the Permian-Triassic Khuff Formation. Others include the Dukhan Anticline, which trends from the south to the northwest, a few kilometres inland from the coast up to the area of Dukhan. This uplift has exposed the fossiliferous Dam Formation (from the Miocene epoch) and has trapped the Dukhan oilfield within the crest of the Dukhan Anticline.

Almost devoid of notable contours, Qatar's highest point is Qurayn Abu Al Bawl (GPS 24.717, 51.047) in the southwest, also listed as Al Galail. This location, at an elevation of 103 metres, overlooks the Saudi Arabian border 19 km away. Access is west from Route 59 at GPS 24.713, 51.069. Please take care regarding photography and other activities here and at all government buildings, as it is next to a security installation. The land gradually drops in elevation from there towards the north. However, there are low hills in the north, and the general flatness makes any rock outcrop noteworthy. Shallow dry valleys, called *wadi* in Arabic, are found throughout the country.

The Khor Al Udaid area features dunes and *sabkha* (mud, sand, and gypsum salt flats). The sands are aeolian (wind-blown) in origin, while the *sabkha*, which often appears solid, can be a quicksand-like trap for unwary drivers. To Doha's west and northwest are karst limestone areas with depressions symptomatic of erosion and sinkholes. North of Doha, the coast is sandy, created following changes in the level of the Gulf, which, when lower over 10,000 years ago, allowed sand from the extensive exposed seabed to be blown inland.

Qatar shares a single land border of 80 km (approx.) with Saudi Arabia, which was ratified in 2001. It has sea borders with Bahrain to the west, the United Arab Emirates (UAE) to the east, and Iran to the north, as well as sea borders with Saudi Arabia to the southwest and southeast. The Qatari/Saudi border runs through Khor Al Udaid, an inlet of the Gulf in the southeast of Qatar. The sea borders with the UAE (the Al Bunduq field) are also managed through joint agreements.

The sea border with Bahrain was also agreed upon in 2001. The ratification resulted in the Hawar Islands, a few hundred metres off Qatar's west coast, being certified as Bahraini territory. Areas disputed with Bahrain and awarded to Qatar at the same time were Al Zubarah [PAGE 167, 298] on Qatar's northwest mainland, the isolated islets of Fasht Ad Dibal northwest of Al Zubarah, and Jinan Island northwest of Dukhan on the west coast.

Be cautious near any of Qatar's international borders, as Bahrain, Saudi Arabia, and the UAE arrest people who are in their territory illegally.

**Climate**

Qatar experiences a desert climate defined by scorching, humid summers and warm winters. During July – the hottest month – the highest temperature officially recorded in the country was at Turayna in the central south, reaching 51.4°C on 2 July 2021. The physical reality of this heat is intensified by coastal moisture; humidity can easily reach 100% when a night fog forms, though it typically hovers around 40% during the day. In the coolest month of January, the daytime temperature might peak at 31°C (with an average of 22°C), while the minimum drops to 12°C.

Rainfall is unlikely at any time of year, with the highest probability between December and March. Winds are usually light, coming from the south in the summer (the Arabian Sea monsoon season) and shifting from the north in winter, when weather come from central Asia. This prevailing northwesterly wind – known locally as Al Shamal – is the primary driver for springtime dust storms. Originating over Iran, Iraq, and the northern Arabian Peninsula, these storms can roll in and shroud the country like a heavy woollen blanket, lingering for several days.

Climate statistics can sometimes be casually stated in public data. For instance, the term 'average temperature' (Celsius) can be misleading. The average July figure in Qatar given by www.holiday-weather.com is 37°C. This 37°C statistic actually represents the average 24 hour mean. While the absolute highest temperature recorded in the country has exceeded 51°C in July – this therefore is a possible maximum you might experience.

NATURE

With Qatar's extreme desert climate, plants and animals face constant stress to survive. An increasingly developed human environment adds to these pressures for many species, though some have taken advantage of new man-made environments.

*Acacia tortilis*

## Flora

Qatar's fauna ultimately depends on its 300+ species of flora. The dominant trees include the 'Ghaf', *Prosopis cineraria*. This large tree, with its feathery leaves, grows in sandy soils (though not usually in dunes) from the central region through to the north of Qatar. The 'Ghaf's leaves can trap moisture from fog, and the resultant water dripping to the ground becomes the tree's own irrigation system. Christ's thorn tree, *Ziziphus spina-christi*, grows in rocky *wadi* environments. Its flowers are a source of prized honey, and its small fruit is eaten by animals and, occasionally today, by humans. The 20-metre height and densely branched habit make it an ideal shade tree for villages. A similar tree, *Ziziphus mauritiana*, has been introduced, probably from Malaysia.

Three species of Acacia are found in Qatar. 'Salam', *Acacia ehrenbergiana*, is found in loose, sandy soils; its appearance varies, but it is usually a very ragged, bushy form, less than 3 metres in height. 'Garat' (Acacia nilotica) resembles Salam, though it is slightly smaller and less bushy. 'Simr', *Acacia tortilis* (also known as *Vachellia tortilis*), is widespread in Qatar and, as with other Acacias, prefers well-drained, sandy soil. This tree is the classic umbrella Acacia, also found in Africa, and unlike the other Acacias of Qatar, its flowers are creamy-coloured rather than yellow. All Acacia species have roots that can penetrate deep into the soil and fractured rock, up to 30 m in depth, in search of water. The trees respond to drought by dropping their leaves, which will regrow rapidly after rain.

On the north coasts and at Al Wakrah, south of Doha, the mangrove *Avicennia marina* grows on muddy areas in the intertidal zone. Its aerial roots absorb oxygen, water, and nutrients in a muddy, stagnant lagoon-type environment, while the leaves excrete the excess salts that result from growing in seawater. In Qatar, around Al Thakira, they grow up to around five metres high. It utilises pneumatophores - pencil-like aerial roots that rise from the anaerobic mud like tiny snorkels - to breathe during high tide.

**The Ecosystem:** This is a vital nursery for the maritime world. Beneath the tangled roots, a hidden universe of juvenile fish, purple swimming crabs, and shrimp finds sanctuary. Offshore, the seagrass beds support the Hawksbill Turtle (*Eretmochelys imbricata*) and grazing Dugong (*Dugong dugon*).

Botanical Diversity: Beyond the mangroves, the surrounding salt marshes and sabkha host a variety of salt-tolerant flora, including the succulent Anabasis (*Anabasis setifera*), the woody Salsola (*Salsola imbricata*), and the thorny Desert Box (*Lycium shawii*).

**Animals**

In historical times, Qatar's land mammals may have included the Asiatic lion and the Asiatic cheetah, along with their prey, such as antelope and gazelle. Today, the number and variety of land mammals, especially larger ones, have been reduced. Smaller mammals are the most common.

The dwarf gerbil (*Gerbillus nanus*), Wagner's gerbil (*Gerbillus dasyurus*), and Cheesman's gerbil (*Gerbillus cheesmani*) are widely dispersed small rodents. Cheesman's gerbil is probably the most readily seen towards dusk in sandy areas. Look for a light russet-coloured rodent about 11 centimetres (cm) in body length with a slightly longer tail and rear legs that are somewhat longer than the forelegs. These are opportunistic feeders, preferring seeds and grain, though they will eat insects if other food is scarce. They probably breed throughout the year, with each litter having up to eight young, and are vital food for owls and foxes. Jirds are related to gerbils, though they are larger, up to 16 cm, with a more rat-like appearance. The Libyan jird (*Meriones libycus*) and Sundevall's jird (*Meriones crassus*) are omnivorous and occupy sandy or rocky desert in Qatar. With its long, kangaroo-type rear legs, the Egyptian jerboa (*Jaculus jaculus*) occupies a similar niche to the gerbil. The more familiar house mouse (*Mus musculus*) and house rat (*Rattus rattus*) join these small rodents in Qatar.

The desert hedgehog (*Paraechinus aethiopicus*) is relatively small, at up to 25 cm. As with most other hedgehogs, this is a nocturnal animal that eats insects and small animals. This hedgehog breeds once a year with a litter of perhaps six young. The Cape hare (*Lepus capensis*) is comparable to the European brown hare in appearance and is up to 68 cm in length. Like most other desert animals, it is active from dusk to dawn, sheltering under vegetation during the day. This animal breeds year-round, producing up to 6 litters annually and 4 leverets per litter. The hare's adult size and the lack of larger predators in Qatar mean it is most vulnerable only when young, except when hunted by humans.

The largest predators in Qatar include three canids and possibly the honey badger (*Mellivora capensis*), which might live in the south of the country. The honey badger is omnivorous, about 75 cm long (excluding the tail), and may have a couple of cubs annually.

An adaptive predator, the golden jackal (*Canis aureus*), has a body length of up to 85 cm and a tail of about 25 cm, with a weight of 14 kilograms (kg. This jackal possibly breeds with feral dogs in Qatar. The species may be reclassified to *Canis lupaster*. Pure animals have a rusty-brown coat with a black back. Like most jackals, this omnivorous animal feeds on small rodents, lizards, and carrion, and supplements its diet with fruit and vegetation. They breed once a year and give birth to up to six pups. Found throughout Qatar, the Arabian red fox (*Vulpes vulpes arabica*) is a subspecies of the red fox, though with a less intense red colour. Ruppell's fox (*Vulpes rueppelli sabaea*) is a pale-coloured, desert-living fox, up to 74 cm long including its tail, and weighing less than 1.9 kg. They breed once a year with up to six pups. Like the jackal, these foxes are omnivorous, eating small animals, large insects, and plant products.

Bats include the desert long-eared bat (*Otonycteris hemprichii*) and Geoffroy's trident leaf-nosed bat (*Asellia tridens*), which are both insectivorous.

*Arabian Oryx*

Reintroduced species include the **Arabian oryx** (*Oryx leucoryx*), which has become the logo of Qatar Airways. The oryx can be up to 175 cm in length, 100 cm at shoulder height, and weigh up to 70 kg, with both sexes having twin horns of up to 65 cm. Their natural habitat is a desert environment, both stony and sandy, where they might roam in family groups of about ten animals. The white colour of the coat helps reflect heat, while in colder weather, the hair raises to expose the darker skin, allowing it to absorb heat.

The Arabian oryx can breed year-round, with a single calf born 8 months after mating. Calves are well camouflaged in desert conditions, having a mid-brown coat. Extinct in the wild by 1972 due to hunting, a breeding population was established in several zoos worldwide, most notably at Phoenix and San Diego Zoos. Animals were reintroduced into their original countries from the mid-1970s.

In Qatar, this reintroduction initially focused on Al Wabra Wildlife Preserve, a private zoo; later, other locations also bred the animal. In winter, the Arabian oryx can obtain its water by eating fresh vegetation, including grasses and leaves. In summer, they would roam to where rain had fallen.

The other major mammal reintroduced to Qatar is the Arabian sand gazelle (*Gazella subgutturosa marica*), locally called 'reem'. Due to hunting, the animal was extinct in Qatar by the end of the 1950s. It was reintroduced in the mid-1990s, notably in the Al Reem Reserve. Males can grow to 110 cm and weigh 30 kg. Both sexes have horns, though the males' are longer. In a safe environment, population growth can be rapid, as this gazelle can breed after about 18 months of age, and about 30% of live births are twins, with a gestation period of just over 5 months.

Arabian sand gazelle

# CAMEL

Qatar would hardly seem an Arab country without the Camel, *Camelus dromedarius*, the dromedary. The word 'camel' comes from the Arabic *jamal* (a male camel). The word 'dromedary', for the single-humped camel variety, comes from the Greek *dromos*, meaning race or racecourse, which is very apt in the world of camel racing today. All living dromedaries are domesticated animals; the wild type disappeared, perhaps 2,500 years ago. This domestication began at least by 1,000 BC, probably in southeast Arabia, when the wild camel population was declining, likely due to human predation.

Male camels can reach 2 metres at the shoulder and weigh 600 kg; females are perhaps 10% shorter and 30% lighter. The single hump is a fat-bearing organ; as fat can release water when metabolised due to a lack of food, it supports better survival during drought. The camel is a herbivore and grazes on the ground and browses on bushes and trees, though nowadays, a most of its diet is supplied as hay or other animal feed. Like a cow, the camel is a ruminant, so it spends much of its day either eating or ruminating. Remarkably, its body temperature can fluctuate by more than 10°C, and it can deal with a 30% water loss; either of these changes would kill most mammals. Fortunately, camels can replenish water at around 20 litres a minute, which is helpful when finding water in a desert climate.

From around 4 years of age, camels can breed, typically giving birth to a single baby after a gestation period of about 15 months. It may then live for some 50 years. In captivity, the dromedary has bred with the llama. In the wild, in areas such as Iran where their ranges overlap, dromedaries can breed with the two-humped Bactrian camel. In Turkey, Bactrian and dromedary camels are bred specifically in Izmir province, producing large, single-humped animals whose males compete in camel 'wrestling' events.

Camels have been used historically for long-distance transport, milk, meat, clothing, and more; they are, therefore, arguably more useful than cattle. Today in Qatar, they are bred for the prestige they bring, especially for racing. Camels are used for short races from about 18-24 months of age; the prime age is around six years, and these older camels can race at around 40 kmph. Though children were previously used as jockeys for their light weight, since 2007, the 'rider' has been a simple robot with a rotating whip to encourage the animal's speed. Prizes can include hundreds of thousands of Qatari Riyals and luxury cars. However, the sales value of the winner, which can reach US1,500,000, must be an added benefit. These high prices are obtained for animals that, like thoroughbred racehorses, have a known and admired lineage. Other camels might take part in camel beauty contests or milking contests. Again, the value of a successful animal might run to more than US1million, with the most expensive camel ever being sold for USD2.72million in the UAE (though rumours say one has been sold for USD9.5million). Camels have been banned from these beauty contests for having Botox injections to enhance their lip pouts. As they say, beauty is in the eye of the beholder.

Camel and calf suckling

## Lizards

Geckos are the most numerous lizards in terms of species and overall numbers. The Arabian desert gecko (Bunopus tuberculatus), rough-tailed gecko (Cyrtopodion scabrum), and Heyden's gecko (Hemidactylus robustus) are all found here. The yellow-bellied house gecko (Hemidactylus flaviviridis), as its name suggests, is the species most commonly seen inside buildings, where it feeds on insects; it may well be the most commonly seen lizard in Qatar. Other lizards include the Persian leaf-toed gecko (Hemidactylus persicus), Arabian short-fingered gecko (Stenodactylus arabicus), Slevin's short-fingered gecko (Stenodactylus slevini), Gulf short-fingered gecko (Pseudoceramodactylus khobarensis), Persian rock gecko (Pristurus rupestris), Arabian desert lizard (Acanthodactylus opheodurus), Blanford's short-nosed desert lizard (Mesalina brevirostris), Hadhramaut sand lizard (Mesalina adramitana), yellow-spotted agama (Trapelus flavimaculatus), Arabian toad-headed agama (Phrynocephalus arabicus), and eastern skink (Scincus mitranus).

*Arabian toad-headed agama*

The strangest lizard of Qatar is Zarudny's worm lizard

(Diplometopon zarudnyi), a limbless subterranean lizard. The largest lizards are the desert monitor (Varanus griseus), which can reach over 90 cm from nose to tail tip. They are active hunters and eat other reptiles, including the Egyptian spiny-tailed lizard (Uromastyx aegyptia), which is slightly smaller at up to 80 cm.

There is one toad species, the African common toad (Sclerophrys regularis), that may have been introduced from Egypt. Though Qatar is a hyper-arid country, these toads are expanding their distribution by using artificial irrigation systems.

**Snakes**

Snakes include the Sindh saw-scaled viper (Echis carinatus sochureki), a venomous ambush hunter of up to 50 cm in length; possibly the desert black snake (Walterinnesia aegyptia), which can exceed a metre in length and is a venomous hunter of small animals; the hooded malpolon or false cobra (Malpolon moilensis), a venomous rodent-eater that grows to over 1.5 m; the flowerpot snake (Indotyphlops braminus), a worm-like snake of only a few cm in length found in soil; the crowned dwarf snake (Eirenis coronella), a small, non-venomous snake of only about 30 cm in length; the crowned leaf-nosed snake (Lytorhynchus diadema), again non-venomous but slightly larger at up to 50 cm; and Clifford's diadem snake (Spalerosophis diadema), a six-foot-long hunter of rodents that is very mildly venomous.

**Insects**

The moths and butterflies of Qatar are thought to number fewer than 35 species, including the blue pansy (Junonia orithya), the clouded yellow (Colias croceus), and the painted lady (Vanessa cardui), whose family is also familiar in Europe.

**Birds**

Over 325 bird species have been recorded in Qatar, excluding introductions such as the red-necked ostrich, which is kept in zoos. Of these, about 119 species are relatively common, 83 are scarce but expected to be seen at some point in the year, 38 are seen regularly but are uncommon, 39 have been seen only once or twice, and about 46 are vagrant species. The overall number of species in Qatar is gradually increasing, principally due to the creation of new human-made environments. These include vegetated areas such as farms, parks, and golf clubs, and, less attractively, rubbish dumps where birds such as eagles, especially steppe eagles, feed.

Invasive species are probably among the most easily seen birds around Doha. The common myna, *Acridotheres tristis*, is an aggressive resident that breeds throughout Doha and its surroundings. Very territorial, it outcompetes and kills the young of similar-sized birds, and lives very freely alongside people. The Indian house crow, *Corvus splendens*, nests in trees and is found towards the coast in areas of human habitation. The house crow scavenges refuse and, like the myna, can live alongside people. From Africa or India, the rose-ringed parakeet, *Psittacula krameri*, is a common resident breeder and, like the myna, probably results from escaped cage birds. This is the parakeet seen in London and other cities worldwide that were not part of its original range. Another parakeet, the larger Alexandrine parakeet (Psittacula eupatria), is also found in Doha. These birds feed on nuts, fruit, and seeds, which can damage cultivation in Qatar.

Common Myna

Off the coast of Doha at Al Aaliya Island (a restricted location north of The Pearl), some 500 pairs of Socotra cormorant, *Phalacrocorax nigrogularis*, nest. This endangered species breeds in winter, always synchronously within any given colony. The great cormorant, *Phalacrocorax carbo*, occurs in lower numbers.

Birds readily seen on the coast include the greater flamingo, *Phoenicopterus roseus*, which is present from around November to April. They might also be found inland at Irkhaya Farm (25.013, 51.163) along with the black-crowned night heron (*Nycticorax*

*nycticorax*), grey heron (*Ardea cinerea*), and purple heron (*Ardea purpurea*).

European Roller

Smaller shorebirds are mostly winter visitors and include the grey plover (*Pluvialis squatarola*), common ringed plover (*Charadrius hiaticula*), little ringed plover (*Charadrius dubius*), Kentish plover (*Charadrius alexandrinus*), lesser sand plover (*Charadrius atrifrons*), greater sand plover (*Charadrius leschenaultii*), common snipe (*Gallinago gallinago*), European black-tailed godwit (*Limosa limosa*), bar-tailed godwit (*Limosa lapponica*), Eurasian whimbrel (*Numenius phaeopus*), Eurasian curlew (*Numenius arquata*), common redshank (*Tringa totanus*), marsh sandpiper (*Tringa stagnatilis*), common greenshank (*Tringa nebularia*), green sandpiper (*Tringa ochropus*), wood sandpiper (*Tringa glareola*), Terek sandpiper (*Xenus cinereus*), common sandpiper (*Actitis hypoleucos*), ruddy turnstone (*Arenaria interpres*), sanderling (*Calidris alba*), little stint (*Calidris minuta*), and dunlin (*Calidris alpina*).

Gulls and terns, which are mostly migratory species, include the slender-billed gull (*Chroicocephalus genei*), common black-headed gull (*Chroicocephalus ridibundus*), great black-headed gull (*Larus ichthyaetus*), steppe gull (*Larus barabensis*), gull-billed tern (*Gelochelidon nilotica*), Caspian tern (*Hydroprogne caspia*), lesser crested tern (*Thalasseus bengalensis*), white-winged tern (*Chlidonias leucopterus*), Saunders's tern (*Sternula saundersi*, seen throughout the year), and whiskered tern (*Chlidonias hybryda*, seen throughout the year).

Inland from Doha, some attractive migrants that should be seen include the flashing blue of the European roller (*Coracias garrulus*), the deeper blue of the Indian roller (*Coracias benghalensis*) - both these rollers are similar in size to a jackdaw or feral pigeon - the blue-cheeked bee-eater (*Merops persicus*), the European bee-eater (*Merops apiaster*), and the Eurasian hoopoe (*Upupa epops*), of which some stay in Qatar rather than moving on during migration.

*Steppe Eagle and Indian House Crows*

Smaller migratory species include the much-sought-after grey hypocolius (*Hypocolius ampelinus*), found in scrub; the rufous-tailed scrub robin (*Erythropygia galactotes*); the spotted flycatcher (*Muscicapa striata*); the red-spotted bluethroat (*Luscinia svecica*); the black redstart (*Phoenicurus ochruros*); the common redstart (*Phoenicurus phoenicurus*); the rufous-tailed rock thrush (*Monticola saxatilis*); the whinchat (*Saxicola rubetra*); the European stonechat (*Saxicola rubicola*); the northern wheatear (*Oenanthe oenanthe*); the Isabelline wheatear (*Oenanthe isabellina*); the desert wheatear (*Oenanthe deserti*); and the pied wheatear (*Oenanthe pleschanka*).

Expect to see the common kestrel (*Falco tinnunculus*) and the western osprey (*Pandion haliaetus*), which is resident along much of the coast and breeds in Qatar. Arriving in winter are the western marsh harrier (*Circus aeruginosus*), pallid harrier (*Circus macrourus*), and steppe eagle (*Aquila nipalensis*).

Less common birds include the crab-plover (*Dromas ardeola*), a distinctive wader with black-and-white plumage and a heavy bill, seen at Simaisma, though the resort's impact may affect their numbers. The North African red-necked ostrich (*Struthio camelus*) has been introduced to the Al Reem reserve.

**Sea Mammals**

Despite being almost landlocked and shallow, the Gulf has many sea mammals. These include the orca or killer whale (*Orcinus orca*), Bryde's whale (*Balaenoptera edeni*), Indo-Pacific bottlenose dolphin (*Tursiops aduncus*), Indo-Pacific humpbacked dolphin (*Sousa chinensis*), spinner dolphin (*Stenella longirostris*), often seen leaping out of the sea and rotating its body, and the dugong (*Dugong dugon*). The dugong can grow to around 3 metres and weigh up to 500 kg. They feed on seagrass in shallow waters, which makes the Gulf an ideal habitat. A single calf is born after a year's pregnancy and is dependent for almost two years, after which it might live for a further 65 years.

*Indo-Pacific bottlenose dolphin*

The Whale Shark (*Rhincodon typus*), the world's largest fish, is found in Qatar's seas. Qatar hosts one of the world's largest seasonal gatherings of these fish (often over 600 individuals) at the Al

Shaheen oil field from April to September. These appear to be seasonal feeding aggregations of mackerel tuna spawn. The whale shark also feeds on marine plankton, consuming small sardines and krill. These are drawn to the warm waters of the Arabian Gulf and use oil platforms as artificial reefs. It's possible, but not proven, that the Gulf waters are also a live birthing area.

### Sea Turtles

The Gulf is home to several sea reptiles, including the hawksbill turtle (*Eretmochelys imbricata*) and the green turtle (*Chelonia mydas*), both of which are found in Qatar's seas. Green turtles are the most common in Qatar's waters, where they feed on seagrass but do not appear to nest, while hawksbills do nest, but the adults move elsewhere to feed in coral reefs. The hawksbill has a hawk-beak-shaped mouth, while the green turtle's is more rounded.

The most detailed knowledge of any turtle is for the green turtle; however, it is likely that the hawksbill has a similar lifestyle in most respects. Only female turtles return to land, and then only to lay eggs; males never return to land after hatching. The female hawksbill may reach maturity around 20 years of age, and the green turtle at 25 years of age or older. A mature adult green turtle may measure 120 cm in shell length and weigh 170 kg, while a hawksbill may measure 85 cm and weigh 65 kg. The eggs are laid on a sandy beach with a relatively shallow slope. In Qatar, Fuwayrit beach is a prime location and is consequently closed during the peak nesting season from 1st April to 31st July.

Turtle mating takes place at sea near the shore, after which the female lays up to 140 eggs; the green turtle repeats this up to 4 times over a few weeks. They then leave, migrating to feeding grounds that may be hundreds of kilometres away. Each turtle returns to breed every 2-3 years, undoubtedly returning to its hatching beach when it matures. As with some other reptiles, the temperature of the environment surrounding the egg decides the sex of the hatchling. More females develop at temperatures over 30°C, and more males at temperatures under 30°C. The impact that global heating will have on the sex ratio is clear and will presumably affect total numbers over the long term unless they relocate to different, cooler areas to nest.

*Green Turtle*

The nesting process is designed to camouflage the location of the eggs, but even so, foxes may find and dig up a nest to eat the eggs. Around 60 days after the eggs are laid, they hatch, and the hatchlings coordinate their eruption from the nest, appearing en masse and scrambling together towards the sea. On their way, hatchlings are predated by ghost crabs (*Ocypode rotundatus*), gulls, and foxes, and in the sea by fish. The result of this predation and other causes of death is that perhaps 990 out of every 1,000 eggs laid may never give rise to an adult. The young turtle may spend the next five years in open waters, feeding on krill and other small marine life, before moving into shallow waters. The green turtle feeds on seagrass and algae, while the hawksbill is omnivorous, though it prefers sea sponges, which, though toxic to many sea animals, do not affect it.

Other sea reptiles include various sea snakes, which are found generally in shallow waters and are best given a wide berth. They include the annulated sea snake (*Hydrophis cyanocinctus*), the Gulf sea snake (*Hydrophis lapemoides*), the reef sea snake (*Hydrophis ornatus*) in shallow water, including sandy-bottomed areas, the yellow sea snake (*Hydrophis spiralis*), and the yellow-bellied sea snake (*Pelamis platurus*), which may reach over two metres and inhabits shallow water. All are extremely venomous, as their venom must remain potent even when diluted in seawater.

**Nature Reserves**

There are 12 land reserves in Qatar, two of which also include marine areas. In most cases, the reserves seem little different in development from places outside their boundaries. Most are freely accessible.

- Ash Shahaniyah covers 12 sq. km in central Qatar. It was a sanctuary for the endangered Arabian oryx from Muaither farm. Today, there is also a pen for ostriches. Admission is 'free' but only through a paid tour with a tour company.
- The 54 sq. km Al Masshabiya reserve is in southwest Qatar, near the Abu Samara border. Here, there are sandy plains, some hills, and valleys. Seasonal grass, herbs, and wild trees grow on sand dunes in the reserve. Arabian oryx, gazelle, and other endangered animals were settled here.
- The Al Eraiq reserve is next to Al Masshabiya and is intended to protect its vegetation from overgrazing.
- In northeast Qatar, 64 km from Doha, Al Thakhira was chosen as a natural land and sea reserve and includes the small island of Um Far opposite the housing at Al Thakhira and natural mangroves. The reserve has rich marine biodiversity and the *Avicennia marina* mangrove.
- The Al Reem reserve lies on the western coast and covers around 16 per cent of Qatar's total land area. It has distinctive calcareous formations alongside the western coast and is recognised under UNESCO's Man and the Biosphere Programme.
- The Al Wasil nature reserve measures around 36 sq. km. It was chosen in line with biodiversity strategy aims and to limit the rapid urbanisation on Qatar's eastern coast.
- Khor Al Udaid, also known as the 'Inland Sea', was made a land and sea nature reserve in 2007 and stretches over around 1,833 sq. km. It has large white sand dunes and presents a unique mix of geological terrains and environmental factors, creating potential natural habitats for various flora and fauna. Despite it being a reserve, 4x4 vehicles use it as a recreation area, and tourist camps line the shore.
- The 53 sq. km Al Rafa reserve is found near the Al Rayyan and Al Wajba areas, west of Doha.
- Smaller reserves include the Sunai reserve, northwest of Doha; the Um Al Amad Reserve, 25 km northeast of Doha; and the Um Qarn, 30 km north of Doha.
- Finally, Irkaya Farm is off the Abu Samra Road about 50 km

west of Doha in the south-central plain of Qatar. Though also a nature reserve, the area is a man-made environment of sewage settling ponds and agricultural pivot fields, and it is these that attract wildlife, most especially birds.

*Pivot field irrigation*

## AGRICULTURE

Perhaps the key reason humans have been able to survive on the Qatar peninsula is access to the sea and a symbiotic relationship with the camel. Searing heat, intense sun, and a lack of rain mean that agriculture in Qatar depends on man-made irrigation, including permanent irrigation. As a result, farming has historically been subsistence-based, with limited scope for crops and a vast range of area needed for animal grazing.

There are no permanent rivers in Qatar, so most water, until recently, was derived from local rainfall, with the runoff fed into localised water catchment features. Qatar's soils are relatively shallow, with high salt levels and low nutrients due to high evaporation and high temperatures. These issues make crop cultivation difficult.

Today, most of the water for agriculture in Qatar is pumped from two aquifers: the Aruma aquifer in southwest Qatar (recharged from the west and Saudi Arabia) and the more critical Rus aquifer northwest of Doha. Agriculture is probably possible over less than 300 sq. km of Qatar, while the actual area in use is around 85 sq. km.

*Date Palms - with bunches of dates*

## DATE PALM

The quintessential tree of Arabia, the date palm (Phoenix dactylifera), is grown over about 24 sq. km in Qatar. In modern agriculture, the date tree is almost entirely dependent on humans for fruit production. The tree is single-sex; therefore, female-flowering trees need a separate male tree for pollination. As male date trees do not produce fruit and thus 'waste' space, an artificial ratio of around one male tree to 100 female trees is created. This means each female tree requires artificial pollination.

Artificial irrigation is needed for date palms in Qatar today, typically by drip-feed irrigation. After about eight years, the tree can produce fruit. Date palms can reach heights of around 20 metres and live for approximately 90 years, depending on the variety. All aspects of the tree and date fruit cultivation are labour-intensive; however, the fruit, which ripens in mid-summer, has a high value, so there is a reward. Ripe dates have a high sugar content, so the fruit, after either drying or being compressed into a mass, is not easily damaged by bacteria or fungus. The date fruit can therefore be stored and used for up to two years. Qatar now has around 600,000 date palms, producing about 21,000 tons of fruit annually.

### Other Agriculture

The salad and vegetable sector is currently undergoing a evolution, with production expected to reach 120,000 tonnes by the end of 2026. Companies like Agrico and QATFA now utilise advanced Nutrient Film Technique (NFT) and vertical stacking to produce Lettuce (Lactuca sativa) and Spinach (Spinacia oleracea) year-round. The Qatari startup VFarms , http://vfarms.qa, 15km northeast of Ash Shahaniyah, cultivates Iceberg lettuce by using atmospheric water generators to harvest moisture directly from the humid Gulf air in their vertical farm facility. This produce has begun to penetrate regional markets; in 2025, Qatari agricultural and processed food exports to the United Arab Emirates and Saudi Arabia reached approximately QAR115M. Despite these gains, the "problem of scale" persists. The indirect energy required for desalination and LED lighting remains a significant overhead. Other greenhouse crops include cucumbers, peppers, strawberries, and tomatoes. Root vegetables grown include beetroot, carrots, onions, and potatoes, Fruits and vegetables are also imported, along with wheat imports of over 250,000 tons.

**Livestock and Fish**

Qatar's metamorphosis from an import-dependent peninsula to a regional leader in food security was jump-started by the 2017 diplomatic crisis. While the state formerly relied on neighbours for 80% of its dairy, it has since achieved a 99% self-sufficiency rate in fresh milk and its derivatives. This was largely driven by Baladna, https://baladna.com/, near Al Khor, which airlifted thousands of Holstein Friesian cattle to a desert 'farm'. This is now equipped with advanced climate-control systems to deal with temperatures up to 50°C to support some 24,000 animals. The industry has matured beyond raw milk and meat into high-value processing, with new facilities producing yogurts, evaporated milk and sterilised cream that were previously sourced entirely from overseas. To maintain scale, producers must import vast quantities of fodder and grain (Zea mays) from international markets, as less than 2% of Qatar's land can support agriculture. Some progress has been made using treated sewage effluent for local hay production.

Manufacturing has followed this upward trajectory, with local consumer brands now dominating the retail landscape. Companies like Qatar Pafki and Albina Snacks have changed from simple re-packaging to full-scale production of corn-based snacks and roasted nuts, while Rosetta Pasta has established an alternative to Italian imports.Qatar's processed foodstuffs have begun to penetrate regional markets. In 2025, the value of these exports reached approximately QAR115M, with the United Arab Emirates and Saudi Arabia emerging as primary destinations for Qatari-made snacks, beverages, and dairy. This however is a two way flow. Sheep and goats meat supplies around 18% of local demand – though beef production is negligible. Qatar's ability to turn a geopolitical blockade into a manufacturing springboard has redefined its role in the Gulf's economic ecosystem.

Qatar is almost self-sufficient in chicken meat – with a annual production of up to 40 million birds a year. It is producing around 140million eggs a year – helping it achieve almost 30% sufficiency.

The number of camels is about 94,000 animals, many of these are electronically tagged. A small proportion of these are used for camel meat.

Fish supplies are increasingly focused on aquaculture off the coast near Al Khor, with about 500tonnes produced – out of a total 15,000 tonnes. Millions of juvenile fish are released into the wild to bolster stocks. Popular fish are Grouper; Kingfish and Mackerel Tuna.

Historic Use of the Sea as a Resource: Excavations at Bin Ghannam Island (also known as Al Khor Island or Purple Island) have revealed ample evidence of the exploitation of fish and molluscs. Tools found include fishhooks dating to 5610 BC. The inclusion of 'purple' in the island's name stems from its being a base for the exploitation of purple dye from the shellfish *Thais savignyi*, a murex sea snail. Vast quantities of the shellfish produce a dye that, after extensive treatment in air & sun, is a variety of 'Tyrian purple', the imperial purple associated with the city of Tyre and used in Rome and elsewhere. Qatar's shellfish created a colour towards the red end of purple, though it would settle to a maroon over time. From around 1400 BC, shell middens show a lengthy timeline of occupation at this site, which apparently was under the Kassites' (of Mesopotamia) control . The occupation appears to have followed a cycle of use, abandonment, and reuse over hundreds of years, perhaps serving as a base for seasonal activities such as pearling.

At Ras Abrouq, on the coast of western Qatar, evidence of occupation dating back to around 5,000 BC has been found, including potsherds and fish remains. Clearly, the coast and sea were exploited by early occupants of Qatar. The exploitation of the pearl oyster (*Pinctada* sp.) has been documented from excavations at more than a dozen sites along the coast of Eastern Arabia, dating from the

6th to the 4th millennium BC. This activity included pearl diving and was a seasonal practice, concentrated between April and September, with the pearls exported, probably originally to Mesopotamia.

~

## POPULATION & MAJOR PROJECTS

**Population makeup**

Qatar is unusual in that around 88% of its residents are not nationals of the country and are unlikely to become nationals. A breakdown of Qatar's current population based on available data, primarily from Total Population 2025 projections: Approximately 3.12 million - Qatari Nationals: Approximately 0.36 million (around 11.6% of the total population) Non-Nationals (Expatriates): Approximately 2.76 million (around 88.4% of the total population). The population growth over the last couple of decades has been extraordinary - in 2004, approximately 744,029 people were resident in Qatar, and in 2014, approximately 2,218,372 people. The driver of this recent growth is the increase in LNG production and export since 1997.

The non-nationals come from diverse countries - India: Approximately 700,000 (21.8%); Bangladesh: Approximately 400,000 (12.5%); Nepal: Approximately 400,000 (12.5%); Egypt: Approximately 300,000 (9.35%); Philippines: Approximately 236,000 (7.36%); Pakistan: Approximately 180,000 (4.7%); Sri Lanka: Approximately 140,000 (4.35%). The remarkable percentages of foreign nationals to Qatari nationals are broadly comparable to those in the UAE and somewhat higher than in Monaco - which has a similar approach to gaining nationality as does Qatar. Looking at the total population - Males: approximately 2.40 million (around 76.8% of the total population) & Females: approximately 0.72 million (around 23.2% of the total population). The gender imbalance is caused by the fact that the vast majority of non-nationals are males, typically in non-technical work. To simplify, they are employed because of their low cost relative to the work they provide - they enable higher profit margins within the value-added output. Breakdown by Age (Total Population): 0-14 years: Approximately 0.41 million (13.1%); 15-24 years: Approximately

0.36 million (11.5%); 25-54 years: Approximately 2.18 million (69.9%) - this is the largest age group, reflecting a large working-age non-national population; 55-64 years: Approximately 0.12 million (4.0%); 65 years and over: Approximately 0.05 million (1.5%).

Figures drawn from a variety of sources, including data.gov.qa and npc.qa (last census 2020), the UN and extrapolation from these.

In essence, non-nationals in Qatar mainly work for and serve each other, forming socio-economic silos.

Most of the non-national population works in companies across construction & infrastructure, oil & gas, services such as retail & hospitality, healthcare, information technology, education & domestic services.

Qatari nationals tend to work in government as civil servants, as well as in finance, banking, education, the armed forces, and the police. There is a mandatory military service requirement - governed by Law No. 5 of 2018, which replaced the original 2013 legislation - of 12 months for male Qatari nationals between 18 and 35 years of age. Females are encouraged to join on a voluntary basis.

**Major Projects**

Projects include gas and oil extraction and support infrastructure, as well as ports Hamad Port, Ras Laffan Port, Hamad International Airport, the metro system, and vast new towns such as The Pearl and Lusail. High-profile events, along with their associated infrastructure, include the 2006 Asian Games, the 2011 Arab Games, the 2021 F1 Qatar Grand Prix, the 2021 FIFA Arab Cup, the 2022 FIFA World Cup, the 2023 AFC Asian Cup (held in 2024). The 10-year contract to hold an annual F1 race, with the first on 8 October 2023, has cemented Qatar's position as a major host for sports events following its successful hosting of the FIFA World Cup. The year gap from the 2021 F1 Grand Prix and the 2023 contract was to allow the 2022 World Cup to be held.

Looking forward, Qatar will again host the Asian Games in November 2030, and in July 2025, the Qatar Olympic Committee officially confirmed it has entered the "Continuous Dialogue" phase with the IOC for the 2036 Olympic and Paralympic Games.

The non-nationals working on these projects have helped fuel Qatar's tremendous population growth. Population growth is expected to continue until 2070, when it may reach 5 million, before gradually declining slightly.

## Towns and Major Divisions

The regional breakdown of population by administrative region (according to Qatar's Planning and Statistical Authority, QPSA) showed that Doha, Al Wakrah to its south, and Al Dayyan to Doha's north on the central east coast accounted for 50% of Qatar's total population. Given that much of Qatar is within a 60-minute drive of the Corniche in Doha, most of the country's towns and villages are within Doha's potential commuter belt.

*West Bay skyline - Doha*

**Doha**: (GPS: 25.291, 51.533; PAGE 50 onwards) By far the largest city in Qatar, all other towns probably serve as suburbs, dormitories, or service towns for Doha. Most of Qatar's key attractions are in Doha, including Souq Waqif, the Museum of Islamic Art, Msheireb Museums, the National Museum, and Katara. Doha's places of interest are listed separately under their names.

**The Pearl**: (GPS: 25.368, 51.551; PAGE 136) An extensive man-made development to the north of Doha. Public transport includes the Legtaifiya Metro station on the Red Line, with free MetroLink buses (05:50-22:00 daily) running into the development. It consists primarily of man-made islands with apartment housing, though hotels, retail, and restaurants abound. The style is a modern take on a European Mediterranean town, intended to evoke an impression of Venice, with waterways and non-Venetian-style high-rise buildings. Many of the apartments are available to buy or on long lease. Other areas in Qatar also have similar purchase options, including Al Khor Resort, Msheireb, and Old Ghanim. The most visited sections of The Pearl are Porto Arabia, Viva Bahriya, and the Qanat Quartier, each of which is enclosed by lagoons with a 'pearl-like' island in its centre.

*The Pearl*

**Lusail**: (GPS: 25.417, 51.503; PAGE 139) About 20 km north of central Doha. Public transport includes the Lusail Metro (Red Line), which has a MetroLink feeder bus service, and the Lusail Tram. Less than 30 years ago, Lusail was an empty *sabkha* and desert. Coastal landfilling and excavation have created a new town and a new coastline. The development is still at a relatively early stage; however, it already includes the 2022 World Cup main stadium, the Lusail Multi-purpose Arena, the Lusail Circuit, and Place Vendôme, another massive shopping mall. The marina area will service sea-based leisure craft and up-market housing. Qetaifan Island will have a range of hotels, including floating hotels. Perhaps the most iconic building is Katara Towers, a crescent-shaped hotel.

**Al Khor**: (GPS: 25.680, 51.496; PAGE 146) Located about a 50 km drive north of central Doha. The bus station feeding into Al Khor is Lusail, next to the metro station, a 50-minute journey. Focused on a sea lagoon with patches of mangrove, including Bin Ghannam Island, this town has a variety of natural habitats. It features a fishing harbour with dozens of dhows and a small retail fish market. Though there are a few historical sites, they are not a 'must-see'. Probably one of the most interesting today is the house of Sheikh Tamim bin Hamad Al Thani's maternal grandfather, Abdullah Bin Nasser Al Misnad. The old house is south of the small harbour, just west of a children's play area on the junction of Al Khor Road and Al Arab St. Within Al Khor are restaurants and accommodation. To the north of the main town, Al Khor Community is purpose-built housing for employees at Qatar Gas and other employers at Ras Laffan, 20 km to the north. Outlying areas include Al Thakhira and Ash Shafallahiyah.

**Ras Laffan**: (GPS: 25.892, 51.560) Located some 80 km north of Doha. Lusail is linked to Al Khor, south of the Ras Laffan industrial area. Ras Laffan is an extensive industrial development and is the major employer in northern Qatar, forming part of Qatar's massive energy industry. To its northwest is Al Jassasiya's Rock Carvings [97].

**Al Ruwais**: (GPS: 26.131, 51.200; PAGE 156) One of the longest drives in Qatar is the 90-minute, 110 km journey between Al Ruwais on the northwest coast and Doha. Bus stations serving Al Ruwais include Al Gharafa Bus Station and Al Khor. Al Ruwais is a port town whose new port, built in 2011, replaced the now-abandoned old port in the town's south. The port primarily handles regional cargo, including fruit, vegetables, and livestock, with shipments from Iran having increased since the Qatar boycott. Doubtless, new sources will appear over the next few years. The port also serves as a fishing port. To the north of the town are sandbar-type islands. Southwest of Al Ruwais are several ruined settlements, including Al Jamal, Al Khuwair, and 24 km southwest, Al Zubarah. The older town of Al Ruwais is just to the east of the modern port, with mangroves to the town's east. Offshore, there are usually dozens of small fishing boats. There are limited accommodation and dining options.

**Al Wakrah**: (GPS: 25.177, 51.604; PAGE 100) It's just over a 20 km drive between Doha and Al Wakrah to the south. Feeder bus stations are HIA, Industrial Area Bus Station, and Al Sudan Bus Station, which go into the souq. There is a metro station, Al Wakrah, on the Red Line; use the MetroLink bus. Al Wakrah is one of the older, still-occupied settlements in Qatar, dating to at least 1845; today, it is rapidly being subsumed by Doha.

**Mesaieed** (Also called Umm Said): (GPS: 24.990, 51.549) Located south of Doha by some 40 km. Bus feeder stations are at HIA for a 90-minute journey. Mesaieed is a significant town founded after the Second World War. Receiving piped crude oil from Dukhan and gas from Ras Laffan and islands near Idd Al Shargi, this is a key industrial area. This flow of gas supports fertiliser, steel, and aluminium plants. A major artificial industrial port services other exports. The town has housing projects - often accommodating thousands of people, enabling much of the workforce to have a short commute. Recreational facilities include cricket and football, and there are restaurants. However, the closest hotels are in Sealine, about 20 km south of Mesaieed, and Al Wakrah, about 20 km north. Just north of Mesaieed is Hamad Port the country's primary seaport for standard commercial, livestock, and construction cargo.

**Dukhan**: (GPS: 25.420, 50.794; PAGE 178) Dukhan is about an 80 km drive west of central Doha. The feeder bus station is the Industrial Area Bus Station for the 90-minute journey. Dukhan is a mid-20th-century town created to service the nearby oil fields. As a 'company town', access requires a permit. The area to its north includes Zekreet and the area around 'Film City'.

## GOVERNMENT, POLITICS AND INTERNATIONAL RELATIONS

Qatar is a monarchy whose head of state bears the title of Amir (sometimes spelt Emir) and the honorific title Sheikh. The ruler is also the overseer of the judiciary and the commander-in-chief of Qatar's military and security forces. Unlike, to an extent, in the United Kingdom and the United States of America, the head of state in Qatar is treated, written about, and spoken of with considerable respect by the very deferential Qatari society. Lèse-majesté (offence against the sovereign, etc.) is a crime in Qatar under Article 134 of the Qatari Penal Code. In cases with no other aggravating factors, conviction carries a sentence of several years' imprisonment.

The Prime Minister chairs the Council of Ministers, and the ministries carry out their respective functions. Semi-government bodies also administer and implement Government policies.

A Shura Council (Consultative Assembly) was set up in 1972, with 45 members who act as individuals rather than as members of a political party (which is not permitted). In 2003, a national referendum was held which approved elections for 30 out of 45 seats; the first such election was in October 2021. In November 2024, Qatar held a national referendum to amend the Permanent

Constitution. An overwhelming majority (90.6%) voted to abolish direct elections for the Shura Council.

Though Qatar is not a democracy, the Government seeks the consensus of Qatar's nationals on its policies and their implementation. Qatar is a member of the Gulf Cooperation Council, a six-member body that also includes Bahrain, Kuwait, Oman, Saudi Arabia, and the UAE.

Qatar's diplomatic dexterity has mended fences with Saudi Arabia over the last few years, a reconciliation mirrored in its restored ties with Bahrain, the UAE, and Egypt was made under the the Al Ula Declaration of January 2021. This return to regional rapport followed a period of friction that served as a crucible for Qatari character, forging a sharpened national identity and a stubborn self-reliance.

Oman has historically remained a local political ally - a relationship that has matured alongside a strategic pivot toward Turkey's industrial and military might. These regional alignments are increasingly serving to counterbalance a deep-rooted Western security architecture. Although the United Kingdom and the United States have served as vital historical partners – with Al Udeid Air Base housing approximately 10,000 US Air Force personnel - Qatar is actively diversifying its defence dependencies to better insulate itself from unpredictable regional changes.

Using the wealth available to its government through Qatar Investment Authority (QIA), Qatar has made considerable investments within the economies of key allies, including Britain, France, and the USA.

∽

GDP, ECONOMY & MONEY: BANKS, ATM AND MONEY IN GENERAL

The Qatari currency is directly pegged to the USDollar, meaning that its exchange rate against other currencies will vary in step with the USDollar. Since 2001, the rates have been fixed at 3.64 QAR per USD.

**Credit & Debit Cards**

Credit and debit cards, alongside Apple Pay and Google Pay, are almost universally accepted across Qatar. From public transport and petrol stations to restaurants and hotels, contactless payment is the standard, except at ATMs. To avoid the high international transaction fees often levied by traditional banks on small purchases, consider specialist card providers such as Starling (for UK residents), Revolut, and Wise. These cards are typically transaction-charge free and integrate directly with digital wallets. This allows using a card for small purchases without incurring cumulative individual transaction charges. When using an ATM or a point-of-sale terminal, always select the option to be charged in the local currency to ensure your home bank sets the exchange rate, avoiding unfavourable conversion mark-ups. Verify exact terms with your card providers prior to travelling. The Qatar financial system includes the Qatar Mobile Payment System (QMPS), a QR-code-based transfer network. While highly efficient for local accounts, prohibitive cross-border fees render it impractical for short-term visitors. Additionally, the state has recently introduced 'Himyan' – the country's first national prepaid debit card for residents. Named after the traditional leather pouch used by ancient Arabian merchants to safeguard their wealth, the Himyan logo is now a ubiquitous sight on local card terminals.

ATMs are easy to find at Hamad International Airport, in major shopping areas, at some hotels, and at petrol stations. Normally, you will be charged a fee per cash withdrawal (see card options above), plus the exchange rate between your card's currency and QAR. Charges will vary depending on the agreement between the banks concerned.

**Cash**

Although Qatar is increasingly a cashless transaction system, be sure you have some Qatari Riyals in cash - it means you can at the very least tip service providers directly in QAR.

Before the Qatari Riyal was established in 1973, Qatar used the Qatar-Dubai Riyal, and before that, the Gulf Rupee. That was an official currency issued by the Reserve Bank of India and the Government of India to address the Indian Rupee currency drain. Today, US dollars are often accepted at tourist attractions. It's essential with USDollars and other foreign currency that the notes are absolutely in mint condition - any slight blemish on a note may mean that it will not be accepted. Hamad International Airport (HIA) has exchange counters in the arrivals hall and ATMs at various points - see ATM use above. Money exchanges are available in towns and many malls. When exchanging major currencies, rates are comparable at any Qatari money change in townr; those in the city generally offer better rates than those at the airport. There are also exchange counters in the airport departures hall, or you could drop your remaining Qatari money into local charity boxes.

Qatar issues currency in notes (Riyals) and coins (Dirhams). The coins are of little value; there are 100 dirhams in 1 Qatari Riyal, and their use is declining. Coins are now minted only in 25 and 50 dirham denominations, each with its value on the reverse and, on the obverse, the date at the top with the emblem of Qatar below. There are several hundred Qatari dirhams to one US dollar (unlike the dirham, AED, of the UAE).

Notes are available in values of 1, 5, 10, 50, 100, 200, and 500 Riyals. Each denomination has a distinct colour palette and images. All have Arabic on one side and English on the other.

∼

### Economy background

GDP (Gross Domestic Product) in US Dollars (2024): $239.1 billion (IMF 2026 Forecast) and its GDP per Capita in US Dollars $76,530 (Current prices) / $131,400 (PPP).

Qatar's oil and natural gas resources are the country's main economic engine and source of government revenue, accounting for around 60% of GDP, 85% of exports, and 70% of total government revenue (depending on fluctuations in oil and gas prices). Key export destinations for its 81 million tonnes (Estimated 2025 performance - Qatar's key energy resource) in 2024 are China: 24%, India: 15%, South Korea: 12%, Pakistan: 9%, Europe (combined - after the decision to 'drop' Russian LNG): 10%, Japan: 4%. Imports of non-food items are overwhelmingly from the USA, China, and Japan. Food imports rely on UAE & Saudi Arabia (both supply processed food from their own imports), India, USA, Turkey and Australia. Sea Freight is critical for bulk products like grain, live animal such as Australian sheep and cattle (both of these animal shipments have been under review), land for processed food from Saudi Arabia and UAE (through the single land border) and air freight for high value fresh product (berries and even flowers).

Again, as a simplification, income from various sources (gas & oil being key) flows to the government - the government then uses these to develop the country through Qatari organisations that employ people (both Qatari and non-Qatari), which in turn creates employment opportunities in service industries such as entertainment, retail, healthcare and so on. Since 1 January 2025, Qatar has implemented a 15% Global Minimum Tax (OECD Pillar Two framework) for large multinational enterprises (those with revenues over €750 million). There currently is no direct income tax, which in many countries creates a flow in the opposite direction, from the population to the government. However, as Oman may introduce income tax in January 2028 (subject to Royal Decree), Qatar and the other GCC states may follow suit. Equally, VAT is currently not levied; however, plans are to introduce it at 5%. This is likely to enable the government to gain more precise insight into the economy if it includes practically every product and service, as is done in Saudi Arabia.

The income from oil and gas that flows to the government is, in effect, a profit share with the production companies. Government spending on this income is the critical engine of the economy. As the government receives much of its income from gas & oil rather than taxation, its spending drives Qatar's high economic growth and per capita income levels. Robust state spending on public entitlements and booming construction spending look set to keep overall economic growth high for many years.

The GDP per capita for wage-earning Qatari nationals is a lot higher than the raw figure of $76,530 (though this does not mean that wages themselves approach this figure). The opposite is also true; low-paid manual labourers may earn around USD300-400 a month.

Qatar's reliance on oil and natural gas is likely to remain for the foreseeable future. Qatar's North Field holds approximately 25.2 trillion cubic metres of proven natural gas reserves - representing 12.1% of the global total. This concentrated abundance ensures Qatar remains the third-largest repository of natural gas on the planet, trailing only the vast, diffuse fields in Russia and Iran. Production is around 81 million tonnes per annum (gas is measured in cubic feet/meters, while LNG output is measured in tonnes; 1 million tonnes of LNG = 1.36 billion cubic meters of gas). This output will double to 142 million tonnes per annum by 2030. The Pearl Gas-to-Liquids plant is the largest of its kind in the world. Proved oil reserves exceed 25 billion barrels, allowing production to continue at current levels for about 56 years. Additional condensates are created as a result of oil & gas extraction. Despite the dominance of oil and natural gas, Qatar has made significant gains in diversification into non-oil sectors, including manufacturing, construction, and financial services. The leisure industry and tourism are also increasing factors. In recent years, these non-oil and gas sectors have accounted for half of the total GDP.

North of Doha lies Ras Laffan. Since 1996, Ras Laffan has served as the engine of Qatar's modern economy. Northeast of Al Khor, it receives methane gas (this gas is the basis of all the downstream gas product) directly from the North Field, which – together with Iran's South Pars – constitutes the world's largest non-associated natural gas reservoir. While the surface maritime boundary is cleanly divided based on the equidistance of the two nations' coastlines, subterranean extraction operates under the geological 'rule of capture', effectively making the shared reserves a competitive draw. By purifying the gas and chilling it to **-162°C**, the methane is condensed into export-ready liquefied natural gas (LNG). Apart from LNG, Qatar also produces Helium, Nitrogen-based fertilisers, Ethylene for plastic production. Shipped globally, this highly concentrated LNG energy generates the primary revenue streams that underwrite Qatar's development.However, much of the diversification away from oil and gas also relies on 'added value' products that make use of that oil and gas. These include petrochemicals (ethylene and methanol extracted from gas by super steam heating), which are fundamental to the plastics industry; helium, fertilisers (ammonia also created from gas, combined later with nitrogen and urea that uses ammonia and $CO_2$); and finally, primarily in Mesaieed, using gas as a power source in Qatar for steel, aluminium smelting and copper & lead recycling.

The major industrial area is the Mesaieed Industrial Area, south of Al Wakrah. The primary industries produce lubricants, fertiliser (as a joint venture with Norsk Hydro using gas as a raw material), fuel additives, vinyl, and chemicals. Using gas as an energy source are aluminium and steel smelters (another joint venture with Norsk Hydro). A major electricity-generating unit uses natural gas as its power source. Construction aggregate is both locally sourced and imported; for example, gabbro, an igneous rock similar to basalt, is imported from Oman. North of Mesaieed is Hamad Port, a man-made commercial container port and coastguard base with an adjacent military port, constructed from 2010 in a former *sabkha area*. It handles general containers, machinery, vehicles, and imported grain and livestock. Hamad Port is associated with the port and commercial district of Um Alhoul. This is a Free Zone for smaller-scale manufacturing, warehousing and logistics, business services, and commercial activities (retail, services, offices).

Um Alhoul also houses a major desalination plant and electricity plant, powered by gas. The Um Alhoul Power (UHP) facility, has hybrid architecture where two distinct desalination technologies operate in parallel.

The Multi-Stage Flash (MSF) units serve as the facility's traditional workhorses. These industrial leviathans harvest thermal waste - low-pressure steam diverted from the gas turbines during electricity generation - to heat seawater in a series of chambers. As the pressure drops in each successive stage, the water 'flashes' into steam, which is then condensed into high-purity distillate. Operating separately from this thermal cycle, the Seawater Reverse Osmosis (SWRO) units use high-pressure pumps to force seawater through semi-permeable membranes, stripping away salts and impurities at a molecular level.

The plants produces about 900 million litres of potable water daily - one providing the steady, foundational capacity, while the other offers the agile, pressure-driven response of modern filtration.

Before entering the national grid, the water from both streams must be made safe for consumption. It is treated with lime (calcium hydroxide) and carbon dioxide to restore alkalinity and achieve the 'sweet' taste required by consumers. Finally, chlorine is added to ensure disinfection throughout the distribution network.

Rather than discharging the hyper-saline brine byproduct back into the Arabian Gulf - where it could distress the local Dugong population and Seagrass beds - the waste is diverted to the QAR1billion Qatar Salt Production Plant. Here, the brine is refined into industrial bromine and table salt.

Once processed, the water is pumped into the Strategic Water Security Mega Reservoirs – which hold a staggering 10.45 billion litres, providing Qatar with a critical seven-day emergency buffer.

Tourism has been a successful area of Qatar's economy &diversification. The number of visitors exceeded 5.1 million (Official 2025 figure), and the country's tourism income in 2024 was USDollar 15.1 billion (8% of its total GDP).

*Calouste Gulbenkian*

## Oil & Gas History

Qatar's history of oil exploration is inextricably linked to oil exploration in the Middle East more broadly, as it was included in the historical commercial contract known as the 'Red Line Agreement'.

This agreement grew out of an arrangement by Calouste Gulbenkian, an Armenian born in Ottoman Turkey in 1869 who became a British citizen in 1902. He was well-connected with the

Ottoman Sultan Abdul Hamid II. Gulbenkian had promoted the prospects for oil in Mesopotamia (Iraq), which was then part of the Ottoman Empire. The prospects were so clear that the Ottoman sultan had large areas of land in Mesopotamia transferred from government ownership to his personal control, thereby nullifying earlier exploration agreements. Over time, German interests obtained small concessions from him in modern Iraq. During this period, most of Persia's territory was granted for exploration under a 1901 agreement with a Briton, William K. D'Arcy, who later unsuccessfully sought exploration rights within Ottoman domains.

The Young Turk revolution in 1908 altered the Ottoman Empire's economic situation in favour of British interests. In 1910, the National Bank of Turkey was set up to support British interests, with Calouste Gulbenkian as a director. He negotiated an agreement between various interested parties, and in 1912, the Turkish Petroleum Co. was founded. Shares were distributed: 25% to Deutsche Bank (also involved in the Berlin-Constantinople-Baghdad Railway project), 25% to a Shell subsidiary (Anglo-Saxon Petroleum), and 50% to the National Bank of Turkey, of which Gulbenkian controlled 15%. D'Arcy was excluded. The outcome was a non-compete clause that the partners would only work in cooperation with each other within the agreed territory - in effect, a form of cartel.

Despite all this manoeuvring, no company was granted an exploration agreement. Finally, in 1912, it was agreed that the Anglo-Persian Oil Company (a successor to D'Arcy) would obtain 47.5% of the Turkish Petroleum Co., Deutsche Bank 25%, Anglo-Saxon Petroleum Co. 22.5%, and Calouste Gulbenkian 5%, after which he became known as 'Mr 5%'. Shortly after this, the Turkish Ministry of Finance granted a concession lease. The First World War paused final negotiations, resulting in the German shares being transferred to the French Government's Compagnie Française des Pétroles (now TotalEnergies).

After the First World War, the United States sought oil exploration rights in the region. Several US companies cooperated as the 'Near East Development Corporation' (NEDC). After several years of negotiations, an agreement was reached for the USA to join the cartel. The shareholding became Anglo-Persian Oil Company, Royal Dutch/Shell, the Compagnie Française des Pétroles, and NEDC, each at 23.75%, with Gulbenkian still at 5%. Gulbenkian's interest in oil was transferred to his foundation as Partex, which was sold to a Thai organisation, PTT Exploration and Production, in 2019. The agreement was signed in July 1928, and the company was named Petroleum Concessions Ltd. The territorial boundaries of the agreement were defined when a map was produced with a red line drawn across it, marking the concession area. The red line ran from Turkey to the south, covering the Levant, Iraq, and the Arabian Peninsula (except Kuwait). This agreement collapsed after the Second World War and the establishment of Saudi Arabia.

Qatar was included in this general situation through a new subsidiary, Qatar Petroleum Co. In Qatar, the first talks for exploration took place in 1922 with Major Frank Holmes (the "Father of Gulf Oil"). The Anglo-Persian Oil Company conducted a survey in 1926, but no oil was found. After a workable oil discovery in Bahrain in 1932, a further concession for Qatar was signed on 17th May 1935 with Anglo-Persian representatives for 75 years. In return, 400,000 rupees were given on signature, 150,000 rupees were to be paid annually, and additional royalties were payable. Britain agreed to supply enhanced security. In October 1938, the first oil well was sunk in Dukhan, and oil was found in 1939. However, due to the Second World War, exports did not begin until 1949.

During the early 1950s, labour for Qatar's oil industry was initially foreign. Later, Qatari nationals were increasingly employed, which led to improved labour rights and higher wages for the workforce.

Offshore oil was explored by the International Marine Oil Company, and Shell Qatar was awarded these fields in 1952. Following this, oil was discovered in 1960 at Idd Al Shaqi (the concession was later acquired by Occidental Petroleum of Qatar). These offshore fields use Halul Island, just under 100 km northeast of Doha, for oil storage and export.

Qatar joined OPEC in 1961, a year after the organisation was formed. In 1973, the Qatari government acquired 25% of Qatar Petroleum Co.'s shares. In February 1977, the company became wholly owned by Qatar's government.

In 1971, while drilling the North West Dome-1 well in search of offshore crude, Shell's engineers struck a geological titan: the North Field. Instead of the anticipated oil, they found a reservoir of non-associated natural gas. At the time, this was a stranded asset; the region lacked pipelines, and the cryogenic conversion of gas to liquid

LNG was still a costly enterprise. Following a phased buyout of Shell, the Qatari government secured 100% of the offshore concession rights by February 1977. This negotiated sovereignty transformed a "disappointing" gas find into a 25.2 trillion cubic metre engine that would eventually fire the nation's future. Production began in 1981 from what would eventually become the world's largest gas field. The first LNG shipment was made in 1997. In 2015, Qatar supplied the UAE with about 7.548 billion cubic metres of gas and Oman with 2.067 billion cubic metres via the Dolphin Gas Project, established in 1999.

The Qatar Government withdrew from OPEC on 1st January 2019 (during the Qatar boycott period), explaining that it wished to increase gas production by 43%. Qatar's total liquids production - comprising crude oil, condensates, and Natural Gas Liquids (NGLs) - is projected to reach approximately 1.9 million barrels per day in 2026. For the year 2025, Liquefied Natural Gas (LNG) production is estimated at 81 million tonnes. This output is slated to rise as the North Field expansions come online, with total capacity reaching 110 million tonnes by late 2026 and culminating at 142 million tonnes per annum by 2030.

∽

## International Transport

This focuses on Hamad International Airport, which supports Qatar's development as an international communications hub. Qatar Airways, with over 220 passenger jets and 30 cargo-only jets, uses the airport as its hub-and-spoke centre, serving over 83 countries and 165+ destinations. Supporting this has been a major redevelopment of Doha Port, next to the Museum of Islamic Art. It is a leisure port, a destination for cruise ships, and a centre for leisure marine operations. Typically, in winter, it has 3 or 4 weekly visits by cruise ships and can handle vessels of more than 183,000 tonnes and 300 m in length.

To the south of HIA is Ras Bufontas, a free trade zone focused on light industry, emerging technologies, and service businesses.

∽

## FOOD PRODUCTION

Qatar's metamorphosis from an import-dependent peninsula to a regional leader in food security was jump-started by the 2017 diplomatic crisis. While the state formerly relied on neighbours for 80% of its dairy, it has since achieved a 99% self-sufficiency rate in fresh milk and its derivatives. This was largely driven by Baladna, https://baladna.com/, near Al Khor, which airlifted thousands of Holstein Friesian cattle to a desert 'farm'. This is now equipped with advanced climate-control systems to deal with temperatures up to 50°C to support some 24,000 animals. The industry has matured beyond raw milk and meat into high-value processing, with new facilities producing yogurts, evaporated milk and sterilised cream that were previously sourced entirely from overseas. To maintain scale, producers must import vast quantities of fodder and grain (Zea mays) from international markets, as less than 2% of Qatar's land can support agriculture. Some progress has been made using treated sewage effluent for local hay production.

Manufacturing has followed this upward trajectory, with local consumer brands now dominating the retail landscape. Companies like Qatar Pafki and Albina Snacks have changed from simple re-packaging to full-scale production of corn-based snacks and roasted nuts, while Rosetta Pasta has established an alternative to Italian imports.Qatar's processed foodstuffs have begun to penetrate regional markets. In 2025, the value of these exports reached approximately QAR115M, with the United Arab Emirates and Saudi Arabia emerging as primary destinations for Qatari-made snacks, beverages, and dairy. This however is a two way flow. Sheep and goats meat supplies around 18% of local demand – though beef production is negligible. Qatar's ability to turn a geopolitical blockade into a manufacturing springboard has redefined its role in the Gulf's economic ecosystem.

The salad and vegetable sector is currently undergoing a similar revolution, with production expected to reach 120,000 tonnes by the end of 2026. Companies like Agrico and QATFA now utilise advanced Nutrient Film Technique (NFT) and vertical stacking to produce Lettuce (Lactuca sativa) and Spinach (Spinacia oleracea) year-round. The Qatari startup VFarms , http://vfarms.qa, 15km northeast of Ash Shahaniyah, cultivates Iceberg lettuce by using atmospheric water generators to harvest moisture directly from the humid Gulf air in their vertical farm facility. This produce has begun to penetrate regional markets; in 2025, Qatari agricultural and processed food exports to the United Arab Emirates and Saudi Arabia reached approximately QAR115M. Despite these gains, the "problem of scale" persists. The indirect energy required for desalination and LED lighting remains a significant overhead.

## CULTURE

This section considers culture, especially family culture, for the fortunate 11% of the population who hold Qatari nationality.

Culturally, Qatar is full of contrasts: jaw-droppingly modern, yet deeply conservative; remarkably insular, yet potentially open. Although most people living in Qatar are not Qatari nationals, this section gives an overview of Qatari nationals unless noted otherwise.

An example of modernity and a desire to emphasise Qatar's historic culture as well as its future, the mother of the Amir, Her Highness Sheikha Moza bint Nasser, conceived the Qatar Foundation to transition the nation from a hydrocarbon economy to a knowledge-based one. This vision birthed Education City, a 12-square-kilometre "multiversity" where Qatari women now significantly outnumber men in higher education. This trajectory is sustained by the Amir's sisters: Sheikha Al Mayassa bint Hamad, who chairs Qatar Museums, and Sheikha Hind bint Hamad, Vice Chairperson of the Qatar Foundation. Their influence has propelled Qatar to intellectual prominence through recent milestones such as Art Basel Qatar and the Web Summit Qatar 2026.

There are two fundamental, almost inextricably linked, areas in Qatar that impact its underlying culture: the role of the family (both nuclear and extended) and of Islam. The Qatari nuclear family - grandparents, parents, and children - forms the key social unit. The extended family, which includes first and other cousins, forms additional units. Finally, the larger social unit, a tribe, provides its members with a social framework and an identity familiar to other Qataris.

~

### Marriage

Marriages are generally arranged with the parents' agreement and, in many cases, organised by the family. Marriages within the extended family account for around 42% of the total (according to the Qatar Planning and Statistics Authority (QPSA), 2016; this has since changed its name to the National Planning Council (NPC)). Within all marriages, 24% are between first cousins. The National Health Strategy 2024–2030 is actively promoting pre-marital genetic screening to address the health implications of this cultural preference. Typically, male Qataris marry at 27, and females at 25. Polygynous marriage is allowed, and QPSA figures show they account for around 8% of marriages. Fertility rates for Qatari females have declined from 4 children per woman in 2007 to 2.4 in 2025.

Marriages are often regarded as an agreement between the families of the bride and groom. A contract, *melcha* (or *milka*), is drawn up and witnessed by suitable people, ideally including the Imam of the major local mosque. Typically, a dowry is paid by the male's family to the female's family after an agreement on the amount.

Unlike in, for example, the UAE, in Qatar, no government marriage gift of money is provided; however, loans (intended to be repaid) might be offered, currently up to QAR 300,000. Part of this may be forgiven with the birth of a child and subsequent children.

The *shabka*, a celebratory event, might be held by the families to present gifts. This is followed by agreeing on the marriage date, which might be weeks or months away. Before the actual wedding night, a 'henna party' may be held for the females of the families, either in a commercial hall specially built for weddings or a hotel's ballroom. On the night of the marriage, an event is held where the bride and women have a separate venue from the groom and men. Usually, only female guests attend the bride's party, perhaps with a strict 'no camera' rule; however, the memory is enhanced when guests receive a gift. At all celebratory events, the chief participants are at one end of the room, and guests always greet them formally. The men's event concludes with sword dancing and traditional music, until, often in a chain of hooting cars, the men's party leads the groom to his new bride.

Traditionally, socialising occurs within the extended family, with male and female members forming separate groups during the week. The Majlis is an essential social arena in Qatari male social life. This is a private or semi-public room (usually attached to the house but with a separate entrance) where men meet to discuss everything from business to falconry. This is where guests may be received - if you are a guest, a small gift such as quality chocolates, incense or a bijou gift from your own country is appropriate. Social activity during the week centres on coffee shops and modern malls, as well as informal groups in parks and beachside locations. At weekends, relaxing with the nuclear family is the focus, though as can be imagined, first cousins of both a husband and wife may be included, as they are also the brother or sister of a spouse.

A significant source of an individual's identity in Qatar is their tribe. A tribe is a group of people who share a common identity that, in many instances, is the belief they are descended from a single man and, by implication, his wives. It may be that a tribe is actually a historical accretion of smaller units that today share a collective identity.

## Names & Titles

Historically, the head of a tribe and also of major sections within a more prominent tribe would have the honorific/title Sheikh (a daughter or wife would be a Sheikha). As Sheikha can also be a female's name, check the family name to see which of the two possibilities it is. If it's Al Thani, you will have the honorific. In Qatar, the Sheikh/Sheikha title is now reserved exclusively for members of the ruling Al Thani family (or, in some instances, their wives from outside the family). The word Amir, which means 'prince' in this context, is reserved for the ruler. These uses and exclusions vary from country to country in the Arab and Islamic world.

A tribe's members will have the tribal name as their family name/surname, for instance, Al Kubaisi (Al means 'the', as in 'one of the members of the tribe'). A member of this tribe might be called Mohammed bin Ali bin Abdullah. His first name, Mohammed, is followed by 'bin', which means 'son of' Ali (his father), who is the son of Abdullah (Mohammed's grandfather). Ibn is a variant of bin. A female has a similar name structure, for example, Fatima bint Ali bin Abdullah Al Kubaisi; here, the first name is Fatima, and 'bint' means 'daughter of' Ali. On marriage, both the man and woman keep their birth names; however, their children have their first name followed by their father's name, and so on.

## Town and Country

Qatar has two intermingling cultures: a Bedouin one, the traditional nomadic society, and the *hadhr*, a culture of settled people. Historically, a tribe may have had a territory acknowledged as its collective land, which others could enter with permission. Traits such as bravery alongside generosity, epitomised through hospitality, are core to Bedouin culture. The Hadhr culture in Qatar is mainly found on the coast. The fixed location for these families allowed for educational establishments to develop. Although the family was settled, male members might be away for weeks, months, or even years at a time as they worked in pearling or commerce overseas. This obliged women to be involved in many areas of society that men might have otherwise occupied.

Falconry, Camel, and Horse Racing are not just "hobbies" but vital pillars of Qatari national identity, actively supported by the government. The Marmi Festival and races attended by the Amir are essential cultural touchstones.

## Social Greetings

Greetings between members of the same sex are a matter of tradition. This may be a 'cheek kiss', once on each cheek if you know each other, maybe twice on the same cheek if you are more than acquaintances, or multiple times if you are friends and haven't seen each other for a long time. A nose kiss may be given if they are perhaps related. Occasionally, a person may kiss another person's forehead; this is a sign of deference. Usually, during these greetings, the right hand is held or placed on the other person's left shoulder.

Verbal greetings in Qatar are often formulaic and lengthy. Qataris enquire about the other person's health and family, and the other person reciprocates. If between men, these enquiries are never about a man's wife, as this is considered disrespectful. Between a Qatari and a non-Qatari, a normal handshake is used; often, friends hold hands for a long time.

Frequently, a key form of communication is in hand gestures - a single gesture can cover several sentences. Be aware of these - and only use them when you are certain of the context they are used in.

Often, even if you have invited a Qatari person or group to coffee or a meal at a restaurant, there will be a good-natured disagreement after the meal over who will have the 'honour' of paying. Each person will be happy to pay, especially if you are the only foreigner. However, if you have invited people, insist on paying and accept their invitations in return.

Within Qatar, although achieving consensus is preferred, decisions are top-down without real delegation of responsibility or authority. This is the form of decision-making in many businesses with Arab cultures and in many other Asian cultures. Even in choosing a restaurant, the senior person is deferred to. In businesses and professional meetings, a person is addressed using their university degree or job title, followed by their first name, e.g., 'Engineer Ahmed' or 'His Excellency Khalid'. To an extent, this explains the importance of achieving certification. A man may be called 'Abu Mohammed' or 'Abu Miriam'; 'Abu' means 'father'. It might also be a sign that he is well-known to the person who addresses him, as they know his child's name, though some men are only called 'Abu Mohammed'. A similar range of address terms is used for women, though the term *umm*, meaning 'mother', is used instead of *abu*.

## QATARI CLOTHING

Clothing for both sexes is expected to be modest, concealing the body. Qatari men wear the white *thobe* (it may be a dark colour in winter), either with a small stand-up collar (Mandarin style) or a Western formal shirt collar. Both styles have cuffed sleeves, often worn with cufflinks. The *thobe* is usually tailor-made for the wearer, with options for material quality, shade, overall design, and fit. Under the *thobe*, lightweight long *sirwal* pants are worn, as well as a vest (undershirt). The *ghutra* headdress is usually a heavily starched white cloth (it may be red and white or another design), formed from a square of material folded once across two corners to form a triangle. The longest edge forms the front, with the apex of the two shorter edges down the back. It is worn in several styles according to the wearer's preference; in Qatar, the most distinctive is the 'cobra' style, which you will recognise when you see it. Under the *ghutra* is a small *ghafiya* cap that provides some grip and prevents oil from the hair from touching it. The black circle of rope, *agil*, on the *ghutra* (often with a long-tasselled cord at the back, a very Qatari style) was previously used to hobble a camel's front legs. Placing it on the head served to secure the *ghutra* in place (and a convenient place to store it); some religious men do not wear this. Men wear formal sandals or possibly shoes, and in addition to cufflinks, they might wear a stylish watch and frequently carry a pen in the *thobe*'s chest pocket. Worn for prestige on special occasions such as weddings is a *bisht* - a traditional long, white, brown, or black lightweight Arabic cloak trimmed in gold thread. The man's ensemble explicitly states the wearer's identity: he is a Qatari.

Qatari women typically wear a black (or another colour) cloak, the *abaya*, which is worn over the shoulders and reaches just above the ground. Over her head, covering the hair and neck, is a scarf, the *shayla*, also known as a *hijab*. Under this *abaya* and *shayla* may well be the latest fashion from New York, London, Paris, or Milan, elaborate Lebanese-style fashion, or simply jeans and a T-shirt, along with Western-style underwear. The 'batoola', the face mask seen in the National Museum, may still be worn by traditional older women.

If you have time - Embrace Doha www.EmbraceDoha.com offers classes in cultural crafts - calligraphy, making incense and more.

### EDUCATION

Before 1949, Qatar had simple schools that focused on teaching the Quran. A school for boys offering a broader education was established in Doha that year, following rising income from oil exploration. Other schools were established in 1954, and the first girls' school opened in 1956. By 1976, there were 130 schools in Qatar, with an equal split between boys' and girls' schools. Today, the number of Qatari government-operated schools is over 208.

Today, education for Qatari nationals and foreign employees of the Ministry of Education is free within the government system. There are three streams of education in Qatar: elementary school (ages 6 to 12), preparatory school (ages 12 to 15/16), and secondary school (ages 15 to 18). Education is compulsory between age 6 to the end of preparatory school. Qatari government schools are single-sex, with English taught as a foreign language.

Since 1964, there have been a variety of fee-paying international schools in the country, catering primarily for the children of non-Qatari nationals. However, Qataris can and do attend. Currently, there are around 340. A wide variety of national curricula are followed, including US (32 schools), UK (131 schools), and Canadian (3 schools). The UK curriculum remains the most prevalent, representing roughly 44% of the private market. This gives students International General Certificate of Secondary Education (IGCSE) and A-Levels, qualifications recognised by almost every university globally, from Harvard to Oxford. In private schools, the history of Qatar is taught alongside the national curriculum. If the student is Muslim, Arabic and Islam are also taught. International schools may be co-educational or single-sex. The Qatari government supports nationals attending these schools with a grant of up to QAR28,000.

The major national university, Qatar University, was founded in 1973. There are now over seven Qatari university-level educational institutions. Within Qatari government universities, scholarships are available to non-Qatari nationals. Additionally, there are 19 foreign university-level establishments in Qatar, mainly from the USA. The first international university was Virginia Commonwealth University, with its campus predominantly located in Education City, which is almost a Multiversity City. Most international academic establishments offer a limited range of courses, as their parent bodies provide the material and tutors. The University of Doha for Science and Technology (UDST), formerly the College of the North Atlantic - Qatar, was elevated to a national university in 2022 and is the primary hub for technical and vocational degrees, balancing the more academic focus of Qatar University. There is some segregation of the sexes in classrooms at several universities. According to QPSA, about 70% of students (in both government and private universities) are female, accounting for around 67% of all graduates. These percentages are comparable throughout the Gulf. For comparison, the figures for the UK (2018) are 57% female students and in the USA (2019), 56%.

The education system is under the authority of the Ministry of Education and Higher Education. Finally, the Qatar Foundation for Education, Science and Community Development, in effect an autonomous body, aims to place Qatar at the cutting edge of education, with a special emphasis on the inclusion of foreign universities.

∽

## Media

Qatar, as an Arab country, is open to Arabic-language printed media from around the world, much as English-language media from the USA is available in London, and British media is available in New York. Some of this media is based in an Arab country. Others with a 'pan-Arab' approach, especially if they are critical of Arab governments, may be based in a non-Arab location, such as London.

Historically, in Qatar, the relatively small population of Arab speakers meant that local Arab-language media received a subsidy (whether direct or through advertising and other support) from the government, as publications would not otherwise be financially viable. This subsidy resulted in censorship, whether government-imposed or self-censorship (in line with the 2014 Cybercrime Law and the recent Law No. 11 of 2025), to align with known government preferences. This was also the situation with English-language newspapers. Support for and overt government censorship were largely removed in 1995. However, laws within the country mean that many press houses continue to self-censor. Currently, there are five major Arabic dailies active in 2026: Al Sharq, Al Watan, Al Raya, Al Arab, and Lusail (which focuses on the economy). Their combined daily print run is estimated at 65,000-75,000 copies, read not only by Qatari nationals but also by other Arabs, including 300,000 Egyptians.

English language papers include the *Gulf Times* (www.gulf-times.com), *The Peninsula* (www.thepeninsulaqatar.com), and the *Qatar Tribune* (www.qatar-tribune.com). Several television stations, including Taalam and Baraaem, are aimed at children. Al Jazeera provides news and current affairs (www.aljazeera.com/live) in both English and Arabic, alongside the Arabic-only Qatar Television (a government operation). Al Jazeera is a private foundation for public benefit, initially funded by an earlier ruler of Qatar. Its news programs are claimed to be free of government political censorship. Indeed, it has replaced other channels in Qatar and other Arab countries as many people's preferred choice for news, thanks to its naturally less Western-centric focus. Despite claims to be free of government political censorship, its editorial coverage excludes many areas of domestic Qatari affairs. Al Rayan TV, however, is under the Special Engineering Office (also known as the Private Engineering Office), a state-owned infrastructure provider. A few magazines include *Expat Woman Qatar* (www.qatarexpatwomen.com) and *Time Out Doha* (www.timeoutdoha.com). Radio stations include Al Jazeera (Arabic and English) and Sout Al Khaleej (Arabic and English, www.soutalkhaleej.fm).

\*\*\*

DO'S AND DON'T'S

These are included for awareness and to help you have a better time, when you visit Qatar. If you have visited any Arab country before, comparable suggestions could be made; though perhaps to a lesser or greater degree.

**Do's**

**Do review your government's travel advice for Qatar.** The geopolitical currents of the region can shift , and staying informed is a prerequisite for a smooth journey.

**Dress modestly in public.** While Qatar is more relaxed than, for example, Saudi Arabia, both men and women should cover their shoulders and knees in malls, markets, and government buildings. Women do not need to wear an Abaya, but carrying a light pashmina or similar large scarf is a versatile "safety net" for entering more traditional areas. Do be cautious also in public areas such as parks, especially when exercising,; women's sports-bras are unlikely to be acceptable.

**Do use your right hand for all social exchanges.** Whether passing a business card in a West Bay boardroom or accepting a piece of *khubz* (flatbread), the right hand is the hand to use. The left hand is traditionally reserved for personal hygiene and is considered "unclean" in a social context.

**Do ask for permission before photographing individuals.** Qatari privacy is a fortress. Under Law No. 11/2025, filming or photographing people without their explicit consent - particularly women - is a criminal offence that can lead to a fine of QAR100,000 or imprisonment.

**Do stand when a senior figure or a member of the Al**

**Thani family enters.** This silent signal of respect is part of Gulf etiquette.

**Do accept the ritual of hospitality.** When offered Arabic coffee (Qahwa) and dates from the Date Palm, take a couple of cups. Shake the cup gently from side to side to signal you have had your fill; otherwise, the "bottomless cup" policy remains in effect.

**Do maintain a positive dialogue about the State.** Qataris are deeply proud of their rapid national development. Avoid the "backseat driver" approach of comparing their governance to Western systems; their loyalty to the Amir is a pillar of social stability.

**Do respect the silence of prayer.** If you see someone praying in a public space, walk behind them. To walk in front is to "cut" their connection to the *Qibla*.

**Do use formal titles.** Address contacts as "Your Excellency," "Sheikh," or by professional titles like "Doctor" or "Engineer" followed by their first name (e.g., Engineer Hamad) until a more casual rapport is established.

**Do carry physical ID:** Under Qatari law, you must carry your passport or Qatari ID (at least a photocopy) at all times. Police may occasionally conduct spot checks in areas like Msheireb or the Corniche.

**Don'ts**

**Don't criticise the Ruling Family, the State, or Islam:** Whether in person or on social media, any commentary deemed insulting to the Amir or the national interest is a "red line" with severe legal consequences.

**Don't Criticize a Person directly:** Things that would cause embarrassment and loss of face to a Qatari should absolutely be avoided. Criticism should be given indirectly, circumspectly, and never in front of others to prevent loss of face. Advice on how to handle any potential criticism is worth seeking from a person known to you both who is more senior than the person you wish to address.

**Don't Discuss Politics and Religion:** Although conversations between friends and family members include politics and religion, these topics are unlikely to be discussed in front of people they are less familiar with. If you are a foreign national in Qatar, conversation about politics and religion should be avoided; discussion about the ruling family should also be cautious. In all cases, a positive, admiring viewpoint is usually the best attitude. Do not discuss your own religion unless you are a Muslim. Proselytising is prohibited by law, and a positive viewpoint of your own religion might be misconstrued as such.

**Don't assume "Yes" means "Agreement":** a person may say "Inshallah" (If God wills it) or "Yes" out of politeness and a desire to avoid "loss of face," even if they cannot fulfil a request. Look for clues of hesitation, or follow up soon after to confirm. In Britain understanding social cue are also sometimes opaque. For example, an invitation might be responded to by a "that would be nice, I will get back to you" - a non British person might feel the invitation was accepted - but the two phrases together usually means disinterest.

**Don't treat the 'delete' button on Social Media as an eraser.** Under Qatar's cybercrime laws, a digital footprint is a permanent ledger. Posts or "likes" that violate public order can be prosecuted years later. WhatsApp texts are considered within this social media context.

**Don't gate crash the "Family Only" sections if you are a man:** Many parks, beaches, and even some restaurant sections are designated for "Families Only" (women, children, and married couples). Single men (often referred to as "bachelors" in local parlance) are strictly prohibited from these zones.

**Don't publicly display affection.** Holding hands is generally tolerated for married couples in international areas, but kissing or excessive physical contact in public will likely result in a firm intervention by the authorities.

**Don't drink alcohol in public.** Unlike the total prohibition in much of Saudi Arabia, alcohol is available in Qatar within licensed international hotels and bars. However, it is strictly illegal to be drunk in public, to drink in the street, or to carry alcohol except when transporting it directly from the Qatar Distribution Company (for residents with permits) to your home.

**Don't bring pork or prohibited items into the country.** Customs at Hamad International Airport are meticulous; pork products and religious materials intended for proselytising will be confiscated.

**Don't assume all medications are permitted.** Qatar has a zero-tolerance policy for narcotics. If you carry prescription stimulants (often used for ADHD) or strong painkillers like Codeine (this has opium as an ingredient, while Tramadol as a synthetic equivalent, you must have the original prescription and a detailed medical report.

**Don't engage in LGBTQ+ advocacy.** Same-sex relations are illegal in Qatar. Public advocacy, including the display of rainbow symbols, is viewed as a violation of public morals and may result in detention or deportation. There were several instances in the World Cup.

**Don't photograph sensitive sites.** This includes military installations, government ministries, and the interiors of certain mosques. If a building looks official, keep your lens capped.

**Don't carelessly use common gestures:** Pointing with a single finger, making a fist, or banging a desk to make a point are not acceptable behaviours. Wearing footwear in a home and showing the soles of the feet (even if covered by socks/tights) or the sole of your footwear should be avoided.

**Don't display the soles of your feet.** When sitting in a *majlis* or a formal setting, pointing your soles at someone is a silent "slap" in the face. Keep your feet flat or tucked away, though in a large group this lack of display might be impossible if people are spread around a room.

**Don't be lose with your Language:** According to the Qatar Penal Code Article (290), "Anyone who makes gestures, dares to say or sing immoral things or perform an infamous deed in a public place or an open space is convicted to no more than six months in prison and to a fine of no more than three thousand riyals, or to one of these two penalties." This is reinforced by article (294): "Anyone who instigates debauchery, dissipation or adultery in public by words, gestures or any other means is convicted to no less than six months and no more than three years in prison." This applies to instances of 'flipping the bird', for example, when in the 'privacy' of your own car.

**Don't eat, drink, or smoke in public during Ramadhan.** During the holy month, the daytime fast is mandatory for all adults in public spaces. Even chewing gum in a taxi is a breach of this code.

**Don't film accidents or "pranks".** Capturing a traffic mishap or filming people for "viral" content is a fast track to a police station. In the digital age, Qatar views the unsolicited lens as a predator.

∽

## OTHER NATIONALITIES IN QATAR

Qatar has, as noted above, a very substantial range of other nationalities; over 80% of the total population is from non-Western countries, South Asia and Southeast Asia dominate. In general, they are in Qatar under a sponsorship system (*kafala* system), where a Qatari organisation or person enables them to acquire a work visa, and after a trial period, a Work Residence Permit, leading to a Qatar Identity Card (QID valid for 1-3 years). This QID typically permits them to work only for the organisation or person named on that card - and to work only in the type of job described. With sufficient notice, it is possible to change the sponsor. This QID is a high-security smart card that serves as a resident's primary legal identity document for areas such as opening a bank account to accessing Hamad Medical Corporation.

How the non-national entered Qatar will vary; the employer might have paid all expenses, or the hopeful worker might have paid them. Inevitably, informal labour exists outside these strict legal frameworks, particularly in domestic and small-scale maintenance sectors. All salaries are required to be paid electronically through Qatari banks. The Qatar Central Bank operates as the central hub for inter-bank transfers.

Especially in service jobs, retail and hospitality, the non-national may be overqualified for the job - they are attracted by better pay and working conditions in Qatar than in their home country. The flow of finance, often into remote areas of their home countries, may have been a key to an extended family's prosperity. Qatar may also be a transit point before legal entry into a different end-destination, such as your own country.

In Qatar, non-nationals in service industries may have excellent English (some might use Gulf English, a patois of Tagalog, Urdu, and so on), some Arabic (again, often a patois), and often several other languages from their home country. After being in Qatar for some months and obtaining the Work Residence Permit (a government-issued legal requirement), the non-national should be well accustomed to dealing with all major nationalities in Qatar, many of whom have different expectations of what service entails. Hopefully, they will meet your expectations.

In Qatar the absolute minimum wage is QAR1,000 per month, with a QAR500 housing allowance (unless accommodation is provided), and a QAR 300 food allowance (unless food is provided). Under the Ministry of Labour's 2026 digital oversight, any employer who fails to transfer these specific amounts via a Qatari bank account faces immediate electronic blocks on their ability to renew residency permits or hire new staff. These minimum also apply to Qatari nationals. However, in practice a Qatari high school graduate in the public sector will be paid roughly QAR 10,000 to QAR 12,000, with QAR 4,000-QAR 6,000 housing allowance and transport allowance.

Where large numbers of (non-Qatari) people are employed at the same location, accommodation (perhaps in a small dormitory-style setting) and transport are usually provided. The white buses common on Qatar's roads transport workers between their accommodation and their workplaces. Where staff numbers are low or spread across a wide area, the above allowance is often given. Senior staff will usually have individual accommodation and transport.

∼

ISLAMIC RELIGION IN QATAR

In AD 628, the Prophet Mohammed sent an envoy, Abu Al Alaa Al Hadrami, to Munzir ibn Sawa Al Tamimi, the Arab governor, based in what is now Al Ahsa, for the Sassanids in Qatar and the surrounding area. Similar requests were sent to all rulers of lands with contact to Madinah (including, according to Islamic tradition, Emperor Heraclius of the Byzantine Empire), where Mecca and Medina, the two core towns under the rule of Prophet Mohammed, are located. The letter asked for Munzir's allegiance to the Islamic faith, which he and some of his subjects agreed to. After more correspondence, Mohammed advised that those who did not become Muslims should pay *jizya*, a tax levied on non-Muslims. After the death of the Prophet Mohammed in 632, a widespread revolt, the Ridda Wars, occurred throughout the Islamic world. The new Caliph sent Abu Al Alaa Al Hadrami to defeat the rebels, which he did. From this date, Qatar increasingly became an Islamic country, primarily Sunni.

Although Christianity was well established in Qatar, Islam gradually became the dominant religion. By the 10th century, probably the entire area was Islamic. Since the Al Saud incursions from 1787, Qatar has increasingly followed the version of Islam, based on the Hanbali school of Islam, that is dominant in Saudi Arabia.

As with Christianity, there are different schools of thought within Islam. The Hanbali school follows the law and culture as given in the Quran, the Prophet Mohammed's sayings, and the records of the companions of the Prophet. This approach is much the same way as the Bible, the sayings and traditions of Jesus, and accounts made by his disciples inform the behaviour of Christians. Unlike some other Islamic schools, the Hanbali school does not accept legal or cultural interpretations from different Islamic schools of thought. The school originated with the Iraqi scholar Ahmed bin Hanbal, who died in AD 855. This school of thought was followed by Imam Mohammed ibn Abd Al Wahhab (the main mosque in Doha is named after him), who lived from 1703 to 1792. The Al Thani ruling family belongs to the Bani Tamim tribe - the same tribe as Mohammed ibn Abd Al Wahhab himself. Imam Mohammed ibn Abd Al Wahhab was a student of several Hanbali theologians who espoused ideas at the extreme of Sunni Islamic thought. Imam Mohammed ibn Abd Al Wahhab gained the support of local rulers to the north of Riyadh. These eventually included the ruler of Diriyah, Sheikh Mohammed bin Saud. These two men collaborated to expand their political and religious territory. By 1818, this covered large areas of Arabia, including the Qatar peninsula. That state, now called the First Saudi State, fell in 1818. A Second Saudi State emerged in 1824, further increasing Wahhabism's influence in Qatar.

The basis of Islam is what has been called the Five Pillars of Islam, which are incumbent on each Muslim:

1. Shahadah: The testimony of faith each Muslim must say, in the form: 'There is no God but Allah (God), and Mohammed is His Prophet'.

2. Zakat: Annual charitable giving, based on a proportion of one's wealth.

3. Sawm: Fasting during the month of Ramadhan. Not eating, drinking, or smoking in public is also prohibited for non-Muslims.

4. Hajj: Making the pilgrimage to Mecca at least once during one's lifetime, if possible.

5. Salat: Prayers five times a day.

The mosque is the first and quintessential Islamic building. In Arabic, the name is *masjid*, which means 'place of prostration'. The

Prophet Mohammed's house, a typical 7th-century Arabic-style house with an internal courtyard, acted as the first mosque. The rooms' ceilings were supported by columns, creating what is now called a hypostyle (meaning 'under columns') mosque. More prominent mosques in Arabia followed this style.

The critical function of a mosque is as a place of prayer to Allah (God). However, it is acceptable to worship elsewhere. Prayers are held five times daily based on solar time (the sun's position in the sky). Therefore, the time of worship varies throughout the year and also depends on the location on Earth. The first prayer is about 10 minutes before sunrise; the second at solar noon; the third in the late afternoon; the fourth when the entire solar disk has sunk below the horizon; and the fifth when the sun would be between 12 and 18 degrees below the true horizon (around 90 minutes after the fourth prayer). Today, technology has immeasurably simplified knowing when prayer is due.

In Islam, it is preferred that men gather in a *masjid Al jumaa* (congregational mosque) for the midday Friday prayers, with an Imam leading the prayers. Most mosques do not have a particular Imam; however, in urban areas, there is a significant mosque to serve a district, the *masjid Al jumaa*, which does. Many of these are named in memory of an individual, such as the Imam Mohammed ibn Abd Al Wahhab Mosque and the State Grand Mosque of Qatar (as in Christianity, churches and cathedrals often bear a person's name; St Paul's or St Peter's Cathedrals are well-known examples).

On entering almost all mosques, a visitor faces the *mihrab* (prayer niche), which faces Mecca (towards Qatar's West-Southwest). This direct relationship between a mosque's main entrance and the *mihrab* is preferred. Though a mosque's purpose is to accommodate prayers, it is possible to pray in any clean, respectable place, for which a small prayer rug can be used as a clean surface. Some major mosques in Qatar have prayer spaces for women on a mezzanine floor so they can hear the prayer service without being overlooked by men.

∽

## Ramadhan

Ramadhan is the holy month when Muslims abstain from eating, drinking, and smoking between sunrise and sunset. Non-

Muslims are affected because it is prohibited to be seen eating, drinking any liquid, smoking or even chewing gum in public places during daylight hours in Ramadhan. Loud music is also proscribed, especially in public places. As a result, most restaurants are closed (though large hotels' main restaurants usually function for non-Muslims) during the day. All bars are closed, and hotels are not allowed to serve alcohol publicly. Working hours are shorter, with later starts and earlier finishes. Qataris look forward to and enjoy Ramadhan as it is a time for self-restraint and spiritual reflection. After evening prayers, friends and family are visited, and social activity continues late into the night.

During Ramadhan, government offices are open from 09:00 to 14:00, Sunday to Thursday. Commercial offices that deal directly with the public will have shorter hours than normal but longer than the government's. Banks may work from 10:00 to 14:00 and 21:00 to 23:00 (check specific timings). Other businesses and smaller shops will also have altered hours, with shorter daytime hours and later closing times. Major supermarkets may have unaltered timings. As Ramadhan follows the lunar calendar, it moves forward by about 10 days each year.

At the end of the days fasting a popular tradition is the "Midfa Al Iftar" (Ramadhan Cannon) which is fired at Souq Waqif, Katara and other locations to signal the end of the fast

**Islam and Culture**

Islam is a crucial part of Qatar's culture. It influences activity during the day due to the importance of prayer times. As has been said, it is also critical in the social interactions between males and females. Clothing and modesty are also influenced by religion, including details about how high a garment should be above a person's ankles. The foods that cannot be eaten (such as pork), how an animal should be killed, and the views on alcohol are all covered by the Quran or sayings of the Prophet Mohammed.

~

UNESCO LISTING

Qatar has a single UNESCO World Heritage Site, Al Zubarah [PAGE 167, 298], a coastal town listed in 2013 as an 'outstanding testimony to an urban trading and pearl-diving tradition which sustained the region's major coastal towns'.

*View from the boardwalk - Al Zubarah*

On the northwest coast of Qatar, Al Zubarah was a pearling and trading centre that flourished from around AD 1760 to 1811. Finds at Al Zubarah include Bavarian jetons (brass tokens) and Chinese porcelain, suggesting it was part of a broader trade network. The town is on a ridge of slightly higher ground, with the sea to its west and *sabkha* to the east. The landscape was created during the mid-Holocene period (about 6,000 years ago), when sea levels in the Gulf were up to 3 metres higher than they are today. During this period, the sea was over a kilometre inland at Al Zubarah. It has since retreated, stabilising around its current position about 1,500 years ago, with *sabkha* replacing the sea.

The entire plain on which Al Zubarah is located is currently devoid of tree cover, reflecting the impacts of heat, wind, drought, high soil salinity, and roaming livestock. Windblown sand and debris cover much of the town area. Periodically, archaeological excavations are made, and new finds are discovered.

The site's location corresponds roughly to the "Cadara" mentioned in the 2nd-century Geographia by Ptolemy. While often associated with Al Zubarah, some geographers suggest Cadara may have lay near

Al Khor/Al Thakhira area. Al Zubarah's very early establishment may have followed Portuguese attacks on other coastal settlements in its region. Later disruption in Iraq, ruled by the Ottoman sultans and the Mamluks, who originally came from the region of modern Georgia, may have increased the population in Al Zubarah. A general relacation of the Utub tribal confederation in northeast Arabia resulted in the Al Khalifa sheikhs settling in Kuwait before 1732. They felt sidelined in Kuwait and relocated to Qatar by 1766.

Basra, in Iraq, was hit by the plague in the early 1770s, which affected its trade and enabled other centres, such as Al Zubarah, to develop. Further migration from the Basra area to Al Zubarah occurred during the Ottoman-Persian War of 1775-1776. During the period when Al Zubarah was inhabited, several smaller settlements in northwest Qatar seem to have been affected, either positively or negatively, by the rise and decline of Al Zubarah. The town follows the legacy of similar towns that developed around the Gulf, many of which traded with Mesopotamia in ancient times and then with the Abbasid and later rulers based in Baghdad. These small towns often served a small hinterland as well as trans-ocean trade.

Following an unsuccessful attack on Al Zubarah by the Persian governor of Bahrain in 1783, Al Zubarah's ruler, Sheikh Ahmed bin Mohammed bin Khalifa, invaded and captured Bahrain, which his descendants have ruled since. The rise of the Al Saud family in Al Diriyah, near modern Riyadh, affected the finances and appeal of Al Zubarah, which paid tribute to the Al Saud from 1787. However, the Al Saud occupation of the Al Ahsa oasis, 140 km southwest of Al Zubarah, also increased Al Zubarah's appeal to many families. Perhaps a critical reason for the town's almost meteoric rise, was that it was a 'free port' unlike to Ottoman taxation at Basra; in effect it was a $18^{th}$ century version of Dubai's modern ethos. In 1809, Al Zubarah was occupied by Al Saud forces. The Ottoman sultan instructed the governor of Egypt, Mohammed Ali, to attack Al Diriyah in 1811, following the Al Saud occupation of the Hijaz and Makkah and Madinah. The Sultan of Oman, Sayyid Said bin Sultan, attacked and largely destroyed Al Zubarah that same year. This destruction and the Al Saud confrontation at Al Diriyah created an opportunity for the Al Khalifa of Bahrain to reoccupy the town, though the occupants then lived in a much smaller area.

The increased assertion of British power in the Gulf complicated disputes between the Al Khalifa and the Al Thani family based in

Doha. During a period of confrontations from 1868 onward, the Al Khalifa family was gradually excluded from the Qatar peninsula. The rise of the Al Thani family was helped by the decline of Ottoman influence, despite the Ottomans having several forts in Qatar and a governor at Al Zubarah. In 1878, Sheikh Jassim bin Mohammed Al Thani captured the town, though his hold was tenuous. Despite the town's decline, its proximity to Bahrain led to the construction of Al Zubarah Fort in 1938. Following this, Britain decided in 1939 that Al Zubarah was indeed part of sovereign Qatari territory; a 1937 memo by the Political Resident at Bushehr stated that it 'definitely' belonged to Qatar.

*Northern House - Al Zubarah*

The ongoing territorial disputes between Qatar and Bahrain were settled by the International Court of Justice in The Hague in 2001. It was decided that Al Zubarah was Qatari territory, while the Hawar Islands (off the west coast of Qatar) were Bahraini.

Despite all the legal attention, Al Zubarah had been covered by windblown sand, which concealed cemeteries, courtyard houses, walls, fishermen's huts, mosques, palaces, and narrow streets. The brief period of Al Zubarah's occupation provides an authentic insight into the organisation of towns in the region during the 18th and 19th centuries.

The town walls of Al Zubarah consist of the original outer wall and a smaller inner wall, which was built after the town's 1811 destruction. The outer wall is around 2,500 m long, with 22 bastions at regular intervals, and extends into the sea to the north to form part of a harbour. This wall, along with the town's overall grid-like layout, suggests a planned town. The smaller inner wall was built later, over earlier structures, and uses older building materials.

Up to 600 separate buildings are enclosed within the outer wall, suggesting a population of over 6,000. Neighbourhoods appear to have been planned. Most parts of the town have courtyard-style housing, which was common throughout the Gulf until an oil economy grew. Some houses seem to have had the iconic wind towers found throughout the region. Many buildings have gypsum decoration, suggesting a degree of wealth.

In the southern area of the town is a large, square, fortified palatial compound of well over one hectare, with nine interior courtyards and a tower on each corner. Functions found in some rooms include bathing areas and date-processing rooms (*madbasa*), which have long troughs to collect date syrup pressed from dates stored in sacks. A smaller compound to the northeast, just over half the size, has been partially excavated and has towers at each corner. Both these compounds may have had an upper floor. A mosque is close to these two residential buildings; early 20th-century photos show it had large columns and arches supporting what is believed to be a multi-dome roof, all covered in plaster. Public squares are also found in this area.

In the middle of the town, 80 metres east of the beach, was a souq that not only engaged in import and export but also appears to have been involved in other activities, including glass manufacture and date processing. On the beach, a small fort marked an area of deeper water to its south. Huts believed to be associated with fishing and pearl diving have also been identified by their post-holes found on the beach. Though there are contemporary with Al Zubarah, this type of hut structure and its function remain prevalent throughout the region.

A couple of wall barriers perpendicular to the original wall extend for a kilometre towards the more recent Al Zubarah Fort. These are thought to have directed traffic toward the town and to act as a defensive shield for water carriers moving between the town and Qalat Murair to its east. A water canal also leads towards Qalat Murair, stopping about 500 metres to its southwest. Though originally functional as a small boat canal, it appears to have been abandoned and partially infilled, probably due to operational or economic failure during Al Zubarah's existence. In places, the barrier walls run over the canal.

Al Zubarah Fort was built in 1938 by the ruler of Qatar, Sheikh Abdullah bin Jassim Al Thani, as a police outpost. It was used as a military fort until the early 1970s. The construction followed a period of confrontation with Bahrain over this area and the Hawar Islands when a Bahraini police fort was built on those islands in 1937. The single-storey fort is of a type common throughout the Arabian Peninsula, with a large open courtyard, a water well, and rooms opening off the square. There is a photographic exhibition about the old town within the fort.

Qalat Murair (Murair Fort; *qalat* is Arabic for fort) (GPS: 25.974, 51.043), along with water wells and a surrounding area of housing, was built in 1768 by Sheikh Mohammed bin Khalifa . Agriculture and livestock pens were to the fort's south and southwest. Its purpose appears to have been to defend the water canal that served Al Zubarah. Today, most of its remains are below the surface. Since it was unoccupied from the early 20th century, the stones may have been reused for building the adjacent Al Zubarah Fort.

About 1,600 m northeast of Qalat Murair is a small fort, Qalat Shuwail (GPS: 25.979, 51.056), which was noted in 1850 by Francis Warden, Chief Secretary to the Government of India at Bombay. It is thought that this fort is also contemporary with the town of Al Zubarah. Both Al Zubarah and Qalat Murair are on ground above the current *sabkha* and earlier sea levels, as shown by wave-cut platforms offshore. The area around Qalat Murair was the location of the freshwater supply for Al Zubarah; this water supply 'floats' over seawater that intrudes inland.

There are scattered mangrove (*Avicennia marina*) areas along the shoreline and on the mudflats. Close to Al Zubarah, and in the general inland areas, salt-tolerant plants are common. Occasional sightings of dugong and common bottlenose dolphin (*Tursiops truncatus*) are made offshore. Socotra cormorant (*Phalacrocorax nigrogularis*) roosts on Um Jatila Island, just off Al Zubarah. Greater flamingo (*Phoenicopterus roseus*) can be seen in winter, close to the shore during high tide. Both green turtle (*Chelonia mydas*) and hawksbill turtle (*Eretmochelys imbricata*) have been seen in the water. Some agricultural areas associated with Al Zubarah were developed 5 km southeast of the town and at Al Jumail, 18 km north of the coast.

## UNESCO Intangible Cultural Heritage

Qatar also has inscriptions on the UNESCO Representative List of the Intangible Cultural Heritage of Humanity:

1. **Falconry** as a sport is included as a UNESCO Intangible Culture. In Arabia, it is an ancient hunting practice mentioned by the Prophet Mohammed. Hunting lodges built in the deserts of Syria and Jordan between AD 680-83 by Umayyad caliphs testify to the sport's prestige. Treatises on falconry were written, with the peregrine falcon (*Falco peregrinus*) and saker falcon (*Falco cherrug*) appearing to be the favoured birds, which they remain today. The history of falconry in the Gulf is little known as it was not, until recently, a written practice. Classically, three species were quarry for falconry: the Houbara bustard (*Chlamydotis macqueenii*), the stone curlew (*Burhinus oedicnemus*), and the Arabian hare (*Lepus capensis*). The introduction of guns in the 16th century reduced the pressure to hunt with falcons and generally reduced wildlife. Today, falconry is no longer for obtaining food but is a sport. Wild falcons are trapped during migration between September and November and then trained. In Qatar, captive falcons can be seen in Souq Waqif [PAGE 76] or near the Sealine Hotel. Various pieces of equipment are associated with falconry in the Gulf: the *burqa* (head hood) used to keep the bird calm; a *wakar*, the stand on which the bird sits; *subuq*, the tethers attached to the ankles; and of course a glove for the man, called a *dass*, *kaff*, or the more modern *mangaleh*. World Falconry Day is celebrated annually on 16th November. Qatar hosts the Marmi Festival, an annual falconry event in January, during which falcons and Saluki hunting dogs are displayed, and hunting demonstrations are held.

2. **Majlis**, the third inclusion is the system of holding a *majlis*, a gathering of people. A *majlis* is a formal space, either a specific room in a building or, in Bedouin society, an outdoor space. It serves several functions, including as a reception for guests, a celebration meeting place, or a discussion area. Today, a *majlis* can refer to a physical space within a home or a public building, or to a personal meeting. In traditional society, a *majlis* is a single-sex meeting. Arabic coffee in a *majlis* can be a formal occasion, with guests often assigned specific places relative to the host.

*Coffee in desert*

3/ **Arabic Coffee**: As a demonstration of generosity and hospitality, Arabic coffee is included in this list. The coffee uses green coffee beans (Coffea arabica); of course, in Saudi Arabia, it might be from the southwest - and Khawlani Coffee, or perhaps from Yemen, in which case let's hope it's Mocha. The process of preparing the coffee was traditionally done in front of guests. The beans are roasted lightly over a fire, pounded with a metal pestle, and placed in a large copper coffee pot, the *dallah al logmah*, with water, then boiled. To add flavour, cardamom, cloves, or other spices are added. After the coffee has been brewed, it is poured into a smaller coffee pot, the *dallah al manzal*, from which it is served into small cups called *finjan*, which look like large thimbles. Usually, the most honoured guest is served first. Arabic coffee is often accompanied by dates, which are eaten first. When you have had enough (after two or three cups, it's polite), return the cup to the server by giving it a slight shake in your right hand to indicate you are finished.

4/ **Practices connected with date palms** Turning from social rituals to agricultural heritage, the knowledge and skills, traditions and practices connected with date palms are another intangible heritage listing. The date palm, Phoenix dactylifera, is the iconic tree of Arabia. Evidence of human consumption has been found on Dalma Island (east of Qatar, off Abu Dhabi's coast), dating to around 5290-4940 BC. The earliest confirmed cultivation of the date palm is from southern Mesopotamia and the northern Gulf during the 4th millennium BC. The Sumerians helped establish early palm oases, making the date palm a significant crop by 2500 BC. The spread and adaptation of date palm cultivation highlight its cultural and agricultural importance in the region.

The nomination text states, "Nurturing the date palm tree - this is specifically related to the knowledge the practitioner uses to provide suitable conditions for the palm's growth and the bearing of its fruit, including various traditional nurturing methods such as planting the offshoots, pruning, irrigation, and assisted pollination."

Apart from the actual date fruit, eaten either fresh or dried, in the West, this dried style is the usual version - numerous secondary products can be obtained from the fruit. Date Paste (Ajwa or majoon al tamar) is a ground paste created from pitted dates used in confectionery, bakery products (like date bread and cookies), and as a natural sweetener. Date Syrup (Dibs) is a viscous, sweet syrup extracted from dates (usually by pressing like a cider press), used as a natural sweetener, condiment, or spread. Dried and ground dates can be processed into a powdered sugar substitute. Dates can be fermented to produce vinegar. In some traditions (in Christian Arab areas), dates are fermented to produce alcoholic beverages. Date Juice: A non-alcoholic beverage made from dates. Animal Feed: Date pits (seeds) are soaked and ground for use as a nutritious feed for livestock, including camels, cattle, sheep, goats, and even chickens. Date Seed Oil: An oil extracted from the seeds, suitable for use in cosmetics, soaps, and some pharmaceutical applications. Date Seed Coffee Substitute: Ground date seeds can be roasted and used as a caffeine-free coffee substitute or an additive to coffee. Traditional Remedies: Dates are used in traditional medicine for various ailments, including sore throats, colds, and digestive issues due to their high tannin content.

Date palm leaves are transformed into many practical objects. The fruit stalks and leaves become brushes, while the long leaflets and midribs are woven into baskets, mats, fans, and hats. Fibres from leaf bases and fruit stalks are twisted into ropes, nets, or cordage. Fronds are also used for roofing and fencing. The stiff leaf midribs become crates, furniture, or walking sticks. Newer technologies are exploring converting palm leaves into hardwood for high-quality products.

5/ **Henna body art**. Moving ahead from date palm traditions to body art, Henna (Lawsonia inermis) is a scraggily flowering shrub whose leaves, when powdered and then formed into a paste (in the Gulf) with water, lemon juice, and sometimes essential oils or sugar to create a smooth paste that allows for good dye release and a long-lasting stain. Henna use dates back to at least the pre-dynastic period in Egypt; a worker's body was found at Hierakonpolis, showing signs of Henna use. At Souq Okaz, near Taif, Saudi Arabia, it was traded and used medicinally in the 6th century AD. Today, in the Arabian Gulf, Henna is widely used to decorate the skin of women attending a wedding. It might be an elaborate design or a simpler application on the sole of the foot - the colour is typically ochre, though 'Sudanese' Henna is a dark Brown. It is used less frequently today as a men's hair dye, often leaving a vivid orange hue. There are several Hadiths (authentic sayings) of the Prophet Mohammed personally using Henna as a dye and mentioning it on women's skin. Henna leaves produce better quality dye in hot weather. The flowers are used to make a rare perfume that is sweet, heady, and somewhat spicy.

6/ **Al Sadu Weaving** (Inscribed Dec 2025) Al Sadu is a traditional form of weaving practised by Bedouin women, using a horizontal ground loom known as *al badwa*. The textile is famously durable, crafted from the natural fibres of the dromedary camel (*Camelus dromedarius*) and the domestic goat (*Capra hircus*). It is distinguished by its bold, rhythmic geometric patterns - most notably the *Shajara* (tree) motif - which serve as a visual language recording tribal identity and migration.

Historically, Al Sadu was the "architecture" of nomadic life, providing the heavy, salt-tolerant strips used for the *bayt al shar* (house of hair) tents. While modern villas have replaced the tent, the craft has transitioned into creating memory filled reception area for homes.

7/ **The Bisht** (Inscribed Dec 2025) The Bisht - a men's ceremonial cloak - is perhaps the most internationally recognised piece of Qatari attire following the 2022 World Cup. This inscription, a joint Arab file led by Qatar, celebrates the meticulous skills of bisht-making, which have flourished in the region for over 150 years. The cloak is traditionally made from fine wool or camel hair. In Qatar, it is designed to be draped over the shoulders, with the right hand free for greetings. The defining feature of a prestige Bisht is the Zari - the intricate embroidery along the collar and sleeves made from metallic thread, often silver dipped in gold. A master tailor can spend up to 15 days hand-stitching a single garment. One might observe that the Bisht serves as a public declaration of the wearer's status and dignity, usually worn only on the most significant life milestones or during state affairs.

8/ **Arabic Calligraphy** (Inscribed 2021) Inscribed as a shared heritage of 16 Arab states, Arabic Calligraphy is the artistic practice of handwriting the 28 letters of the Arabic alphabet to convey harmony, grace, and beauty. From its development as a means of recording the Quran, it has evolved into a sophisticated Islamic art form. Traditional practitioners use a *qalam*, a pen fashioned from dried reeds or bamboo, and ink traditionally mixed from honey, black soot, and saffron.

The fluidity of the cursive script allows for "infinite geometry," in which letters can be stretched or transformed into complex motifs, such as animals or architectural shapes. In modern Qatar, this ancient practice has found a new canvas in "calligraffiti," where the elegance of the *Thuluth* or *Kufic* scripts is applied to urban walls, effectively bridging the gap between the manuscript and the metropolis.

9/ **Harees** (Inscribed 2023) Harees is a quintessential communal dish made from coarsely ground common wheat (*Triticum aestivum*) and meat - typically lamb or chicken. Its preparation is an exercise in patience: the wheat is cooked for hours in salted water, then the meat is added, and the entire mixture is beaten into a smooth, porridge-like consistency with a large wooden spoon called a *mizrab*.

The listing highlights the "communal knowledge" of its preparation, particularly during the Holy Month of Ramadhan. It is a dish designed for sharing; the final product is served in large platters with a pool of clarified butter (ghee) at the centre.

10/ **Al Ardha** (Inscribed March 2026) Al Ardha is the traditional Qatari sword dance that serves as a performance of "martial poetry." Originally a war dance performed before battle to stir the tribes' spirits, it is now the centrepiece of National Day celebrations. Men stand in two parallel rows, swaying to the rhythm of the *Iddah* (drums), while a leader known as the *Shaiyal* chants lines of heroic poetry that are repeated by the "row people."

# CHAPTER 5
# HISTORY

Qatar's history is interwoven with that of the surrounding regions, and much must be inferred from the broader regional picture.

In Wadi Fatimah at Saffaqah, an archaeological site in central Saudi Arabia, thousands of lithic remains from the Acheulean Period (1,760,000-130,000 years ago). In that period, Saffaqah lay in the headwaters of the major extinct river Wadi Sahba, which flowed east towards what is now the Gulf, in the area of Khor Al Udaid in Qatar. This natural route along a fertile river valley allowed humans to travel very easily during an 'Out of Africa' event into the region. The earliest dated evidence of humans in Qatar is 'Abbevillian' stone cores (dating to around 600,000-500,000 years ago), discovered by Dr Julie Scott-Jackson and a University of Oxford team. These cores were found in southwest Qatar, near the Saudi Arabian border, at sites collectively named 'Kapel'.

The Gulf's water volume has varied with the rise and fall of ice cover in the northern and southern latitudes over the last 300,000 years. Seawater levels have risen by about 120 m over the last 15,000 years, covering what must have been an ideal habitat used by both animal and human populations. At times, rising sea levels created swamps to the south of Qatar, effectively making it an island. As recently as 7,000 or 8,000 years ago, the area now occupied by the Gulf was a broad historic river flowing through a fertile valley flood plain to the north of Qatar.

On the west coast, at Al Daasa, 6 km southeast of Dukhan,

pottery from the Mesopotamian Ubaid civilisation (6500-3800 BC) has been excavated from a seasonal fishing settlement. Also from this period, 18 cairn burials have been found on low hills just northwest of Al Khor, north of Doha, including a pit burial covered with limestone slabs.

More recent evidence of human occupation has also been found on nearby Bin Ghannam Island (Al Khor Island) in the Al Khor lagoon. Here, fragments of tools, shells, and fish have been carbon-dated to between 5610 and 5080 BC. Ceramics from the Dilmun civilisation (2000-1750 BC, Bronze Age) have also been found, along with evidence of circular huts, post-holes, stone-lined pits, and fire hearths. Kassite pottery from Mesopotamia (1530-1160 BC) was widely distributed over this island. It is to this period that the name 'Purple Island' refers to Bin Ghannam Island, as the Kassites traded in the colour-fast dye 'Tyrian purple', obtained from a shellfish, *Thais savignyi* (now called *Hexaplex kuesterianus*), found at this island [PAGE 150]. Pottery from Sassanid Persia (AD 224-651) and from AD 1700-1900 has also been excavated. This small island, covering less than 17 hectares, was worked for some 4,000 years.

At another long-established site, Ras Abrouq, north of Zekreet on the west coast, Ubaid period (c. 6500-3800 BC) potsherds have been found. Also at Ras Abrouq are some 100 Seleucid period (312-63 BC) burial cairns.

∼

### ANCIENT HISTORY

The first definitive historical reference to Qatar is by Pliny the Elder (AD 23-79) in his *Natural History*, where he mentioned a tribe called the 'Catharrei'.

Qatar became subsumed by the rising power of the Sassanids, the new ruling dynasty in Persia. In AD 224, Ardashir I, the Sasanian king, defeated Artabanus V, the Parthian king, and founded the Persian Sassanid Empire, becoming Shahanshah (King of Kings). He conducted military excursions around Yamama (south of modern Riyadh) in 240, where he is reputed to have killed the ruler. Farther east, Mazun (modern northern Oman) became a province of the Persian Empire under the Arab Julanda governors. Shahanshah Shapur II (309-79) occupied Yamama following ship raids from Arabs into the Persian coast. He set up a buffer kingdom that eventually was ruled by the Arab Lakhmid rulers, who may have been the source of those raiding ships. Shapur II also set up frontier posts along the eastern coast of Arabia, running through Qatar to northern Oman, and crossed west into the Hijaz and Syria. In 363, after the Battle of Ctesiphon in Persian Mesopotamia between Rome and Persia, the Roman Emperor Julian was killed, marking a high point in Persian suzerainty of the Gulf region. Following a period during which little Persian activity is known, further expansion into Arabia occurred during the rule of Shahanshah Khosrow I in 532. This included the Red Sea areas of Hijaz and Yemen, bringing Qatar from the western edge of the Persian Empire towards its geographical centre. However, Arabs again raided into Iran. The new Shahanshah Khosrow II occupied northeast Arabia and deposed the Lakhmid dynasty in 600. The Lakhmid kingdom, which acted as a buffer state, having been removed, the next wave of Arab invasions would have unopposed access into the Persian Empire.

## CHRISTIANITY

Christianity was established in Qatar before the middle of the 4th century AD, possibly as a result of the relocation of monks following persecutions by the Persian Shahanshah Shapur II. His action may have been a reaction to the Roman Emperor Constantine the Great's support of Christianity after his Edict of Milan in 313. Shapur II may have believed that Christians posed a threat to Persia.

A publication, the 'Vitae Ionae', tells the story of a monk who lived during the time of Catholicos Barbashemin (343-346). It mentions a monastery of Rabban Thomas in 'Beth Qatraye' (modern Qatar). Beth Qatraye was one of several Christian establishments belonging to the Eastern Church in the Gulf area, which included Sir Bani Yas Island (near Abu Dhabi), Bahrain, Darin Island (on the coast near Dammam), and Rew-Ardashir in Fars, northwest Persia, which oversaw the others. Rew-Ardashir was under the administration of the bishop (later Catholicos) of Seleucia-Ctesiphon, the Persian capital. Beth Qatraye was also the name of the ecclesiastical province that covered the current regions of Kuwait, Eastern Saudi Arabia, Bahrain, and Qatar. The neighbouring province of Beth Mazunaye (the Persian province of Mazun, modern Oman) was noted as attending the Markabta Synod, represented by their Bishop Yohannon.

In 576, a bishop mentioned a monastery in Beth Qatraye that participated in the Synod of Mar Ezekiel, the patriarch of the Eastern Church from 570-581. Mar Ezekiel personally visited the region and reported on the pearl fishing to Shahanshah Khosrow I. Beth Qatraye hermit monks asked that Patriarch Ishoyahb I (582-95) of Seleucia-Ctesiphon correspond directly with them, effectively creating their independent role in Qatar. In 613, Ishaq an-Naynuwi was born in Beth Qatraye and later became Bishop of Nineveh in modern Iraq. After he died in about 700, he became St Isaac of Nineveh. After the establishment of Islam, Beth Qatraye became a tax collector for the Muslim rulers until the end of the 7th century. During the rise of the Qaramita state, which was based in Bahrain from 899, Beth Qatraye disappeared from records.

∼

### THE RISE OF ISLAM

Qatar's first contact with Islam came in 628, when the Prophet Mohammed sent an envoy, Abu Al Alaa Al Hadrami, to Munzir ibn Sawa Al Tamimi, the Sassanid governor of Qatar. Similar requests were sent to rulers of lands having contact with the Hijaz in western Arabia, where the Prophet Mohammed lived. The letter asked Munzir ibn Sawa Al Tamimi to declare allegiance to Islam, which he and some of his subjects accepted. After more correspondence, Mohammed advised that those who did not become Muslims should pay *jizya* (taxation on non-Muslims). After the death of the Prophet Mohammed in 632, a widespread revolt occurred throughout the Islamic world. Abu Al Alaa Al Hadrami was again sent by the new Caliph, Abu Bakr, to eastern Arabia to defeat the rebels, and he succeeded.

The next military action by the Caliph in the region was against Persia. Since the Persian rulers had eliminated the Lakhmid buffer state in 600, the Islamic empire had an open door to the rich land of Persia. In 633, the Arab conquest of Persia began, and the Persian capital Ctesiphon (south of modern Baghdad) was occupied in 637. This was a remarkable campaign conducted at the same time as the Byzantine areas of Palestine and Syria were also being conquered by the Caliph; the Islamic war front stretched across a vast area. By 651, the entire Persian Empire was occupied. The last Sassanid ruler (Yazdegerd III, 632-651) was killed by an inhabitant of Merv in central Asia during his long retreat after the occupation of Ctesiphon. Qatar was now firmly within a new Arab Muslim empire.

After the rise of the Islamic Abbasid Caliphate in 750, the capital of Islam moved from Damascus, near the Mediterranean, to Kufa in southwest Iraq and then to Baghdad in 762. This transfer of power to the region north of Qatar led to an extraordinary flow of wealth from the Gulf into what was then the world's most populous city. Baghdad's splendour was recounted in the *One Thousand and One Nights*; however, little is known about Qatar's history during this period. The only archaeological site dating to this period is the possible governor's palace at Murwab in northwest Qatar.

From 874, a form of Shia Islam was developed by the Qarmatians in southern Iraq. In 899, they took advantage of a rebellion in Basra, Iraq, against Abbasid rule. They seized power in Bahrain, Qatar, and Eastern Arabia, periodically controlling as far southeast as the coast of Oman. They became the most powerful force in eastern and central Arabia, exacting tribute and customs dues until they were defeated in 976 by the Abbasid Caliphs. Around 1067, the Qarmatians were finally overpowered. A successor state was ruled by the Uyunid dynasty, which also held sway over eastern and central Arabia under Abbasid allegiance.

The occupation and destruction of Abbasid Baghdad by the Mongol prince Hulagu Khan in 1258 ushered in a period of Ilkhanate rule over Syria, Iraq, and Persia by his successors. Qatar was on the periphery of this state, whose capital was in Tabriz, Iran. Although it is known that the Bahrain-based Usfurids ruled eastern Arabia from 1253 onward, Qatar was often a vassal of the growing power of the Kingdom of Hormuz. This was based on Hormuz Island at the eastern entrance to the Gulf and was itself a nominal vassal to various Persian princes, who were often vassals themselves to empires like the Ilkhanates. It was a complicated and often-changing power structure.

The power balance in the region was destroyed with the arrival of the Portuguese in the Gulf in 1507. They quickly defeated the Kingdom of Hormuz and then occupied the island from 1515, setting up forts in the Gulf, including three on Bahrain.

Portuguese Indian Ocean Ships 1541

Another major power, the Ottoman Turks, appeared in the Gulf region from 1514. They campaigned against Persia's Safavid rulers, and in 1538, the Persian town of Basra (in modern southern Iraq) became an Ottoman town. This gave them a port on the Gulf, from which they could campaign against Portugal and Safavid Persia. The 1555 peace treaty between the Ottomans and the Safavids allowed the Ottomans to focus on the Portuguese and the petty states in Arabia. Between 1550 and 1560, there were frequent clashes between them. The coastal town of Qatif on the eastern Arabian mainland, opposite Bahrain, was occupied by Portugal. Al Ahsa, an inland town 70 km west of Qatif, was occupied by the Ottomans.

To complicate the power structure, Shah Abbas the Great, the ruler of Persia's Safavid dynasty, occupied Bahrain in 1602. Subsequently, Bahrain was ruled from Behbahan, a Persian town near the northern end of the Gulf. Another power had appeared: the

English East India Company. In 1622, Persia, joined by an English fleet, defeated Portugal and occupied the island of Hormuz.

Qatar was surrounded by intense competition for territory, by four powers - Ottomans, Portuguese, Safavids, and the English East India Company. Despite this, it does not seem to have been occupied by any of them. Presumably, however, ships from Qatar's small ports were forced to pay protection and customs duty to those various powers.

By 1670, Qatar came under the rule of the Arab tribe, the Bani Khalid, after they had conquered Al Ahsa from the Ottomans. Taking advantage of Persia's increasing weakness following its disastrous defeat in Afghanistan in 1711, Oman occupied Bahrain in 1717. However, by 1736, Persia, under its new ruler, Nader Shah Afshar of the new Afsharid dynasty, had reoccupied the island, once again bringing the eastern areas of Arabia under Persian domination.

## THE START OF QATAR'S MODERN HISTORY

Qatar has a more defined history from the mid-18th century. A series of events resonate in the region's modern politics, where alliances were made and then broken, with former allies almost inevitably attacking their previous partners.

In 1732, members of the Al Bin Ali family from Kuwait, who were part of the Utub tribal federation, are thought to have settled in what would become Al Zubarah [PAGE 167, 298] on the west coast of Qatar. Later, between 1762 and 1768, the Al Khalifa family, also part of the Utub, moved from Kuwait to Al Zubarah under the leadership of

*Sheikh of Qatar's Fort Doha*

Shaikh Mohammed bin Khalifa. Al Zubarah grew, partly because of instability elsewhere in the region and the lack of customs charged by its ruler. The town developed trading links through the Gulf and attracted traders from Basra who settled there after fleeing Iraq during the Ottoman-Persian wars of 1775-79.

In 1782, a skirmish took place on the island of Bahrain between a group from Al Zubarah and Bahraini merchants. The resulting deaths on both sides escalated the incident. An invasion of Bahrain from Al Zubarah succeeded in destroying Manama, the main town. Part of the spoils was the ship used by Bahrain's Governor to collect customs. In retaliation, plans were made in Bahrain to invade Al Zubarah with 2,000 soldiers sent from Persia, who still claimed rule over the island. In May 1783, the Omani Sheikh Nasr Al Madhkur, the governor (or, more likely, the vassal ruler) of Bahrain and Bushehr under the Persian Shah Ali Murad Khan, landed his troops outside the town but was defeated by a combined force from the town and the surrounding region. Compounding this defeat was an attack on Bahrain itself on the same day by Utub Tribe members from Kuwait who set fire to Manama. By July 1783, Shaikh Ahmad bin Mohammed Al Khalifa had captured Bahrain with a force from Al Zubarah. Following that, large numbers of people moved from Al Zubarah to the island of Bahrain.

From 1787, Al Zubarah came under increasing attacks from Al Diriyah (near modern Riyadh), led by Amir Abdulaziz ibn Mohammed Al Saud, ruler of the First Saudi State. Following the Al Saud capture of Al Ahsa (in today's eastern Saudi Arabia), many refugees fled from there and arrived in Al Zubarah in 1795. Al Saud forces, however, exacted taxes from Al Zubarah as a protection payment.

From the death of Shaikh Ahmad bin Mohammed Al Khalifa in Bahrain in 1795, two of his sons jointly ruled Bahrain and Al Zubarah. One, Sheikh Abdullah bin Ahmed Al Khalifa, ruled until 1842. In 1797, the Al Khalifa family moved to Bahrain, starting the decline of Al Zubarah. A series of attacks on Al Zubarah by Omani forces between 1799 and 1802 ended after the Al Khalifa obtained support from the Al Saud family.

Al Zubarah was then the target of a combined attack in 1809 by Al Qassimi forces (from Ras Al Khaimah) and Al Saud forces. It was occupied by them, giving Britain and Oman, who had existing struggles with both, a new conflict centre to consider. In 1811, a combined British/Omani force attacked Al Zubarah and the Al Qassimi/Al Saud forces, leaving the town in ruins.

**British Engagement**

The political result of these conflicts was that, from 1811, the Al Khalifa family again became the dominant power in Qatar. Britain supported them through various agreements, including the critical General Treaty of 1820 (which also involved Abu Dhabi and Ras Al

Khaimah) and a later Treaty of Perpetual Truce of Peace and Friendship in 1861.

Britain increased its impact on Qatar in 1821, when an East India Company vessel bombarded the town of Al Bidda (now part of Doha) as retaliation for what was said to be piracy committed by its inhabitants. This action forced between 300 and 400 people to flee temporarily.

Al Bidda was involved in a later turning point in Qatar's modern history. A contender for power in Bahrain, Sheikh Abdullah bin Ahmed bin Khalifa, made an alliance with Shaikh Isa Bin Tarif Al Bin Ali of Al Bidda, a leading power in the region and, incidentally, Sheikh Abdullah's earlier military opponent. They fought a battle at Fuwayrit (often called the Battle of Umm Suwayya) on 17th November 1847 against Sheikh Mohammed bin Khalifa, ruler of Bahrain and Al Zubarah. Shaikh Isa Bin Tarif was killed, and his ally, Sheikh Abdullah bin Ahmed, escaped to Persia. Following the battle, Sheikh Mohammed bin Khalifa attacked and destroyed Shaikh Isa's base of Al Bidda and moved its population to Bahrain. This population migration created a power vacuum, which allowed the rise of the Al Thani family, the current rulers of Qatar.

~

## Pearl Diving

One of the oldest professions in the Gulf region is pearl diving. Archaeological evidence dating back to the Late Stone Age (6,000-5,000 BC) suggests that the trade and spiritual beliefs within the Gulf included the natural pearl.

In the early modern era, as stability increased and the Gulf's economy integrated into international markets, the Gulf's pearl industry boomed. Divers from Oman's Batinah Coast and the Yemeni island of Socotra, almost 3,000 kilometres away by sea, came to the Gulf to dive for this valuable resource. By around the middle of the 19th century, there could have been few families on the coasts of Eastern Arabia or Western Persia who did not have men working in the pearl business.

Historical records illustrate the extent of pearl diving and the profits it generated. The value of the pearl market is estimated to have grown by over 600% between 1790 and 1905. Pearls from the Gulf generated about US1.75 million in income a year from 1830, rising to US4 million by the early 20th century. In his 1829 book *Travels in Assyria, Media and Persia*, James Silk Buckingham wrote that pearls from Bahrain brought in approximately £200,000. In the same period, James Wellsted, in his 1838 book *Travels in Arabia*, reported that there were over 4,000 boats engaged in pearling between Bahrain and Oman. Pearls from the Gulf were traded to India, the Ottoman Empire, Persia, China, Europe, and North America. Sheikh Mohammed bin Thani of Qatar told William Palgrave in 1877: 'We are all from the highest to the lowest, slaves of one master, Pearl.'

*Pearl Diver*

The British Political Resident, John Lorimer, wrote in his *Gazetteer of the Persian Gulf* that the Qatar industry was worth £625,933 in 1873/74 and £1,076,793 in 1904/05. Lorimer also noted that there were 350 pearl boats in Doha.

Two species of molluscs were sought for their pearls. The Akoya pearl oyster, *Pinctada imbricata fucata*, grows to a shell length of 60-80 mm and produces as a by-product 'Lengeh shells' (named after the Iranian port), which are used for products such as buttons. The second, larger species, *Pinctada margaritifera*, commonly known as the black-lip pearl oyster, grows to 200 mm in length.

Pearl grounds on the western shore of the Gulf run from Kuwait to Musandam in Oman. They also extend on the Persian side of the Gulf, from near Bushehr (opposite Kuwait) to Lengeh (opposite Musandam) in the south.

Pearl diving was a seasonal activity from June to September with two diving periods: the big dive, a 60-day journey, and the small dive, a 40-day trip. Each season, dozens of pearling boats left Doha for coastal banks rich with oysters. The ship's captain, the *nakuda*, commanded the whole operation, including the pearl divers, *ghawas al lulu* (*lulu* is Arabic for pearl). On the diver's fingers and toes was leather protection, *khabbal*, to protect against sharp rocks and shells. A wooden nose peg, *fitaam*, stopped seawater from entering the nose under deep-water pressure, and oil-soaked cotton plugs blocked the ears. They used a knife to cut the shellfish off the rock and a basket, *dadjin*, to put their catch in.

A diver used two ropes to descend, which his assistant, the *saib*, held from the ship. The diver would remain underwater for 60 to 90 seconds, reaching depths of up to 20 metres. Each vessel could carry up to 40 divers, each diving perhaps 40 times a day. A crew could gather 8,000 pearl oysters a day. In colder waters, some divers greased their bodies against the chilly water, much as ocean swimmers do today.

These divers lived on credit given by their captain, who owned and worked the boats and kept the crew. Many of the divers were slaves, transported from East Africa, typically through Zanzibar and Oman, and then to individual towns across Arabia. Pearl merchants, *tawawish*, in turn, advanced loans to boat captains before the diving season. The pearling industry, therefore, functioned on borrowed capital. The captain would collect all the pearls, sell them to the merchant, and then pay the divers in cash. Despite risking their lives, they received the smallest proportion of the sale; the slaves, of course, were dependents of their 'owners'. Each season, the system depended on success, with financial ruin for everyone down the chain a possibility.

By 1924, however, the region's pearling industry was already falling into rapid decline. A primary factor was the development of the cultured pearl industry in Japan, initiated in 1916 by the entrepreneur Mikimoto Kokichi. From then on, the number of boats in the pearl fishing fleets dwindled. The men travelled elsewhere to look for work, perhaps to Baku, Iraq, and Persia, where oil production had already started.

**Oil, Gas, and Modern Development**

Oil and natural gas have been a critical part of Qatar's economy for almost 100 years. The Anglo-Persian Oil Company surveyed Qatar in 1926, but no oil was found. After an oil strike in Bahrain in 1933, a Qatari concession was signed on 17th May 1935 with Anglo-Persian representatives for 75 years, in return for 400,000 rupees on signature and 150,000 rupees per annum in royalties; Britain agreed to provide enhanced security. In October 1938, the first exploratory oil well was sunk in Dukhan, Qatar's west coast, and oil was discovered in late 1939. However, due to the Second World War, exports did not begin until 1949.

Over this period, the dispute with Bahrain over Al Zubarah continued, and in 1936 it expanded to include the Hawar Islands, just off the Qatari central west coast. A Bahraini police fort was built on the islands, and Bahrain imposed a ban on trade and travel to Qatar. Qatar followed this by building Al Zubarah Fort [PAGE 168], completed in 1938.

*Sheikh of Qatars Fort Doha*

Following Britain's announced withdrawal from 'East of Suez' in 1968, the Gulf sheikhdoms' future political situation needed to be addressed. For many months, it appeared that Qatar would become part of a union that would include Bahrain and the now-constituent states of the United Arab Emirates. Ultimately, on 3rd September

1971, Sheikh Khalifa bin Hamad Al Thani, the then Heir Apparent and Prime Minister (and soon-to-be ruler), declared Qatar a separate, independent sovereign state.

In 1971, Qatar discovered the North Dome Gas Field in the Gulf; this field straddles the maritime border between Iran and Qatar as the South Pars/North Dome Gas Field. Production began in 1981, and it eventually became the world's largest gas field.

On 27th June 1995, Sheikh Hamad bin Khalifa Al Thani (since his abdication, known as The Father Amir), the father of the current ruler, Sheikh Tamim, assumed power. During his reign, the State of Qatar saw massive economic, social, and cultural development.

The Al Zubarah dispute with Bahrain was settled by the International Court of Justice in March 2001. Al Zubarah, the Fasht ad Dibal sandbank, and Janan Island were confirmed as territory of Qatar, while the Hawar Islands and Qitat Jaradah Island were settled as Bahrain's territory.

From 5th June 2017, Saudi Arabia, the UAE, Bahrain, and Egypt instigated a political and economic blockade against Qatar. This followed years of disputes in the late 20th & into the 21st centuries, rather than only reflecting those from a few centuries ago. A notable event included the withdrawal of their ambassadors from Qatar on 5th March 2014. Qatar was visibly shocked by the 2017 situation, and vehemently denied the various accusations and demands, which included that it should shut down the Al Jazeera media network, curb diplomatic ties with Iran, close the Turkish military base, and end Qatar's alleged support for state terrorists and extremist groups. The blockading nations accused Qatar of destabilising the region and undermining their security. Qatar decried the boycott as a violation of its sovereignty and international law. The blockade and the resulting focus on self-sufficiency have strengthened Qatar's national identity and solidified the unity of its nationals. The blockade was officially resolved on 5th January 2021.

Qatar's first general elections were held on 2nd October 2021 for 30 of the 45 seats in the Shura Council. In November 2021, Qatar held its first Formula 1 race as a replacement for the cancelled Australian Grand Prix during the COVID-19-affected season. Qatar has subsequently signed a 10-year contract to host the race from 2023.

The year following the resolution of the blockade, the 2022 FIFA World Cup was held in Qatar. This enhanced Qatar's standing, especially in the Arab world. Qatar's management of such a large, multinational event also boosted its global reputation for handling massive events. The unparalleled platform showcased Qatar's intangible culture and destination appeal, boosting long-term tourism.

**International Relations**

Established in 1996, the centrally located Al Udeid Air Base is one of the most strategically significant military installations in the Middle East. It serves as a pivotal hub and Combined Air Operations Centre for United States regional operations, playing a crucial role in regional military activity. In addition to a significant American presence, Al Udeid also hosts elements of the United Kingdom's Royal Air Force and, of course, Qatar's Amiri Air Force. This multinational presence underscores the base's role as a cooperative security location. The base has been instrumental in supporting United States military operations in Iran, Iraq, Syria, Afghanistan, and other regional hotspots. Turkey has also had military personnel based in Qatar since 2015, at a base northeast of Al Udeid. These foreign military presences have allowed Qatar to develop an initial focus on national issues to one with a regional core and international ambitions.

With the wealth it can spend, Qatar is an astute negotiator, facilitator and goodwill accumulator. Qatar's diplomacy is transactional and far-reaching; a USD400million Boeing 747-8 gifted to the American presidency carries as much weight as complimentary hosting of 400 Taliban delegates. With support from the military and core political alignments, bolstered by the success of the sporting events it hosts, Qatar has become a locus for dispute resolution. This has increased with the USA's current preference to avoid multinational bodies such as the UN. Qatar has acted as a facilitator in areas as disparate as Ukraine, Venezuela, central Africa, the Levant and Afghanistan.

## CHAPTER 6
# THE AL THANI FAMILY

The Al Thani family can be traced back to a branch of the Maadhid tribe, whose eponymous founder, Maadhid bin Musharaf, claims descent from the Banu Tamim (children of Tamim) tribal confederation, one of the largest in Arabia, which has existed since at least the 6th century AD. The confederation's name and the current ruler of Qatar's name are the same, an indication of the persistence of naming in Arab culture. The family takes its name from Sheikh Mohammad bin Thani bin Mohammad Al Thamir (the Thani here has become the family name).

From the 17th century AD, the family lived in Ushayqir, 170 km northwest of Riyadh, in present-day Saudi Arabia. At some time around the start of the 18th century, they were settled at the Yabrin (Jabrin) oasis, 280 km southeast of Riyadh. During the 1740s, they moved to Qatar, firstly near Sikak in the south, then to Al Zubarah, and eventually to Fuwayrit.

**Rise of the Al Thani**

The battle of Fuwayrit in 1847 and the subsequent Al Khalifa move to Bahrain created a power vacuum in Qatar. Under the leadership of Sheikh Mohammed bin Thani, the Al Thani family made a strategic migration from Fuwayrit (in the northeast of Qatar) to the growing settlement of Doha, near Al Bidda, between 1848 & 1850.

The Perpetual Truce of Peace and Friendship, signed in 1861 by Britain with Shaikh Mohammed bin Khalifa Al Khalifa, collapsed in Qatar in 1867 following a series of incidents. After Sheikh Jassim bin

# THE AL THANI FAMILY

Mohammed Al Thani was imprisoned by Sheikh Mohammed bin Khalifa Al Khalifa, a battle against Bahraini forces in Qatar ensued, which the Qatari side won. Sheikh Jassim was released in exchange for Bahraini prisoners. Later in the year, 24 boats from Bahrain and 70 ships from Abu Dhabi, with a combined total of 2,700 men, attacked Qatar and destroyed the towns of Al Bidda and Al Wakrah. Despite this, Qatari forces were powerful enough to attack Bahrain, destroying 60 boats and killing 1,000 men. These conflicts led Britain to force a change of ruler in Bahrain, confiscate all his ships, and impose a large fine of $100,000.

Shaikh Abdullah Al Thani (ruler of Qatar centre), Shaikh Muhammed Al Mana (right) and Salith

## The Leadership of The Al Thani Family

The British Political Resident in the Gulf, Colonel Lewis Pelly, signed a treaty with Sheikh Mohammed bin Thani in 1868. This treaty acknowledges Qatar as a separate political entity, rather than a part of Bahrain, and the Al Thani family as its leaders.

Following a conflict within the Al Saud family, Midhat Pasha, the Ottoman Governor of Bagdad, reoccupied eastern Arabia in 1871 and also occupied Qatar. Despite Britain's alarm, the Ottomans then incorporated Qatar into the *sanjak* (administration area) of Najd (Eastern Arabia) in 1872 as a *kaza* (small administrative region). Sheikh Mohammed bin Thani was appointed as the *qaim-makam* (sub-governor), once again supporting his dominant role in Qatar. In 1878, Sheikh Mohammed's son, the future *qaim-makam* Sheikh Jassim bin Mohammed bin Thani (Al Thani), attacked and defeated the residents of Al Zubarah, who were allies of Shaikh Isa bin Ali Al Khalifa in Bahrain, and he also captured the nearby Al Murair Fort. In the following years, Bahrain once again tried to regain control of Al Zubarah, probably assuming Britain would support them against the newly confirmed Ottoman *qaim-makam*; however, Britain did little.

The Ottomans came under pressure due to historical local rivalry. In 1882, Abu Dhabi occupied Khor Al Udaid in southeast Qatar. Sheikh Jassim bin Mohammed Al Thani, the new *qaim-makam*, was not supported by the Ottomans in regaining it. He retaliated by raiding 300 km southeast of Khor Al Udaid into the Liwa Oasis in the southwest of the modern UAE, the original home of the Abu Dhabi Al Nahyan Sheikhs.

A conflict between the Ottomans and Sheikh Jassim followed a simmering dispute after the newly appointed Ottoman Governor of Basra, Mehmed Hafiz Pasha, arrived in Qatar from Al Ahsa with 340 armed men. Sheikh Jassim relocated to Al Wajbah, 13 km west of Doha, with men from several tribes. After unsuccessful negotiations, the Ottomans captured and imprisoned several men on a ship, the *Merrikh*. Following this, the Battle of Wajbah took place in 1893, with over 4,000 men supporting Sheikh Jassim. Both sides had large losses; however, the Qataris defeated the Ottomans. The result was that Mehmed Hafiz Pasha withdrew to Al Ahsa, and the Ottoman Sultan then deposed him as governor. This defeat consolidated Sheikh Jassim's position and reduced the Ottomans' ability to govern.

The Ottomans officially renounced sovereignty over Qatar in 1913, though they stayed in Doha until 1915. On 3rd November 1916, Britain signed a treaty with Sheikh Abdullah bin Jassim Al Thani that provided him with a diplomatic shield. Qatar gave up its independence in foreign affairs in exchange for Britain's support against external threats; similar agreements had been made throughout the Gulf. Despite this, Britain continued to show little interest in Qatar's internal affairs until oil exploration negotiations began in 1922.

The path to the formal independence of Qatar was a result of the January 1968 announcement that Britain would withdraw its military presence from The Gulf (East of Suez as the concept was called) by the end of 1971. This created a strategic scramble to fill the impending political vacuum, leading to the February 1968 Dubai Accord, which proposed a "Federation of Arab Emirates" comprising nine states: the seven Trucial States, Bahrain, and Qatar. However, the potential union was fraught with friction from the outset. Bahrain, then the most populous and administratively advanced, sought a proportional representation that the others feared would lead to its hegemony, while Abu Dhabi and Qatar – both growing oil powers – were wary of subsidising their neighbours without significant control. The transition to independence was accelerated by the 1968 British announcement of a full military withdrawal from the Gulf by the end of 1971. Initially, Qatar sought security through the "Federation of Arab Emirates" – a proposed nine-state union alongside Bahrain and the seven Trucial States (now the UAE). However, the project was plagued by deep-seated regional rivalries. Bahrain, then the most populous, demanded a dominant legislative voice that the others feared, while the Al Thani family was increasingly wary of diluting their authority or subsidising a collective treasury.

The friction reached a breaking point in October 1969 during a meeting in Abu Dhabi. Jim Treadwell, then the British Political Agent in Abu Dhabi, delivered a note from the British government that was perceived as an overbearing ultimatum to finalise the union. In a decisive display of independence, Sheikh Ahmad bin Ali Al Thani walked out of the negotiations, effectively signalling the end of the nine-state dream. With its significant oil revenues and the nascent potential of its offshore gas fields, Qatar calculated that the risks of "going it alone" were preferable to a marriage of convenience where its domestic policy would be subject to the competing whims of its neighbours. Bahrain declared independence on 14 August 1971, and Qatar followed on 3 September (until 2007 this was Qatar's National Day), choosing a path of strategic solitude that allowed the Al Thani to craft a modern state on their own terms.

The Amir of Qatar Sheikh Tamim and the then President of Ukraine

## 21st Century Qatar

In the 21st century, the then-ruler, Sheikh Hamad Bin Khalifa Al Thani, abdicated in June 2013, and his son, Sheikh Tamim bin Hamad Al Thani, the current Amir of Qatar, became ruler.

His later education was in the United Kingdom at Sherborne School (which now has schools in Qatar) and Harrow School before graduating from the British Royal Military Academy Sandhurst in 1998. Sandhurst was also attended by Sheikh Hamad in 1971, and by numerous other leaders of the Arabian Gulf States over several decades. Sheikh Tamim's extensive time abroad has contributed to his fluency in English and French, in addition to his native Arabic.

Sheikh Tamim prioritises practical results and order, a trait possibly honed through his Sandhurst and subsequent Qatar military discipline. This envelops both domestic and foreign policy, which is also centred on mediation and strategic independence.

Domestically, Sheikh Tamim has focused on fostering a strong national identity rooted in Islamic traditions while pursuing economic diversification and sustainable development, as outlined in the Qatar National Vision 2030.

On the international stage, Qatar under Sheikh Tamim has carved out a significant role as a key mediator in regional and global conflicts. His foreign policy is characterised by maintaining open channels of communication with a wide range of international and regional actors, allowing Qatar to act as a crucial intermediary.

# CHAPTER 7
# EXPLORERS OF QATAR

An idea of life in Qatar before today is provided by some travellers who have passed through the area.

Lieutenant J.H. Grubb of the Indian Navy (Bombay Marine) in 1822 described Bidda as a 'most miserable place: not a blade of grass nor any kind of vegetation near it; the water good, obtained, they said, at some distance. The anchorage in the inner harbour is very good, four fathoms, being about one-eighth of a mile from the shore, surrounded by a reef nearly dry, which forms a complete basin, the entrance to which is very narrow, but deep, and free from danger. Not so in approaching it, as the water is very shoal about seven miles out, there being two and a half fathoms, sand, and a good deal of sea in a north-wester.'

William Gifford Palgrave, a Victorian traveller who was a Jesuit priest at the time, visited Qatar in 1863, en route from Bahrain to Oman. His journey was probably funded by Emperor Napoleon III, part of his probing of the Levant and Arabia. Palgrave assumed the name Seleem Abu Mahmood El Eys, a Syrian physician. He wrote

But if the people of Qatar have peace within, they are exposed on the land side to continual marauding inroads from their Bedouin neighbours, the Al Manasir and Al Murra. Hence the necessity for the towers of refuge which line the uplands : they are small circular buildings from twenty-five to thirty feet in height, each with a door about half-way up the side and a rope hanging out, by this compendious ladder the Katar shepherds, when scared by a sudden attack, clamber up for safety into the interior of the tower, and once there draw in the rope after them, thus securing their own lives and persons at any rate, whatever may become of their cattle. For to scale a wall fifteen feet high is an exploit beyond the ingenuity of the most skilful Bedouin.

On landing at Al Bidda we went right to the castle, a donjon-keep, with outhouses at its foot, offering more accommodation for goods than for men. Under a mat-spread and mat-hung shed within the court sat the chief, Sheikh Mohammed bin Thani:, a shrewd wary old man, slightly corpulent, and renowned for prudence and good-humoured easiness of demeanour, but close fisted and a hard customer at a bargain ; altogether, he had much more the air of a business-like avaricious pearl-merchant (and such he really is), than of an Arab ruler.

In the 20th century, the descriptions of foreign visitors create a vivid impression of the country.

In January 1904, Hermann Burchardt, the German explorer and photographer, arrived in Doha after travelling by sea from Kuwait into Al Uqair and overland via Al Ahsa. He went to the Turkish Fort, located south of the Amiri Diwan (a reception and administrative complex for the ruler). This fort was between Al Bidda and Doha, and Burchardt was 'quartered with the Commander, a major'. Burchardt described that 'three neighbouring towns are distinguished. Doha, with the garrison, and Al Bidaa, and As-Solata. The garrison consisted of 1 *tabur* (an armed unit of approx. 250 men) with two old cannon. Soldiers, military officers, and administrative officers with their families dwell in miserable mud houses, and the state of health is not good; particularly common are eye diseases. At one time scurvy was also common; better nutrition for the soldiers has eliminated this disease completely'. He continued, 'in reality the Turkish influence extends no further than the reach of rifles and canon' from the fort.

Robert Cheesman worked in Iraq from 1920-23 as an assistant to Sir Percy Cox, the High Commissioner of Iraq in the British administration. In 1921, Cheesman travelled through Saudi Arabia and arrived in the small port town of Al Uqair. There he used the organisation of Abdul Aziz Al Qusaibi, the ship-owner, and the support of Abdulaziz Al Saud, who ruled the central and eastern areas of what is now Saudi Arabia. In April, Cheesman boarded a 'Baghala' type of dhow near Al Uqair and crisscrossed between the western shore of Qatar and the eastern shore of the Saudi coast in the

Gulf of Salwa, describing how shallow the water was, as the boat needed to be pushed despite being 1/4 mile (400 m) from shore. He wrote, 'Here the Qatar coast is a sandy shore; scrub grows close to the sea and across one to two miles of undulating sand-dunes until the hills are reached, which appear featureless and level-topped, running parallel with the coast and rising from 200 to 300 feet'.

THANK YOU 🙏
for buying this Qatar guide
I do hope you found it useful.
A review will help others know whether this guide is right for them compared to other guides to Qatar.
It will also let us know what we need to improve.

# CHAPTER 8
# ARABIC LANGUAGE

Arabic Text

Arabic is spoken by between 400 and 490 million people worldwide. For others, it is the language of Islam, the divine tongue of the Quran, but its significance extends far beyond that. It is one of the six official languages of the United Nations, a vital tool for diplomacy and trade. In its earliest form, Arabic developed in northwest Arabia, with several other languages contributing to its development. Arabic's use was reinforced with the rise of Islam. The Prophet Mohammad delivered the Quran in spoken form, revealed he said by the angel Gabriel as the actual word of God, spoken in Arabic. It was then transcribed into written Arabic. Written Arabic script has had slight modifications since Mohammed's time.

As Islam spread, the script was adopted by other languages, such as those used in the Persian Empire. Urdu also uses the script, as it developed several centuries later. Different Arab regions created their own unique phonetic and grammatical shifts, and a multitude of spoken dialects emerged. Today, while Modern Standard Arabic (MSA) serves as a unifying force, spoken Arabic varies significantly from country to country. MSA is the formal language of news, education, and official documents, understood across the Arab world. However, a speaker of a Moroccan dialect, for example, might find it challenging to understand a Qatari dialect in everyday conversation. This is comparable to some regional dialects or conversational slang in the British Isles being almost unintelligible to a person from another English-speaking country, or even within the

British Isles. However, until recently, written Arabic was a standard and formal script throughout the Arab world. The interesting change occurred when mobile phones, which offered text messaging, arrived in the Arab world (from 1998). The system and keyboard only accepted left-to-right texting, and so "Arablish" (sometimes called Arabizi - a portmanteau of Arabic and English) texting developed. This remained until the early 2,000s when Arabic text was widely introduced - some Arabs still use the Western script out of habit. In the French speaking regions "Francio" was the equivalent.

The Arabic alphabet, with 28 letters, is written from right to left. There must have been countless smudged documents as students' right hands moved over the wet ink. While it's flowing and connected, characters might seem daunting to a beginner; it is an alphabet like any other. Once a learner grasps the individual letter forms and how they change depending on their position in a word - much as English letters change slightly when written in a cursive form - the process of reading and writing becomes very manageable. Unlike a logographic language like Chinese, where each symbol represents a word or concept, each Arabic letter represents a sound, much like in English. The primary challenge is that short vowels are typically marked with diacritics, which are often omitted in printed texts, leaving readers to infer them from context.

Beyond the script, the language is built on a root system. The majority of Arabic words derive from triliteral roots, such as k-t-b (ك-ت-ب), whose core meaning in Classical usage is 'writing'. Some philologists suggest an underlying sense of this particular root as 'bringing elements together' – reflected in extended usages – though this is secondary and not uniformly attested as the root's original meaning. By applying different vowel patterns, prefixes and suffixes to this root, a family of related words is created, including *kitab* (book), *kataba* (he wrote), and *maktab* (office or desk) or even – to illustrate the gathering aspect - *katiba* (a battalion or a troop of horses).

Countless Arabic words have been adopted and transformed into other languages. Spanish and Portuguese, in particular, adopted many terms during the centuries of Islamic rule on the Iberian Peninsula, including words like azúcar (sugar) and algodón (cotton), both of Arabic origin. English also owes a debt to Arabic for terms such as *alcohol, algebra, coffee* and *zero* - often through convoluted routes.

# ARABIC LANGUAGE

| English | transliteration | Arabic |
|---|---|---|
| hello | marhaba | مرحبا |
| how are you | kayf halik | كيف حالك |
| I am fine | ana bikher | أنا بخير |
| what's your name? | ma ismik | ما اسمك |
| my name is …. | ana ismi | انا إسمي |
| welcome. | ahlan wa sahlan. | أهلاً وسهلاً |
| good morning. | sabah alkhair | صباح الخير |
| good evening. | masa alkhair | مساء الخير |
| yes | naam | نعم |
| no | laa | لا |
| welcome, help yourself | tfadhal | تفضل |
| thanks. | shukran - | شكراً |
| goodbye | maa assalama | مع السلامة |
| sorry | asif | آسف |
| please | minfadhlak | من فضلك |
| about / almost | yaani | يعني |
| where is the | ayn al | این ال |
| company | ash-sharika | الشركة |
| hospital | mustashfaa | مستشفى |
| hotel | alfunduq | الفندق |
| restaurant | mataam | مطعم |
| supermarket | subermarket | سوبر ماركت |

| | | |
|---|---|---|
| museum | mathaf | متحف |
| this is expensive. | haadha ghaali | هذا غالي |
| no it's cheap. | la inaha rakhisa | لا إنها رخيصة. |
| thobe | thoob | ثوب |
| ghutra | ghutra | غترة |
| aqal | agaal | عقال |
| black cloak (for women) | abaya | عباءة |
| headscarf (for women) | shayla | شيلة |
| veil covering face | niqaab | نقاب |
| face mask | birqa | برقع |
| furniture | athaath | أثاث |
| chair | kursi | كرسي |
| table | attawlah | الطاولة |
| bed | assirir | السرير |
| carpet | sajada | سجادة |
| jewels | mujawharat | مجوهرات |
| gold | dhahab | ذهب |
| silver | fudha | فضة |
| are these made of real gold | hal hadhih masnuwiat min aldhahab alhaqiqi | هل هذه مصنوعة من الذهب الحقيقي |
| vegetables | khudrawaat | خضروات |
| onion | basila | بصلة |

| | | |
|---|---|---|
| cabbage | alkarnab | الكرنب |
| tomatoes | tamatim | طماطم |
| cucumbers | khiar | خيار |
| radishes | fjul | فجل |
| beans | faswlaya | فاصوليا |
| potatoes | bitata | بطاطا |
| fruits | fawakah | فواكه |
| watermelon | albatikh | البطيخ |
| lemon | liamun | ليمون |
| orange | alburtaqali | البرتقالي |
| dates | tawarikh | تواريخ |
| banana | mawz | موز |
| peaches | khukh | خوخ |
| grapes | aanb | عنب |
| walnuts | eayn aljamal | عين الجمل |
| I want to drink | ared an ashrab | اريد أن أشرب. |
| juice | aasir | عصير |
| orange juice | aeasir alburtuqal | عصير البرتقال |
| apple juice. | aasir altafahu. | عصير التفاح |
| coffee | qahwa | قهوة |
| tea | shai | شاي |
| bread | khabaz | خبز |
| rice | aaruz | أرز |
| cheese | jbin | جين |
| one egg | bidha | البيض |

| | | |
|---|---|---|
| how much is a dozen eggs? | kam hu dazinat min albida? | كم هو دزينة من البيض؟ |
| meat (beef) | lahm | لحم |
| lamb | lahm kharuuf | لحم خروف |
| chicken | dijaaj | دجاج |
| fish | samak | سمك |
| shoes | jooti | جوتي |
| clothes | malaabis | ملابس |
| shirt | qamis | قميص |
| traditional pants | sirwaal | سروال |
| trousers | bantaloon | بنطلون |
| suit | badhla | بذلة |
| a dress | fistan | فستان |

Arabic Numerals

Algebra and zero, of course, are fundamental parts of modern mathematics. The numbers we use today, known as Arabic numerals, originated in ancient India, possibly in the 3rd century BC, and were further refined there over the following centuries. Like Hindi, the numbers are written from left to right, unlike Arabic. Often, when giving, for example, a phone number, a person will emphasise that it must be written from left to right. The relevance of the number's position relative to other numbers in showing its value was used earlier by the Babylonians in their 60-unit system, and this may have influenced the subsequent adoption of positional numbers into the Arabic system, which itself was widely used in the Arab world by the 9th century AD. The concept of 'zero', which was previously understood, was fully incorporated in the Arabic numerals then.

Arabic numerals made the jump to Europe through an Italian mathematician, Leonardo of Pisa. He studied in North Africa and published his book *Liber Abaci* in 1202, which championed the new system for its efficiency. Hence, the term 'Arabic Numerals' (they arrived from the Arab speaking world) rather than Indian Numerals. General uptake in Europe was slow, but by the 16th century, the numerals' practicality for bookkeeping, trade, and complex scientific calculations gradually led to their acceptance. They largely displaced Roman numerals across Europe, enabling much quicker and more provable calculations.

| 1 | ١ | wahid |
|---|---|---|
| 2 | ٢ | ithnan |
| 3 | ٣ | thaltha |
| 4 | ٤ | arbaa |
| 5 | ٥ | khamsa |
| 6 | ٦ | sitta |
| 7 | ٧ | saba |
| 8 | ٨ | thamaniya |
| 9 | ٩ | tisa |
| 10 | ١٠ | ashara |
| 20 | ٢٠ | ishroon |
| 30 | ٣٠ | thalathoon |
| 40 | ٤٠ | arbaoon |
| 50 | ٥٠ | khamsoon |
| 60 | ٦٠ | sittoon |
| 70 | ٧٠ | saboon |
| 80 | ٨٠ | thamanoon |
| 90 | ٩٠ | tisoon |
| 100 | ١٠٠ | mia |

**A Final Note**
Qatar is a land that thrives on the "Social Contract" of mutual respect. You may observe residents navigating these rules with a certain fluidity, but as a visitor, you lack the "cultural currency" to buy your way out of a mistake. Adhering to these guidelines ensures you are seen as an invited guest rather than a digital intruder.

The above is intended to be helpful and to raise awareness when dealing with a Qatari or an organisation; obviously, circumstances will impact any outcome and require note-taking. A short-term visitor is likely to come and go in Qatar without even considering these points.

Churches: Several churches have premises in Doha within a complex, especially to the south of the F-Ring Road at the junction with the Doha Expressway at Mesaimeer (often referred to as Abu Hamour by residents). Their congregations include Coptic Egyptians and various denominations from India and the Philippines, including Catholic and Protestant. The principal day for services is Friday (the day off for most workers) and Saturday; services are also held on Sunday. The most striking detail about the complex is its "anonymous" exterior. By law, these buildings cannot display crosses, steeples, or bells on their facades.

Always read your country's foreign ministry's advice on Qatari culture, and, if possible, consider registering for alerts about Qatar. Some countries are more cautious or informative than others.

UK: www.gov.uk/foreign-travel-advice/qatar/local-laws-and-customs

USA: travel.state.gov/content/travel/en/international-travel/International-Travel-Country-Information-Pages/Qatar.html

# CHAPTER 9
# INDEX

Abu Samra - International Border - - 10
Accessibility (special needs travellers) - - 37
Agriculture - - 261
Airport - - 6
Al Jassasiya (Al Gasasia) Rock Art - - 152
Al Karana bird watching - - 180
Al Khor - - 146
Al Khor Zoo & Panda House - - 147
Al Reem Biosphere Reserve - - 173
Al Ruwais - - 156
Al Shaqab Horse Racing Academy & Equestrian Club - - 115
Al Thakhira - - 149
Al Thani Family - - 325
Al Wakrah - - 98
Al Zubarah - - 167, 298
Alcohol & Drugs - - 5, 26, **42**
Animals (wild) - - 246
Arabic Language - - 334
Arrival Into Qatar - - 2
Ash Shahaniyah Camel Race Track - - 183
Aspire Park - - 121
ATM - - 8, 64, 271
Banks - - 271
Barzan Towers - - 145

Bin Ghannam Island / Purple Island - - 150
Birds - - 253
Bus - - 12, 19,
Camel - - 62, 77, 104 (rides), 128 (for sale), 151, 168, 183, 191, (racing), 249
Car Hire - - 21 onwards
Cash - - 272
Central Qatar - - 179
Children - - 14, 21, 24, **32**
Climate - - 34, 241
Clothing Qatari - - 286
Clothing To Consider Wearing - - 33, 90
Corniche / Harbour Promenade - - 22, 50, 56, **60**
Culture (of Qatar) - - v, 33, 40, **282**
Customs (imports) - - 5, 6
Date Palms - - 262
Dhow Harbour - - 45, 50, **70**
Doha - - 50 onwards, 267
Doha South And East - - 96
Driving - - 10 land border, **21** onwards
Dukhan - - 178
Economy & Money - - 271,
Education - - 287
Education City - - 109 onwards
Eid - - 48 holiday dates
Embassies - - 31
Explorers Of Qatar - - 330
Falcon Club, Al Gannas - - **131**, 190
Falcon Souq - - 45, **76**
Fish Market - - 62
Freiha abandoned village - - 166
Fuwairit Beach - - 153
Gas LNG - - 241, 272-275, 280,
GDP - - 271, 274, 276
Geography - - 242
Transport - Getting Around - - 14
Ghost Villages in western Qatar - - 139
Government, Politics And International Relations - - 270
Hamed International Airport - - 6
Health - - 2, 3, 32, 35, 36, 37, 43, 57,

History Of Qatar - - 310
Holidays And Religious Occasions - - 47
Hotels - - 224
Imam Mohammed Bin Abdulwahhab Mosque - - 90
Insurance - - 3, 4, 5, 10, 11, 26, 32,
International Airport - - 6 onwards
Irkhaya Farm (bird watching) - - 252
Islamic Religion In Qatar - - 72, 90, **295**
Katara - - 129
Khor Al Udaid / Khor Al Adaid - - 105
Land Arrival - Road from Saudi Arabia - - 10
Language Phrases - - 334
LGBTQ+ - - 293

**Libraries**
Dar Al Kutub Al Qatariya - - 82
Qatar National Library - - 112
Museum of Islamic Art - - 66
Lizards - - 109, **251**
Lusail - - 139, 268
Lusail Boulevard - - 140
Metro - - 16
Mudhlim & Musfur Caves - - 180

**MUSEUMS**
Arab Postal Stamps Museum - - 141
Children's Museum by OliOli- - 131
Lawh Wa Qalam - - 113
Mathaf Arab Museum of Modern Art - - 117
Msheireb Museums - - 59, 83
Museum Of Islamic Art - - 65
National Museum Of Qatar - - 60
3-2-1 Qatar Olympic and Sports Museum - - 123
Sheikh Faisal Bin Qassim Al Thani Museum - - 184
Nature of Qatar - - 244
North and West from Doha - - 152 onwards
North and Northeast from Doha - - 146
Oil - - 273, 277
Oryx - - 248
Panda House (for two Pandas - Suhail & Soraya) - - 148
Pearl Diving - - 302, 318
Photography & Video - - 39 restrictions, 45

Pigeon Towers Katara - - 132, 134
Places To Visit - - 50
Population - - 241, 265
Qatar Airways - - 2, 6,
Qatar National Library - - 112
Qatar Photography Centre - - 134
Ramadhan - - 48 dates, 293, 296
Regular Events In Qatar - - 189
Restaurants - - 198
Road Safety - - 24, 30, 43
Safety - - 19, 32
Sea Arrival - Cruise - - 8
Service Providers - Tours, - - 53
Sheikh Abdulla Bin Zaid Al Mahmoud Islamic Centre - - 72
Sim Cards - - 12
Snakes - - 253
Souq Al Wakrah - - 100
Souq Waqif - - 73
Special Needs Travellers - - 37
Taxi / Uber / Karwa - - 10, 27, 33
The Pearl - - 136
Tour Providers - - 53
Towns And Major Divisions - - 267
Tram - - 15, 28, 86 Msheireb, 118 Education City, 141 Lusail
Travel Advice by your Government - - 32, 37, 46
Tour Suggestions - - 51
Uber - - 10, 27, 33
UNESCO Listing - - 298
Water Taxi - The Pearl - - 138
Weather - - 33, 244
West Bay - - 93
West Doha - - 109 Rayyan, 121 Aspire
Zekreet Fort - - 177

www.ingramcontent.com/pod-product-compliance
Lightning Source LLC
Chambersburg PA
CBHW050327010526
44119CB00050B/700